Stimulating Creativity

VOLUME 2

Group Procedures

STIMULATING CREATIVITY

VOLUME 2
Group Procedures

MORRIS I. STEIN

Department of Psychology
New York University

ACADEMIC PRESS   New York   San Francisco   London

A Subsidiary of Harcourt Brace Jovanovich, Publishers

To
S V
and
P V

BF
408
.S747
vol. 2

ACADEMIC PRESS, INC.   68525
111 Fifth Avenue, New York, New York 10003

United Kingdom Edition published by
ACADEMIC PRESS, INC. (LONDON) LTD.
24/28 Oval Road, London NW1

Library of Congress Cataloging in Publication Data

Stein, Morris Isaac, Date
    Stimulating creativity.

    Bibliography: v. 1, p.   ; v. 2, p.
    CONTENTS: v. 1.   Individual procedures.—v. 2.   Group
procedures.
    1.   Creation (Literary, artistics, etc.)
2.   Problem solving.   I.   Title.
BF408.S747   153.3'5   72-77340
ISBN 0−12−664202−8 (v. 2)

Contents

Preface   vii
Acknowledgments   xi
Contents of Volume 1   xiv

PART V   GROUP PROCEDURES   1

XII   Introduction to Group Procedures   3
Some Characteristics of Groups   4
Before Making Final Arrangements for Group Procedures
  to Stimulate Creativity   17

XIII   Brainstorming   25
Theory   27
Setting Up for a Group Brainstorming Session   30
An Introduction to the Research Studies that Follow   37
Studies of the Two Principles and Four Rules   44
Studies of Outcomes   52
Studies of Process   70
Attempts to Increase the Effectiveness of Brainstorming   104
"Training"   113
Maltzman's Basic Procedure   114
Summary   137

XIV   Creative Problem-Solving   142

Theory   143
Training Programs   144
Evaluation Studies   163
Summary   170

XV   Synectics   172

Synectics, Inc. Training Programs   174
Synectics Education Systems Training Programs   177
Synectics in Comparison with Other Group Techniques   179
Theory and Technique of Synectics   185
The Participants in a Synectics Meeting   191
Synectics' Problem-Solving Process   196
Synectics in Action   202
Setting up a Synectics Group within an Organization   205
Synectics Groups in Real Company Situations   209
Synectics for Education   211
Evaluation   215
Summary   219

XVI   A Study of Cognitive and Personality-Insight Approaches   222

Theory of the Creative Process in This Study   223
The Two Approaches   224
Participants   228
Results   230
Summary   232

PART VI   OTHER PROGRAMS   235

XVII   Diverse Organizational and Company Programs   237

Description of Programs   238
Evaluation of Some Existing Programs   247
Summary   249

PART VII   CONCLUSION   251

XVIII   A Summary and a View toward the Future   253

Individual Techniques   254
Group Techniques   267
Research Considerations   279

References   286

Subject Index   293

Preface

This book is an outgrowth of one of the earliest creativity studies in post-World War II United States concerned with the psychological and social factors affecting creativity. After the results were presented to various lecture and seminar audiences, on nearly each occasion there were one or more persons who would ask: Can creativity be stimulated? If yes, what are the techniques for doing so? What assumptions underlie them? How effective are they?

To find the answers to these questions I became involved in a search of the literature (primarily research) and this led to the present two-volume work. The first volume presents procedures designed primarily to help individuals who can then work alone or in groups. The second volume contains procedures for groups of individuals. That procedures are divided in this manner should not deter any one reader or group from selecting what they think they can use, regardless of the section in which it appears.

The first volume also contains my theoretical orientation to creativity. I used it in my empirical research and it also served in organizing the material presented here. This orientation, succinctly stated, is: Creativity is a process that results in a novel work that is accepted as useful, tenable, or satisfying by a significant group of people at some point in time. As a process it consists of overlapping stages—hypothesis formation, hypothesis testing, and the communication of results—all of which follow a preparatory or educational stage which is not always uniquely part of the creative process. In each stage one may see the effects of *intra*personal and *inter*personal factors. All these factors reflect the fact that creativity occurs in a social context and is a function of the transactional relationships between the individual and his environment—the creating individual is both affected by and affects his environment.

This statement and other related matters, such as criteria of creativity, set the stage for discussion of the aforementioned individual and group procedures, and also prepare the reader for a presentation of procedures specially suited for each stage in the creative process.

The relevance of procedures for stimulating creativity to the stages of hypothesis formation and hypothesis testing will be immediately evident. On other occasions, however, especially when we discuss the communication stage of the creative process, the relevance of the procedures to creativity may not be so readily apparent. The reason for this may well be that when many persons think about creativity, they limit themselves to the creating individual, whereas in my approach, while the creating individual is the center of attention, he is not all there is. He is seen as creating in a social context and thus as affecting and being affected by the persons and social forces in his environment. Stimulating creativity, therefore, involves not only stimulating the individual but also affecting his social milieu and the people in it. If those around the creating person do not value creativity, if they do not provide the necessary supportive environment, if they do not accept the creative work when it is completed, then it is likely that the creative individual's efforts will encounter serious if not insurmountable obstacles. Since creativity is a process, it is necessary to keep in mind not only the creating individual but also the direct and indirect forces in the social environment that affect him. Knowledge of such forces, in addition to what it can do to help the creating individual, can also be used to stimulate creativity further.

In addition to the statement about the creative process there are other background statements such as the effects of an individual's cognitive and personality characterisitics on his behavior. This discussion is intended to provide additional theoretical background and rationale for the individual procedures. By the same token, the discussion of some of the characteristics of groups is intended to highlight for the reader some of the problems in group behavior with which techniques for stimulating creativity have to cope as well as to indicate some assets of groups that can be built upon.

The aim in selecting the procedures discussed in this two-volume work was to be as thorough and as diversified as possible in the hope of maximizing their usefulness for readers concerned with the sciences, arts, engineering, humanities, business management, and everyday aspects of living. But at least two shortcomings need to be noted at the outset. No work such as this can hope to be up to date on publication. There is always some creative person, somewhere, who is developing a technique for stimulating creativity, and his work came to our attention after the manuscript was completed.

Further, this book contains a larger proportion of techniques for technological and consumer-related product areas than it does of techniques for the arts and humanities. Such a disproportion reflects the status of the field. There is less information available on the deliberately designed techniques in the arts and humanities, other than those involved in good teaching, than in the areas mentioned.

In presenting the various individual and group procedures for stimulating creativity, we have tried to include sufficient detail so that readers who become curious enough to try the procedures will have a basis on which to proceed. We would also like to encourage these persons to consult the original descriptions of the procedures, for although there may be some redundancy in such reading it may frequently add some piece of information or detail that would be beneficial for a successful experience.

While the material presented here is intended for use, it is not intended to be a guide to the perplexed who seek instant creativity. By presenting the theoretical rationale underlying the various techniques and the research on their assumptions and effectiveness, we do hope to provide readers with a more solid basis than is currently available for making their various choices. Where systematic research was not available we do cite available anecdotal evidence and are careful to point out that it is anecdotal. And when we have felt that research findings needed further substantiation, as occurred on numerous occasions, we asked for further replication.

Hopefully those who try the various procedures described here will make their experiences, their failures as well as their successes, known in appropriate publications. Such information together with the efforts of future investigators in this area will help us come closer to learning more about what kinds of procedures for stimulating creativity should be used by what kinds of individuals under what kinds of conditions to achieve creative results. If these two volumes also turn out to be a step in this direction, then their purpose will have been fulfilled.

Acknowledgments

There are a number of persons who have been most helpful in the various stages of development of these volumes. Chief among them is my colleague Professor Joseph Weitz of the Psychology Department at New York University who read an early version of the manuscript and parts of the later one. To him I am indebted for his insightful criticisms. To Alexander Biel, of Ogilvy and Mather, I am indebted for numerous discussions. To Professor Harold Basowitz, with whom I have been associated at the Research Center for Human Relations in the Psychology Department of New York University, I am most indebted for his help in coping with countless administrative details. To Barbara Fried I am grateful for many a beneficial dialog, in which she brought to bear her own knowledge of creativity. To Myron A. Coler, Professor of Continuing Education and Director of the Creative Science Program at New York University, I am most grateful for the many opportunities he gave me to discuss ideas contained here. And to the Lewis and Eugenia Van Weazel Foundation I want to convey my appreciation for their support of The Creative Science Program which provided me with data and information.

There is another large group of persons to whom I am grateful, those whose work is cited at length in these volumes and to whom I sent my descriptions of their work for comments and criticism. While I followed their suggestions in correcting my description of their work, when it came to the matter of evaluation and interpretation the final word had to be mine.

I am also indebted to all those unnamed seminar participants who gave me the opportunity to test out my material with them. And, of course I am thankful for all the inputs accumulated during the years from my co-workers and students with whom I worked on research designed to understand the creative process.

I am grateful to Mrs. Eleanor Cunningham for her secretarial efforts throughout much of the time this work was in preparation, and to Mary Insinna, Sue Ellen York and Stephanie Meketansky for the secretarial aid they gave me in the final stages of the two volumes. I am most appreciative of the ever-present patience, guidance, and helpfulness of the Academic Press production staff. Finally, I want to express my appreciation to the Public Health Service for its support through a Career Award (5K06-MH18679) to me from the National Institutes of Health.

Excerpts on pp. 13-15 from D. C. Pelz and F. M. Andrews, *Scientists in organizations*, copyright 1966, John Wiley and Sons, Inc.

Excerpts in Chapter 13 from A. F. Osborn, *Applied imagination* (3rd ed.), 1963, by permission of Charles Scribner's Sons.

Excerpts in Chapter 13 from S. J. Parnes, *Creative behavior guidebook*, 1967(a), by permission of Charles Scribner's Sons.

Excerpt on pp. 34-35 from E. De Bono, *Lateral thinking: Creativity step by step*, copyright © 1970 by Edward De Bono. Reprinted by permission of Harper and Row, Publishers, Inc.

Excerpt on pp. 50-51 from S. J. Parnes, Effects of extended effort in creative problem solving, *Journal of Educational Psychology* 52, 117-122. Copyright 1961 by the American Psychological Association and reproduced by permission.

Excerpts in Chapter 13 from T. J. Bouchard, Jr., Personality, problem-solving procedure, and performance in small groups, *Journal of Applied Psychology Monograph* 53, February 1969, No. 1, Part 2. Copyright 1969 by the American Psychological Association and reproduced by permission.

Excerpts on pp. 62, 78 from E. Weisskopf-Joelson and T. S. Eliseo, An experimental study of the effectiveness of brainstorming, *Journal of Applied Psychology* 45, 45-49. Copyright 1961 by the American Psychological Association and reproduced by permission.

Excerpts on pp. 76-79 from R. Hyman, On prior information and creativity, *Psychological Reports* 9, 151-161 (1961). Reprinted with permission of author and publisher.

Excerpts on pp. 82, 83, 93, 94 from D. W. Taylor *et al*., Does group participation when using brainstorming facilitate or inhibit creative thinking? *Administrative Science Quarterly* 3, 23-47 (1958), by permission of the Society for Personnel Administration.

Excerpts on pp. 85-86 from M. D. Dunnette *et al*., The effects of group participation on brainstorming effectiveness for two industrial samples, *Journal of Applied Psychology* 47, 10-37. Copyright 1963 by the American Psychological Association and reproduced by permission.

Excerpts on pp. 92, 104-106 from P. C. Dillon *et al*., Brainstorming on a "hot" problem. Effects of training and practice on individual and group performance, *Journal of Applied Psychology* 56, 487-490. Copyright 1972 by the American Psychological Association and reproduced by permission.

Excerpts on p. 103 from G. S. Rotter and S. M. Portugal, Group and individual effects in problem solving, *Journal of Applied Psychology* 53, 338-341. Copyright 1969 by the American Psychological Association and reproduced by permission.

Excerpt on p. 113 from M. D. Dunnette, Are meetings any good for solving problems? Copyright © *Personnel Administration* 29, 12-16 (March-April 1964). Reprinted by permission of the International Personnel Management Association, 1313 East 60th Street, Chicago, Illinois.

Excerpts on p. 115 from I. Maltzman *et al.*, A procedure for increasing word association originality and its transfer effects, *Journal of Experimental Psychology* 56, 392-398. Copyright 1958 by the American Psychological Association and reproduced by permission.

Excerpts on pp. 129-132 from I. Maltzman *et al.*, Experimental studies in the training of originality, *Psychological Monographs* 74, No. 6 (Whole No. 493). Copyright 1960 by the American Psychological Association and reproduced by permission.

Excerpts in Chapter 14 from S. J. Parnes, *Creative behavior workbook*, 1967(b), by permission of Charles Scribner's Sons.

Excerpt on p. 165 from S. J. Parnes and A. Meadow, Effects of "brainstorming" instructions on creative problem solving by trained and untrained subjects, *Journal of Educational Psychology* 50, 171-176. Copyright 1959 by the American Psychological Association and reproduced by permission.

Excerpts on pp. 181-183 from W. J. J. Gordon, *Synectics*, copyright © 1961 by William J. J. Gordon, Reprinted by permission of Harper and Row, Publishers, Inc.

Excerpt on pp. 203-204 from G. M. Prince, *The practice of creativity*, copyright © 1970 by George M. Prince. Reprinted by permission of Harper and Row, Publishers, Inc.

Excerpt on p. 213 reprinted with permission from W. J. J. Gordon, *The metaphorical way*, Porpoise Books, 1971; available from Synectics Education Systems, 121 Brattle Street, Cambridge, Massachusetts.

Excerpts on pp. 241-243 from L. R. Bittel, Brainstorming: Better way to solve plant problems. Reprinted by special permission of *Factory*, May 1956. Copyright Morgan-Grampian, Inc., May 1956.

Excerpts on pp. 243-246 from J. E. Bujake, Jr., Programmed innovation in new product development, *Research Management* 12, 279-287 (1969), © 1969, John Wiley and Sons, by permission of John Wiley and Sons, Inc.

CONTENTS OF VOLUME 1: Individual Procedures

Part I Plan of the Work

Chapter I   Introduction

Part II Theory and Criteria

Chapter II   The Creative Process
Chapter III   Criteria in Studies of Creativity

Part III Individual Procedures

Chapter IV   Introduction to Personality Procedures
Chapter V   Affecting Personality Characteristics: Role Playing, Hypnosis,
                 and Psychotherapy
Chapter VI   Introduction to Cognitive Procedures
Chapter VII   Altering States of Consciousness

**Part IV Procedures for Affecting the Individual Stages of the
         Creative Process**

Chapter VIII   Affecting the Preparatory (Educational) Stage
Chapter IX   Stimulating Hypothesis Formation
Chapter X   Making Hypothesis Testing More Effective
Chapter XI   Affecting the Communication of Results

PART V

GROUP PROCEDURES

The chapters of Volume 1 of this work concerned themselves with procedures that an individual may utilize by himself or with the aid of another person for stimulating his creativity. But among the procedures for stimulating creativity there are also those that have been developed for work with groups of persons. To these we now turn.

Again we wish to emphasize the fact that the division of the techniques to stimulate creativity into individual and group procedures is to some extent arbitrary. The reader should not be hampered by this division and should select what he can utilize effectively regardless of whether it has been presented as an individual or group procedure.

Chapter XII

Introduction to Group Procedures

Four group procedures for stimulating creativity will be considered—brainstorming, creative problem-solving, synectics, and a personality-insight approach. Brainstorming, more than the other techniques, emphasizes a cognitive approach. To be sure, personality factors are relevant to brainstorming, but the real emphasis is on "loosening up" thought processes, keeping oneself from evaluation, and coming up with as many ideas as possible. The material on brainstorming, while based on the work of its originator, Osborn, also draws heavily on the work of Parnes, president of the Creative Education Foundation at the State University College at Buffalo. Parnes and his co-workers have continued much of Osborn's work and have made contributions of their own. They have added various procedures to brainstorming and developed an integrated program called Creative Problem-Solving. This will be the second procedure discussed in this chapter. Parnes and his group have also conducted studies of the various assumptions underlying brainstorming and of the effectiveness of both brainstorming and creative problem solving for the stimulation of creativity. Brainstorming may be used as an individual or group procedure. Our focus in this section is on brainstorming as a group procedure. Its use as an individual procedure was discussed in Volume 1, pages 209-221.

The third group procedure for stimulating creativity, synectics, was devised by Gordon (1961) and has been further developed both by Prince (1970a) and

3

by Gordon himself (1971). Synectics is similar to brainstorming in its goal—to encourage the conception of novel ideas and products. It also shares with brainstorming the assumption that cognitive processes are important to the creative process, and it tries to foster their development by encouraging the use of methods similar to those used in brainstorming. Its uniqueness, however, especially as manifest in the works of Gordon (1961, 1971), lies in the use of metaphors and analogies and related problem-solving mechanisms. In synectics there is also greater awareness of a person's psychodynamics, and use is made of this knowledge "to bring the person out" and to help him manifest his potentialities. Prince's work with synectics makes greater use of group dynamics. There is much overlap between Gordon's and Prince's efforts. The works of both men were drawn upon for the discussion of synectics in this section.

The fourth part of this section devotes itself to a discussion of a personality-insight approach to stimulating creativity. This approach was utilized primarily for research purposes at the Center for Programs in Government Administration at the University of Chicago. It takes up a number of problems left unanswered by the other procedures, such as the relative significance of personality and cognitive factors in creativity and the relationship between the kind of training a man has received to stimulate his creativity and the kind of organization in which he works. In both brainstorming and synectics, individuals may possibly learn what their personal problems relating to creativity are; in the personality-insight approach effort is purposely directed at this matter, although within prescribed limits. Such considerations do not go as far as in group or individual psychotherapy, but do go further than is usually expected in industrial and managerial situations.

Persons involved in group procedures for stimulating creativity may be individuals who work with each other, or they may be persons who have met for the first time in the training session and in that session work together as a group. These people may also work either as individuals or as part of a team in their daily working activities. Therefore, although procedures are presented in this section as group techniques, it is hoped that individuals will not be put off from reading this material since it is not limited to groups. Individuals may find techniques here that could be useful to their own creativity. Similarly, it is to be hoped that both individuals and groups will find worthwhile ideas in a later chapter (Chapter XVII, pp. 237-249) devoted to a discussion of diverse company programs to stimulate creativity.

SOME CHARACTERISTICS OF GROUPS

So that we shall have a better framework for assessing the kinds of problems and difficulties that groups may experience which result in the inhibition or restriction of their creativity and creative potential, and to have a better understanding of the kinds of problems that the group procedures for stimulating creativity are designed to overcome, we shall turn now to a consideration of a number of relevant characteristics of groups.

Patterns of Communication

One of the frequent problems encountered between or within groups lies in the area of communication. Either appropriate individuals do not get the information they need, or some individuals become burdened or overloaded with information. This faulty dissemination of information can not only inhibit the group's creativity but can also undermine the members' morale and lessen the effectiveness with which they organize themselves for any cooperative or mutual endeavor. Part of the problem in the dissemination of information may be attributed to the manner in which the patterns of communication between group members are defined. How effective a group may be in the solution of problems may vary as a function of available channels of communication. This is the result of studies conducted by Bavelas (1948, 1950) and Leavitt (1951). It is the latter's research that we shall now consider.

In Leavitt's work each of five subjects was given a card on which there were five symbols taken from a master group of six. Each symbol appeared on four of the five cards, and one symbol appeared on all five. The subjects' task was to determine which of the symbols they shared.

The subjects were seated around a table on which there were panels that separated them from one another. In the panels there were slots between contiguous subjects. If the slots were open, messages could be passed between subjects; consequently, by opening and closing the slots the experimenter could control or test various communication channels.

In any one problem-solving task—to discover the single shared symbol—the six subjects were given 15 trials. And to test the effectiveness of a communication network or to study the way in which it works, the subjects were given 15 problem-solving tasks. Leavitt concentrated on four communication networks as shown in the accompanying diagram.

the circle , the chain , the "Y" , and the wheel .

These four channels varied in their degree of centralization. The wheel has maximum centralization; the circle has no position that is more central than any of the others; and the chain and "Y" networks are in between, with the "Y" more centralized than the chain.

Among the results of Leavitt's work we find that the problems were worked on more efficiently in the more centralized networks than in the less centralized ones. However, when the participants were asked to what extent they were satisfied with what they were doing, which might well be regarded as a measure of morale, it was found that the less centralized networks received the better ratings. Thus, subjects in the wheel network passed fewest messages for a correct trial and had the fastest single correct trial. But when they were asked how personally satisfied they were with their task, those subjects in the circle network had the highest score.

The work by Bavelas and Leavitt stimulated others to study similar problems and their efforts, as reviewed by Shaw (1964), suggest that the earlier findings need some qualification. In summarizing the findings of the later studies, Shaw also reported that more decentralized networks involved the sending of more messages, and participants in these networks had higher satisfaction scores. But when efficiency, measured by such variables as speed and accuracy, was looked at, then the data did not consistently support the earlier findings. It was learned that there were 10 out of 16 comparisons in which decentralized networks produced more errors, and in 22 out of 36 comparisons decentralized networks resulted in faster solutions than did the centralized networks. Shaw suggests that the variations may be ascribed to variations in the complexity of the tasks used in the experiments. Leavitt's experiment (which involved the exchange of symbols on cards) used a relatively simple task, while other researchers devised tasks involving constructing sentences or mathematical problems, which were more complicated. Keeping complexity of task in mind, Shaw found that in decentralized networks the fact that more messages were sent and higher satisfaction ratings were obtained held both for simple and complex tasks. But when the criteria were speed of solution and frequency of error, the interaction with task complexity was found to be significant. When problems are simple, centralized networks produce faster solutions; when problems are more complex, the decentralized networks produce faster solutions. When problems are simple, more errors are made when the network is decentralized; but when the problem is complex, more mistakes are shown in the centralized network. It would then appear, according to Shaw (1964) that centralized networks are good to collect information in one place. But if we expect to do something with this information, then decentralized networks are better.

As we shall see in the discussion of group techniques to stimulate creativity, the orientation here is not only to open up channels of communication within an individual and to free him to give ideas, but also to encourage communication between individuals so that participants can use communication networks flexibly to meet the demands of problems and not get trapped by any specific network where the responsibility for solving the problem falls on one person to the exclusion of the others. There is also encouragement to build on each other's ideas and suggestions, for none of them is the private property of any one participating member.

Group Climate

Another characteristic of techniques for stimulating group creativity is the creation of a certain kind of "group climate." Specifically, a definite attempt is made to have groups become nonevaluative. It is felt that if members of a group evaluate each other's responses, they will inhibit the free flow of ideas. In synectics, especially in the form used by Gordon (1961, 1971), for example, there is a great deal of freedom—any participant may express himself in any way he wishes and in any language he wishes. And a specific rule in brainstorming bans criticism, in the hope that this prohibition will help create a freer, more easygoing atmosphere and environment in which the participants will be better able to think up, verbalize, and develop ideas.

A group environment per se frequently results in the members' becoming less inhibited than each would otherwise be. This freer atmosphere manifests itself in participants who are more likely to take risks in solving a problem when they are in a group than when they are alone. Wallach and Kogan (1965) have called this phenonemon the "risky shift"—the taking of more risks within a group than if alone. They studied five-member student groups who were brought together to discuss such questions as, should a patient with heart trouble risk an operation that might cure him, or should he resign himself to a more restricted life? Should a low-ranking chess player try a risky play in a tournament and stake his reputation on it?

Three experimental conditions were used. In one of them, the group discussed the problem and arrived at a consensus. In another, no group discussion was permitted, but each member stated his opinion in turn until all of the decisions were the same. And in a final condition, there was group discussion, but no attempt was made to reach a consensus. The individual members recorded their decisions privately.

The results of this study were that in those groups that engaged in discussions, the risky shift had occurred whether or not they had come to group agreement. The opinions of the groups that had not discussed the problem showed a verging effect but did not shift in the direction of taking risks. Thus, the process of group discussion, and not information about the opinions of others or the pressure to conform, seemed to be a critical factor in the risky shift. Wallach and Kogan apparently believe that during the discussion, individuals come to feel that the group as a whole shares responsibility, and if the suggested idea fails, then all have had a share in it. Consequently, participants are likely to take bigger risks in the group than if each were alone in assuming responsibility for his suggestion.

Homogeneous and Heterogeneous Groups

One of the questions confronting managers in industry that also confronts those involved in setting up groups intended to be creative (or to be trained to have greater creativity) is how to compose the groups. Specifically, should the group consist of individuals who have the same personality and attitude or abilities, or should the individuals in the group be as different from each other as possible? Should groups be heterogeneous or homogeneous with respect to their members' personalities and abilities? On what should the characteristics of group composition depend?

Hoffman (1959) and Hoffman and Maier (1961) studied the behavior of homogeneous and heterogeneous groups in problem-solving situations. In the first experiment Hoffman (1959) selected subjects in terms of similarity and dissimilarity of personality profiles, as measured by the Guilford-Zimmerman Temperament Survey. Three types of four-person groups were established: A homogeneous group in which the personality profiles of the group members correlated highly and positively with each other; a second type of group in which the members' personality profiles correlated highly but negatively with each other; and a third type of group in which correlations among the personality profiles were essentially zero.

Three hypotheses were tested in this study. (1) When the problem involves quality alone, the heterogeneous groups produce higher-quality solutions than homogeneous groups. (2) When the problem involves both quality and acceptance, the heterogeneous groups either do not agree on a solution, come up with novel solutions, or are against change. Homogeneous groups, on the other hand, do not produce novel solutions and they either do not agree or do not accept alternatives that are offered them. (3) Homogeneous groups do not show a relationship between satisfaction with solution and its quality. Heterogeneous groups show a positive relationship between degree of satisfaction with solution and quality of solution.

The first hypothesis, concerned with quality alone, was tested with a problem in which the students were told that they were a guerrilla team that had just blown up an enemy bridge, and that in order to return to its home base the team had to cross a heavily mined road. There were ropes, lumber, and other kinds of materials that could be used to effect the crossing, and the group's problem was to decide on the best method for crossing the road safely and quickly and without leaving any traces. Solutions were rated in terms of feasibility, safety, concealment of clues, and amount of time taken to solve the problem.

The behavior of 17 heterogeneous groups (combining Type 2 and Type 3 groups described earlier) were compared with that of the homogeneous groups (Type 1). In terms of quality of solution, the heterogeneous groups scored significantly (at the .05 level) higher than the homogeneous groups. That these differences are probably related largely to the personality differences of the groups is reflected in the fact that course grades, sex composition of the groups, and sociometric attractiveness of the group did not account for the obtained differences.

The second hypothesis, designed to test the relationships between quality and acceptance of solutions and homogeneity of groups, was studied with a problem in which three individuals perform three different jobs in hourly rotation. For the sake of efficiency their supervisor asks them to work in fixed positions instead of rotating. The solutions to this problem are classified into three groups: Old solutions, in which the group does not change or continues rotation with a different time interval between changes; new solutions, which involve complete acceptance of the supervisor's solution even with some minor modifications; compromise or inventive solutions, in which work procedures that were not part of the roles themselves were assigned so as to take advantage of individuals' abilities and to allow participants to be free of monotony. There was no significant difference between homogeneous and heterogeneous groups in the number of old, new, and inventive solutions arrived at. Considering the inventive solutions alone, it would appear that where nonhomogeneous groups were involved in conflict, the resolution of the conflict yielded creative ideas. Only 16% of the 12 homogeneous groups produced inventive solutions, whereas 41% of the 17 heterogeneous groups did so.

The third hypothesis had to do with satisfaction of the participating members in the two situations. It will be recalled that it was predicted that positive relationships would be obtained between quality of solution and degree of satisfaction with solution in the homogeneous groups. The finding was, interestingly enough, that practically all the homogeneous groups were satisfied with their poor solutions. The heterogeneous groups also did not show the hypothesized relationship; the expectation that they would be less satisfied with a poor than with a good solution was not confirmed by the data. The third hypothesis was also not confirmed for the second problem. The differences, although in the right direction, were not statistically significant.

Thinking that the generality of the findings in the just described study was limited—that heterogeneous groups produced solutions of higher quality than homogeneous groups but their satisfactions with their solutions were similar—since only two problems were used, Hoffman and Maier (1961) undertook another study in which subjects were selected as in the first experiment, the two problems in the first experiment were repeated, and three new problems were added. These problems emphasized differences between group members and therefore should have made the problems more complex and put more stress on the heterogeneous groups. In this kind of situation the quality of the solutions achieved by heterogeneous groups, as well as the degree of their satisfaction with their solutions, might or might not be reduced.

An example of a more complicated problem was the "Student Assistance Fund" problem, in which each subject in the four-person group was told he was a student qualified to receive assistance from the university fund. He was also told that he needed $1,500, whereas the fund contained only $3,000 (if each of the four were to get this amount, $6,000 would of course be needed). The group had to decide how to divide the available money and had to develop a method for allocating the money in the future. Thus, there was potential conflict in the group because the money could not be divided equally and still fulfill each student's needs. Second, students were also given conflicting standards for allocating the money among themselves. In scoring the solutions to this problem, only the future method for allocating funds was evaluated, but data were also obtained from the subjects on their satisfaction with the solutions and with the amount of influence each felt he had in arriving at the solutions.

The findings of the first study were supported in this one. Solutions achieved by heterogeneous groups either did not differ in quality from those achieved by the homogeneous groups or they were definitely very superior. Homogeneous groups never did better than the heterogeneous ones. Specifically, this was true on three out of four problems—the heterogeneous groups produced better solutions than the homogeneous groups. There were differences between the groups on the fourth problem, and solutions to this problem were generally of poor quality. This is an especially important point to be remembered when we turn to the research evaluating the various techniques for stimulating creativity. There, too, the research data indicate that a technique may work well with one kind of problem but not with another. Of course, we would eventually like to know what kind of problem each technique is best suited for.

An interesting finding in this study was the interaction between sex and personality factors as they related to problem solving. Using the subjects from both groups, the investigators were able to study the effects of mixed-sex groups and heterogeneous personalities as compared with same-sex groups and homogeneous personalities. The effects were different for the two problems studied (since only two problems overlapped between the first and second studies). On one problem, as the ratio of women to men in a group increased, there was a decrease in the difference between the homogeneous and heterogeneous groups (but only one group was studied in which there were all women). On the other problem, high-quality solutions were found primarily among the mixed-sex groups. In discussing these results the investigators suggest that where the problem allows for alternatives that the group itself generates, a same sex group consisting of heterogeneous personalities will yield higher-quality solutions. But where the problem itself contains the alternatives, then adding a mixture of the sexes to the mixture of the personalities will produce the higher-quality solutions. This may be the case, but first it is necessary to eliminate possible effects of sex differences on the first problem. This problem seems to be a more "masculine" kind of problem (i.e., more dependent on a male's experience) in which women might not have very much to offer, as compared to other problems which would more likely be in the realm of the female students' experience.

It will be recalled that, after the experiment, subjects had to indicate the degree of satisfaction they felt with their solutions. Analysis of these data showed that there were no differences in satisfaction between the two groups. The heterogeneous groups, therefore, did not achieve their higher quality scores at the cost of satisfaction with the solutions by the individual group members.

The final finding in this study that is of interest is that, more important than quality of solution as a factor in determining a subject's satisfaction, was the subject's satisfaction with the amount of influence he had over the decision about a solution. Thus, if subjects believed they exercised their expected amount of influence on the decision, then they were satisfied with the decision of their group. Therefore, the investigators suggest that when the group consists of individuals with different points of view, if these people express their points of view, and if the differences are used in the final solution, the solution is very likely to be of very high quality. Individuals need not have the same amount of influence, but they must see that all points of view are attended to, and that all relevant viewpoints play a role in the final solution. All group members need not be active participants in the group's discussions, but if they are dissatisfied, then they must make their attitudes known. In sum, high-quality solutions that are accepted can be obtained from groups that are made up of persons with different points of view, provided these viewpoints are expressed and used by the group in coming to a final decision.

The two studies just cited involved four-person groups. There have also been experiments on two-person groups (dyads). There, the data indicate that dyads heterogeneous in attitudes and homogeneous in abilities were more creative than those which are heterogeneous or homogeneous in both. Training in the other member's viewpoint improves the creativity of heterogeneous dyads; low interpersonal attraction is negatively correlated with creativity; and the more creative each member of a dyad is, the higher the creativity of the two-person team.

Where a great deal of cooperation among members is required in performing an actual task, especially where a chain of acts is required of the group and each individual provides a separate link (e.g., in a maze study where groups have to master a complex interlocking system of levers), a homogeneous group is likely to be more efficient. One extremely slow member could keep the whole group from progressing at a satisfactory rate. Although a recalcitrant member can hinder the progress of a discussion group, arriving at a decision too quickly on the basis of opinions already held is unwise in some situations. A heterogeneous group is more likely to discuss the problem adequately and hence arrive at a more satisfactory solution. Thus, there is an optimal mix of personal characteristics for any given group project. The optimal mix for simple routine tasks includes fairly similar kinds of individuals, whereas for complex tasks requiring creativity the mix should be more diversified. (These studies are reviewed in Krech *et al.*, 1962.)

Group Aging

Groups, like individuals, age. This is not simply a matter of growing older chronologically and living with the problems and difficulties that some individuals consequently experience in keeping their creativity at a high level. Such problems do exist in groups, but more relevant is a quality of aging related to an individual's experience on the job. Some persons (whether in research, management, sales, or other fields, and regardless of status) learn certain techniques for performing their jobs and for getting along with others that gradually rigidify. These people become constricted; their behavior is well described in Merton's characterization of the bureaucratic personality (Merton, 1957).

Just as individuals develop rigidities, so do combinations of individuals in groups. The amount of time a group has stayed together may be a factor in its creative vitality. As a group ages, it may become less and less sensitive to new ideas, new processes, and creative developments. It is conceivable that the techniques to be described can "shake" a group out of its fixed patterns. Unfortunately, there is no research evidence on this point. Nevertheless, if this were true, then one of the reasons for stimulating creativity through group techniques would be that things might have been worse without them. Another potential effect of the techniques is that during the course of a group creativity stimulating session individuals learn something more about creativity than they knew before participating in it. They might develop some creative ideas while in the program, and even if they do not continue with creative activities when they return to their jobs, they may have acquired greater appreciation and understanding of the creative processes through which their associates, superiors, and subordinates on the job achieve their creative ideas and products.

What is the evidence for some of the effects of the "aging" process in groups? Torrance *et al.* (1957) studied bomber crews, comparing temporary and permanent three-man crews. When he gave them arithmetic problems, he found that the temporary crews had a higher percentage of correct solutions. To learn about some of the factors that might be responsible for this finding, he asked his subjects to write stories about a hypothetical conference and found that the low-status members of the permanent crews made fewer references to disagreement than did the high-status members. In temporary crews the low-status members made just as frequent references to disagreements as did high-status members. Presumably, the low-status members in permanent crews did not feel as free to disagree.

The other studies of a systematic character come from research conducted in research and development organizations in industry. One of the first studies with these groups is that by Shepard (1956) in which he asked research directors to rank teams or sections on various criteria, including creativity. Data were then obtained on the length of time the men had spent in the groups, and highest- and lowest-ranking creativity groups were compared. The highest-ranking groups were found to be less than 16 months in group age, and after that the rankings declined with increasing group age. Members of the groups also ranked the groups, and their ranks on creativity also showed a drop with increasing age, but there was an increase in creativity levels when the groups were 2-5 years of age.

Pelz and Andrews (1966) selected 83 research groups and obtained a variety of data on them which they related to group age. (Group age was defined by Pelz and Andrews as the average number of years that each man belonged to his group. Thus, a group that had been in existence a long time might still be regarded as "young" if it had been recruiting new members.) A series of very interesting findings then became available.

Scientific Contributions and Usefulness

Pelz and Andrews obtained data on their groups' scientific contributions and their usefulness to their organizations. The data were then adjusted to eliminate the effects of extraneous conditions. The adjusted scores showed a general decline in scientific contribution as the groups grew older. For usefulness the curve was curvilinear with a peak at 4 or 5 years of group age. Comparing older and younger groups, they found that the older ones were more relaxed, less secretive, and more specialized. If the older groups maintained their interaction with others and kept up intellectually, then they also kept up their vitality.

The performance of individuals in the groups and not the groups as such were rated by colleagues on "scientific contribution" and "over-all usefulness to the laboratory," and these ratings were averaged for each group.

Shepard's (1956) data on scientific contribution were confirmed. He too found a high peak early in the life of the group. There is, then, a decline between 2 and 3 years of group age; a rise at 4 and 5 years of group age that does not exceed the earlier peak; and finally a decline at 10-12 years of group age.

The data for overall usefulness show a rise at 4-5 years, followed by a drop at 6-7, a slight upward turn at 8-9, and finally another drop at 10-12. Pelz and Andrews suggest that new members stimulate a group to think in new scientific and technical ways. Usefulness, however, involves solving a problem efficiently in ways that proved themselves in the past. It takes several years for a group to develop this effectiveness.

Communication and Cohesiveness

Pelz and Andrews also studied the communication and cohesiveness patterns of these different age groups. Communication was measured by the frequency of contacting supervisors and colleagues and the total amount of time spent in contacting them. Cohesiveness was measured by the proportion of "most significant colleagues" chosen from the work group members using the "ratio of total within-group choices to total possible within-group choices [pp. 246-

247] ." This ratio turned out to be independent of group size. The findings were as follows. Initially, communication declined and cohesiveness increased; as the men got to know each other better, they selected each other as "significant colleagues." However, a reverse trend set in after 4-5 years. Cohesiveness dropped to a point where some of the oldest groups saw their chief a few times a month and their colleagues even less often. These groups could hardly be called groups.

Competition and Age

Pelz and Andrews found that competition between colleagues declined up to 6-7 years and then rose after that. Between groups, competition rose initially and thereafter dropped. Secretiveness within and between groups rose slightly at first; after that there was an irregular decline. Apparently, older groups gain security and assurance, according to these researchers; hence they are more relaxed, less competitive, and less secretive.

Perceived Similarity

It was also found that members of groups saw themselves as similar to each other up to 6-7 years of group age, when competition was lowest. Then competition rose and the extent to which they saw themselves as similar dropped.

Breadth of Problem Area

What was the effect of aging on preference for breadth or narrowness of problem area? Older groups become less interested in broadly mapping new areas and more involved in probing more deeply into narrow areas. Groups that were able to combine specialization and breadth and were internally cohesive and externally competitive were at the peak of their power.

Role of Administrator

The administrative chief plays different roles with younger and older groups. The greatest benefit to younger groups was on scientific contributions if the chief was a source of original ideas. Older groups looked to the chief as a "neutral sounding board" and benefited from him primarily by using him as someone on whom they can test their own ideas.

The supervisor of an older group who is effective in his role encourages group members to challenge each other. He acknowledges his group, pointing out the contributions of each person and not taking credit for himself. He can have his group compete with other groups, preferably outside the organization. He should try not to allow the group to become too specialized. Members need to maintain their breadth to be vital as a group.

For a younger group an effective supervisor is one who is a technical leader and supplier of original ideas, and who encourages ideas from group members without challenge or criticism, since the young group needs the freedom to work without fear of criticism.

Effects of Competition and Secretiveness

Earlier, competition was mentioned as a characteristic of groups, but how does it affect performance? Pelz and Andrews say that competition between colleagues was associated (but not significantly so) with higher performance only in younger groups. Competition *between* groups was associated with higher performance in older groups.

Secretiveness, which was found generally to be mild, inhibited younger groups in their performance but was of some benefit to older groups.

Diversity

When diversity (which Pelz and Andrews defined as "disagreement on technical matters [p. 257]") existed within groups, it was found to be helpful on scientific matters to both young and old groups and useful in older groups. If an older group could keep interested in new areas, it was an asset, just as it was a handicap if the group preferred narrow specialization.

One very interesting new measure developed by Pelz and Andrews was a measure of "intellectual tension," made up of two variables—perceived similarity and secretiveness (i.e., the extent to which group members see themselves as unlike each other and secretive). Younger groups were handicapped by this tension and older groups were helped by it.

Leaderless Groups

In most real-life situations where a group is called together for creative problem solving there is likely to be a leader. The leader may be an executive of a corporation, a research director, a scientific or technical supervisor, or a manager. But, when the group begins to work creatively and if in fact the group leader is to function as a working member, he must try to become a group member, or the group will not be able to function properly. If the leader cannot assume this role, then he may have to exclude himself from such activity. This does not mean that the administrative or scientific head of a real group does not play a role in the creative process. He does, but in certain parts of the process it is best that he behave like a member of the group.

Other groups, by the very nature in which they were set up to work creatively, are leaderless. For this type of group and for the type described previously, it is well to consider characteristics of leaderless groups. In this regard we are fortunate to have a balanced overview of leaderless groups' assets and liabilities by Maier (1967).* What follows is based on his work.

*This article was also published in Maier and Solem (1970).

Assets

(1) A group has more information and knowledge than each of its members. Even if any one member of the group knows a great deal, the unique information that another individual has can sometimes make a significant contribution. (2) A group can develop a greater number of approaches to a problem than an individual can. Individuals may become fixated on a single approach, and while this may also be true of groups, the individuals in a group can counteract each other's behavior and rigidity. (3) When individuals participate in solving a problem, there is a greater probability that the solution will be accepted by the group members and carried out. When groups solve a problem, there is a greater feeling that they are responsible for making it work, whereas if an individual solves a problem by himself he still must convince and persuade others to accept the solution. (4) A group that participates in the development of a decision has greater comprehension of the decision. If an individual arrives at a decision, he must then communicate it to those who have to carry it out, which entails danger of communication failure. On the other hand, where a group has participated in the decision, it not only understands the decision better but is also aware of the various alternatives that have been considered.

Liabilities

Just as leaderless groups have assets, so they have liabilities for problem solving. Maier (1967) points to the following.

(1) Some individuals feel under pressure to conform in group situations. Thus, they are likely to keep their disagreements to themselves in order to arrive at a consensus. Confronted with the force of a majority opinion, they are likely to accept it regardless of its soundness. Maier and Solem (1970), for example, found that minority opinions had little influence on solutions reached in leaderless groups, even when these opinions were the correct ones. And of course there is the well-known Asch (1952) experiment in which some individuals who were asked to give their judgments after a series of suggestions had already been offered were swayed in the direction of the erroneous judgments, even though those judgments disagreed sharply with their perceptions.

(2) Another characteristic of group problem-solving behavior that Maier points to is the effect of what he calls "valence of solution." The valence of a solution is essentially a turning point between the idea-getting process and the decision-making process. Thus, when groups of three or four people engage in solving a problem in a leaderless group situation, some or all of the individuals in the group may offer solutions to the problem. The number of positive and negative reactions to each solution is algebraically summed, and each solution is then given a *valence index*. Maier (1967) reports that the first solution that received a positive valence value of 15 tends to be adopted by all members of the

group about 85% of the time. And they behave in this manner regardless of the quality of the solution. Moreover, after the valence of 15 has been reached, solutions of higher quality have little chance of being considered. A critical valence of 15 is not affected by the nature of the problem or the exact size of the group. It should be noted that the valence index of any solution is not a measure of the number of persons supporting the solution but merely the algebraic sum of positive and negative statements. Hence, a vocal minority can push a solution by supporting it actively, or skilled group manipulators can influence a group to a degree in excess of their proportionate membership in the group.

(3) In leaderless groups an individual may appear who dominates the group and exerts more than his share of influence over it. He does this by participating vocally to a greater degree and thus affecting the valence index. Through persuasion and persistence he can wear a group down so that the remaining members have to give in. Neither his persistence nor his powers of persuasion are related to problem-solving ability, so that the person who is actually the best problem solver but who lacks these skills may not stand much chance of upgrading the group's solution. But Hoffman and Maier (1970) point out that merely appointing someone as a leader can create a problem because the appointee then tends to dominate the discussion and to exert an inordinate influence on its outcome.

(4) When a group is presented with a problem, its goal presumably is to seek and find a solution. In the process, however, individuals may get involved in converting others with neutral stands and arguing against those with opposing points of view. All of this proselytizing can result in contests to win an argument rather than in efforts to find the best solution. Some group members' conflicting "secondary goals" can be of such intensity as to obstruct a group's progress toward its goal.

There is much research on group behavior that cannot possibly be covered here, but let the foregoing suffice for our purposes. The studies cited serve to illustrate a variety of group characteristics and how they might affect a group's behavior. Although group creativity was not the focus of these studies, there is no doubt that channels of communication, group climate, group age, etc. affect group creativity just as they affect group effectiveness in other areas.

BEFORE MAKING FINAL ARRANGEMENTS FOR GROUP PROCEDURES TO STIMULATE CREATIVITY

Each of the group procedures to stimulate creativity is designed in its own way to overcome some of the problems that were previously discussed, as well as others. Of course, these procedures are not only useful when there are problems; they can also be of value when problems do not exist. The fact is, however, that they are most likely to be used when problems arise or when there is dissatisfaction with the group's creativity. In this situation, it is not necessarily true that a creativity stimulating procedure is the method of choice. There may be other things that can be done. Although attention in this book is focused on procedures to stimulate creativity, our concern is also that they be used appropriately. We believe that in some instances other procedures may be more appropriate to solving the problems and removing the restrictions that block creativity. In addition, we also believe that before a person undertakes a group technique for stimulating creativity he should also consider some means of evaluating its future value. Therefore, we now turn to a consideration of several questions that are among those that should be asked before final arrangements are made for group procedures to stimulate creativity. The questions are: Is a group procedure for stimulating creativity needed? Should there be an in-house training program? Or should groups be sent to training programs outside the organization? Who in the organization should be sent for training? What kind of creativity program should be selected? What criteria will be utilized to evaluate the significance of the program for the individual and for the organization? While answers to these questions vary depending on the individual circumstances, several general comments are in order that can serve as general guidelines.

Need for a Group Procedure—Diagnostic Surveys and Psychological Testing

Before undertaking a group program for stimulating creativity, it is appropriate to ask whether there are problems or obstacles to creativity that can be solved in other more appropriate and less time consuming ways. A solution needs to be congruent with the problem. Hence, the first problem that needs to be solved is what kind(s) of problem(s) exist. It is conceivable in some situations, even if one or more individuals in an organization are sent to group programs, that they may be unable to make effective use of what they learn because there are still problems in the organization which militate against the manifestation of creativity.

Management of an organization may be quick to say that the problem is the lack of creativity in the organization, but the lack of creativity is sometimes a symptom of other existing problems or attitudes that militate against creativity. For example, does the organization really value creativity or does it want more efficient productivity? What are the value orientations of top management, supervisory, scientific, and technical personnel? Is there congruence and agreement as to values placed on success and creativity within the organization? What is the nature of and how effective are the formal and informal channels of communication? What is the character of interpersonal relationships within the organization? What is the quality of supervision? Are supervisors competent in carrying out their roles? Are subordinates qualified to fulfill their roles? How are work problems selected or assigned? How are the outcomes evaluated? What is the quality of supporting services and personnel in the organization? Are the rewards in the organization offered to reinforce creative behavior or only to encourage more efficient and productive behavior?

These are some of the questions that need to be answered in evaluating the current status of an organization insofar as its creativity is concerned. Answers may be obtained through interviews or diagnostic surveys (Pelz & Andrews, 1966; Stein, 1959a-e). These can be administered either by the organization's own personnel department or with the aid of some outside consulting group. Not infrequently, they may reveal some of the bottlenecks to creativity that need to be cleared up by administrative decisions and programs within the organization. If these obstacles are not eliminated, problems may continue to exist, and money spent on programs to stimulate creativity will be wasted. Appropriate decisions that rectify existing problems may unleash a number of creative developments for organization problems that had inhibited the utilization of the creative potential available in the organization. For example, unresolved interpersonal conflicts might have reached a point where more time and energy is spent on them than on creative activity. Changing the reward system so that creative developments are in fact rewarded might bring an increased number of creative ideas and products to the fore. By uncorking some of the problems in the channels of communication, better understanding of the organization's goals may develop, and the creative efforts of the personnel may be more directed and less diffuse. All of these and similar problems need to be dealt with by management, whose responsibility they are. The buck should not be passed to the creativity program for it does not have the power nor the responsibility for dealing with such matters.

Just as there is a need for further data and understanding of the characteristics and problems of the organization, there is also a need to gather information about the psychological characteristics of the individuals who are counted on for creativity. Many organizations are sorely lacking in such information. It has been our experience with Research and Development organizations that each of them, if asked, could come up with an up-to-the-minute inventory of its physical plant and equipment, but few could provide information and data about the psychological characteristics of its personnel that could be used as a basis for assessing their creativity. Before deciding on a group creativity program, such psychological data must be collected. It may well be that the relative lack of creativity in the organization is due to the large number of personnel who were selected for their jobs without having the necessary characteristics for creativity. This is a case where there are too many Indians and no chiefs. Another possibility is that individuals may be found in the organization who possess the psychological characteristics for creativity but who are not in situations that make use of their abilities. They may be so inundated with detailed technical work, paper work, or administrative activities that they have little time to do the work for which they were employed.

Whatever the case, it is most desirable before embarking on a creativity stimulating program to have appropriate data about the personnel involved. Such data can be collected through interviews, surveys, or psychological testing programs.

Preparing an Organization for Diagnostic Surveys and Psychological Testing

If an organization has not had experience with diagnostic surveys and psychological testing, it must prepare its personnel at all levels for what is to come. Preparation can take place at group meetings to which all echelons are invited to hear the program presented and to ask questions. Essentially, the groups are told that top management wants to take the pulse of the organization. It wants to learn what assets it has insofar as creativity is concerned. Consequently, a questionnaire that covers the areas of communication, values, roles, rewards, etc. will be administered in the organization to persons representing all echelons. In addition, a psychological assessment program will also be undertaken.

This statement plus some additional elaboration is often sufficient to get the ball rolling and then the floor is opened to questions. The following are typical questions:

(1) How was the survey constructed? And how valid and reliable are the tests? In response the men are told how the questionnaire was constructed and to whom it has been administered. With regard to the psychological tests, the group is told how they were constructed, with whom they have been used, and some general statement as to the uses that were made of them. Our aim is always to answer the questions as completely as possible without interfering with the goals of the program.

(2) Will the test data be anonymous? Every person in the group wants assurance that no personal data will be revealed to others with whom they are working. They want to be certain that none of the information or answers they give will be used by management for promotions, salary increases, or for making job assignments. We have always provided such assurance and respected the desire for anonymity. The matter of anonymity is discussed with top management before the program is begun, and their approval is obtained for: (a) the use of code numbers by participants instead of their names on the questionnaires or the tests; (b) informing those in management not to make a request to see the data on any one person; (c) analyzing group data so that the size of the groups would not be such as to make them easily identified by management. These are sufficient assurances.

(3) A third rather popular question about surveys and psychological tests is whether the participants will be informed about the results. For the survey they are told that group data will be presented at one or more meetings of all those involved. If a psychological testing program is involved, then the men are told that the information will also be presented as group data. (We frequently find

that once the psychological data are presented as group results, the men want individual reports, and different plans have to be made for this.)

(4) The participants also want to know what use will be made of the survey and psychological tests results. Our practice has always been to tell them the truth—the results will be used to assess the organization in terms of creativity; to take a reading now on the organization and compare it with data to be collected two years from now to see how the organization has changed; to determine whether there is a need for selection of new personnel or for reallocation of current personnel.

These last two possibilities stir the most interest and/or anxiety among the participants, as might be expected. Their queries, however, give us an opportunity to point out that a good personnel program is one that tries to place a man in a situation in which he will be happy and in which he will make most effective use of his abilities and potentialities. Consequently, whatever data will be collected will be only part of the data that will be available for the decision on any change. Psychological test data will be considered together with job histories and evaluations, etc. before any decisions are made. Furthermore, our experience has been, and indeed it has been borne out by some research (Brim *et al.*, 1969), that people do not object so much to tests that are used to select and evaluate other persons' abilities for jobs that they themselves might not qualify for. They only object to the use of tests when they fear that tests would be used to keep them from positions they want.

When the nature of their objections to tests is made manifest and when the participants are told how the tests will be used, there is more cooperation and, although all skepticism is not dispelled, the tests are taken. Of course, to maintain the participants' confidence they need to be kept informed as to how the tests are used.

Top management also has some queries, and two representative ones are:

(1) Will their decisions be determined by the surveys and/or the tests? At the beginning we have to convince top management of the value of the surveys or tests. After the data are in, we have to convince them to use their own judgment and to evaluate the test results against their own experiences before arriving at a decision. Test and survey data should always be used in conjunction with other data. In addition, survey and test data should not be used to do dirty work. If someone is to be fired, then it should not be done shortly after the results are in. It is hard to convince the participants that the test or survey data were not the only pieces of information available. If management wants to fire someone, hopefully they will do so before the survey and psychological data are collected.

(2) The second major management question is, if a test battery were used as a condition of employment for selection purposes, might the company be turned

down by prospective employees? Whether or not this happens, we believe, is a function of the job market. When the job market is tight, applicants are more likely to accept a testing program. When jobs are plentiful, it is conceivable that applicants may look askance at an organization using tests.

These objections to testing could be diminished if those in the organization responsible for psychological testing introduce the matter and conduct the tests as casually as they set up interviews for the prospective employee with top management. Just as prospective employees may be made anxious about "the front office" or "the boss," they may be made anxious about the tests. If the purpose of testing is explained, if the prospective employee is told that test data will be used together with such additional information as previous job history, recommendations, interviews, etc. to help place him in a position that will be of significance to both him and the organization, then it is likely that few problems will be encountered. On the other hand, problems may arise if those responsible for testing feel uncomfortable with what they are doing, or if they say something like, "And, *now*, we would like you to take some psychological tests. I hope you don't mind; personnel insists on it." Just as one would not say this about interviews, this should not be said about tests. After the prospective employee has taken the test, he will see for himself how the tests are used. If the tests are not used properly and he objects or tells other prospective employees not to take them, he is no doubt right. If the tests are used properly, then word is likely to spread about this too. Prospective employees will be so informed and few, if any, problems are likely to occur.

There is, then, much to be gained from a good survey and psychological testing program. It provides data that can highlight problems and obstacles to creativity which, if resolved, could release much creative potential, even without a creativity stimulating program.

There are other uses of a survey and psychological testing program. If the problems cannot be resolved by management and it is necessary to undertake a creativity stimulating program, then the data collected can serve diagnostically and help in deciding what kind of a creativity stimulating program to select. Also, a survey and psychological testing program may provide baseline data that may later be of value in determining whether or not a creativity stimulating program has been of value. Both these matters will be considered further later.

An In-House Training Program?

One of the advantages of an in-house program is that the program can be tailored to the organization's needs. It can be developed to focus specifically on the problems that are of interest to the organization, and it can be scheduled at the convenience of the participants. However, an in-house program may be expensive in terms of personnel, and it is necessary to ascertain that it is economically worthwhile. It may well be that utilizing the services of a consultant or sending company personnel to a creativity training program may suit the needs of most organizations. In answer to the problem of scheduling an appropriate time for sending personnel to a creativity training program, one may as well face the fact that there just is not any convenient time. One time is as good or bad as another.

Who in the Organization Shall Be Sent for Training?

Ideally all of the personnel in the organization. The more persons conversant with the creative process, the more likely it is that an atmosphere will emerge that will be conducive to creative developments. There will be greater appreciation and understanding of the problems that confront the individual and greater regard for him and the process through which he solves such problems. It is impractical, of course, to think that all personnel will participate in a creativity stimulating program. Some selection needs to be made. A possible rule of thumb is to consider those persons who had once been but who no longer are creative, as well as those persons who had been counted on to be creative by virtue of their training and experience but who are not manifestly creative. In both these instances, data gathered in interviews with the potential candidate's peers, subordinates, and superiors, as well as from survey questionnaires and psychological tests, could serve as a good basis for a proper determination.

If possible, it would be desirable to avoid sending someone from the personnel department unless he is really qualified. Otherwise it is much more desirable to send those individuals who will use the creativity techniques, for they are in a better position to provide some evaluation as to the techniques' potential significance for the organization. If one person is to go, he should be from the latter group. If someone from personnel is to go, for whatever reason, then he should be accompanied or followed by someone who will use the techniques.

One group of people who frequently get to go to seminars away from the home office are those who need or merit a trip or who can take in the seminar while they are involved in other organization business in the vicinity of the seminar. Such individuals are frequently poor choices because their selection was not determined by how appropriate they were for the seminar and the seminar for them.

What Kind of Creativity Program Shall Be Selected?

The answer to this question is also best decided when survey and psychological test data are available. If surveys or psychological tests are not used, then information needs to be gathered in interviews or group discussions with company personnel. The question is, what do company personnel seem to be lacking for manifesting creativity? Are they constricted cognitively? Do they have personality problems? Or is it a matter of difficulties in interpersonal relationships? If the problems are as specific as these, then a selection could be made of one or more of the procedures that follow. On the other hand, most situations are likely to be fairly complex, and for them the best approach is to ask for consultations with those responsible for creativity stimulating programs. The advice of the representatives of different programs can then be evaluated in terms of the organization's needs. Additional guidance may be obtained from other organizations that have had prior experience with the different creativity stimulating programs.

What Criteria Will Be Used to Evaluate the Program for the Individual and for the Organization?

Criteria can and will no doubt be selected all along the way for evaluating a creativity stimulating program. However, it is best if the criteria are set up before a program is selected. Such criteria are likely to be more practical and significant than those developed after the program is completed. One can always add to the criteria even after the program is completed.

The major criterion that most organizations are concerned with is the payoff in terms of actual profitable works produced within a reasonable time. This is the most practical and hard-headed criterion. In setting up this criterion it is important to set a reasonable time limit and realistic goals.

Other criteria might involve the kinds of questions included in the survey mentioned previously. After enough people have gone through the creativity stimulating program, has morale improved? has communication improved? has the quality of interpersonal relationships improved? etc.

Also, if psychological tests were administered prior to the start of the creativity stimulating program, then six months and/or a year after the training period, the tests should be readministered to learn if any changes occurred.

These, then, are some criteria that need to be kept in mind and which can be added to as one prepares to evaluate the effects of a program to stimulate creativity. With these criteria and the questions previously presented in mind, let us now turn to the various group programs for stimulating creativity from which selections can be made.

Chapter XIII

Brainstorming

The best known and probably most widely used procedure to stimulate creativity is brainstorming. It was originated in 1938 by Alex F. Osborn in response to his dissatisfaction with the "usual" business conference. Osborn, as did so many other business executives, came to regard the usual business conference as a waste of time because, although the business meeting would be called to deal with one or more important problems, it usually did not yield anything of value. Therefore, Osborn developed brainstorming as a means of achieving "organized ideation [Osborn, 1963, p. 151]" in group meetings held in his advertising company, Batten, Barton, Durstine, and Osborn. These group meetings began to be called *brainstorming sessions* because " 'brainstorming' means using the *brain* to *storm* a problem [Osborn, 1963, p. 151]."*

In 1953 Osborn set forth the rules and principles of brainstorming in his book entitled *Applied Imagination*. The book actually includes more than information about brainstorming. In fact, it concerns itself with all phases of the creative

---

*A more picturesque way of thinking of this term comes from Bittel (1956) in which an idea from a secretary helped an engineer solve a problem. In describing this situation, Bittel says, "The secretary seeded a cloud of confusion with an idea that released a brainstorm [Bittel, 1956, p. 101]."

problem-solving process. The book became quite popular and according to information on the jacket cover of the copy used for purposes of this chapter (1963 third revision and 14th printing), the book has gone through fourteen printings yielding a total of 120,000 copies.

In 1954 Osborn founded and became president of the Creative Education Foundation and in 1955 the first Creative Problem-Solving Institute was established and sponsored jointly by the State University College at Buffalo and the Creative Education Foundation also located in Buffalo.

At the present time Dr. Sidney J. Parnes is director of the Creative Education Foundation. While Osborn pioneered, popularized, and promoted brainstorming, Parnes, through his own efforts and those of his associates or others in the field, provided the research and theoretical rationale for its assumptions, uses, and effectiveness.

It is important at this point to interrupt the discussion to make two points of semantic clarification so as to minimize any possible confusion:

(1) It is conceivable that some confusion may be stimulated by the terms brainstorming and creative problem-solving because Osborn and Parnes have been involved in both, and both procedures are, in fact, related. To minimize the confusion between brainstorming, discussed in this chapter, and creative problem-solving, discussed in the next chapter, it should be said that brainstorming is a procedure for *idea generation*—a procedure that involves the suspension of judgment and evaluation so as to allow an individual the opportunity to come up with ideas without fear of censorship or criticism. However, at times, the procedure is also extended to include a second step in the creative process. This additional step does involve evaluation—evaluation of ideas that come to the fore when judgment, etc., is suspended. In brief, the primary emphasis in brainstorming is on the coming up with ideas when judgment and evaluation have been *deferred*.

It is apparent from what has been said that brainstorming may be used throughout the problem-solving process wherever new or more ideas are necessary. But, brainstorming is only one procedure used for arriving at these new or more ideas. There are others, such as those discussed throughout this book. All of these procedures plus others have been collated, initially by Osborn and later by Parnes, into an integrated program called Creative Problem-Solving. The title "Creative Problem-Solving" when capitalized refers to this combination of approaches, but brainstorming, by itself, may result in creative problem solving (words not capitalized) and hence initiate the possible confusion referred to previously.

(2) The second point of semantic clarification that needs to be made is that Parnes prefers limiting the use of the term brainstorming to characterize the work of *groups* using it to achieve creative solutions. When *individuals* working

by themselves are involved Parnes prefers calling it *deferred judgment*. Other workers in this area more commonly use "brainstorming" for both conditions. We have followed this more common practice although we have tried on occasion to adopt Parnes' use. In both conditions it should be apparent that judgment is deferred.

With these brief introductory statements in mind let us now turn to the theory underlying brainstorming. Later we shall present a rather large body of research information. The presentation of theory that follows is based primarily on Osborn's (1963) *Applied Imagination* and secondarily on Parnes' *Creative Behavior Guidebook* (1967a) and *Creative Behavior Workbook* (1967b).

THEORY

For Osborn "the creative problem-solving process" consists of "(1) *Fact*-finding. (2) *Idea*-finding. (3) *Solution*-finding [Osborn, 1963, p. 86] ."

Fact finding consists of two parts: problem definition and preparation. The former involves selecting and highlighting the problem while the latter involves assembling information related to the problem.

Idea finding involves producing ideas through idea generation and through the combination of and extrapolation from existing and available ideas.

The third phase of the creative problem-solving process, *solution finding*, involves evaluating ideas and adopting one of them for further development and eventual use.

Osborn recommended brainstorming for the second, "idea finding," phase of the creative problem-solving process. Brainstorming as we said is a method for coming up with ideas without regard to their evaluation. This does *not* mean that evaluation is disregarded forever but rather that it is only deferred. Osborn carefully separated evaluation from idea generation for fear that evaluation, if it came too early, might adversely affect the number and quality of ideas produced in attempting to solve a problem.

This orientation in the brainstorming procedure as Osborn himself points out, has a long history. A technique very similar to brainstorming has been used by Hindu religious teachers for more than 400 years while working with religious groups. "The Indian name for this method is *Prai-Barshana. Prai* means 'outside yourself' and Barshana means 'question.' In such a session there is no discussion or criticism. Evaluation of ideas takes place at later meetings of the same group [Osborn, 1963, p. 151] ."

It is apparent then that Osborn believed that an individual could *deliberately* set out to come up with ideas that would provide creative solutions to problems; and what held for an individual also held for groups of individuals. He therefore recommended brainstorming to help overcome the restrictive and rigidifying effects of evaluation that occurred in most business conferences. On the group level, therefore, Osborn saw a brainstorming session as "nothing more than a creative conference for the sole purpose of producing a checklist of ideas—ideas which can serve as leads to problem-solution—ideas which can *subsequently* be evaluated and further processed [Osborn, 1963, pp. 151-152]."

Efforts devoted to deliberately coming up with ideas for creative solutions could be facilitated by following two major principles and four major rules.

The two major principles are: *deferment of judgment* and *quantity breeds quality*. The four major rules are: (1) *Criticism is ruled out*; (2) *freewheeling is welcomed*; (3) *quantity is wanted*; and (4) *combination and improvement are sought*.

The Two Principles

Deferment of Judgment

Thinking, according to Osborn, involves both a "judicial mind" and a "creative mind." The former "analyzes, compares and chooses" (i.e., evaluates), whereas the latter "visualizes, foresees and generates ideas [Osborn, 1963, p. 39]." The judicial mind "puts the brakes" on the creative mind, and these brakes need to be removed so that ideas can be generated. To remove these brakes, the first principle of brainstorming—*deferment of judgment*—has to be observed. The individual verbalizes or writes down his ideas without concern for their value, feasibility, or significance (all of which are, however, considered later). Yet he does not engage literally in free associations, for this might result in fruitless ideas: "instead of literally deferring judgment, we are, in reality, using 'limited-criteria' thinking—these 'limited' criteria being dependent on the way we state the problem [Parnes, 1967a, p. 68]." For example,

> In using the principle of deferred judgment, we don't say, "List ideas that come to your mind by free association." Instead, we say, "List ideas *with respect to such-and-such a problem.*" When we list uses for a broom, for example, we are setting the criteria of "uses" and "broom" in our minds as we allow our automatic associative processes to go to work. In other words, we are saying, "I will entertain any idea that comes to my mind with respect to *using a broom* in some way. . . ." Hence I *am* judging (and ruling out) *automatically* any thought or idea that comes to my mind that is not pertinent to "uses for a broom" [Parnes, 1967a, pp. 68-69].

Expressed differently, the problem as stated "sets" the individual, and his thought processes do not run on at random, but operate within the more limited framework of what Parnes calls *primary criteria*, for example, "uses" and "broom" in the sample just presented. What, then, is deferred? According to Parnes, *secondary criteria* are deferred. These secondary criteria include such evaluative thoughts as: Will it be too expensive; Will it take too long to do; Will it require too many people to do it?

Quantity Breeds Quality

The second principle of brinstorming is that *quanitity breeds quality*. The rationale for this dictum originates in associationistic psychology, which (see Volume I, pages 86-88) assumes that our thoughts or associations are structured hierarchically. The most dominant thoughts in this hierarchy are those which are most habitual, common, or usual, and are therefore likely to be, from other points of view, the "safest" and most acceptable to others. It is necessary to "get through" these conventional ideas if we are to arrive at original ones. After the dominant ideas have been reviewed and rejected, additional effort has to be expended in order to generate fresh associations. Implicit in this view is that somewhere in the repertoire of an individual's associations there are some that are original or others that, if combined properly, can yield creative results.

The Four Rules

The two basic principles just described, deferment of judgment and quantity breeds quality, give rise to four essential rules for a brainstorming session.

1. Criticism Is Ruled Out

All criticism and evaluation are put off until some future date. This key rule is the means of implementing the principle of deferred judgment. It is so critical that when brainstorming is conducted in a group, some chairmen or leaders ring a bell whenever any member of the group criticizes another's ideas or is self-critical or apologetic for that which he has himself suggested.

2. Freewheeling Is Welcomed

Participants are to feel free to offer any idea; as a matter of fact, the wilder the idea the better, for "it is easier to tame down [an idea] than to think [it] up [Osborn, 1963, p. 156]." The intent of this rule is to help the individual feel more relaxed and less inhibited than he might in ordinary circumstances by encouraging him to and implicitly rewarding him for using his imagination. It relieves him of responsibility for evaluation.

3. Quantity Is Wanted

This rule is a restatement of the second principle of brainstorming, that the more ideas suggested, the greater the probability that an original one will come up.

4. *Combination and Improvement Are Sought*

The intent of this rule is to motivate participants to build on others' ideas by showing how already offered ideas might be improved or combined in various ways with other ideas. This rule not only encourages the development of additional ideas, but also offsets any feeling of embarrassment individuals might experience at not having been the first to think of an idea.

To summarize, these two principles and four rules constitute brainstorming's fundamental orientation to the generation of ideas irrespective of whether this orientation is practiced by an individual or by a group of individuals; to achieve a creative solution the idea-generation stage is separated from and is followed by idea-evaluation. There are no specific guidelines on how to evaluate a list of ideas developed through brainstorming, probably because Osborn, brainstorming's originator, assumed that people are more practised in idea evaluation than idea generation. Nevertheless, should an obstacle be encountered in the process of idea evaluation and should more ideas be needed, the brainstorming process following the two principles and four rules can be reinstituted.

SETTING UP FOR A GROUP BRAINSTORMING SESSION

Brainstorming with a group of individuals is a bit more complicated than with a single individual—not because of complications in the process but because of the number of persons involved. A review of the literature highlights several important pointers regarding group composition, problem selection, etc.—some points of which may also be of value to individuals using brainstorming. After these pointers have been discussed we shall turn to a presentation and discussion of research studies of the principles and rules of brainstorming as well as related matters.

Group Composition

Brainstorming, as we have said, involves a deliberate attempt to make effective use of what is known about the creative process. This holds true not only for the development of creative solutions to problems but also for the selection of people involved in the process. To randomly select individuals to participate in a brainstorming session and to expect them to come up with creative ideas is rather unrealistic. This is not to say that all possible participants do not have the potential for creativity, rather it is to highlight the point that maximization of the probability that brainstorming will prove valuable requires thoughtful selection of participants and leaders. We now turn to some of the more critical issues involved.

Participants

Participants should have knowledge and/or experience with the field in which the problem is based. If there are participants who have no previous experience with brainstorming then they should attend an orientation session at which they learn what to expect. This meeting could include a discussion of the fundamentals of thinking and forming ideas as well as the basic principles of brainstorming. Use can also be made of slides, movies, etc., available from the Creative Education Foundation.

It is helpful for the group to include a few "self-starters" to get the ball rolling. If they dominate or monopolize the group it may be necessary to tell them to hold back. As Bristol (1958) put it, "In choosing your panel member, it is wise to choose at least one or two people of known creative ability. You may find it wise, also to choose a few panel members who are not too close to your problem, because their ideas may reflect a more refreshing approach to your problem [p. 145]."

Executives who "have been over-trained in the usual kind of non-creative conference [Osborn, 1963, pp. 159-160]" are undesirable as participants. All members of a brainstorming group should hold the same administrative rank within the organization so as not to feel inhibited in their superiors' presence.

Brainstorming groups can be established throughout an organization. Guests from other parts of the organization could be invited to any core group so that more and more people gain experience in solving problems creatively.

The optimal size of an *idea-finding* brainstorming group is twelve persons. The critical point is not so much the size of the group as that it should be an even number of persons. For idea evaluation or decision making, according to Osborn, one might want an odd number of participants. In the idea-finding group in addition to the leader, associate leader, and recording secretary (who is not really a participating member of the group) the group can consist of five regular or core members and five positions that can be filled by nonregular members or visitors.

Obviously, both men and women can constitute a brainstorming group. And a group so composed can frequently add more rivalry, excitement, and zest to the group process.

Leader

The group leader's personality, his knowledge and experience with the problem, and his knowledge and experience in brainstorming are all critical considerations in his selection. "You will want to choose him with great care, because your chairman can mean the success or failure of your brainstorming session. You want to choose a keen-witted, friendly person who is able to be both a 'driver' and a 'relaxer,' that is, someone who can keep the session atmosphere friendly and informal [Bristol, 1958, p. 144]."

The leader has to fulfill several very critical functions. He has to process the statement of the problem so that it is stated in a workable manner. He has to select participants who will be able to follow brainstorming's two principles and four rules. He has to prepare new participants. He has to provide a warmup session for the group and prepare the total group prior to the brainstorming session. And, he has to conduct the session in terms of brainstorming principles and in such a manner as to enable the group to manifest its full potentiality.

Associate Leader

The associate leader should have the same characteristics as the leader. He helps the leader as is necessary and should also be able to take over the leader's function should it become necessary to do so.

Recording Secretary

A secretary who is a nonparticipating member of the group records participants' ideas and suggestions. These may be recorded in a telegrammatic fashion but with enough data so that their general sense is not lost. If the topic discussed is very technical then a secretary with technical knowledge has to be selected. On some occasions two secretaries have been used to keep up with the rapidity of the flow of ideas. On such occasions the secretaries take turns in recording every other suggested idea. Tape recorders may also be used but they need not replace the secretaries.

It is a good idea to number ideas as they are recorded. The leader then has a ready tabulation of the number of ideas produced which he can use to tell a group how well it has done and to spur it on to even greater production.

When ideas are recorded they are not noted with the name of the suggestor. "The need for group congeniality far outweighs the good of granting individual credit [Osborn, 1963, p. 178]."

The Problem

If brainstorming is to be effective it is necessary to state the problem properly. Brainstorming is not for all problems. According to Osborn it is indicated for problems that require idea finding rather than judgment. The problem to be selected is one that lends itself to many alternative possible solutions. Brainstorming cannot be of much help with a problem such as "when should we introduce such-and-such a new course"; But, it can be used to produce ideas for tests that would help in arriving at such a decision.

A problem should be specific rather than general. An example given by Osborn is that a general question may be that of introduction of a new synthetic fiber. To be more specific it should be altered to ask what ideas would help to introduce the new fiber to weavers and mills or to introduce the new fiber to dress houses and cutters, etc.

If a problem is a complex one it should be broken down into component subproblems and each should be worked on separately (Bristol, 1958). A brainstorming session may even be devoted to breaking down a problem into its subunits. And, then, a separate brainstorming session can be devoted to each unit.

The Process

Prior to the brainstorming session the leader prepares about a 1-page memorandum in which the time and place of the brainstorming session is given as well as well as a very simple statement of the problem. The memorandum also includes the background of the problem and examples of the kinds of ideas that are desired. If necessary, illustrations and other exhibits should accompany the memorandum.

This memorandum is circulated to the participants at least 2 days before the brainstorming session so that they can become acquainted with the problem and allow their ideas to incubate.

When the participants report at the time selected for the brainstorming session, the leader starts off new participants with a warmup session using some very simple problem (improving men's pants is one suggested by Osborn) unrelated to the problem they will finally work on.

The leader presents the problem and answers questions. The four brainstorming rules are stated: "(1) *Criticism is ruled out.* (2) *'Free-wheeling'* is welcomed. (3) *Quantity is wanted.* (4) *Combination and improvement are sought.*" Then he calls for ideas and suggestions from the group.

Just as soon as a hand goes up the leader asks the person to state his idea. If too many hands go up, each person in turn is given a chance to state one idea. No one is allowed to read his ideas from a list if he brought such to the meeting. The lists can be given to the leader before the meeting and their contents should be given at the meeting.

As people verbalize their ideas, one idea may stimulate a related idea. These are called "hitch-hikes," and they are given priority of statement in the brainstorming process. It is important that a participant have some way of signifying (e.g., snapping his fingers) that he has a hitch-hike so he can be given priority by the leader. A participant might well make a note of his ideas so that he doesn't forget them.

When the group seems as if it is running dry, the leader might encourage the participants to come up with more ideas by telling them how well they have already done or by urging them to come up with "about 10 more ideas," etc. He can suggest his own ideas during these slow periods or come up with idea-spurring questions as: What other uses can one make of such-and-such? How can such-and-such be changed in terms of color, sound, motion? Etc.

As ideas are suggested they are noted by the secretary. Experience has shown that 30 minutes is an optimal period for a brainstorming session. However, some practitioners suggest 15 minutes or less and some as much as 45 minutes.

Brainstorming in Action

The following is an excerpt of an idea-generating brainstorming session quoted from De Bono's [1973, pp. 158-159] book, *Lateral Thinking: Creativity Step by Step*. It was to redesign a teaspoon.

...A rubber spoon

...I feel that the secondary function of a spoon which is that of transferring sugar from the basin to the cup has largely disappeared and that a teaspoon in the shape of an egg whisk would be much more efficient.

...(Put down egg-whisk.)

...And make it electrically driven.

...Incorporate a musical box for the aesthetic function.

...Have something like a pipette tube which you dip in the sugar with your finger over the top and transfer sugar in that way. Then the sugar would be provided with a dispersing agent so that you would entirely lose the pleasure of stirring.

...Going back to the egg whisk I think one ought to have a sort of screw thing, rather like an electrical swizzle stick. The axle would be hollow...

...(Can I interrupt here? You are beginning to tell us how you would make it and that is not the function of this session.)

...No, I am just describing what it looks like.

...(Could you describe it more simply?)

...A rotating spoon?

...No it's got a screw. You know, a propeller type screw.

...You push it up and down?

...No it's electric, you just press the button on the top.

...It seems to me this is too complicated. Now you have an ordinary sugar tongs and each individual would have his own sugar tongs and would pick up a couple of lumps of sugar. The tongs have two ends and you could create turbulence just as easily as with a spoon.

...Doesn't this restrict you to lump sugar?

...Yes, small lumps. But you can still get the quantity of sugar you want.

...(What shall we put down there?)

...Tongs.

...What about something like those ashtrays which spin as you press them.

We could have something that you placed over a cup and as you pressed it, it opened out to release some sugar and at the same time spun to stir the sugar in.

. . .If there is so much fun stirring in sugar then perhaps we ought to have some sort of inert sugar which people who don't like sugar could use in order to enjoy stirring in.

. . .A once off spoon made of sugar.

. . .A device which contains sugar and which is moved up and down in the cup. But if you don't want sugar you keep a gate closed.

. . .I would like to take up the idea of electricity but not using a battery or anything like but using the static electricity present in the body.

. . .This idea of a screw. One could do it on the autogiro principle. As the screw went up and down the fluid would make it revolve.

. . .Like a spinning top.

. . .A vibrating table that would agitate everything on it—whether you had sugar nor not.

. . .What about a sugar impregnated stick.

At the end of the brainstorming session participants are asked to keep the problem in mind for the next day allowing themselves further opportunity for incubation. They are later contacted by the leader who notes their new ideas if they have come up with any. A list of all ideas is then compiled and after the leader ascertains that ideas are stated succinctly and clearly, and properly classified if necessary, is presented to the evaluation group.

Evaluation Group

In brainstorming idea generation is separated from idea evaluation. Therefore after the ideas are compiled they are presented to an evaluation group consisting of five persons. There is an odd number in an evaluation group to avoid ties in arriving at decisions. A brainstorming group, it will be recalled, consisted of an even number but such a group was not involved in decision-making or evaluational activities.

Osborn tells us that an evaluation group can be constituted in various ways. It can consist of all of the members of the previous (idea-generation) panel, some members and some nonmembers of the idea-generation panel, or it might be made up of a completely different group of people [a procedure recommended by Bristol (1958)].

However this group is constructed it should be composed of individuals who will have direct future responsibility for the problem. As an aid in deciding the relative merits of the various ideas the evaluation group may use a checklist of criteria. They might ask themselves whether the idea is simple, timely, costly, feasible, etc. Those ideas that are selected are reported back to the idea-generation group so members of that group can still maintain a sense of participation in arriving at a creative solution to the problem.

It will also very likely be necessary to persuade others in the organization to accept an idea or a tentative working model of an idea. This may require knowledge and experience in marshalling arguments and being persuasive. Finally appropriate techniques need to be used in introducing the final work to the audience at large.

At each step in the total process there may be the need for additional new ideas. Under such circumstances a brainstorming session and the process, as described previously, can be begun again.

Errors and Pitfalls to Be Avoided

There are certain mistakes that should be avoided if the effects of brainstorming are to be maximized. Bristol (1958) suggests the following:

1. Failing to get support for your brainstorming program of at least one of your superiors.
2. Boasting prematurely about brainstorming and getting your colleagues to expect too much.
3. Failing to indoctrinate your panel adequately.
4. Submitting the unscreened list of ideas to people unfamiliar with how brainstorming works. It is best to keep the unscreened list confidential.
5. Failing to see that the next steps are taken [p. 145].

Osborn also suggests as two reasons why brainstorming may not work: the failure to follow instructions (by the group leader as well as the participants) and exaggerated expectations. What can be expected is that some sessions may produce final answers, provided the problem has been stated simply enough; some sessions may produce planks for plans; some sessions may produce checklists that are guides to stimulate further thinking; some sessions may produce approaches to subsequent solutions.

Its Uses

To avoid unrealizable expectations it is necessary to recall Osborn's (1963) assessment of brainstorming as "only one of the phases of idea-finding which, in turn, is only one of the phases of the creative problem-solving process [p. 191]." He adds,

Let's bear in mind that group brainstorming is meant to be used—not as a substitute—but as a supplement, and especially in these three ways:

1. *As a supplement to individual ideation* Individual effort is an indispensable factor in creative problem solving. Brainstorm sessions should never be considered as a substitute for such effort. Group brainstorming serves solely as a supplemental source—a means of generating a maximum number of potentially usable ideas in a minimum of time.

2. *As a supplement to conventional conferences* The usual conference is necessarily judicial, both in spirit and in function, and therefore relatively unproductive of ideas. This does not mean that brainstorm sessions should supplant conventional conferences. It merely means that conventional conferences can be profitably supplemented by an occasional brainstorm session—if and when creative thinking is the primary purpose.

3. *As a supplement to creative training* In over 1,000 courses in creative thinking, group brainstorming has been used as one of the teaching methods. This type of self-demonstration does much to induce a more creative attitude and to develop fluency of ideas. By the same token, participation in brainstorm sessions can help improve the average person's creative ability, not only in group effort, but also in individual effort [pp. 191-192].

By way of emphasizing the nature of the relative contributions of both individual and group brainstorming it should be noted that Osborn said, "Despite the many virtues of group brainstorming, individual ideation is usually more usable and can be just as productive. In fact, the ideal methodology for idea-finding is a triple attack: (1) Individual ideation. (2) Group brainstorming. (3) Individual ideation [Osborn, 1963, p. 191]."

This then is a summary of the theory and assumptions underlying brainstorming, the factors to be considered in setting up a brainstorming session, and the factors to keep in mind to maximize the benefits to be reaped from its proper use. Needless to say many more details may be obtained from reading Osborn's (1963) and Parnes' (1967a, b) basic works.

With the foregoing as background information we shall turn to a rather large number of research studies that were designed to cast light and understanding on the assumptions, processes, outcomes, and training effects involved in brainstorming. Since the material to be covered is so diverse it is best that we consider by way of preparation a number of characteristics of the research in this area.

AN INTRODUCTION TO THE RESEARCH STUDIES THAT FOLLOW

Brainstorming is the most researched of all the procedures for creative problem solving. It has been scrutinized from practically every angle and in terms of almost every variable. Some of this research was initiated and carried out by brainstorming's adherents and supporters, who sought to provide it with a scientific basis and rationale. A second group of investigators seemed, at least implicitly, to have reacted against the overzealous and overenthusiastic statements made about brainstorming by its supporters. Some of the latter probably felt that statements such as "brainstorming yields 80% more ideas" had a better place in advertising than in research literature on creativity. Then when this second body of researchers presented their work with all the objectivity of scientific articles, one wondered if there was not a note of glee and satisfaction when stated results were not so favorable to brainstorming. It should therefore not be surprising to the reader that studies by adherents of brainstorming support brainstorming while some other publications support it less strongly or not at all.

In any case, both to provide the reader who may be interested in brainstorming with a guide to the published literature and as an introduction to what follows in this book, it is necessary at this point to consider several characteristics of published research studies.

Subjects

In almost all of the studies the subjects are college students. They are not even a representative sample of college students but are usually students in a psychology class where one of the requirements is that they must give a stated number of hours to participation in psychological experiments. This is supposed to be a learning experience for the student and, of course, the faculty member, if he is the experimenter, gets the subjects and the data for his research.

One of the difficulties in using college students lies not only in the fact that they are not representative of the adult working population to whom we would like to extrapolate the results but also that they are not always very motivated for the experiments in which they participate. The results of their effort may reflect only a minimal level of what one could obtain in real life with motivated subjects. This too is an open question for which we require more information.

What has just been said is true for any experiment in which college students are used but in the area of creative problem solving, generally, or brainstorming, specifically, there is still another problem—how well trained the subjects are in a specific technique. In studies that do concern themseleves with the effects of training it is usually assumed that all subjects are trained in a specific technique and that all subjects will be equally capable of following the instructions. Thus one group of individuals is not expected, insofar as having been well trained in his particular approach, to be at any greater advantage or disadvantage in using deferred judgment than is a group involved in solving a problem using critical judgment. Now, if the proponents of brainstorming are correct in assuming that we are all more accustomed to working on problems using critical judgment than we are in solving problems using brainstorming's rules and principles, then no matter how clearly the instructions are stated they will not make up for this deficiency in experience with brainstorming as a problem-solving procedure. It would take time and training to have available subjects who are as well prepared to accept brainstorming instructions or to defer judgment as they are to be proficient in critical problem solving.

It is also frequently assumed in the studies to be presented that while subjects may differ in personality characteristics such individual differences "cancel out" and do not put one technique at a greater advantage over another. If this is so, it is a most desirable state of affairs. The fact of the matter is that it is only assumed to be so, but there is no evidence that it is so, and because the number of subjects studied is relatively small it is possible that individual differences do not cancel out.

It should be indicated that while in some instances it may be desirable to do studies where it is assumed that individual differences cancel out there is also much to be learned from studies in which subjects are selected because they are in fact different from one another. This theory when properly utilized in an experimental design where various creative problem-solving techniques are also used may well lead us to find that some of the procedures are particularly well suited for some individuals and not others. Without studying the personality and intellectual characteristics of the subjects, and such study as we shall see is unusual, we will gather rather little information on this score.

Problems

Just as there may be creative problem-solving techniques that some people find more useful than others, so there may be problems which may be solved more creatively with some techniques than with others. To cast light on this matter not only requires sufficient knowledge and experience with a problem-solving technique but also requires knowledge of the characteristics of problems used. There are many ways in which problems differ from each other, e.g., pure and applied, real and unreal, logical and illogical, or in other terms related to a problem's content and structure. Furthermore, information should be available on the relationship between problems selected for study and problems in various areas to which creativity may be applied.

Among the problems used in studies of brainstorming's effectiveness are those which require the subject to make up titles for stories, to think up the consequences of an event, or to think up the uses for such commonplace objects as a coat hanger and a brick. These problems come from existing tests of cognitive abilities or creativity such as those developed by Guilford (1967) or such as the *AC Test of Creative Ability* (Harris & Simberg, 1959). Other problems used come closer to real life; one such problem concerns itself with how to increase tourist trade to the United States. Still others are unreal or fantasy problems, one of which involves thinking up as many benefits or disadvantages as possible that may accrue because a person developed an extra thumb on each hand.

These and other problems are selected because they are regarded as measures of the cognitive characteristics presumably involved in creativity. Others are selected because pretesting has indicated that they "pull" a goodly number of ideas and because they do not put one group at a greater or lesser advantage over another. Occasionally we find a problem with direct relevance to a field of work. Never do we find a statement relating to a problem's structural characteristics which would allow generalization to other problems where brainstorming may be used.

Instructions

One of the important characteristics of studies in this area are instructions given to subjects. The purpose of the instructions is to set the subjects so that they will behave in such a manner as to allow for a proper test of the hypotheses in the experiment. However, several important problems arise in this regard.

For example, one of the important hypotheses in the brainstorming literature is that if judgment or evaluation operates in the idea-generation stage it will interfere with the production of ideas. To test this hypothesis one approach that has been used is to give each of two sets of subjects different instructions, one of which presumably involves more judgment or more evaluation than the other. Researchers using this approach have employed various kinds of instructions. One experimenter asked one group of his subjects to make up *clever* titles for stories and his other group to make up *appropriate* titles for the same stories. A second investigator used the instructions *to be creative* and *to be practical*. And, a third research group asked one half of their subjects *to be critical* and the other half *not to be critical*. In each of these instances the first instruction (to be *clever, creative*, and *critical*) represented the attempt to involve the subject in more judgment and evaluation than he exercised when he was instructed to be *appropriate, practical*, and *not critical*. The latter are "freer instructions." The freer instructions presumably establish the conditions that we seek to establish in brainstorming. Hence, the panel should yield not only more ideas but also more better ideas than when they are confined to the more restrictive condition imposed by the instructions to be more judgmental and evaluative.

It may indeed be true that subjects who are instructed to be "clever" or "appropriate" are indeed being so. In research the extent to which subjects behave cleverly or appropriately is reflected in the final results. *But, before* the subjects start responding they are not trained or given experience in determining or in knowing whether they are giving clever or appropriate responses. Some subjects may not know or they may not share some of the same criteria as those used by raters or the experimenters. Maybe if subjects and experimenters openly shared the same criteria the new results might be different from already obtained results.

There is still another matter. How do we know that the instruction to a subject to be appropriate is freer for him than the instruction to be clever. It may be less difficult, it may be equally difficult, or indeed it may be more difficult for some individuals. The fact of the matter is that we do not know these relationships at present.

The experimental design is such that the study should only be conducted with subjects for whom one set of instructions results in a freer condition than does another set of instructions. It is insufficient to believe that the instructions as transmitted are adequate. It is important to know that the instructions have "taken" and whether they have or not should be determined in some way other than with the same test that is used to determine the number and quality of ideas produced.

What has been said about not knowing all of the effects of the instructions is equally applicable whether simple sets of instructions are used such as those that have been discussed or whether more complete instructions are used, which encompass the two principles and four rules. Indeed, in a study by Parloff and Handlon (1964), in which they did use the more complete instructions and in which they tried to determine what indeed was going on in the subjects' behavior, they learned that subjects produced more ideas not because deferment of judgment affected their capacity to generate ideas but because it affected their standards so that they were more willing to report ideas they would otherwise have rejected.

This is an important finding for it tells us what may happen when people are asked to follow brainstorming instructions. However, the research problem is not really over at this point. It may still be that subjects who defer judgment produce more and better ideas than individuals who do not defer judgment. All that can be said is that in the studies previously mentioned and in those which shall be presented one cannot be certain that researchers were actually studying individuals who deferred judgment. *And*, if subjects were not deferring judgment then the researchers were not conducting a good test of brainstorming's hypotheses.

Criteria

In the studies covered, the experimenter had to establish criteria to determine the number of ideas subjects offered and to evaluate their quality. To determine the number of ideas is not extremely difficult but it also is not that easy. What the experimenter was obviously interested in was the number of *different* ideas and, at times, there are problems in determining when an idea or suggestion is really different from a previous one and, if it overlaps with a previous idea, then it must be determined what degree of overlap is required before it will be regarded as a new and different idea. This is a difficult but not insurmountable problem, and, in reality, once such criteria are worked out then they may be systematically applied *within* an experiment. Thus it is reasonable to expect that within any one experiment there will be no special advantage to a group using brainstorming and a group not using brainstorming. However, a problem does arise when one wishes to compare the results of two experiments using the same problem and presumably the same problem-solving procedure. If experimenters do not spell out their criteria for quantity of ideas, and they rarely if ever do, then proper comparisons and understanding are impossible.

Criteria for quality of response are a much more difficult matter than those for quantity. In some experiments the matter of quality of response is presented as total number of "good" or average number of "good" responses; and in some experiments more qualitative criteria are used. But "good quality," "high quality," or simply "quality" of responses is arrived at in at least three different ways:

(1) One is a statistical definition of quality which really is infrequency of response or how rarely a response or idea is given to a problem. In other words the experimenter, using this approach, simply lists how many times an idea or suggestion is offered. The less frequently it is offered the higher its quality.

The problem with this approach is that it is highly dependent on the subjects participating. Not all groups may be equal in generating unique ideas. Consequently, what may be a unique idea in one group or one experiment may not be unique in another. This again makes it impossible to compare data from different experiments since brainstorming may be good in one experiment but not in another, and this discrepancy may be related to the level or capacities of subjects involved. Since there are test problems which are used in several experiments one may wonder why experimenters do not share their data and establish a dictionary of responses. This dictionary would eventually tell experimenters whether they are dealing with responses uniquely given to a problem or whether the responses are really dependent on the group studied.

The uniqueness criterion as a measure of quality is related to the idea that a creative response is rare. In this there lies a good deal of potential confusion, for "rareness" is not necessarily the same as "uniqueness," which again is not necessarily the same as creativity. Sometimes a creative solution may well depend on the use of something quite commonplace. We shall present a study later (see p. 76-78, Hyman, 1960) in which this was the case. It is a study in which the statistically unique solution was not necessarily the creatively workable or effective solution.

(2) The second way that has been used to determine the quality of an idea is to use raters' judgments or qualitative ratings of ideas. If the statistical counting

procedure is supposed to stand for objectivity then when raters are used the approach is subjective. Since raters vary from experiment to experiment, data from two studies are not necessarily comparable. Assuredly the effects of raters may be constant within an experiment, and neither the control group nor the experimental group are at an advantage. However, as has happened in at least one study* the experimenters did not really go along with the raters' judgments. Because they were bound by the strictures of the experimental design these experimenters did not let their judgments intrude. But, the fact of the matter was that they felt their raters' judgments were too conservative. Had they not been so conservative, the results might have been different. Raters can effect the outcome of studies yet no systematic criteria are utilized in selecting them. Thus individuals with some unknown characteristics make ratings which are then regarded as the basic data of the experiment.

(3) The third criterion for evaluating responses involves a combination of the two criteria just described. And, then, of course, the averaging process used may obscure the relative contribution of quantity and quality factors.

To illustrate some of what we have just mentioned, as well as to further prepare the reader for what follows, several details should be noted.

First let us deal with frequency of response. It should be noted that when a test is used in one experiment the experimenters concern themselves with what they call *uncommonness* of response, but the same infrequency of response in another study is called *uniqueness* of response and the reader should not be confused. Responses are assigned numerical values by experimenters. Thus a very infrequent response may be given the highest score. More frequently given responses obtain lower scores with the most frequently given responses receiving a "0."

When raters are used they also assign numerical values to responses. The experimenters may decide that only responses receiving a certain average value may be used in evaluating results. Let us say that experimenters decide that a response with an average score of 4 should be regarded as a good quality score. But this score of 4 may be arrived at in different ways. If two raters are used, for example, both may have assigned a rating of 4 to the response. But, the average rating of 4 may be received by a rating of 5 by one rater and a 3 by another. Thus, the experimenter can lose sight of the fact that one rating is below and another is above the accepted criterion. Some of the synonyms for quality that raters use in the different studies include judgments of cleverness, attractiveness or least time consuming. When a subject's responses are judged for cleverness (Christensen, Guilford, & Wilson, 1957, p. 85) he may have been asked for titles that are "interest arousing, catchy, inviting or novel." And his responses are

* See Weisskopf-Joelson and Eliseo (1961).

rated by judges in terms of one of five categories of cleverness. In another study (Weisskopf-Joelson & Eliseo, 1961) subjects were asked to come up with brand names for a cigar, a deodorant, and an automobile. In this study the quality score was based on judges' ratings of attractiveness.

Finally there is the third category of criteria in which both objective and subjective factors are used to obtain quality scores. This is true of the *AC Test of Creative Ability*. In one part of this test the subject is given five problem situations and asked for least expensive and least time-consuming solutions. Judges then evaluate the suggestions for how little they would cost in time and money.

We see, then, that experiments designed to provide a test of hypotheses stimulated by brainstorming or experiments designed to provide further understanding of brainstorming are quite diverse in their experimental design, problems used, criteria employed, etc. When we add to this that there is little if any replication of the studies, we see then that there is not much of a solid research foundation for many of brainstorming's characteristics. However, that is the status of the field. Nevertheless, with the foregoing information about the characteristics of research in this area, the reader is now better prepared for the research studies themselves that follow.

STUDIES OF THE TWO PRINCIPLES AND FOUR RULES

Principle 1: Deferment of Judgment

The first principle of brainstorming whether carried out by an individual or group is to defer judgment. It is implemented by two of the four brainstorming rules: (1) *Criticism is ruled out* and (2) *Freewheeling is welcomed*.

This principle is sometimes the butt of skeptics' jokes who distort it and make it sound as if the end result of brainstorming is a set of wild ideas because *no* judgment is exercised. The fact is that, as we have said, in the total brainstorming process judgment is not lacking. It is first only *deferred*. Evaluation and judgment do come back into the brainstorming picture after the individual or group has come up with ideas as a result of deferred judgment.

There are two sets of research studies that contribute information on the validity of the first principle. In one the attempt is made to get the subject to defer judgment or rather to engage in less judgment by telling him to follow one rather than another set of instructions which differ in terms of how much judgment is involved. In the second set of experiments, groups of subjects are given a more complex set of instructions which usually involve all four rules of brainstorming or something quite close to them. This second set of studies will be discussed later under the heading of "Studies of Outcomes." It should be apparent however, that outcome studies and those considered here are really quite similar in that they both concern themselves with the first principle.

A study by Christensen *et al.* (1957) is an example of a study designed to investigate the effects of deferred judgment. They presented their subjects with a series of short stories and asked them to compose titles for these stories under two sets of instructions—one of which was believed to call for more evaluation than the other. For the *more* evaluative instructions subjects were asked to compose "*clever* titles." These titles were to be " 'interest arousing, catchy, inviting, or novel' [Christensen *et al.*, 1957, p. 85] ." These titles were also to be appropriate. For the *less* evaluative instructions subjects were asked only to compose "*appropriate* titles."

The results of this experiment were: When subjects were asked to produce clever titles, and were presumably more evaluative, they produced fewer titles than when they were asked for appropriate titles and were presumably less evaluative. This result is consistent with the first principle of brainstorming: deferment of judgment should lead to an *increase* in the number of responses.

But, how is quality effected? According to the first principle not only should deferred judgment result in more responses but it should also result in more higher quality responses than when judgment is not deferred. On this point the Christensen *et al.* (1957) data reveal that under the more evaluative condition subjects do in fact, and contrary to the first principle of brainstorming, produce a larger number of high quality (clever) responses than when the subjects are less evaluative. In addition, since clever responses were rated for *degree* of cleverness the results of this study further revealed that under the more evaluative condition the *average* degree of cleverness was higher than under the less evaluative condition. Thus instructions that presumably led the subjects to be more evaluative in their behavior produced fewer ideas but more high-quality ideas and ideas of higher average quality than in instances when they were not so instructed. Therefore, the first brainstorming principle is only partially supported. It is supported in that deferment of judgment leads to an increase in *number* of ideas but not to an increase in the quality of ideas.

Several objections were raised by Hyman (1960) to the Christensen *et al.* (1957) study. (1) They did not counterbalance the instructions. In all experimental conditions the one involving "free instructions"—instructions asking for "appropriate" responses—preceded the one involving "clever" instructions. Consequently, obtained effects may be due to practice. (2) The task of making up titles does not appear very similar to other tasks involving creativity. There may not be very much creativity involved in the plot-titles task employed by Christensen *et al.* (3) The subjects in the Christensen *et al.* experiment were not really trained in the brainstorming technique and therefore probably did not invoke and make use of the principle of deferred judgment.

Hyman (1960) then set about conducting a series of experiments in which he tried to take these criticisms into account. In one of them he presented twenty-eight new program engineers at the General Electric Company with four different but equivalent types of problems that were taken from the *AC Test of Creative Ability*. These problems involved: thinking up consequences for various occurrences (consequences problems); suggesting reasons to account for empirical relationships (hypothesis formation problems); suggesting improvement for common problems (sensitivity to problems); and suggesting uses for common objects (other uses problems). Each engineer worked with half of the problems under the instruction to "be creative" and with the other half under the instruction to "be practical." Instructions were counterbalanced so that one half of the engineers worked first with problems with the instruction to be creative and then they worked on other problems with the instruction to be practical; the other half of the subjects first worked on problems with the instruction to be practical and then worked on other problems with the instruction to be creative.

When the engineers were instructed to be practical, they did in fact produce a larger number of responses than when they were instructed to be creative. This result supported Christensen *et al.* and the principle of deferred judgment, since to "be creative" presumably involved more evaluation than to "be practical." This was a general effect based on combining the number of ideas for all problems worked on. This effect was not manifest in the data obtained for each of the problems considered separately. The instruction to be practical did not produce more responses than the instruction to be creative for each problem used.

There were differences between problems in effects produced which were as follows: The obtained effect was manifest with the *consequences* and *other uses problems*. When subjects presumably deferred judgment they produced more consequences of various occurrences and suggested more uses for common objects than when they were so instructed as to become more judgmental. However, this effect was *not* produced when subjects were asked to suggest reasons to account for various empirical relationships (*hypothesis formation problems*) and when they were asked to suggest improvements in common problems (*sensitivity to problems*). No greater superiority was found for either the instruction that involved judgment or the one that involved deferment of judgment when working with *sensitivity to problems*. And, indeed, a reverse (and statistically just significant) effect was found for the *hypothesis formation problems*. With these problems the instruction to be practical and hence less evaluative produced *fewer* ideas than the more evaluative instruction to be creative.

To obtain data on quality of ideas produced, Hyman scored all obtained responses for uniqueness of response. Analysis of data so obtained revealed that, once again, counter to the deferment of judgment principle, the more evaluative instruction produced more responses that were unique than did the less evaluative instruction. Furthermore, this difference in favor of the evaluative instruction held up for all four problems used in this experiment.

Summarizing the results of the two studies just presented, we may say that deferment of judgment, if it was achieved by the less evaluative instructions to the subjects, results in more responses than a set of instructions that involves more evaluation. The latter evaluative instructions, however, contrary to the first principle of brainstorming, results in better quality responses. It also appears that these results are a function of the problems studied. They appear in developing titles to stories, in developing ideas about the consequences of various occurrences, and in thinking up uses of commonplace objects. These effects do not occur in considering number of ideas to a test of *sensitivity to problems*, and they are reversed for quantity of ideas when subjects worked on *hypothesis formation problems*.

The expectation that deferred judgment would also result in better quality ideas did not obtain. The evidence was that for each of the problems studied, better quality ideas were produced when subjects were asked to be more rather than less evaluative in their behavior.

Additional evidence on the validity of the first brainstorming principle will be presented later when we consider studies of outcomes.

Principle 2: Quantity Breeds Quality

The second principle of brainstorming is that quantity of ideas results in quality of ideas. It is asserted that with the production of a larger number of ideas there is both a larger number of quality ideas and a higher average quality of ideas than would be found with a smaller number of ideas. This principle is associated with the third and fourth rules of brainstorming: *quantity is wanted* and *combination and improvement are sought*.

Implicit in the second principle is an extension of the first, deferred judgment. If judgment is deferred then quantity will be increased and if quantity is increased then quality will be increased.

Two groups of studies will be considered here. The first focuses on the correlation between quantity and quality of ideas. The second group of studies involves the hypothesis that better quality responses will occur later rather than earlier in a sequence of responses.

Correlational Studies

In the manual accompanying the *AC Test of Creative Ability* (Harris & Simberg, 1959) correlations are presented between quantity and uniqueness of responses for different parts of the test battery. Data for these correlations were collected from thirty-six individuals who varied in their manifest creativity. All of the correlations are very high and the average correlation between quantity and uniqueness, for the same part of the test, is +0.85.

Parnes and Meadow (1959) studied the relationship between quantity and quality (where quality was a combination of uniqueness and value) for two problems: How many uses can you think of for a hanger, and how many uses can you think of for a broom? These problems were presented to subjects who had not been trained in brainstorming. The results of this experiment indicated that the correlation between quantity and quality was high. Under brainstorming conditions the correlation between quantity and quality was +0.67 for the hanger problem and +0.71 for the broom problem. Under nonbrainstorming conditions the correlations were not very different: +0.64 for the hanger problem and +0.81 for the broom problem. A positive correlation between quantity and quality was found whether or not brainstorming was used.

In another study, Parnes (1961) investigated the frequency of good ideas among "high" and "low" producers of ideas. The former were persons who had produced more than the median number of ideas in the sample studied, and the number of ideas produced by the latter was below the median. As hypothesized, Parnes found that high producers did indeed produce more good ideas than did the low producers.

These studies support the second principle of brainstorming that number of ideas and quality of ideas are related. And, furthermore, this relationship holds whether or not one uses brainstorming instructions.

There is still another datum that needs to be added to the picture—no matter what is the nature of the instructions used there are some people who simply produce better quality ideas than do others. This finding was obtained by Christensen *et al.* (1957) who, as reported earlier, asked their subjects to work on problems with the instruction to be clever and the instruction to be appropriate (which presumably involved less judgment). They found a correlation of +0.62 between the number of clever ideas their subjects produced under both conditions. "It appears," say Christensen *et al.* (1957, p. 86), "that individuals are more or less disposed toward making clever responses whether or not they are explicitly instructed to do so." Consequently, it may not really matter whether one asks an individual to defer judgment or not; he will still behave in the way he wants to. And, if he is so disposed, he will produce novel responses.

Time and Effort Devoted to the Production of Ideas

The second principle of brainstorming states only that a relationship will exist between quantity and quality of ideas. It does not say when in a sequence of ideas, the better ideas will occur. However, according to the theory of association one would suggest that the first ideas to come to mind are the more usual or more commonplace ones. The more unusual ones, the more unique ones are likely to come later. Insofar as direct statements on this matter by the adherents of brainstorming are concerned, we find, for example that Parnes (1961, p. 120) says that "the *best* idea will come late in the *total production period*."

In the study by Christensen *et al.* (1957), referred to previously, there are data on the relationships between four variables and time. One of these is total number of responses and the other three are measures of quality—uncommonness of response, remoteness of response, and cleverness of response. Each of these three quality measures was based on a different psychological test. For uncommonness of response two unusual uses tests were used as well as one figure concepts test and two number associations tests. For remoteness of response four problems in the consequences test were used. And, for a study of the relationship between time and cleverness the plot titles test was used both with the instruction to write appropriate titles and the instruction to write clever titles.

Results of this analysis of the relationship between total number of responses and time indicated that the rate of producing ideas did not vary much as a function of time. But, in support of the second brainstorming principle, two of the three quality measures—uncommonness of response and remoteness of response—were higher later rather than earlier in a sequence of ideas. The same result was not obtained with the third quality measure—cleverness of ideas.

In 1961 Parnes reported an investigation in which he studied subjects who were not trained in brainstorming. He gave them 5 minutes to list all possible uses they could think of for a wire coat hanger. The quality score used for these responses was a composite made up of ratings both of uniqueness and value.

There were two groups of subjects in this experiment. One group was registered for but had not yet taken a creative problem-solving course. The other group was composed of students enrolled in other courses. The median total number of responses was obtained for each group and for each group two subgroups were established: those whose total number of responses was above the group median and those whose total number of responses was below the median. Therefore, within each group Parnes had two subgroups. One subgroup was of "high" producers and the other was of "low" producers. For each subgroup the total number of responses was further subdivided into two halves and the average quality of response in the second half was compared with that obtained in the first half. The results indicated that in all instances, whether the analysis was carried out with the high or the low producers, the quality of ideas in the second half was greater than in the first half.

This study led Parnes to two additional experiments reported in the same paper (Parnes, 1961). In the experiment just reported subjects were not trained in brainstorming and they had 5 minutes to work on the wire coat hanger problem. In the second experiment Parnes used the same problem but this time with subjects who had already been trained in brainstorming. They had a longer period, 15 minutes (instead of 5 minutes), to list all the uses they could think of for the coat hanger. Parnes then divided the 15-minute time period into three

5-minute segments. This enabled him to do two things. First, he could investigate whether over the total 15-minute period there was a relationship between time and quality of response. Secondly, he could take the first 5-minute segment, divide it in half, and he would have an experiment very much like the one with the high and low producers who also had 5 minutes to work on the hanger problem. The difference between the two experiments was in the subjects' experiences with brainstorming. In one the subjects did and in the other the subjects did not have training in brainstorming.

When Parnes analyzed the quality of ideas produced in each of the three 5-minute segments he found that significantly more quality ideas were produced in the last segment than in either of the first two. And the first two 5-minute periods did not differ from each other.

Then when Parnes divided the first 5-minute segment in half so that he could compare the relationship between time and quality of ideas for trained and untrained subjects he did *not* find support for the results of the first study. In other words, while untrained subjects who worked on a problem for 5 minutes gave more quality responses in their second 2 1/2 minute period than in the first, subjects trained in brainstorming did not show this result.

Parnes (1961) also reported on still another body of data. These data were collected from one-hundred eighty subjects who were *not* trained in brainstorming and who had participated in an earlier experiment by Meadow and Parnes (1959) in which they worked on the plot titles test for 3 minutes. Parnes (1961) took the data for these subjects, divided their 3-minute working period in half and analyzed the data to see if there were more good quality ideas in the second than in the first half of the 3-minute period. No such result was found.

In discussing these disparate findings Parnes says,

> Thus we have data suggesting: (a) for *untrained* subjects, significantly more good ideas among *later* ideas in a *5*-minute period, but not significantly more in a *3*-minute stint; (b) for *trained* subjects, significantly more good ideas among *later* ideas for a *15*-minute period, but not significantly more for a *5*-minute stint. Theorizing from the four sets of related data, it might be suggested that subjects will get at least as many good ideas in the second half of their total idea output regarding a creative thinking problem as in the first half, but that with increasing production time, the proportion of good ideas in the second half will increase over the first half. It might be further theorized that untrained subjects will show this increasing proportion more rapidly than trained subjects, who have already learned to be more creative in their early ideas. In a sense, both trained and untrained subjects seem to be stimulating their creativity by *extended* effort in idea-finding. For the trained subjects, a 5-minute period (on the type of problem used) does not seem to be long enough to elicit *extended* effort on their parts. . . . However,

for untrained subjects 5 minutes *did* seem to provide enough time to call for *extended* effort [Parnes, 1961, pp. 120-121].

There are other variables that may also affect Parnes' results. It is not always clear from the published reports whether subjects, before they start working on a problem, are told how long they will have to work on it. If they were told, it is conceivable that they could pace themselves. When they see that the end of their time is approaching they may make a concerted effort to come up with better quality ideas. Consequently, positive relationships can be found in both the experiment with 5-minute time periods and the experiment with a 15-minute period. But the results would not be found in the first 5-minute segment of the 15-minute period because within the context in which it appears the subjects' attitude is just not the same as when the 5-minute period appeared alone.

Another factor affecting the nature of the results is the kind of problem used. In Parnes' (1961) studies he used the coat hanger problem but in the 3-minute experiment be used data collected by Meadow and Parnes (1959) with the plot titles test. Parnes did not find the hypothesized results with this problem. But this could have been anticipated from the study by Christensen *et al.* (1957) in which the same problem was used for the study of the relationships between quality of response and time and they too found no positive relationship between these variables for the plot titles test. However, when other tests or problems were used a relationship between quality of response and time was obtained. Consequently, before definitive statements are made about the relationships between different variables and quality of response, studies need to be carried out with a variety of problems.

Still another factor that may affect the nature of the obtained relationship between time and quality of response is the measure of quality. Parnes's measure of quality in the previous studies is a score based on the *combination* of ratings of uniqueness and value of response. However, when Christensen *et al.* obtained their positive relationships they used measures of uncommonness and remoteness of responses both of which are closer to uniqueness than to value. It is conceivable that the value subscore could have had a negative effect on the results. It would be interesting to see what would happen to Parnes' results if each of his subscores was studied separately. Would each subscore show the same or different relationship with time as did the total score?

Summarizing the data obtained in studies of the second principle that *quantity breeds quality* we find that correlational studies generally support the principle. Furthermore, the correlational relationship occurs whether brainstorming or nonbrainstorming instructions are used. In addition, some of the evidence suggests the likelihood that some people are disposed to produce quality responses regardless of how they are instructed to work on a problem. Hence, if one wants quality it may be worthwhile to concentrate on learning how better to select the right persons—a matter which has received little, if any, attention in this area.

Other studies indicate that when quality is measured by some kind of statistical or "distance" measure, like uncommonness or remoteness, then quality increases with quantity and time as the second principle of brainstorming suggests. But when the measure is more qualitative like cleverness it does not. It should also be noted that the relationship between time and quality of response may be affected by the nature of the problem used and amount of time available to the subject to work on it. Some time periods may be too short for the effects to be manifest.

STUDIES OF OUTCOMES

In addition to studies of the principles underlying brainstorming there are available two kinds of outcome studies or studies of the value and effectiveness of brainstorming. The first consists of reports in which brainstorming was used to solve problems in real-life situations. The second consists of laboratory studies in which the effectiveness of brainstorming was studied under controlled conditions. The problems used in this second category of studies are not very practical nor are they directly related to real life. They are "laboratory" problems. Participants in these laboratory experiments were usually college students who received course credit for their participation in the experiments. Although they might have been involved and motivated for their work it is unlikely that they had the same motivation as one who had a real job in which he tried brainstorming to solve a problem "as if his life depended on it."

The criteria of effectiveness used for the real-life studies are practical achievements and accomplishments and for the laboratory situations the criteria are number and quality of ideas.

The supporters of brainstorming frequently make the point that in addition to its practical value for solving problems brainstorming also results in better or more satisfying interpersonal relationships among the group members that use it. In light of this we shall present in this section information gathered from subjects who participated in different kinds of problem-solving procedures and consider their attitudes and opinions about their experiences.

Two other issues will also be discussed at the end of this subsection. (They appear at the end—not because they are less important than others but because insufficient work has been done with them.) The first issue is what kind of person would do well with brainstorming or some other procedure for solving problems. The second issue relates to what kinds of problems respond better to one procedure than another.

Another major interest of investigators in this area has been the brainstorming process itself. These investigators studied variables that could affect what went on in the process (e.g., the difference between reporting ideas verbally or in a written manner) or variables that could affect the outcome of the process (e.g., the raters and the manner in which their ratings could affect the nature of the results produced).

Reports from Real-Life Situations

It is important to bear in mind that the reports of effectiveness of brainstorming in real-life situations presented are almost solely reports of achievements or outcomes. This means first that we do not have available reports of any failures—if they occurred. Secondly, we do not know for certain just what the process was through which the outcomes were achieved. It may have been primarily or solely through brainstorming or it may have been through the use of brainstorming plus some other procedure. We think that in the studies presented in this chapter brainstorming itself was primarily involved while in studies presented later (pages 248-249) brainstorming may very likely have been used together with other procedures (Edwards, 1966) to achieve creative results. With these cautions in mind we turn to the reports themselves.

Bristol (1958) tells us that brainstorming was used in an effort to increase the use of long-distance telephone calls. Telephone company employees produced sixty-one ideas in an idea-generating session. When these ideas were screened forty-one remained as potentially useful. And, of these forty-one, sixteen were put into use.

Osborn (1963) reports several other successful experiences. The Richmond, Virginia chapter of the National Association of Social Workers generated two hundred ideas through the use of brainstorming and at least fifty of these were put into operation. The problem of improving and increasing the use of downtown bus service was brainstormed by the Greater Lawrence Chamber of Commerce. Twenty-nine ideas were produced and found to be both practical and workable. Fifteen panelists of the Catholic Community Church in Neuilly-sur-Seine, it was also reported by Osborn (1963), brainstormed the question, "How to make our community more livable?" and produced two-hundred seventy-six ideas and eighty-two more ideas were added after the group session through individual efforts. Of all these ideas produced through either group or individual brainstorming seventy were found usable.

Brainstorming then, as we have just seen can produce what we would regard as important primary results—ideas that help solve existing problems. But there are also valuable secondary interpersonal effects in group situations that are associated with the very process of solving problems. Thus, Osborn (1963) includes among the values of brainstorming sessions: improvement of morale, revelation of attitudes toward supervisory problems, and improved mutual understanding among supervisory personnel. Moreover, the sessions are found to be enjoyable and to encourage initiative on the part of those who participated in them so that they would be able to cope more effectively and creatively with future problems.

We see then that brainstorming has been used with a good deal of success. But we have not come across reports of failures. Maybe it never fails. What is more likely is that if and when it fails it is less likely to be written up and published.

Reports from the Laboratory

It will be recalled that studies in which subjects were given instructions that were designed to lessen their inclination to evaluate ideas or which were designed to have subjects defer judgment (e.g., studies in which subjects were asked to give responses that were *appropriate, practical*, and *not critical*) yielded an increase in number of ideas produced. But, contrary to expectation instructions designed to increase a subjects' judgmental orientation (e.g., they were told to be *clever, creative,* and *critical*) yielded more quality ideas and better average quality ideas than did the less judgmental instructions. These studies contribute to our knowledge of the outcomes of brainstorming and need not be repeated here. Among those studies reported here there are those which also focus on instructions, but here the instructions are more extensive and more in line with those used in actual brainstorming sessions. In these studies also the experimental design is more complex than in the previously cited ones.

Meadow, Parnes, and Reese (1959) compared the effects of brainstorming instructions with the effects of instructions that emphasized quality of ideas on previously trained subjects who were asked to generate ideas for problems. The fact that the subjects were previously trained is a critical characteristic of this study because it is one of the few where such is the case. The subjects received their training in a course on *Creative Problem-Solving*. The content of such a course will be presented in the next chapter. At this point suffice it to say that it involves training in a variety of procedures designed to attain creative solutions. One of these procedures that receives a great deal of emphasis is brainstorming.

To groups of subjects equated for training experience two problems from the *AC Test of Creative Ability* (Harris & Simberg, 1959) were presented. In one they were asked for as many uses as they could think of for a *broom* and in the other they were asked to do the same for a *coat hanger*.

When instructed to brainstorm a problem subjects were told to forget about being concerned with the quality of their ideas and to concentrate only on quantity of ideas. For the nonbrainstorming instruction subjects were told to strive for quality of ideas. And to further emphasize quality they were told they would be penalized for bad ideas.

Ideas were rated separately for uniqueness—the extent to which a suggested use differed from the conventional use of either a broom or hanger—and for value—the extent to which a suggestion had usefulness in terms of social, economic, or aesthetic factors. In rating ideas for each variable a three-point scale was used. An idea was regarded as "good" if its combined score for both variables was a 5 or a 6. Results are based on the number of good ideas produced.

The experimenters in this study balanced a number of variables, consequently, they also studied the effects of order on the instructions. That is, they concerned themselves with whether it made a difference in whether brainstorming instructions were used first and then followed by nonbrainstorming instructions or vice versa.

The results of the study indicated that more good ideas were produced with the brainstorming instructions than with the nonbrainstorming instructions. Furthermore these brainstorming effects were stronger in the experimental condition where brainstorming preceded rather than where it followed nonbrainstorming.

For all practical purposes we are more interested in the comparison of both brainstorming and nonbrainstorming when both are in the first experimental position. And, these data indicate that the average number of good ideas produced by groups trained in brainstorming and told to use brainstorming is significantly greater than the average number of good ideas produced by groups trained in brainstorming and told both to strive for quality in their ideas and that they would be penalized for bad ideas. Implicitly the second group was told not to use brainstorming since they would be penalized for bad ideas. (As an aside it should be pointed out that results presented here are general effects. They do not hold for all problems—a matter we shall take up later.)

In essence then, the study by Meadow *et al.* (1959) is congruent with what is said about brainstorming. Brainstorming, although it instructs the subject to concern himself only with quantity and not with quality will nevertheless produce more quality ideas than a procedure that focuses on quality alone. Procedures that emphasize quality presumably are among the more common and more conventional approaches to problem solving. Therefore, it is appropriate to mention another study referred to as a pilot study in another of Parnes' works (1963). In this study the outcomes produced by a brainstorming conference were compared with those produced by a conventional conference. While Parnes does not present details of the experiment in this report (Parnes, 1963) he does say that the brainstorming conference produced a significantly larger number of good ideas on one of the problems used and that the results were in the same direction on the other problem used. Parnes also says in this report that *group* brainstorming was compared with individual conventional thinking and once again group brainstorming was found to be superior.

The results of the two studies just presented are somewhat different from those obtained in the studies cited at the start of this section. In the latter studies, emphasis on quality produced more quality responses but in the former studies (Meadow *et al.*, 1959, and Parnes, 1963 studies) brainstorming instructions that did not emphasize quality produced more quality responses.

There are other differences between the latter two studies and those cited earlier. The earlier studies involved work with individual subjects but the others involved groups of subjects. We cannot say whether the difference in results obtained stems from this or some other difference between the studies. It is not always clear from the published material to which of the specific variables involved specific effects or outcomes may be attributed. It is important to keep this in mind for we would like to suggest on the basis of studies to be presented that one be a bit cautious in accepting completely the presented positive results for brainstorming. In the studies already presented in this section we have noted that brainstorming outproduces problem-solving procedures involving criticisms both in total number of ideas and number of *good* ideas produced. Studies to be presented raise some question about the results regarding quality of ideas, and one of the ways they do so is by presenting results in terms of *average quality* of ideas produced.

We turn first to a study by Brilhart and Jochem (1964) which studied number of ideas and quality of ideas as effected by procedures involving the separation of idea generation and idea evaluation. Then we shall present two studies in which, among other variables, the *average quality* of ideas was used.

Brilhart and Jochem (1964) were interested in the total number of ideas and in the number of good ideas produced by three different procedures, or what they call different patterns for solving problems.

Pattern A they called "ideas-criteria," because it involved first getting ideas and then evaluating them. It consisted of five steps: (1) analysis of the problem; (2) brainstorming according to Osborn's rules; (3) consideration of criteria to be utilized for choosing the best idea; (4) evaluation to select best idea; and (5) report of best solution.

Pattern B, called "criteria-ideas," was one in which criteria preceded the development of ideas. It differed from pattern A in that steps (2) and (3) in the preceding paragraph were transposed so that pattern B consisted of the sequence: (1), (3), (2), (4), (5).

Pattern C, called "problem-solution," was composed of three steps: (1) analysis of the problem; (2) simultaneous generation and evaluation of ideas; and (3) selection of best solution. This pattern was regarded as very similar to critical problem solving.

A total of 27 five-man groups were involved in this experiment, and they were led by student leaders trained by Brilhart. Three problems were used:

(1) library problem—in which subjects were asked for ideas to prevent the mutilation and stealing of articles from a library; (2) tourist problem—in which subjects were asked how to get more European tourists to visit the United States; (3) education problem—in which subjects were asked for ideas to maintain the quality of current education in the face of an increasing school population and teacher shortage.

In addition to their problem-solving instructions, the subjects were also told that the groups whose solutions for each of the three problems received the highest average rank by expert judges would receive $15. It was hoped that this reward would stimulate cooperative group behavior.

Subjects presented all their ideas and their choice of best idea for judges' evaluation. Ideas were scored for quantity and quality. For quality, each idea was rated on a five-point scale by the two authors for (a) feasibility, (b) effectiveness, and (c) generality. An idea was called good if it received at least two ratings of 4 and one of 3 by both raters on these three scales. An idea which was rated good by one rater and not the other was discussed by the raters who then had to arrive at a decision whether to call it good or not.

Turning to the results of this study we find that patterns A and B each produced more ideas than pattern C. In other words, those patterns that separated idea generation from idea evaluation yielded about 50% more ideas than the pattern in which ideation and evaluation were combined.

Considering the number of *good* ideas produced, it was found that pattern A which involved the separation of ideation and evaluation, and hence involved deferred judgment, was significantly superior in the number of good ideas produced to that produced by pattern C which involved the combination of ideation and evaluation. Neither pattern A nor pattern C differed in the production of good ideas from pattern B where criteria for evaluation of ideas preceded idea generation. Thus pattern A produced the largest number of good ideas and pattern C the smallest.

If there is further substantiation of the Brilhart and Jochem study then it would appear that brainstorming's effectiveness is not necessarily due solely to the *deferment* of judgment but to the separation of idea generation and idea evaluation (or judgment), since Brilhart and Jochem's data indicate that it does not matter if in the *same* problem-solving situation idea generation or idea evaluation comes first*—what does matter is that they be separated.

Pattern A, it will be recalled is most like brainstorming, in which generation of ideas and evaluation of ideas are not only separated but the evaluation is

---

*It is important to emphasize in the *same* situation so that the reader will not be confused and will see that there is *no* similarity between the order sequence in the Brilhart and Jochem study and in the Meadow *et al.* (1959) study. In the former, the parts were separated but occurred in the same setting. In the Meadow *et al.* study brainstorming and critical problem solving occurred in different experimental sessions. But both experimental situations could occur in the first and the second experimental position.

deferred so that it *follows* idea generation. Pattern B involved a consideration of evaluational criteria *before* brainstorming the problem. Therefore here judgmental criteria are not deferred until after idea generation, they are just separated from idea generation. The results, as has been shown, indicate that there is no difference between these two patterns of solving problems in terms of the total number of ideas produced. And, there is no difference between these two patterns in terms of number of good ideas produced. Therefore, it is not *deferment of judgment* that is the critical phenomenon but the separation of idea generation and idea evaluation. Assuredly, since aspects of brainstorming are involved in both patterns, what we have said is limited to the one characteristic of brainstorming mentioned but not to its others.

Finally, it should be pointed out that separation of idea generation and idea evaluation, no matter which comes first, is better than a combination of both in the same process when one considers the total *number* of ideas. On the other hand, pattern A, which came closest to brainstorming, produced significantly more quality ideas than the procedure that combined idea generation and idea evaluation. The procedure (pattern B) which involved evaluation followed by idea-generation fell between the other two patterns in terms of quality of ideas produced. Combining the data for both number and quality of ideas we find that the procedure that comes closest to brainstorming comes off very well.

Now we turn to a study by Weisskopf-Joelson and Eliseo (1961) and introduce the variable *average quality* of ideas produced and discuss how different procedures effect it. In this study the investigators concerned themselves with the brand names offered by their subjects for a cigar, a deodorant, and an automobile. Their subjects were studied in six groups of seven individuals (both males and females) each. Half of the groups were instructed to use brainstorming and hence to defer the use of critical judgment. The other half of the subjects were instructed to emphasize quality rather than quantity and to strive for "good, practical ideas. Let's try to avoid stupid or silly ones [Weisskopf-Joelson & Eliseo, 1961, p. 46]." The task or goal for both kinds of groups was to develop attractive brand names for a cigar, a deodorant, and an automobile. Judges evaluated the "attractiveness" of these names to obtain a quality score.

The results of this study indicated that the brainstorming, noncritical (deferred judgment) condition produced a significantly larger number of ideas than did the critical condition. However, for all three products the *average quality* score of the responses produced under the presumed evaluative condition was greater than the average quality of the responses produced under the nonevaluative condition. This is accounted for according to the experimenters, by the fact that both groups produced about the same number of high quality responses but the noncritical condition produced more ideas of low quality.

Another study in which average quality of ideas produced was used as a variable was one carried out by Bouchard (1969). He compared group brainstorming with group critical problem solving using two experimental conditions

—carefully written instructions and feedback—which he thought would enable him to counteract some of the negative aspects of group behavior. He analyzed the heuristics involved in both problem-solving situations and reasoned that in group critical problem solving the best solutions were obtained if individual members focused on carefully defined goals and kept criteria of quality and relevance in mind. Discussion in group critical problem solving is kept on the track by criticism of poor and irrelevant ideas.

Group brainstorming, on the other hand, "involves a lessening of critical judgment and use of primary process or a sheer associative type of idea-generating mechanism [Bouchard, 1969, p. 12]." The group brainstorming process "is supposedly facilitated by other group members who provide unique stimuli which constantly prod the associative mechanism, thereby generating more and better suggestions [Bouchard, 1969, p. 12]."

In both problem-solving situations Bouchard believed that interpersonal and social-emotional problems could interfere with the smooth flow of the problem-solving process. He thought he could overcome these by writing out instructions for his subjects as explicitly as possible.

The rationale for using feedback was as follows: Bouchard reasoned that in group problem-solving situations a participant focuses his attention not on what the other person says but rather with what he himself will say. Such behavior is more likely to interfere with what is regarded as more basic to brainstorming than to critical problem-solving. In brainstorming colleagues' suggestions are supposed to have stimulus value for other ideas. If a person does not pay much attention to another's ideas and concentrates only on his own suggestions, then the group brainstorming process would be interrupted. To counteract this problem Bouchard used a feedback situation in which subjects listened to a 5-minute tape of their performance and then continued working on the assigned problem. Bouchard believed this "task-relevant feedback" would "help achieve an optimal distribution of attention and information input [Bouchard, 1969, p. 12]." It would also "facilitate interpersonal communication." Concretely, in the feedback condition, subjects worked on an assigned problem for 5 minutes. They then stopped for 5 minutes to listen to a tape of their behavior and then continued working for another 10 minutes on the problem. All told, then, 20 minutes were involved in the feedback condition. In the nonbrainstorming condition subjects worked for 20 minutes without stopping, on the assigned problem.

Male college students participated in Bouchard's study. They worked on the education and thumbs problem. Feedback and nonfeedback conditions and order of problems worked on were counterbalanced. Time of day (which pilot work indicated was important) was also taken into account. The study also included an investigation of the effectiveness of nominal brainstorming groups with other problem-solving groups. A questionnaire to gather opinion data from the subjects on their experiences was also administered. Both of these shall be considered later. Results obtained with nominal groups will be presented on pages 80-104 and questionnaire data will also be presented on pages 63-65.

The instructions to subjects in the critical problem-solving situation were that they should: (1) analyze the problem; (2) keep in mind whether suggested solutions meet a criterion; and (3) present solutions that are meaningful, useful, and defensible—where criticism occurs it should be directed against ideas and not people; (4) all speak up. The subjects involved in group brainstorming were instructed in the four principles of brainstorming and then instructed appropriately for the feedback situation if it was relevant. The subjects in the group critical problem-solving condition were also appropriately instructed for their experimental condition.

All instructions, as we said, were written out and could be easily referred to by the subjects if they needed to do so. In the feedback condition, it will be recalled, subjects worked on an assigned problem for 5 minutes, then they listened to a 5-minute tape of their interactions, and finally they returned to work on the problem for a final 10 minutes. In the nonfeedback situation subjects worked straight through for 20 minutes on assigned problems.

Subjects' ideas were evaluated for quantity and quality. The latter varied with the problem used. For the thumbs problem a "practicality-importance" criterion was used and for the education problem an "effectiveness" measure was used. Specifically, in the practicality-importance measure each idea was evaluated on a five-point scale. If an idea was considered impractical or unimportant, it received a score of 0. If it was considered highly practical or very important, it received a score of 4. If the sum of two raters' scores equalled 4 on this problem, it was regarded as of "good" quality.

For effectiveness, responses were rated on a five-point scale by two judges. If a response was regarded as making no conceivable contribution to the solution of the problem or if it was regarded as an impossible solution, it received a score of 0. If the response was regarded as clearly being a major contribution to the possible solution of the problem, it received a score of 4. An idea was given a final "good" for the education problem if the sum of the ratings it received from two judges totaled 6 or more.

Results in this study are presented in terms of total number of ideas, total number of good ideas, and average quality of ideas.

There are, as one might infer from the presented description of the study, numerous analyses that could be carried out. We shall confine ourselves only to Bouchard's comparison of the group brainstorming and group critical problem-solving conditions with and without feedback because these are most germane to the issue at hand.

The results of this analysis are as follows:

(1) Group brainstorming is superior to group critical problem solving when the data for both feedback and nonfeedback conditions are combined. This result held for total number of ideas and number of good ideas but not the

average quality of ideas. This result is not likely to be of value to persons concerned with practical results, for it is unlikely that a practical situation would make available *both* feedback and nonfeedback data.

(2) Under nonfeedback conditions, group brainstorming was almost, but not quite significantly, superior to group critical problem solving. This experimental condition is most comparable to that used in other studies in this area. It involves a straightforward comparison of group brainstorming with group critical problem solving without feedback in either condition. And, the results indicated that group brainstorming was superior to group critical problem solving, but not significantly so, for total number of ideas and total number of *good* ideas but not for the average quality of ideas.

(3) When the effects of feedback are studied, group brainstorming is again superior to group critical problem solving (in the total number of ideas, and total number of good ideas but not in terms of average quality of ideas). This, according to Bouchard, is due not to feedback helping brainstorming but conversely to feedback having a bad effect on critical problem solving. Because of this datum and because, on an overall basis, no significant effects could be attributed to the feedback or nonfeedback conditions, it is not likely that anyone would want to use feedback in either critical problem-solving or brainstorming conditions.

Integrating the evidence from all studies cited (including those involving only instructions) we find that when brainstorming or instructions designed to effect the use of evaluation are used more ideas are produced than when critical judgment or evaluational procedures are employed.

However, with regard to the number of quality ideas produced, the data are quite equivocal—while adherents of brainstorming seem to find a larger number of quality ideas with a brainstorming rather than with a nonbrainstorming procedure, this finding does not find complete support among all other investigators. Most of these investigators find that there is either no difference in the *number of good* ideas produced in the brainstorming and nonbrainstorming conditions or that the *average quality* of ideas is also no better in the two conditions or is actually higher in the nonbrainstorming condition. This last finding, according to Weisskopf-Joelson and Eliseo (1961) occurs because while the two procedures do not differ in *number* of good ideas produced the brainstorming conditions produces more ideas of lower quality. Later we shall present some information from a study by Parloff and Handlon as to why more lower quality ideas are produced by the brainstorming procedure.

A finding that needs further study is one that suggests that *deferment* of judgment may not be as critical as the brainstormers claim that it is for the *separation* of idea evaluation from idea generation. Either may precede the other; they should not, however be combined in the same process.

Of what value are the results of the presented studies to people concerned with practical application? Before answering this question it needs to be said that all of the studies and results presented are in need of replication, and before this substantiation is available one must proceed with all necessary caution.

Two sets of investigators addressed themselves to the practical applications of their results. With the foregoing caution in mind this is what they had to say.

Weisskopf-Joelson and Eliseo (1961, p. 48) say that "If it is the purpose of problem solving to produce a specific number of ideas of highest possible quality, these best ideas will tend to be of higher or equal quality when the noncritical method is used. . . . A possible exception to this rule occurs when a very small number of responses is required. There the two methods tend to be equally promising, with a slight advantage of the critical method."

The advantage of the noncritical method is based on the larger number of ideas produced. Therefore, if the critical method would be used to develop a larger number of ideas then it would have an advantage. But, this advantage might be overcome by the larger number of participants and longer time required to produce the larger number of ideas. By the same token any advantage that may accrue to the noncritical condition that is an advantage may also be counterbalanced by the time and effort involved in evaluating the quality of the larger number of ideas among which will be a goodly number of lower quality ideas.

Bouchard (1969) in considering the possibility of practical applications of his work said that if one wants a set number of good ideas and if this is not a large number then "brainstorming is no better than critical problem solving and not worth the trouble [Bouchard, 1969, p. 20]." If a few more good ideas are desirable, then brainstorming is more desirable. And since these statements are made on the basis of subjects not trained in brainstorming the guidelines suggested are likely to be minimal suggestions.

We are inclined to agree with both sets of investigators that currently, and until there is more information available, there is little to recommend a noncritical procedure over a critical one. Slightly more higher quality ideas may be produced in the former condition but it will also take a longer time to evaluate all ideas produced in that condition and a goodly number of them are not likely to be worthwhile.

We also agree with Bouchard that as future work in this area continues attention should be paid specifically to how well groups *trained* in brainstorming perform because, at present, results attributed to brainstorming may only be minimal results since subjects using it have generally not been trained.

In addition to the importance of waiting for data on trained subjects, those concerned with the practical applications of the data should also await future data from studies that focus on several other issues to be considered.

Opinions and Attitudes

Brainstorming's value, according to its supporters, is reflected not only in the effects it has on the ideas it produces but also on the effect it has on its participants. According to Osborn (1963), for example, brainstorming has positive effects on such group factors as cohesiveness, morale, and the like. What do the research data show? Unfortunately, not all investigators gather data on this issue, and we are limited to reports from two studies. One is the study by Brilhart and Jochem (1964) in which patterns of problem-solving activities were studied where two of the patterns separated idea generation from idea evaluation, and the third combined these two activities. The second is a study by Bouchard (1969) in which brainstorming was compared to critical problem-solving activities that involved the presence and absence of feedback as variables.

In the Brilhart and Jochem (1964) study subjects rated their satisfaction with each of the three problem-solving patterns. Their ratings did not differ for any of the patterns; the subjects were equally satisfied with each of the three patterns. However, when the subjects were asked which pattern they would choose if they themselves were to lead problem-solving groups, they said they preferred pattern A in which idea generation was followed by idea evaluation (this pattern was closest to the brainstorming procedure) and they also preferred pattern C in which ideation and evaluation were combined. It is interesting to note that although the subjects did not know the results, pattern C, with which they said they were satisfied, was the least effective of all procedures.

The subjects in this experiment did not show much preference for pattern B. On all counts this procedure was almost as effective as pattern A, which was closest to brainstorming. In pattern B subjects separated but did not defer evaluation since idea evaluation preceded idea generation.

In essence, then, the Brilhart and Jochem experiment showed no difference between brainstorming and critical problem solving on a measure of satisfaction and a question concerning which procedure subjects would want to use in working with groups.

In the study by Bouchard (1969) the differences in questionnaire ratings were not very large but where differences appeared, although they were not statistically significant, they were in favor of the critical (nonbrainstorming) condition.

Bouchard asked the subjects in his problem solving groups how much they enjoyed working with their associates. In terms of absolute ratings both those who were in the brainstorming groups and those who were in the critical problem solving groups were on the positive side (i.e., said they enjoyed working with their associates) but the latter rated their enjoyment significantly higher than the former. This measure of group cohesiveness did not square with Bouchard's impression of what was going on.

The second question, also regarded as a measure of group cohesiveness, also yielded favorable ratings for both brainstorming and critical problem-solving groups. The average score of both groups indicate that they would be disappointed if they were told that their "group did not do a good job [Bouchard, 1969, p. 29]." Although the difference was not significant, it was again in favor of the critical problem-solving group who would be "more" disappointed. Using Bouchard's interpretation, the critical problem-solving group members were more committed to their group than were the brainstorming group members.

While the second question concerned itself with how the individual would feel if he were told that the *group* did not do a good job, the third question asked the individual how he would feel if he were told that *he* did not do a good job. Answers to this question were around the midpoint. Nevertheless, those in the critical problem-solving condition said they would be more disappointed than those in the group brainstorming condition.

The two groups were on the positive side when it came to saying whether they enjoyed working on their assigned problem but here ratings obtained from the critical problem-solving groups were significantly higher.

When asked about their satisfaction with their own or their group's performance both brainstorming and critical problem-solving groups gave neutral ratings on the average, and although the ratings of the critical problem-solving groups were higher, they were not significantly so.

Members of the critical problem-solving group felt that the procedure they used was a significantly more effective way for solving problems than was true of groups using brainstorming.

The participants were then asked whether they felt nervous during the group working sessions. The average ratings were not significantly different from each other and members of both groups were "rather nervous."

Finally, the participants were asked whether they felt judged or under pressure from the other group participants. The average ratings were on the positive side. Although the difference in average ratings for the brainstorming and critical problem-solving groups was not significant it was the brainstorming group that felt under somewhat more pressure.

In sum then these ratings indicate that the group critical problem solving condition came off better in terms of more positive ratings than did the group brainstorming condition. This result is counter to the experimenter's observation as we have noted and it is counter to the experiences reported about groups in real-life situations using brainstorming. It is unfortunate that other experiments do not use such questionnaires since their information could have helped resolve this apparent contradiction. At the moment we are left with the following possibilities:

(1) The responses to the questionnaires were not valid. This is not likely for there is nothing to suggest that they should be valid for one condition and not for another.

(2) Subjects in this experiment were simply not good observers and reporters. For example, they were not good observers of the effects of feedback, one of the variables in another part of the study. On the same questionnaire the effects

of feedback were evaluated and subjects said that feedback helped them in their work while the data showed that not only did it not help them but that it actually hindered the effectiveness of those in the critical problem-solving condition.

(3) It is more difficult to evaluate one's behavior in the group brainstorming condition. This may be a possible factor since the participants had really not had much experience with brainstorming, and the enjoyment they registered and other positive experiences they had with critical problem-solving may not have been so much a result of the procedure they used but of the *novelty* of the procedure they used. They may have disliked brainstorming because it was new to them. Had the participants been practiced in brainstorming, the ratings for this procedure might have been higher than they were.

(4) There is still the possibility that the data are quite valid and that for whatever reason, either because of experience or because of the intrinsic nature of the process, the critical problem-solving procedure is more satisfying. In this regard it should also be pointed out that reports cited here for positive reactions in real-life situations to brainstorming come from Osborn who was intimately involved in regarding brainstorming as effective. Secondly, reports from real-life situations were based only on the experience with brainstorming and not on the experience with the two techniques for problems solving. Therefore in the real-life situation a comparative judgment was not made as was the case in the laboratory study.

(5) There is the possibility that in responding to the questionnaire participants gave Bouchard what they *thought he* wanted. This might account for their more positive ratings of feedback (which didn't work) and for the more positive ratings of the critical problem-solving groups.

As we said, it is too bad that others have not used a questionnaire such as Bouchard's in their studies, for such questionnaires might have provided enlightening data.

Before leaving this topic it should also be pointed out that future researchers might consider using questionnaire data or other means to select subjects who are really involved in what they are doing. Bouchard reports some average ratings that reflected neutrality of attitude. One might ask whether these neutral ratings did not also reflect indifference or lack of sufficient involvement in the procedure. If so, the procedure may not have been subjected to proper testing.

In summary then, opinion and attitude data indicate that there is very little difference in the social and emotional characteristics of brainstorming and non-brainstorming groups. What difference there is is usually on the side of the latter, the critical groups. They, it appears are more cohesive, better motivated, enjoy their procedures more, and are more satisfied with their procedures than is true of brainstorming groups.

While the balance tilts in favor of the critical procedure, it needs to be pointed out that subjects in the studies presented were very likely more experienced and more practiced in critical problem-solving. Therefore a proper evaluation of the social-emotional factors in group creative problem solving needs to await the collection of data from groups trained and experienced in group brainstorming.

Personality Factors

There are three basic elements in the problem-solving process: the characteristics of the problem, the procedure employed, and the individual (considered in terms of his psychological characteristics) who employs the procedure to solve the problem. It is the procedure that has received most attention in this field. The other two components have received very little attention, and it is to what is available on these matters that we now turn. First we consider personality factors.

Bouchard (1969) in research that has already been discussed in this chapter, used a variety of personality measures to study the characteristics of his subjects before they participated in his studies. When the studies were completed he related these personality data to the criterion—number of good ideas—to learn the personality characteristics that could produce the largest number of good ideas under varying problem-solving conditions. We shall present only his results for group brainstorming and group critical problem-solving because only they are germane to the present discussion.

Considering the relationship between number of good ideas and personality variables in the group brainstorming condition, Bouchard presents data from two studies. Hence, here is one of those rare instances of replicated data. We find that the first five variables of the California Psychological Inventory (Gough, 1957), dominance, capacity for status, sociability, social presence, and self-acceptance all correlate significantly with the criterion in the two studies. These five variables constitute the first factor (obtained from a factor analysis) of the test, and is called *interpersonal effectiveness*.

Other personality variables which correlated significantly with the criterion in group brainstorming were: expressed inclusion and expressed control variables from the Firo-B test (Schutz, 1958) and the extroversion-introversion score from the Myers-Briggs Type Indicator (Myers, 1962). Bouchard suggests that the judging-perceiving scores from this last test should also be regarded as having been cross validated. Even though the correlation was not significant in the second sample it was of the same magnitude as in the first study.

Turning to group critical problem solving we find that sociability from the California Psychological Inventory, and the expressed-inclusion, expressed-affection, and wanted-affection scores of the Firo-B test all correlated significantly with the criterion. Two factors from the California Psychological

Inventory (I and IV, respectively, interpersonal effectiveness and conventionality) almost achieved significance for the critical problem-solving condition.

In integrating his findings, Bouchard suggests that considering all group-problem-solving conditions in his study (including both brainstorming and critical problem-solving) only the sociability scale and one factor score, interpersonal effectiveness, are "consistently (but not always significantly) related to performance [Bouchard, 1969, p. 25]." Gough, as Bouchard points out, developed these variables to predict social participation. Therefore, if one is involved in the selection of persons who would be involved in group problem solving, he would do well to select them in terms of the sociability score and interpersonal effectiveness factor of the California Psychological Inventory. Some of the characteristics of the individuals so selected would be reflected in Bouchard's report of Gough's definition of the high scorer (Gough, 1957, p. 10) on the sociability variable. He is seen as "outgoing, enterprising, and ingenious, as being competitive and forward, and is original and fluent in thought."

What has just been said refers to individuals in the different problem-solving groups studied by Bouchard, but turning to the personality correlates of the number of good ideas, Bouchard, in group brainstorming sessions, found that some of them are similar to those manifest in the behavior of high sociability scorers while others possess somewhat different characteristics. Combining available information, Bouchard (1969, p. 26) says, "High scoring subjects in the brainstorming groups have well-developed social skills, are outgoing, enterprising, original, verbally fluent, fluent in thought, somewhat aggressive, dominant, and controlling, and yet concerned with feelings of others. They possess self-assurance and are spontaneous, expressive, and enthusiastic."

And when we turn to the selection of individuals for group critical problem solving, more attention might be paid to their desire to be integrated and accepted by groups and to their bent for conventionality.

We would also suggest that there may be a group of individuals who score high on socialization who may also do well in group brainstorming. While there are individuals who find great security in societal conventions and have properly integrated them into their own personalities, being quite constructively critical in what they do and being quite effective in group critical problem solving, there are also, on the other hand, people who although socialized may wish to free themselves from the constricting effects of socialization. They would like to be free to express themselves and they may find opportunity for such freedom in brainstorming situations where the leader or experimenter makes the utilization of freedom quite socially acceptable.

Finally, as a matter for future study we might quote Bouchard on the use of personality factors in the selection of individuals for group brainstorming. He says, "The correlation between personality and performance under the various group problem-solving procedures suggests that proper subject selection can increase performance in brainstorming groups more than in critical problem-solving groups [Bouchard, 1969, p. 26] ." We are not certain that proper subject selection will have a greater effect on brainstorming than on critical problem solving as Bouchard suggests, but the investigation of personality factors in both areas is certainly necessary.

Characteristics of Problems

The third important ingredient in effective problem solving, in addition to the problem-solving procedure used and the problem solver involved, is the problem itself. There seems to be little attention paid to the basic structural characteristics of the problems used in the studies of brainstorming, or for that matter to the characteristics of problems in any study of the procedures of creative problem solving. The problems seem to be selected in terms of practicalities, so that if one investigator gets results with them then they are used by others, or problems are selected because some gross difference between them should be reflected in differences in their ease of solution. These problems are selected because they are "real" or "unreal" or potentially real or unreal. And, finally, problems are selected because in some other studies they have been related to creativity.

Because so little attention has been paid to the structural characteristics of problems, one cannot theorize and set up tests for checking hypotheses on what creative problem-solving procedures might be best for what kinds of problems. Also, because information on the structure of problems is lacking, one cannot even try to generalize from the kinds of problems used in laboratory studies to the kinds of problems that might be found in real-life situations.

In view of all this, all that one can do in a review of this sort is to call attention to the fact that not all creative problem-solving procedures work the same way with all problems. While this statement is accurate, it is hardly sufficient for any recommendations.

To illustrate what we have in mind, we will cite the data from two studies. These studies were not selected for any special criticism, for one can no doubt find similar illustrations in other studies.

Meadow *et al.* (1959), in their study of group brainstorming and critical problem solving that we reported earlier, concerned themselves with the order of these two procedures. In testing for the effects of order on the procedures, the investigators used two problems. In one, subjects had to think up uses for a wire coat hanger, and in the other subjects had to think up uses for a broom. The problems and procedures were used both in the first and second positions of the experimental design. The investigators report that significantly more good solutions were given to the hanger problem when it was used first. And, while more good solutions were obtained with the broom problem in the second test period, this number was not significantly different from that obtained with the same problem in the first test period. Also, "more good solutions were produced in the first period under the brainstorming instructions than under the nonbrainstorming instructions, and that there were more good solutions to the hanger problem than to the broom problem [Meadow *et al.*, 1959, p. 415]."

These results are then reported without any rationale for why the coat hanger problem should lend itself to brainstorming and the broom problem should not. The investigators do not follow up a report of their finding with a statement as to what it is in the characteristics of a coat hanger that do not exist with a broom that makes the former more amenable to brainstorming than the latter. It is not sufficient to say that brainstorming improves flexibility (number of responses) and originality (number of unique responses). We also need to know with what kinds of problems brainstorming, if it is effective, should be used. Problems used in studies of brainstorming are usually selected because previous experience indicates that they lend themselves to many responses or to unique responses. Such information is not very useful when it comes to deciding whether brainstorming will be helpful for work on a new problem. Maybe there is no possible help for this matter since by definition a "new problem" is one whose characteristics are not known. If that is the case then an alternative approach would be to test out a technique such as brainstorming on a range of problems that would include insight problems, trial and error problems, etc. In Chapter XVI we shall discuss other creative problem-solving procedures and point out how they may be better for some problems than others.

Let us take another example. This example comes from Bouchard's (1969) work in which, it will be recalled, he concerned himself with brainstorming and nonbrainstorming conditions with and without feedback. In this study, Bouchard worked with two problems also used by other investigators—the *thumbs* and *education* problems. The thumbs problem is an unreal problem—it is not likely to occur. In this problem the subject is asked to imagine that everyone had an extra thumb on each hand. This thumb would be like the one we already have only it would be on the other side of the hand, and it could work like the present one. With this information the subject is then asked to come up with ideas as to "what practical benefits or difficulties will arise when people start having this extra thumb? [Bouchard, 1969, p. 8]."

The education problem is one in which subjects are told that with the increasing birthrate school enrollment would be higher in 1970 than "today"—the date of the experiment, so that the reader must make allowance for the fact that the study was conducted in 1969. Because of the vastly increased enrollment possibilities, subjects are asked to come up with ideas to the question, "What different steps might be taken to insure that schools will continue to provide instruction at least equal in effectiveness to that now provided? [Bouchard, 1969, p. 8]."

Results of one of the studies in which these problems were used indicated that the thumbs problem yielded more ideas and more good ideas than the education problem. But the education problem yielded a higher mean quality of ideas than the thumbs problem. There was no interaction, in this study, between problem-solving procedure and problem.

A second analysis of this study involved an analysis of the data where only the 15 minutes of working time available to all groups was considered (this involved omitting time for feedback and cutting off the last 5 minutes of ideas produced by nonfeedback groups).

This analysis revealed that once again the thumbs problem yielded more ideas than the education problem but there was an interaction between problem-solving procedures and problem. "The significant Procedure X Problem interaction for total *number* of ideas is due to the fact that the critical problem-solving groups do very poorly on the thumbs problem relative to the other problem and procedures [Bouchard, 1969, p. 19, italics mine]."

These data are very interesting in that they call attention to the fact that experimenters must concern themselves with variance due to problems. However, as presented, the results are limited. Indeed, the education problem is more "real" than the thumbs problem, but does that mean that the results can be generalized to all other real problems—like the hanger or broom problems—or is there a more limited class of problems to which results may be generalized? Hopefully, future research would concern itself more with the means of classifying problems, as relates to the psychological processes involved in solving them, their basic structural characteristics, etc. And, when such data become available, it would then be most desirable if creative problem-solving techniques would be studied for their effectiveness with a range of problems of known characteristics. Results of such studies may then enable one to make a better decision as to which of the available problem-solving techniques is, on a probability basis, best suited for the available problem.

STUDIES OF PROCESS

The purpose of a process study is to make clear what variables or what characteristics of the process account for or effect obtained results. Previously presented outcome studies focused on the end product, e.g., how does what is produced by brainstorming compare with what is produced by some other procedure? In this section we are not concerned with the end state but with what affects the end state.

The first study provides information on two issues. The first is a seemingly unimportant methodological one—does it matter whether subjects write out or speak their ideas? This is generally regarded as so unimportant that experimenters usually do not make a point of telling us how ideas or suggestions for problem solutions were recorded. It is generally assumed that experimenters taped subjects' responses so that a complete record is available for later analysis.

But electronic recording may well alter the psychological aspects of the problem-solving situation. Therefore, by focusing their attention on the method of recording responses, Parloff and Handlon (1964) cast very important light on and make an important contribution to a critical substantive issue—why, as has been reported in some studies, does brainstorming yield more ideas, but ideas with lower average quality, than nonbrainstorming procedures?

Another matter that demands our attention in this section has to do with raters of responses. This matter also receives little, if any, attention in outcome studies. Experimenters, in presenting the procedure involved in their outcome studies, are usually clear in telling us about criteria used in evaluating obtained responses, yet they do not tell us much, if anything, about their raters. At times this may not matter because raters are so highly trained that characteristics of raters are not important. On other occasions, where evaluation is open ended, then it may matter, and it may also matter when we turn to considerations in real-life situations. On this issue we shall present comments by Weisskopf-Joelson and Eliseo (1961) and a study of the problem by Hyman (1960).

The last issue to be taken up in this section is one referred to in the literature as the difference between "real" and "nominal" groups. Previously presented outcome studies involved "real" groups. A real group is simply a group consisting of a stated number of people—3, 4, 12, etc. And when one speaks of group brainstorming, one usually means brainstorming a problem by a real group of individuals working on it in concert. However, the question has been asked, how does having a group work together affect the brainstorming process? Specifically, is it best for the production of number and quality of ideas to have all subjects work together in a group, or would it indeed be better to have each participant brainstorm a problem by himself and then bring together ideas generated by all the participants *as if* they had worked together? These latter groups are called "nominal" groups.

For some reason, the relative effectiveness of nominal and real groups has attracted the attention of numerous investigators who have concerned themselves with the effects of a host of variables. It is to this and the previously mentioned research that we now turn.

Writing Responses, Willingness to Report Ideas, and Standards of Evaluation

There is evidence in some previously reported studies that brainstorming may yield more ideas than other procedures for solving problems, but the *average* quality of these is lower than those produced by nonbrainstorming procedures. In other words, both brainstorming and nonbrainstorming procedures may yield the same number of high quality responses, but brainstorming yields more low quality responses and hence the drop in average quality of response. Why does this happen? This is the question that Parloff and Handlon (1964) undertook to answer in their study.

Parloff and Handlon felt that it was important to differentiate between a person's capacity to *generate* ideas from his *willingness to report them*. Not only does the creative problem-solving process involve idea generation and idea evaluation as the brainstorming proponents and others have suggested, but it also involves the subject's willingness to *report* ideas generated. What is it that affects the subject's willingness to report ideas so that he reports more ideas when instructed with brainstorming than when he is instructed with nonbrainstorming instructions is what Parloff and Handlon sought to determine. As we shall see, the answer they come up with is that when working with the deferment-of-judgment principle the subject lowers his standards.

The problem as stated by Parloff and Handlon is as follows:

> It is generally assumed that the suspension of critical judgment operates to decrease inhibiting or interfering forces and thereby permits the generation of a greater number of creative ideas. However, the studies which purport to find a positive relationship between reduction of critical judgment and an increased number of good solutions to problems do not constitute conclusive evidence that the effect is due to the increased "generation" of good quality ideas. Similar results might be produced if the reduction of critical judgment enabled the individual to report ideas already available to him, which he would ordinarily reject as trivial or worthless. Such ideas may be valued far more by a judge than by the person reporting them [p. 18].

Their study, then, aimed at trying to understand whether the qualitative changes in responses "can be explained in terms of alterations in the 'availability' of responses or in terms of shifts in the subject's standards for selecting a solution from his available alternatives [p. 18]."

In their research, Parloff and Handlon (1964) studied the relationship between brainstorming instructions and quality of response with twelve pairs or teams of girls. Six of these pairs were regarded as mutually congenial, and six pairs as mutually uncongenial. Congeniality was based on congeniality *rankings* the girls gave each other; hence, there is no basis for knowing the absolute level of congeniality. The pairs had to solve both "real" problems ("How can we solve the teacher shortage?"; "How can a shy girl go about meeting a boy she regularly sees on a bus?"; "How can foreign tourists be encouraged to visit the United States?") and "unreal" problems ("What would the consequences be of having an extra thumb on each hand?"; "What would the probable results be of a mutation that would increase the rate of physical maturation but not mental maturation?"; "What would be the advantages and disadvantages of having the power to read minds regardless of the distance?").

The procedure in the experiment was as follows. Each girl was first asked to work individually on each problem for 10 minutes, writing as many solutions as occurred to her (specific instructions for this are not indicated). The pairs were then assembled, but before any work was undertaken by them, each girl was given 2 more minutes to work on the problem individually. To give the girls practice in working as a pair, they were then given one of the real (the teacher problem) and one of the unreal problems (thumbs problem) to solve under "neutral" conditions ("Work together in any way which seems most comfortable to you [p. 21]").

The girls worked in pairs under both low-critical and high-critical conditions. In the low-critical condition, for which the instructions were essentially the same as in brainstorming, the stress was on refraining from criticism, and the girls were urged to give free rein to their imaginations. In the high-critical condition the importance of doing their best was stressed, and they were urged to analyze and scrutinize each idea carefully and to select only the good ones. In both conditions the girls were asked to work together to produce new ideas. Each idea that the pair agreed upon together as new and appropriate was to be entered by one of the individual members. They were also told that tape recordings of their group sessions would be made in order that individual as well as team scores could be derived.

Thus, Parloff and Handlon (1964) had two sources for the solutions they were to evaluate: (1) transcriptions of the complete tape recordings and (2) reports submitted in writing by each pair. The transcripts of the recordings permitted determination of the number and quality of solutions expressed. This was the operational definition of "generation of ideas." The written solutions submitted by each team represented the ideas that they were mutually *willing to offer* the examiner as the product of their collaborative effort.

The procedure for scoring the solutions was as follows. All solutions were first screened for novelty. A solution was regarded as novel if the idea had not been submitted by either member of a pair during the individual testing period. Each solution generated (written or unwritten) by a pair was transcribed onto a board and screened by examiners. These ideas were compared with the solutions submitted by the members of the same pair during the individual resting period and all ideas determined to be redundant for a given pair were eliminated. Novel ideas were then submitted to two judges, who assessed their quality without knowing their source. The criteria for quality were derived from the work of D. W. Taylor, Berry, and Block (1958) in evaluating solutions to similar problems. The criteria for judging the solutions to "real" problems were: "(1) *effectiveness*, or how well the proposed solution solves the problem; (2) *feasibility*, or how readily the means suggested for the solution are available; (3) *clarity*, or how clearly the solution is spelled out. In the judging process effectiveness was most heavily weighted [Parloff & Handlon, 1964, p. 22]" (but no systematic weighting procedure is indicated in the paper). For the "unreal" problems the criteria were: "(1) *significance*, or how important the suggested consequence is; (2) *probability*, or how likely it is that the suggested consequence will occur; (3) *clarity*, or how clearly the suggested consequence is spelled out. For these problems, the greatest weight was given to significance [p. 22]." Judges classified these solutions as good, indifferent, or poor. The judges first worked independently and then met to reconcile their differences.

The results of this study were: (1) A greater number of ideas and a greater number of good ideas were *written down* under the low-critical condition. (2) When verbalized or taped solutions were analyzed, it was found that a greater number of ideas were generated under the low-critical condition. These two points are consistent with what we would expect from the data on brainstorming (e.g., Meadow & Parnes, 1959). (3) But there was *no* significant difference in the number of *good* solutions that were verbalized under the high- or the low-critical conditions. If anything, there was a tendency for the girls in the high-critical condition to verbalize more good ideas than was true of those in the low-critical condition. Thus, although the pairs functioning under the low-critical condition produced significantly more ideas than those under the high-critical condition, since there was no significant difference in the number of good ideas produced, the assumption that the number of ideas is positively related to the number of good ideas is not supported. (4) As in the Hyman study (1960), Parloff and Handlon (1964) also found that there was an effect due to type of problem; more good solutions were verbalized for the unreal than for the real problem. Analysis of the solutions verbalized but *not* reported in writing revealed that significantly more ideas were verbalized for unreal than for real problems. (5) Congeniality of the pairs did not have any significant effects on the results.

In essence, the results of this study indicate that the effect of high-critical and low-critical conditions upon the quality of ideas depends on whether the data are restricted to those ideas that are submitted in writing or include the total number of ideas verbalized by the subjects. Under the high-critical condition 88 good solutions were verbalized by the girls but 67 of them were not subsequently written. Under the low-critical condition 73 good responses were verbalized but only 26 remained written. This suggests that the low-critical condition did not enhance the production of good ideas, but did increase the probability of their being reported. Thus, suspension of critical judgment may simply lower a subject's reluctance to report ideas without substantially increasing his idea production; that is, deferring judgment does not alter a person's generative capacity.

Parloff and Handlon (1964), therefore, make an interesting point with regard to brainstorming training; they suggest that we must investigate whether the individual is being trained to be "creative" or *to alter his standards* so that they conform more closely to those of the judges.

One major problem bedeviling research in the area of creative problem solving is the establishment of meaningful criteria for evaluating the quality of the solutions. Thus far the concern of most investigators has been with establishing interjudge reliability. However, a further stumbling block in experimental work in this area is the possible lack of congruence between the subjects' evaluation of their productions and the judges' evaluation. To the degree that this congruence is overtly or covertly improved by training of the subject, the subject will appear more "creative" [p. 25].

This last point is very interesting because the proponents of brainstorming believe that the training and the instructions per se will serve to increase both the quantity and the quality of responses. In fact, however, what may happen is that during training, individuals learn how to develop standards that will be congruent with those that are accepted by judges.

Parnes interprets these findings somewhat differently.

. . .it isn't necessarily so that they learn to develop standards congruent with those of the judges; it is more a question of their coming up with many criteria, and being more likely to take into account relevant variables that the judges might consider but which they might have overlooked without a broad search of criteria. This is what gets people in difficulty in general—not considering enough criteria and, therefore, going off half cocked. It is interesting to note that our students note that one of the most significant results of our course in that they "take more things into consideration in making a decision" [Parnes, 1972, personal communication].

Collating all the data presented thus far, the data are stronger for supporting the hypothesis that deferred judgment results in the production of more ideas, but it is not very strong and possibly on the opposite side with regard to quality of response. Further exploration of a question raised by these studies indicates that when an individual is instructed to defer judgment, he does not necessarily take that instruction to mean to generate more ideas but rather to alter his standards of evaluation.

Hyman (1961) arrives at a similar conclusion that change in standards of evaluation may be involved in the effects of differences in instructions to subjects. In the study in which Hyman provided his subjects with different kinds of information and then asked them to assume constructive and critical attitudes to these data, he studied the intercorrelation between the rated creativity of ideas and the subjects' satisfaction with a given solution. The correlations presented by Hyman are -0.46 for responses obtained under the constructive condition and

+0.42 for the critical condition. "This difference, which is significant at the 0.01 level, would suggest, if it is replicated in future experiments, that the evaluation variable has brought about a shift in kind of solution which S is trying to achieve [Hyman, 1961, p. 160]."

Raters—The Locus of Evaluation and Criteria

In previously reported studies where quality of subjects' responses was a critical variable, quality was most usually determined by raters and not by the individual who came up with the idea or who made the suggestion. Experimental conditions in which raters evaluate quality of response are analogous to real-life situations where a supervisor listens to a subordinates' various ideas and selects from the offerings or together with the subordinate decides on the suggestion that will be worked on. In other situations where an individual works alone, or even where he works with others, the considerations are such that the individual himself has to select one or more ideas that he will follow up.

One question which therefore arises is whether results in previously reported studies involving only raters' evaluations would be supported if one considered subjects' evaluations. Essentially, would the results of studies which say that quantity and quality of ideas are not significantly related (contrary to the assumptions made in brainstorming) be supported if one studied quality of responses where locus of evaluation was in an external rater as well as if the locus of evaluation was within the subject making the suggestion.

This problem was studied by Hyman (1960) as part of a series of three experiments. The forty-eight subjects in the study had all participated in creative engineering courses at the General Electric Company. These forty-eight subjects consisted of three groups of sixteen people each. Two of the groups participated in one experiment each and the other in two experiments. The experiments were essentially similar in orientation: to investigate the relationship between quantity and quality of ideas. They differed only in the problems used.

There were five different types of problems in the three experiments—consequences, hypothesis formation, sensitivity to problems, other uses, "and a task which asked the respondents to suggest ways for bringing about a desired situation [Hyman, 1960, p. 29]."

Two different sets of instructions were used and they were counterbalanced in each of the three experiments. One instruction asked subjects to strive for quantity and the other asked them to strive for quality. When the focus was on *quantity* subjects were asked to list as many ideas as they could. They were to write down all appropriate ideas. For the *quality* condition subjects were asked to write down only creative ideas.

All subjects worked with both sets of instructions. In any one experiment one-half of the subjects worked on two problems with one set of instructions

and then they worked on another two problems with the other set of instructions. The other half of the subjects followed a reverse order.

Two raters judged the responses for creativity. Their judgments involved
"uncommonness," which meant that an idea was among the 50% most infrequent responses, and their subjective rating of quality.

The results of this set of experiments indicated that the quantity instruction
produced more responses than did the quality condition. For problems that were
common to the three experiments, 68% more responses were developed under
the quantity condition than under the quality condition. Insofar as quality is
concerned, no significant relationships were found between quantity and
quality.

Thus far Hyman's study was similar to others. But then he added a new
variable. He asked the subjects to review their ideas and to select that one idea
for each problem that they considered their best solution. When subjects'
choices were related to judges' evaluations, no relationship was found. Subjects
and judges did not agree. Hyman says that "this lack of correlation is due to the
failure of subjects to agree among themselves as to what constitutes a good
solution [Hyman, 1960, p. 32]." This may be so, but had the problem been a
real problem and had the disagreements occurred it would have been interesting
to have both subjects and raters go ahead and actually develop their solutions.
Then it would have been interesting to compare the creativity of the solutions.
There are numerous occasions in real life where a person's ideas may be turned
down or devaluated in terms of creativity, but which in the course of time are
found to be quite creative. Such practical experiences are most usually impossible to demonstrate in one experiment and hence we are left with the finding
that subjects who generate ideas and judges who evaluate them are not in
agreement.

Hyman pursued the matter further. Since he already had judges' evaluations
of the responses, he studied the ratings that a subject's selected single best
response obtained and found that this was not significantly related to the
quantity condition.

Also, in addition to asking subjects for their single best answer he asked
them to encircle all ideas they thought "worthy of further consideration." Considering two problems that were used in three experiments, Hyman found that
under the quantity condition subjects regarded only 9% of their responses as
worthy of follow-up and under the quality condition they considered 15% of
their ideas as worthy of follow-up. These data are consistent with those found in
other studies. Thus the relationship (or rather the lack of relationship) between
quantity and quality is found not only when judgments of the ideas are made by
raters, but also by the participants themselves.

Finally, since Hyman already had judges' evaluations of the subjects' ideas, he
calculated what proportion of those ideas which the subjects themselves thought

were worthwhile to follow up were regarded as creative by the judges. Calculating these data, Hyman found that under the quantity condition judges felt that 11% of the participants' choices were creative. Under the quality condition judges regarded 19% of the participants' choices as creative. Again these data are consistent with other data that it is not the quantity condition that results in better quality responses, as suggested by brainstorming, but rather the quality condition.

The data just cited suggested to Hyman a possibility entertained by other investigators also—"that the quantity condition may result in decreased efficiency because it may lead the thinker into spending a greater proportion of his time upon ideas of poorer quality [Hyman, 1960, p. 32]."

Turning now to raters' criteria we find an interesting comment in the paper by Weisskopf-Joelson and Eliseo (1961) and some analytical material in a paper by Hyman (1961). Raters' criteria are important in studies of techniques designed to stimulate creativity, for these criteria are employed in evaluating ideas produced by the different procedures. If the criteria are faulty then erroneous evaluations may occur. Indeed, criteria do not pose problems in all studies. They only pose problems in those studies in which there is leeway or some opportunity for subjectivity to become involved in the ratings. In other studies such as those where uniqueness is involved, it depends essentially on a counting procedure. This is a more objective criterion than one like judging an idea in terms of its value or attractiveness.

Weisskopf-Joelson and Eliseo (1961), it will be recalled, asked their subjects to develop brand names for an auto, a deodorant and a cigar. Suggestions were then evaluated by raters. Raters in this study were other college students. The experimenters obviously accepted the raters' ratings as their data but they could not refrain from making a comment about their raters' judgments. They point out that among their raters' highly rated brand names there were three that the raters regarded as very attractive. However, the experimenters themselves regarded these three suggestions as conventional and less attractive. This, as the experimenters say, suggests the possibility that "the imaginative ideas of the brainstormers were wasted on the conservative taste of the judges. Perhaps judges and consumers with greater preference for unusual brand names could throw a more favorable light on brainstorming [Weisskopf-Joelson & Eliseo, 1961, p. 49]." The possibility exists therefore that, in this study, brainstorming was at a disadvantage because of the attitudes of the raters toward the ideas suggested.

Attitudes can quite obviously have subjective effects, but so can other factors which on the face of it can appear quite objective. Thus, for example, some raters may be steadfast in how they think something should be done. If it is done their way or the way they approve of then it is creative; if not, then it is not creative. Thus, the views of these raters may appear quite objective, but how they hold on to their views may reflect something of the problems involved.

While the kinds of problems to which we have just referred to may occur in many studies, not all investigators concern themselves with them. One who does is Hyman, who in one of his studies (Hyman, 1961) found that while he counted on three raters to evaluate his subjects' ratings, he could use only the data obtained from two of them. Ratings obtained from one of them were so in disagreement with the other two that they had to be discarded. But while he did discard his third rater's material, Hyman also investigated more closely what happened.

The problem that was put to the subjects was a technical engineering problem and the raters disagreed how it should be solved. The two raters who agreed with each other gave low ratings to solutions that involved the use of certain materials ("crystals as temperature sensors"), and gave high ratings to those answers that did not use temperature-sensing mechanisms. "Thus, these judges seemed to be employing, firstly, an originality criterion (only unusual or unconventional answers were classified at the high end) and, secondly, a quality criterion (an elaborated answer typically got rated a step higher than a similar answer that had less detail) [Hyman, 1961, p. 155]." The third rater used only a quality criterion—one that involved the use of specifications. If specifications were low then his ratings were low. This latter judge rated some temperature-sensing answers high and others low but the other two judges always rated them low (Hyman, 1961, p. 155).

The material presented here on the differences in raters' frames of reference is interesting not only because it sheds light on some of what is going on in the study of brainstorming but also because of its future usefulness in another regard. One of the aspects of the creative process that has received very little attention is the role of the critic—the art critic, the movie critic, the book reviewer, etc. The data presented here, as well as the kind of study that yielded such data, are stepping stones to setting up procedures for gathering more information in this regard in the future.

While it is fruitful to gain insight and understanding into the criteria that make up raters' evaluations, it would also be worthwhile if experimenters who study brainstorming would be familiar with each others' criteria or evaluations and replicate each others' work. Otherwise there is unnecessary confusion. As we have seen in studies where judgments of quality have to be made, different investigators use different criteria of quality. Consequently, one cannot be certain that the lack of consistency between experimenters in obtained results is a result of criteria or other matters.

Hyman (1960) in his studies of quantity and quality found no relationship between a quantity instruction and quality of ideas as his raters rated them. As Hyman points out, the supporters of brainstorming do find such a relationship but others do not. However, since he used two problems in some of his experiments that Parnes used in his, Hyman had his raters rate subjects' contributions in terms of Parnes' criteria—uniqueness and value. The results were in line with

Parnes' results but they were not statistically significant, probably because a small number (N = 16) of subjects were studied. The question is still open whether Parnes' data would not be confirmed with larger numbers of subjects whose ideas would be rated with the same criteria used by Parnes.

Hyman, it will be recalled, had his raters use a criterion of uniqueness and some subjective judgment of their own about the creativity of the responses. He also had his subjects select their own best responses in some experiments. In the experiments just considered when Hyman had the ideas rated on a nine-point scale of quality, he found that the rated quality of these single best ideas was poorer under the quantity than under the quality condition.

In light of all these variations in criteria, it is apparent that agreement on criteria would be a prerequisite for further research, so that a solid basis would be available for understanding brainstorming better.

Effects of the Group on Brainstorming—("Nominal" versus Real Groups)

One of the questions that attracted a great deal of attention in the brainstorming literature concerned itself with the effect of working on a problem in a group on the number and quality of ideas produced. The question asked could be stated this way: If we have twelve persons to work on a problem would it be better to divide them into real working groups (e.g., 3 groups of four each) or, would it be better to have each of the twelve individuals brainstorm the problem by himself and then assemble their responses into 3 "nominal" groups of four each, *as if* they had worked together? Would the number and quality of ideas produced by *real* groups be better or worse than the number and quality of ideas produced by nominal groups?

Two comments are in order before presenting research designed to answer the stated questions. First, the question does *not* involve a test of brainstorming but only a test of the effects of working in a group on brainstorming. Some persons, as pointed out by Parnes (1963), persist in regarding the literature presented in this section as reflecting on the value of brainstorming. Therefore, to repeat, the studies focus directly on group effects.

Secondly, another confusing element in the research is that it may sometimes be regarded as concerned with the differences between group and individual brainstorming. This confusion can be traced to the fact that some authors correctly refer to one of their experimental conditions as group brainstorming but they incorrectly refer to the other condition in which they assemble individual efforts into artificial groups as individual brainstorming. It is obvious that any group only because of its size will perform better than an individual. To avoid this confusion it is important to bear in mind that the studies that follow concern themselves with the differences between *real* groups and *nominal* (or artificial) groups.

On *a priori* grounds one might argue in favor of real groups because individuals in a group may have a stimulating effect on each other. Each person can bolster another's morale. When a member of a group, a person might find in the group's acceptance sufficient security to take risks and offer ideas he would not offer alone. A group composed of individuals of varying backgrounds and experiences may offer many diverse ideas which could then be combined into additional new ideas; such new ideas might not have been developed without the diversity existing in the group.

While these possibilities favor group brainstorming one could argue against them by saying that an individual working alone would not be confused by others' ideas; he could expand on his own ideas as he sees fit; he does not need to waste energy being competitive; he may be able to express himself fully without interruption from others; and, finally, some persons simply prefer working alone to working with others.

These are some of the arguments in favor of brainstorming problems in real groups and some of the arguments in favor of nominal groups. Again, the issue is not brainstorming but the effects of working in a group on brainstorming.

Research in this area was stimulated by the work of D.W. Taylor and his associates who conducted the first study (Taylor *et al.*, 1958) on real and nominal groups using brainstorming. Subjects in this study were ninety-six Yale seniors and juniors. At the time of the experiment all of the subjects were students in Taylor's class on the Psychology of Personnel Administration in which on various occasions they engaged in small discussion groups. From these students forty-eight were selected at random to be part of 12 four-man actual groups. It should be repeated once again at this point to stress the matter than unlike other studies involving actual groups this one was composed of individuals who had had *prior* experience working in groups.

In addition to 12 four-man actual groups, forty-eight subjects were selected at random to work by themselves. These subjects were to brainstorm their problems alone and then their suggestions were to be assembled into 12 nominal groups of four individuals each. These individuals had not worked together but their responses were assembled *as if* they had worked together.

Three problems were used in this study which were selected because they were found to be of interest to the subjects, because they produced "many and varied" responses, and because brainstorming could be used with them. The problems were: (1) tourists problem—How to get more European tourists to visit the United States, (2) thumbs problem—What kinds of "benefits or difficulties will arise when people start having an extra thumb?", (3) teachers problem—How to persuade people to go into teaching so that with increasing birthrate the quality of education would be maintained.

Each problem was read aloud to the subjects. They did not have a copy of the problem and if questions arose the problem was reread to them. Also, as part of the instructions, subjects read part of a published article that was favorable to brainstorming. And, finally, subjects were told that their responses would be machine recorded. They were not to write their responses "because writing was slow and inaccurate [Taylor *et al.*, 1958, p. 30]." (That responses were spoken and taped but not written became an important matter for subsequent studies.)

The results of this study were: (1) On each of the three problems used, the average total number of ideas produced by real *groups* (37.5) was significantly greater than that produced by *individuals* (19.6). This does *not* relate to the difference between real and nominal groups but only to the difference between real *groups* and individuals. The former do better than the latter and as Taylor *et al.* (1958) point out, this result is consistent with what one finds in the writings of brainstorming's supporters—that groups are stimulating and therefore the average number of ideas suggested by groups is higher than that produced by individuals.

This finding, while interesting does not tell us about the effects of the group on brainstorming. Does it inhibit or facilitate it? To answer this question three additional analyses were carried out in which nominal and real groups were compared and the results indicated: (2) Nominal groups produce significantly more ideas than do real groups. (3) Nominal groups produce more unique ideas than do real groups. Uniqueness is, however, only one measure of quality. The authors therefore used other measures, three for each of the problems, (e.g., "feasibility," "effectiveness," and "generality"). Using these three measures as well as uniqueness, the experimenters report that (4) "In brief, the performance of the real group is inferior to that of the nominal groups on all three problems with respect to each and all of the measures of performance employed [Taylor *et al.*, 1958, p. 43]."

As a consequence of this result the investigators conclude "that group participation when using brainstorming *inhibits* creative thinking [Taylor *et al.*, 1958, p. 43]." To account for this the authors suggest that when working in a group individuals feel less free of criticism than one might suppose. The authors point out that they have no evidence for this but suggest it may be at the root of the matter. The author's second suggestion to account for the result is that persons working in a group are likely to follow the same line of thought and such sameness would cut down on the diversity of ideas produced.

The experimental use of real and nominal groups caught the imagination of many investigators, and they were stimulated to study the effects of numerous variables on the relative superiority of nominal over real groups. In the main, results of these studies supported the Taylor *et al.* (1958) findings.

These other studies were stimulated by the findings just reported. However, before we report these studies, we would like to report another of the Taylor 1958 findings which is not as strongly in favor of nominal groups. One cannot help but wonder if investigators who followed Taylor *et al.* put sufficient weight on this finding and if so why they felt that it was worthwhile to pursue a study of the effectiveness of real over nominal groups.

The data in the Taylor *et al.* (1958) study that we refer to were generated in response to the question whether the obtained difference in unique responses favoring nominal over real groups would still be maintained if one controlled for the fact that nominal groups produce more ideas (of whatever sort) than real groups. In answer to this question Taylor *et al.* (1958) analyzed their data for each of the problems used in the study. They found that after adjusting for total number of responses produced by nominal and real groups there was *no* significant difference between the two of them in number of unique responses for either the tourists or teachers problems. For the thumbs problem a significant difference was found in favor of the *real* groups who produced the larger number of unique responses.

Taylor *et al.* carried out another similar analysis where they controlled for the number of responses produced and focused on the three quality measures they used for each of the three problems. Once again they found no differences between nominal and real groups on quality measures of feasibility, effectiveness, and generality for either the tourists or teachers problems. However a significant difference in favor of the *nominal* groups was found with the thumbs problem. On this point the authors say "that the superiority of nominal over real groups on the three quality measures is largely a matter of difference in number of responses and only to a limited degree, if any, a matter in the quality of the ideas produced [Taylor *et al.* 1958, pp. 44-45]."

Summarizing these last two findings in which total number of responses were controlled, we learned that there were no significant differences in number of unique responses and in three other measures of quality for the tourists and teachers problems. These problems, as we have previously referred to them, are real or potentially real problems. For the third problem, the thumbs problem, an unreal problem, the results are contradictory. When total number of responses are controlled and number of unique responses are studied then real groups are superior while other measures of quality (in this instance "probability," "significance," and "generality") are used then the evidence is in favor of nominal groups.

These differences in measures of quality and in control of number of different responses seems to have escaped the attention of most investigators who studied a whole host of factors and whose findings favored nominal over real groups. It is to this research that we now turn.*

---

*As previously indicated, the Taylor *et al.* (1958) work concerned itself with the effects of the group on brainstorming. For the sake of clarity and emphasis it should be reiterated that, as pointed out by Parnes (1963), Taylor *et al.* were (1) not comparing a conference using brainstorming with a conventional conference, (2) not comparing a brainstorming group with conventional individual thinking, and (3) not concerning themselves with the validity of the principle of deferred judgment. *(continues on page 84)*

Significant Prior Experience in Groups

The subjects in the Taylor *et al.* (1958) experiments were students who had experience working together in classroom discussion groups. But such group experience is probably not as intense or as significant as that occurring in real-life situations. To consider the effects of such prior experience Dunnette, Campbell, and Jaastad (1963) studied the effects of brainstorming on the be-havior of nominal and real groups when their constituent members were research scientists and advertising personnel who had had experience working together in real-life situations.

Nominal and real groups were composed separately for the research scientists and the advertisers. Creative thinking with an emphasis on brainstorming had

---

Although they focused on the differences between nominal and real groups using brain-storming, several studies which did not focus on brainstorming but which concerned themselves with related matters need mentioning.

Taylor *et al.* (1958) compared real and nominal groups where all used critical thinking—instructions emphasized number and quality of ideas. They found that nominal groups were better than real groups on both variables.

This finding was consistent with a study by Tuckman and Lorge (1962) which, while it did not use brainstorming or real and nominal groups, found that group performance rarely exceeded the performance of the best group member, and the performance of the best group member was often inhibited by the group.

Parnes and Meadow (1963) report a study in which ten real groups of four individuals each were compared with ten nominal groups of four individuals each. The former used the principle of deferred judgment and the latter used "conventional thinking procedures" which emphasized the production of quality ideas. The broom and hanger problems were used and none of the subjects had prior training in the use of deferred judgment.

The results of this study indicated that groups that used deferred judgment produced significantly more good ideas on both experimental problems than did the nominal groups.

In the same paper, Parnes and Meadow (1963) also report comparing the ten real groups in the study just mentioned with another ten nominal groups that used deferred judgment. In the write-up of this study we are told quite specifically that subjects received only written instructions and they recorded their ideas in pencil. (We infer that in the previous experiment subjects also wrote out their own ideas. The subjects in Taylor's experiment had their responses tape-recorded which as we shall see later in the text is a rather important matter.) Another difference between the Parnes and Meadow (1963) and Taylor *et al.* (1958) studies is that subjects in the former experiment were allowed 5 minutes for each problem. Taylor's subjects had 12 minutes for each of their problems.

The results of this experiment indicated no difference between real and nominal groups. But contrary to Taylor's findings "the tendency was in favor of the actual groups using the principle of deferred judgment in open discussion [Parnes and Meadow, 1963, p. 318]."

A third study is mentioned briefly by Parnes and Meadow (1963) in which many of the details of the experimental design are missing but they say they compared conventional thinking with deferred judgment in untrained groups where subjects hand recorded their responses. In this study they say they found "a higher productivity of good ideas by the deferred judgment groups, significant on one task and in the same direction on the second [Parnes and Meadow, 1963, p. 318]."

been discussed with all subjects prior to the experiment. As the experiment began subjects were instructed in brainstorming. The problems were read to the men, and they were also given dittoed copies of the problems. The subjects responses were tape recorded as in the Taylor *et al.* (1958) experiment. And, as in the Taylor *et al.* study, 4-man nominal and real groups were used.

However, there were also differences between the Dunnette *et al.* and the Taylor *et al.* experiments. The Taylor *et al.* subjects were either in the nominal group or the real group, while in the Dunnette *et al.* experiment they were in both. We shall discuss order effects later (page 98) but at the moment it should be indicated that the order of nominal (individual) and real groups were counter-balanced. Half the time one came first and half of the time the other came first.

Instead of three problems as in the Taylor *et al.* study Dunnette *et al.* used four problems. They used the three used by Taylor *et al.*, teachers problem, (called education problem here) tourists problem, and thumbs problem. The fourth, people problem, was one in which subjects were told that at age 20 the average height of Americans increased to 80 inches and their average weight doubled. Subjects were asked to come up with responses as to what adjustments and consequences followed.

For purposes of data analysis Dunnette *et al.* (1963) used two criteria: the number of different responses and a quality score. The quality score used in this experiment was a rating of *effectiveness* for the *education and tourists* problems and a rating for *probability* for the *thumbs and people* problems. Ratings of one rater (whose reliability was not terribly high when compared with a sample of ratings from another) were used.

The results of this study indicated that nominal groups produced significantly more (about one-third) responses than did real groups; and that nominal groups were also superior to the real groups in the quality measure. Consequently, Dunnette *et al.* conclude that "The evidence is clear-cut: brainstorming is most effective when undertaken by individuals working *alone* in an atmosphere free from the apparently inhibiting influence of group interaction [Dunnette *et al.*, 1963, p. 36]."*

Dunnette (1964) finds further support for his skepticism about the effect of groups in problem-solving situations by citing the work of Tuckman and Lorge

---

*Rotter and Portugal (1969) raised the question about the effects of having the same subjects work on different problems when they were in the nominal- (individual) and in the real-group situation. They therefore used the *same* problem in both and also found nominal groups to be superior to real groups in number of ideas. Quality of ideas was not studied. In addition to the suggestions offered by Taylor *et al.* (1958) and Dunnette *et al.* (1963) as to why nominal groups are better than real groups, Rotter and Portugal suggest that real groups may be at a disadvantage because of time limits used. Individuals, they suggest may work in spurts and not all individuals may have had the time to record their spurts in the time allowed. Further discussion of the Rotter and Portugal (1969) study are presented on pages 101-103.

(1962) who studied the effects of individual and group behavior in nonbrainstorming situations. They found according to Dunnette (1964, p. 16) that "The group performance rarely exceeded the performance of the best member individually. In fact, the performance of the most effective member was often inhibited and was not, therefore, reflected in the group solution." Consequently, Dunnette adds "Their study leads us to view with extreme pessimism the possibility that meetings can be so constituted and conducted as to be worth the time taken in group problem-solving endeavors."

Dunnette *et al.* agree with Taylor *et al.* that the reasons real groups are less effective than nominal groups may stem from the possibility that real groups get stuck thinking along one line and the lack of consequent diversity cuts down on number of ideas produced. Also, they suggest that some individuals are inhibited by the presence of others in the group.

There are other findings in this study which will be discussed in another context later. One of them is that there are differences in results attributed to the kinds of groups studied—advertising personnel were more severely effected by brainstorming in a real group than were researchers. Secondly, the data on the effects of order suggest that real-group brainstorming preceding nominal-group (individual) brainstorming may be valuable as a warmup procedure. Also, once again some of the effects could be attributed to the kinds of problems used.

We shall, as we said, return to each of these later. At this point, to collate the results of both studies we may say that nominal groups do produce significantly more ideas than do real groups. Both studies agree that nominal groups are better than real groups with regard to quality of ideas (putting aside the need to control for number of ideas produced). The agreement, however, is based on a rather weak foundation. First, in the Dunnette *et al.* (1963) study the quality measure was based on one of the three variables used by Taylor *et al.* (1958). Secondly, in the Dunnette *et al.* study quality-rating data from one experimenter were used and her data were admittedly not very reliable when compared with a sample of ratings obtained from another rater. (3) The Taylor *et al.* results indicate that their three-variable quality results show that nominal groups are no different from real groups on the tourists and teachers problems but they do differ on the thumbs problem. In the Dunnette *et al.* study a difference is found on the teachers (called education) and tourists problems for which data are combined. For the thumbs problem the data are unclear since quality ratings for this problem were combined with a people problem which was not used by Taylor *et al.* In sum then, the evidence favors the nominal over the real group for quantity but not so strongly for quality. What are the factors that account for the obtained superiority of nominal over real groups?

Writing and Speaking Responses

Bouchard conducted a series of experiments on brainstorming and in one of them he was able to compare the relative effectiveness of real and nominal groups. He too found that the results were in favor of the nominal groups. However, when he compared the differences he found between real and nominal groups with those found by Taylor *et al.* (1958) and Dunnette *et al.* (1963), he learned that the difference between his two groups was smaller than those reported in these other studies.

Parnes and Meadow (1963), as reported in the footnote on page 84, did not replicate D.W. Taylor's findings when they compared real groups that deferred judgment with nominal groups that used conventional thinking procedures. As a matter of fact, they found that groups using deferred judgment produced significantly more good ideas with the experimental problems than did the nominal groups. In another study by these same investigators when real and nominal groups were compared under conditions where both of them used deferred judgment no differences were found between the two groups. If anything, the authors report there was a "tendency" in the results in favor of the real groups.

Bouchard in his own work then went ahead and compared his data with those obtained by Taylor *et al.* for number of responses to problems which the studies shared. (The D.W. Taylor rather than the Dunnette *et al.* study was selected because both the Bouchard and Taylor *et al.* study involved college students.) He found that there were smaller discrepancies between number of responses between real groups in the two studies than between the nominal groups. For example, in the Taylor *et al.* study, real groups had an average of 38.4 responses for the tourists problem and Bouchard's real groups averaged 35.3 for the same problem. Turning to nominal groups, Taylor *et al.* reported an average of 68.3 responses and Bouchard's nominal groups reported an average of 39.3 responses.

The question then was, why was the difference in number of responses for the real groups smaller than the difference in number of responses for the nominal groups?

According to Bouchard (1969) any one or a combination of the following factors could be involved: (1) The subjects in the two experiments heard different introductory comments and hence were differently prepared for what was to follow. (2) The time limits used in the two experiments were different. Bouchard used a 10-minute time limit and Taylor *et al.* a 12-minute time limit. (3) Bouchard's experimental subjects had before them copies of the problems they worked on so they could refer to them as they wished. But Taylor's subjects did not. (4) Bouchard's subjects *wrote* out their ideas in one condition and spoke them in another. In Taylor's experiment subjects spoke their responses in both nominal- and real-group conditions.

Probably as Bouchard suggests the differences between his and Taylor *et al.*'s data lie in the different ways they collected their data. For gathering responses from real groups both Bouchard and Taylor *et al.* had their subjects speak their responses which were then tape recorded. Consequently, there is relatively little difference in the data collected by the two sets of investigators from real groups.

On the other hand, when Taylor *et al.* (1958) collected data from individuals who were later to constitute nominal groups these data were again spoken and tape recorded. But when Bouchard collected data from his nominal groups they wrote out their responses.

The matter of how subjects' responses were recorded may also account for why Parnes and Meadow (1963) did not replicate the Taylor *et al.* (1958) findings. As Bouchard (1969, p. 10) says, "Parnes and Meadow (1963) report that they had their Ss record their own ideas in pencil as they spoke them. Apparently the individual Ss wrote their answers also since this is normally the way the test which they used as a problem is administered." In other words if real-group responses and nominal-group responses are written one is not likely to find as big a difference, or any difference at all, between real and nominal groups.

It would seem, therefore, as Bouchard's data indicate, that Taylor *et al.* results which point to the superiority of nominal over real groups may well be accounted for, in part, by the different ways in which Bouchard and Taylor *et al.* recorded data from real and nominal groups.

What are the effects of writing and speaking ideas on the number of ideas produced (the criterion on which the studies were compared)? Horowitz and Newman (1964), according to Bouchard, found that it takes 10 minutes to write out what it takes 2 minutes to speak. According to Horowitz and Newman subjects who are told to speak their responses develop an intolerance of silence. They speak to fill a possible void. Also, while speaking may exhaust a person's repertoire of responses faster than writing, writing may result in fewer responses because for some persons writing may be equated with commitment. To avoid giving the impression that they are committed to an idea they will avoid writing it down and hence produce fewer ideas. Whatever the reasons, asking subjects to write ideas leads to the production of fewer ideas than might be produced were they asked to speak them.

Group Size

Studies of the relative effectiveness of nominal and real groups usually have been limited to 4-person groups. This is at the lower end of group size recommended by Osborn (1963). He suggested that the optimal size of a brainstorming group was somewhere between five and ten. Bouchard (1969, p. 26), after comparing nominal with real groups, suggested that "there may be more rapidly diminishing returns in nominal groups than real groups" as a function of group size. Consequently, he argued, if one extended the working period long enough, the growth curve for a nominal group would cross over that of an actual group, at some point at a group size of four individuals and the actual group would eventually be superior. Bouchard and Hare (1970) reasoned that the crossover would occur if the members of the nominal groups, when they worked individually, would produce many common ideas and a few original ones. Group members, however, having listened to each others' contributions would not waste their time repeating each others' ideas and go on to new and different ideas. On this basis Bouchard and Hare decided to go ahead and study the effects of group size.

The experimenters worked with one hundred sixty-eight male students. Half of them brainstormed a problem individually and half brainstormed the same problem in groups of five, seven, and nine persons. The problem they all worked on was the thumbs problem. Participants were observed on closed circuit TV as they went about solving the problem and their responses were tape recorded. Their scores were based on the number of different ideas they generated.

Analysis of the data indicated that the nominal- and real-groups' data do not cross. As a matter of fact as group size increased the discrepancies between nominal and real groups increased. Consequently, Bouchard and Hare (1970) suggested that if groups larger than four had been used in previous studies comparing nominal and real groups, the results in favor of the nominal groups would have been even more striking than those already reported.

Presence of Experimenter

One of the criticisms leveled against studies of the relative effectiveness of nominal and real groups was that the experimenter was present when real groups worked together in a group situation but not necessarily present when the individuals who made up the nominal groups worked. It was conceivable that experimenter's presence might have inhibited production of ideas by real groups, and therefore, they did less well than nominal groups. Bouchard and Hare (1970) raised this point and controlled for it by conducting a study in which they used closed circuit TV to watch both the individuals and the groups while they were at work. No experimenter was physically present in either situation. Even under these conditions nominal groups performed better than real groups.

Sex of Experimenter

In the experiment conducted by Dunnette *et al.* (1963) (cf. page 84) when subjects worked in real groups the experimenter was a female. Bouchard and Hare (1970) wondered whether the female experimenter might not have inhibited the men in the real group. If so, the real group would have been at a disadvantage compared to the nominal group because members of the nominal groups produced their ideas working alone but male members of the real groups might have been inhibited from speaking their responses in front of a female.

Bouchard and Hare found support in their belief in a study by McGuigan (1963) who demonstrated the effects of sex of experimenter in other experiments.

To study whether sex of experimenter could account for obtained differences between nominal and real groups Bouchard and Hare (1970) investigated the effects of both a 30-year-old male professor and a 21-year-old female undergraduate on the results they obtained.

Analysis of the data revealed that none of the obtained differences between nominal and real groups could be attributed to experimenter's sex.

Feedback

In some studies of the relative effectiveness of nominal and real groups one of the suggested reasons for the obtained results is that persons in groups are negatively affected by the presence of others. Specifically when working in a group an individual may be preoccupied with what others think of his ideas and therefore his effectiveness is restricted. Consequently, it is not surprising that nominal groups, composed of individuals working alone and not hampered by thinking of others' opinions, do better than real groups.

To overcome these possible negative effects Bouchard introduced a feedback procedure (which we considered previously, pages 58-60) and studied its effects on nominal groups, real groups using brainstorming, and real groups using critical problem solving. It will be recalled that in the feedback condition subjects recorded their ideas for 5 minutes, then listened to a recording of their responses for feedback and finally had another 10 minutes to produce more ideas. In the nonfeedback condition, subjects worked for 20 minutes straight through on their problems.

The thumbs and education (teachers) problems were used and scored for number and quality of ideas as indicated on page 60. Using these data Bouchard studied quality of responses in his experimental conditions. He also presented data on *average* quality of response. Thus, Bouchard analyzed his data in terms of number of responses, quality of responses, and average quality of responses.

The results of this study for number of ideas and number of good (quality) ideas were that nominal groups were significantly better than real brainstorming groups, who were significantly better than real critical problem-solving groups. This held true whether or not feedback was used.

Also, in this study, the thumbs problem yielded more responses than did the education (teachers) problem. And, when mean quality of ideas was the criterion no differences were found between real and nominal groups [similar to the finding in the Taylor *et al.* (1958) study], and the education problem received a higher average score than the thumbs problem [as in the Dunnette *et al.* (1963) study].

A further analysis of the data performed by Bouchard was one in which he studied his data when they were based on the first 15 minutes of work in the nonfeedback condition and the first 15 minutes in the feedback condition. Results were essentially the same as those first reported—nominal groups outperformed real groups, and the other results were also similar.

Thus, even the opportunity for feedback does not upset the result that nominal groups perform better than real groups. But one should bear in mind the differences pointed out insofar as problems and criteria are concerned.

Types of Problems

In the studies surveyed, which are doubtless among the most important ones comparing real and nominal groups, there is a great deal of consistency in problems used. With the exception of the Parnes and Meadow (1963) study, all the other studies reported use of real and unreal problems.

The *real* problems are those which could occur and the two that fall into this category are the teachers (education) and tourists problems. Let us reiterate our definitions. In the first, case subjects are asked to come up with ideas for how to cope with a teacher shortage; while in the second case, subjects are asked for ideas on how to stimulate Europeans to visit the United States.

Two problems in the studies are unreal. Again let us review these problems and their definitions. One of these is the thumbs problem in which subjects are asked for the consequences that would occur if people grew another thumb on each hand, while in the people problem, subjects are asked what consequences would occur if people grew to 80 inches and if their average weight doubled.

In the studies reported, reference is often made to obtained differences that could be attributed to the types of problems used. Thus, when Bouchard (1971) considered number of ideas as his criterion, he found that more responses were given to the unreal problem, thumbs, than to the real problem, education (teachers). On the other hand, when mean quality of ideas was considered the difference was in favor of the real (education) problem. Effects produced by real and nominal groups therefore depend on type of problem used.

We shall return to this matter in a moment. At this juncture evidence regarding another type of problem—a "real hot problem"—will be described.

Real and unreal problems, as they were employed in the studies reported, are unlikely to be as interesting or as significant to student subjects as a critical contemporary (in the 70's) problem—e.g., the Vietnam crisis. This was the problem that Dillon, Graham, and Aidells (1972) used with students at the University of California at Berkeley in their study of real and nominal groups. Essentially, Dillon *et al.* asked their subjects to brainstorm the question of how people might influence the foreign policy of the United States as a result of the United States' invasion of Cambodia in the spring of 1970.

The results of this study, which, considered other matters to be presented later in addition to the difference between real and nominal groups on a "hot" problem, were in favor of the nominal groups in terms of number of ideas—quality of ideas was not evaluated. Indeed, although there is no way of determining this accurately, as the authors of this study themselves say, "the differences between individuals and groups seem to be larger than those found in previous studies [Dillon *et al.*, 1972, p. 490]." To account for this the authors suggest the possibility "that people find it much more difficult to adhere to the rules of brainstorming when they are dealing with problems that they are interested in and care about. Thus, the general superiority of individual over group brainstorming appears even more pronounced when the problem is real and when motivation is high [Dillon *et al.*, 1972, p. 490]."

In the early research on the relative effectiveness of real and nominal groups, the issue of the characteristics of problems was also brought up. Taylor *et al.* (1958) selected the tourists, thumbs, and teachers problems for their research on the basis of pretesting in which they found these problems to be of interest to students who were subjects in the studies. The problems were productive of many different responses and they were also appropriate for use with brainstorming.

Parnes and Meadow (1963) point out that Taylor *et al.* (1958), who found evidence favoring nominal over real groups, did not present evidence for the validity of their tests insofar as creativity was concerned. Parnes and Meadow, who did not support the D.W. Taylor findings, used the broom problem for which they present correlations with several of Guilford's measures of functions regarded as related to creativity.

It is indeed important to use valid tests and we would suggest that investigators not be satisfied only with correlations with other psychological tests. The tests they use should also be correlated with manifest creativity.

Criteria and Their Interactions with Problems

Both quantity and quality have been used to evaluate ideas produced by subjects in real and nominal groups. The quantity measure is reasonably straightforward and is based on a count of the number of different ideas produced. For quality the measures that have been used include uniqueness as well as ratings on separate variables. These variables were first used by Taylor *et al.* (1958), and other experimenters [e.g., Dunnette *et al.* (1963) and Bouchard (1969)] selected from them.

The criterion of number of different ideas is, as we said, reasonably straightforward and need not concern us here—although in saying this we are not unaware of the problem of deciding what is "different." In turning to the quality criteria, we are further aware of the fact that there is nothing sacrosanct about these criteria and that studies can and will vary on this score. Our comments, therefore, should not be regarded as limited to just these criteria but they should be regarded as instances to be kept in mind in using all other kinds of criteria.

Let us consider each of the qualitative criteria in turn. One is uniqueness. Some studies have reported that the number of ideas and uniqueness may be correlated, and this needs to be checked out in any experiment. Furthermore, it is conceivable that the relationship between these two criteria may not hold for each problem studied.

The results obtained by Taylor *et al.* reflect the significance of the point we are trying to make. In their study, through the use of analysis of covariance Taylor *et al.* controlled for differences in total number of responses when they focused on uniqueness. It will be recalled that in terms of number of unique responses, the nominal groups were superior to the real groups for the thumbs and teachers problems, and the data just reach significance for the tourists problem. However, when the data are looked at when number of responses is controlled for by covariance, then there is *no* difference between real and nominal groups for unique responses on the tourists and teachers problems. And, on the thumbs problem, there is a difference at the 0.02 level in favor of the *real* groups—a reversal of all other findings that favor nominal groups.

It is unfortunate that other investgators did not use the uniqueness criterion in their work and use it the way Taylor *et al.* did, so that we could then tell whether the reported finding is supported. Uniqueness seems to be a favored criterion in studying other aspects of brainstorming, but it does not figure when nominal and real groups are compared. Again, it should be noted that we mention this specifically because, while all other results favor nominal over real groups, when total number of responses is controlled and uniqueness is studied, the results favor the *real* groups.

Let us now turn to the other qualitative measures. Taylor *et al.* (1958) used ratings on "feasibility," "effectiveness," and "generality" for both the tourists and teachers problems—the "real" problems. But for the "unreal" problem, the thumbs problem, the variables were "probability," "significance," and "generality." Each of these was rated on a five-point scale. Furthermore, although three raters were employed in the study, all of them did not rate all the variables on each of the problems. Rather, raters rated all problems for one set of three variables. Later intercorrelations between variables indicated that the intercorrelations were rather low—in part probably accounted for by the procedure used. But data in the studies by Dunnette *et al.* (1963) and Bouchard (1969) indicate that there are difficulties with rating reliabilities of these variables.

With at least some question in mind about the reliability of rating these variables, we then find that later studies do not use *all* three rating variables for each of the three problems but they select from these variables. Dunnette *et al.* (1963), for example, use "effectiveness" to evaluate responses for the real teachers (what they call the education) and tourists problems and "probability" to study responses for the unreal thumbs and people problems. Bouchard (1969, p. 14) reports that in one of his studies he also used the "probability" scale to evaluate responses to the unreal thumbs problem but because of the lack of reliable ratings in his other studies he discarded it and used a "practicality-importance" scale for this problem. For the teachers (education) problem he, like Dunnette *et al.* used the effectiveness variable.

Thus we find that studies in this area vary a good deal in terms of criteria, but let us go a step further and look at the data when quality ratings for each of the problems are studied under conditions that control for total number of responses given by subjects. Here we find that Taylor *et al.* (1958) report that differences in favor of the nominal groups over the real groups are obtained only for the thumbs problem. They say (p. 41) "Thus for thumbs, but not for teachers and tourists problems, there is a superiority of the nominal over the real groups on the three quality measures over and above that accounted for by a superiority in total number of responses."

And, in Bouchard's study (1969), when he investigates differences between nominal and real groups using a "mean quality score," which also involves a control for number of total responses, then he too does not report effects due to character of group whether real or nominal. He says (p. 18), "For mean quality of ideas, the only significant main effects are due to differences between problems. The education problem receives a higher mean rating than than the thumbs problem. There are no single main effects or interactions."

It is apparent, therefore, that when studies of the differences between real and nominal groups do not control for total number of responses produced, differences between real and nominal groups do not obtain. When the differences do not obtain we wonder, therefore, if what we have here is something we observed previously in studies of standards of evaluation (pages 71-76). In those studies, it will be recalled, it was suggested that groups using brainstorming outproduce groups using nonbrainstorming because they lower their standards of evaluation. Similar factors may account for the differences between nominal and real groups. In other words, individuals who constitute the nominal groups produce a large number of ideas because their standards of evaluation may be lowered when they are instructed to brainstorm a problem. However, when subjects brainstorm a problem in a real group, they may not feel as free to lower their standards of evaluation. Taylor *et al.* (1958) suggest that brainstorming in a group may inhibit creativity because group members are, for one reason or another, concerned with what one person will think of another. Taylor *et al.* are correct in assuming that participation in the real group inhibits number of responses, but insofar as quality is concerned, we wonder if participation in the real group does not also inhibit and forestall lowering of the standards of evaluation.

In summarizing the data in this section, it is suggested that when both nominal and real groups use brainstorming the former outperform the latter in number and even quality of ideas. But, when quality is studied as a function of number of ideas then differences wash out. Caution is recommended in regarding the superiority of nominal groups because of what has just been said and because further work needs to be done on reliability of criteria and replication of the research design.

Also, a survey of the studies reveals the possibility, to be tested in further research, that working in a real group may control *or* inhibit the lowering of standards of evaluation which may occur in individuals when they work alone and whose efforts are later used to constitute efforts of nominal groups.

Individual Differences—Professional and Personality

Dunnette *et al.*(1963) and Dunnette (1964) studied the effects on advertising and research personnel when they participated in nominal groups and when they participated in real groups. They found that both advertising and research personnel produced significantly more ideas in the nominal than in the real groups. However, when mean quality of ideas was the criterion then it was apparent that experimental condition had a differential effect on the advertising and research personnel. For research personnel no significant differences were obtained between subjects who participated in nominal or real groups. Although trends in the data favored the nominal groups, these were not significant. For advertising personnel, however, the differences in mean quality of ideas was in favor of the nominal groups at the 0.05 level.

Data on the relationships between personality characteristics and number of good ideas produced in individual and group situations are presented by Bouchard (1969). His work was such that one could compare correlations between personality characteristics and number of good ideas in two studies. Unfortunately, almost all of the significant findings are not replicated (which may be due, according to Bouchard, to differences in the experiments). The one personality variable that is correlated with number of good ideas in individual and group brainstorming situations is *sociability* as measured by the *California Psychological Inventory*.

In summary then there is one study indicating that two professional groups (advertising personnel and researchers) produce significantly more ideas in nominal rather than real groups. However, when mean quality of ideas is the criterion, research people do not show any difference whether they are in real or nominal groups but for advertising personnel there is a difference. Advertising personnel produce a higher mean quality of ideas in nominal groups.

In the one study which concerned itself with personality characteristics relationships between them and number of good ideas (the criteria reported) held up in one condition and not in the other. One variable, sociability, correlated significantly with number of good ideas in both nominal and real groups. We shall consider other relationships between personality variables and criteria in this area later when we consider attempts to increase the effectiveness of real groups (cf. pages 104-108).

Group Cohesiveness and Ego-Involving Problems

Usually, in experiments involving nominal and real groups, the members of real groups are not selected because they like each other or because they work well together but rather on some random basis. They usually happen to be members of some class which is participating in the experiment, and they are selected in some unbiased way from among the members of the class. Consequently, to refer to them as "real groups" is to use the word "group" rather loosely. The individuals who comprise the real group have little if any history of working together. And we certainly do not know if they want to be together. Therefore we do not know whether they constitute a cohesive group whose members can work together with a minimum of interpersonal friction.

Because of the importance of cohesiveness for problem-solving behavior, Cohen, Whitmyre, and Funk (1960) selected it as one of the variables they studied in differentiating between the effectiveness of nominal and real groups. Unfortunately, however, in actuality they did not work with groups but with nominal and real *pairs* of individuals. To that extent, their work is not completely congruent with the other studies reviewed in this area. Nevertheless, if the study does not fit in exactly with other studies it does provide some interesting results that might be explored further in future studies of groups of individuals.

In addition to cohesiveness, Cohen *et al.* also studied the effects of training and types of problems on the behavior of nominal and real pairs of subjects. The subjects were affiliate nurses. Those who were trained had had a 10-hour course in creative thinking. (The characteristics of this course are not described.) Those who had not participated in the course had had only one session in which they were given an explanation of creative thinking. It was ascertained that the subjects felt comfortable with each other.

All subjects ranked all persons in their respective trained or untrained groups in terms of preference as a brainstorming partner. They also ranked the members of their respective groups in terms of brainstorming skills. One of the results of the study was that there was a significant correlation between preference rank and perceived skill rank.

Cohesive pairs were then formed with the trained and untrained subjects. Cohesive pairs consisted of nurses who preferred working with each other, and noncohesive pairs were those who ended up with partners who were among their least preferred choices. Thus, there were cohesive and noncohesive pairs, and finally there were nominal pairs (two people who had actually not worked with each other but whose efforts were collated as if they had worked together).

Two types of problems were used in this study. One type consisted of problems used in other studies—the tourist and thumbs problems, and the other type, called ego-involving problems, were problems that confronted nurses in their daily professional activities. One of these ego-involving problems was called the *discharge problem* in which subjects were asked to discuss the benefits and problems that would occur if all psychiatric patients would leave their hospitals and return to their homes. The other ego-involving problem, the *treatment problem* involved the development of games, toys, and gadgets for psychiatric patients. This second problem proved to be too difficult and was dropped from the analysis of the data.

The results of the study indicated that on the two neutral problems, the tourist and thumbs problems, cohesiveness and training did not turn out to be critical variables for total number of ideas or for number of unique ideas. Similarly, they were not critical variables for the ego-involving discharge problem when number of ideas was the criterion. However, both training and cohesiveness were critical variables with this problem when number of unique ideas was the criterion. Those pairs who were both cohesive *and* trained did better than all the other pairs. Untrained and cohesive pairs performed significantly better than nominal pairs. Noncohesive trained pairs did not do better than their untrained counterparts.

It should also be pointed out that noncohesive and untrained pairs and nominal untrained pairs did not differ from each other on number of ideas or number of unique ideas. These two sets of pairs are most similar to real and nominal groups in other studies. Therefore, while other studies reveal a difference in favor of nominal groups over real groups this study does not reveal any difference between nominal and real pairs. Using these results as a baseline, the aforementioned results for both training and cohesiveness become all the more interesting.

Summarizing the results of this study it then appears that cohesiveness and training are critical variables when an ego-involving problem is used. And, then, the effects are manifest only when the criterion is uniqueness of ideas. It should be noted that cohesiveness was determined by choice of partner as a brainstorming partner. This preference was found to be correlated with perceptions of the other's skill in brainstorming. Therefore, cohesiveness between the pairs was based not solely on preference for the other but also by preference that involved brainstorming as a skill.

In talking about groups, whether or not we focus on their cohesivenss, it is important to bear in mind that "there are groups, and then there are groups (Parnes and Meadow, 1963, p. 319)." Groups differ as Parnes and Meadow say in terms of types of leaders, personalities of group members, and group "atmospheres." Future research should take all of these characteristics into account.

Order of Work

Various studies have already been reported to support the proposition that nominal groups outperform real groups. However, the possibility exists that certain advantages may accrue from the separate and distinct experiences in both individual and group situations. When brainstorming a problem alone, an individual may follow his own style and pace of work without interruption or distraction by others. Then, when he works with others in a group, he may be stimulated to think about and consider possibilities that might not otherwise have occurred to him. Consequently, the positive effects of individual and group brainstorming sessions might be maximized if an individual were not limited to either individual or group brainstorming but could participate in both. Indeed, Osborn (1963) himself suggested that the order of experience might be first to work alone on a problem, then to participate in a group effort on the same problem, and finally to turn once again to individual efforts. The sequence he suggested was: individual, group, individual. This tripartite sequence has not been studied. Research has concerned itself with the effects of two sequences— individual followed by group and group followed by individual.

It should be clear at the very beginning that when the term "individual" is used it refers to individuals who compose nominal groups, and when the term "group" is used it refers to a real group. Therefore, the sequence individual-group, for example, means a nominal group followed by a real group. It does not mean a sequence in which the effectiveness of an individual working alone is compared with that which he produces in the group or that which he produces before and after a group experience.

Again, our focus is on effects produced when individuals (nominal groups) and real groups both use brainstorming instructions.* With this in mind we turn to the following studies.

*Because studies in the text refer to order effects when brainstorming instructions are used, it would be well to report the effects of order in related studies when brainstorming is not used at all or is not used by both groups.

Taylor *et al.* (1958) studied subjects half of whom first worked alone and then together with others; the other half of the subjects worked in the reverse order. Regardless of the conditions under which they worked, the subjects were instructed in the importance of generating a quantity of ideas and ideas of quality. Subjects were instructed to achieve their ideas through critical thinking. Results of this study indicated that it did not matter whether group or individual came first or whether quantity or quality were studied. The investigators found indirect support for their work in the studies by Tuckman and Lorge (1962) and Campbell (1968).

Meadow *et al.* (1959) did not compare order effects with nominal and real groups, and therefore they differ in this regard from other studies on order. They focused on order effects when subjects participated in a group using brainstorming and a group not using

Dunnette *et al.* (1963), in their previously reported study of researchers and advertising personnel, investigated the effects of order. Their findings show that order did play a significant role in the production of ideas. When group (real) brainstorming *preceded* individual (nominal group) brainstorming, it was more effective than when it followed it. This effect was more apparent with the researchers than with the advertising personnel, and it was significant only with the quantity measure but not with the quality measure. Consequently, the authors say [p. 36] that their findings "suggest that group participation may be useful in 'warming up' for individual brainstorming sessions."

In 1964 Dunnette, in discussing a question that was the title of his talk "Are Meetings Any Good For Solving Problems?", suggested that a practical application of the results of his research would lead to the use of group sessions to *share information* but *not ideas* or suggestions about problems that require solution. Groups would not be used to evolve ideas or suggestions for problem solution. In this approach individual group members, after listening to information about a problem would then go off by themselves to work out or to come up with solutions to the problem. Bouchard (1969) picked up this idea and reasoned that if information were shared in a brainstorming group and if an individual ordinarily would not have had this information working by himself, then he would profit from experience in group brainstorming followed by individual brainstorming. In his study, Bouchard did not, in fact, check whether or what kind of information was transmitted, but rather he compared the effects of the combination of group and individual experiences with the effects of individual experiences.

When Bouchard's subjects came to the experiment, they were assigned to various conditions. In one condition, subjects had 20 minutes to work on their assigned problems. These 20 minutes were divided so that the subject spent 10 minutes working with the group on the problem and the next 10 minutes work-

brainstorming and who presumably used critical thinking plus a penalty for bad responses. Furthermore, subjects in this experiment were equated for experience since all were members of a class in creative problem-solving. Subjects, as we indicated, participated in both brainstorming and critical problem-solving conditions.

The problems in this study were the broom and hanger problems from the *AC Test of Creative Ability* (Harris & Simberg 1959). Responses were scored for uniqueness and value, each on a three-point scale, and the criterion of good response was attained when the combined ratings on the two subvariables was 5 or 6.

Results of this study indicated that brainstorming instructions produced significantly more good solutions when they came before rather than when they followed nonbrainstorming instructions. No differences were found when nonbrainstorming instructions came first or second.

There were also effects on the relationship of order and problem. Significantly more good solutions were obtained to the hanger problem when it was in the first than in the second test period. But no difference between first and second test periods obtained when the broom problem was used.

ing alone. This G(roup)-I(ndividual) condition was then followed by 20 minutes devoted to the I(ndividual)-I(ndividual) condition in which subjects spent 20 minutes working alone on the assigned problems. The order was balanced so that while half of the subjects participated in GI followed by II, as just described, the other half of the subjects followed the sequence of two periods of individual work (II) followed by periods of group and individual work (the GI condition).

For completeness' sake it should be pointed out that the problems used in the study were counterbalanced and that prior to the experiment proper the use of brainstorming was illustrated on videotape. Following the videotape the group brainstormed two practice problems to get accustomed to each other and the technique. In the individual condition subjects wrote their responses and in the group condition they spoke them.

The results of this study indicated that when the criterion was total number of ideas or total number of good ideas there was no difference between the GI and II conditions. However, when the criterion was mean quality of ideas and when the problems were unreal—thumbs and people problems—then the II sequence was better than the GI sequence.

Thus while Dunnette may be correct that experience in a group may have a warm-up effect on the individual experience, Bouchard's data indicate that such a sequence is no better than the same amount of time working individually and collating the responses into nominal groups. Conversely, if a difference does exist then it involves unreal problems which are worked on alone.

To account for the superiority of the II sequence, Bouchard suggests that the GI sequence may have been hampered by the lack of an opportunity for incubation. He suggests the possibility that in the GI sequence subjects moved from the group brainstorming session to the individual brainstorming session without a break. If they had had such a break, subjects might have had time for their ideas to incubate. During the break they would not have felt under pressure, and they would have had more time to think. Then, when the break was over, they might have come up with more and better ideas. Since they had no break none of this was possible and the subjects were unable to take advantage in the individual brainstorming session of what was stirred in them in the group.

A second possible reason for the obtained superiority of the II sequence over the GI sequence, according to Bouchard, was that subjects in the group brainstorming session may not have listened to what others said and therefore did not utilize information that might have been imparted to them when they worked individually.

The GI sequence may also have been at a disadvantage, according to Bouchard, because the subjects in this condition were not trained in group brainstorming. Had they had such training, the group part of the GI sequence may have yielded better results than it did.

In all this we would like to call attention to the fact that in II condition subjects did not have to change their manner of reporting responses. In both parts subjects wrote their responses. Subjects did not experience any disruption in the pattern of their behavior. Such disruptions did occur in the GI condition. In the G part of the condition, subjects spoke and in the I condition they wrote. The change in condition may have prevented them from "gathering up steam" and restricted the number of ideas they produced.

The superiority of the II condition was manifest with the unreal problems, but primarily when mean *quality* but not quantity of ideas was the criterion. This, we would like to suggest, might occur from a variety of circumstances. Unreal problems, such as having two thumbs on the same hand, lend themselves to "silly" responses. In the group condition this could have a contagious effect since suggestions are spoken. One spoken silly idea could stimulate the production of another silly idea. In the individual condition, however, not only is this contagion lacking but the process of reporting ideas itself could increase the mean quality of responses. In the individual condition subjects have to write their responses. Writing involves more commitment and a resulting rise in quality. The combined effects of two commitment-writing periods (as in the II condition) could lead to greater quality than two periods of work in which only one period involves commitment and the other period involves a possibly contagious effect as could occur in the G part of the experiment.

Rotter and Portugal (1969) added two experimental conditions to those used by Bouchard and their results cast interesting light on the problem. Bouchard, it will be recalled, used two experimental conditions: II—two periods of individual brainstorming of essentially 20 minutes of individual work, and GI—10 minutes of group brainstorming followed by 10 minutes of individual brainstorming.

Rotter and Portugal used somewhat shorter time periods than did Bouchard. In their II condition subjects worked for 16 minutes on their problems, and in the GI condition they worked for 8 minutes in the group condition and 8 minutes in the individual condition. In the two added conditions subjects had 16 minutes of group brainstorming (a GG condition) and in IG condition in which 8 minutes of individual work was followed by 8 minutes of group work. Thus, in contrast, to Bouchard, Rotter and Portugal actually studied the effects of all combinations of group and individual effort and so were able to get better understanding of the effects of order on nominal and real groups.

There were other ways in which the Rotter and Portugal study also differed from the Bouchard study. First, when Bouchard had his subjects engage in individual work that was later to be assembled into the productions of nominal groups, he instructed his subjects to *write out* their responses. But when real groups worked on problems they *spoke* their responses. Rotter and Portugal, on the other hand, asked both individuals and groups to write their responses.*

*See page 102 for footnote

Second, in the Bouchard study when subjects moved from one condition to the other they were instructed that in the second condition they *could* use ideas that came up during the first. In the Rotter and Portugal study, as subjects moved from one condition to another, they were told they could *not* use ideas suggested in the first condition.

On an *a priori* basis we do not know what effects such differences in the experiments might have on the results. Whatever their effects, they do not seem

---

*It will be recalled that Bouchard (1969) investigated the relative effectiveness of nominal and real groups and compared his data with comparable data from Taylor *et al.* (1958). Bouchard did not find as large a discrepancy between the means of his nominal and real groups as did Taylor *et al.* (1958). Specifically, he found that both the Taylor *et al.* (1958) data and his data for real groups were quite similar but that they were rather different for the nominal groups. Bouchard argued that in all probability the reason his nominal groups were so different from nominal groups in other studies could be attributed to the fact that when the subjects of his nominal groups worked individually they wrote their responses and this limited or curtailed their productivity. Bouchard's real groups and both the Taylor *et al.* real and nominal groups spoke their responses.

Bouchard's suggestion that the difference in results could be accounted for by written rather than spoken responses by nominal groups is not supported by Rotter and Portugal's results.

Rotter and Portugal asked both their nominal and real groups to write out their responses. Before we compare the data from all three experiments, it should be pointed out that all used 4-man groups. Taylor *et al.* and Bouchard studied male subjects and while Rotter and Portugal studied both males and females, only their data for males will be presented. The three experiments differed in time used—Taylor *et al.* used 12 minutes, Bouchard 10 minutes, and Rotter and Portugal 8 minutes. All three experiments used both the tourists and teachers (education) problems.

In comparing the data from the three experiments, we shall focus on the mean total number of responses and focus on Bouchard's (1969, p. 10) Table 6 which collates his and the Taylor *et al.* (1958) data. When we add to this the male data from Rotter and Portugal (1969, p. 340, Table 3) we learn the following:

On the tourists problem both Taylor *et al.* and Bouchard had their real groups speak their responses and Rotter and Portugal had theirs write their responses. If writing slows down or curtails productivity then Rotter and Portugal's mean data should be lowest. In fact for the tourists problem the means for all three studies [in the order of Taylor *et al.* (1958), Bouchard (1969), and Rotter and Portugal (1969)] are: 38.4, 35.3, and 37.0. But for the education problem Rotter and Portugal's groups, which should be lowest, is, in fact, highest. Using the same order of studies the means are 32.6, 27.0, 58.0. Turning now to the nominal groups for the tourists problem, the data are 68.3 and 39.3, which are the basis for Bouchard's suggestion that writing responses has a negative effect on the production of responses. However, if the discrepancy between the two means is a function of speaking for the first and writing for the second then Rotter and Portugal's data, in which subjects also wrote their responses, should be closer to the second than the first mean. In fact this is not true. For the tourists problem the means are then 68.3, 39.3, and for Rotter and Portugal 78.0. Turning to the education problem the data are not so discrepant, but once again Rotter and Portugal's results are closer to the Taylor *et al.* data. The means are: 63.5, 30.0, and 61.5. Therefore it appears that writing may not be the critical variable. Just what it is that accounts for the differences between Bouchard's and the other's data is not clear.

to alter the primary point that nominal groups are superior to real groups. Rotter and Portugal found that individual (nominal) groups produced significantly more responses than did real groups, and mixed groups were also significantly superior to real groups. Also, within each mixed condition, whether individual work preceded or followed group work it was still superior. Therefore, Rotter and Portugal say (1969, p. 340) that the finding that individual work is superior to group work "holds true whether individual work precedes, follows or is independent of group work." And, further, they say "one may argue that production of ideas is simply a function of the proportion of time spent in an individual situation [Rotter & Portugal, 1969, p. 340]." Mixed groups do better than real groups not because they contain diversity of experience (individual and group) but because part of the mixed groups involved individual experience. Thus, to the extent that an experimental condition involves individual experience it is superior to an experimental condition limited only to group experience.

It will be recalled that Dunnette *et al.* (1963) reported that when group (real) work preceded individual work it had a warming-up effect on the individual work: the sequence group-individual was superior to the sequence of individual (nominal group) work followed by a group (real) condition. This result was not supported by Rotter and Portugal. They found that both of their mixed conditions (in which either individual or group work came first) were about equal, with only a slight, and certainly not significant difference in favor of the real groups.

It is not clear why the results of the two studies are contradictory. It may be related to differences between the two experiments. Dunnette *et al.* allocated 15 minutes to each of the experimental (group or individual) conditions; Rotter and Portugal used 8 minutes for each. The Dunnette *et al.* subjects spoke their answers in both the individual and group conditions, whereas Rotter and Portugal had subjects write their responses. Finally, Dunnette *et al.* studied adult males employed in industry who were either research scientists or in advertising. Rotter and Portugal studied students.

There are other results of the Rotter and Portugal study that should also be reported. One related to the effects of type of problem and the other related to sex of subject. More solutions were obtained for the tourist problem in the GI condition than in the IG condition. And, for the teacher problem, more solutions were found in the IG than in the GI condition. No effects could be attributed to problems alone.

Finally, on an overall basis, males produced more ideas than females. No significant interactions were obtained between sex of subject and any of the experimental conditions. In light of this finding, it should be pointed out that most, if not all studies in this area are based on male subjects, and future studies should certainly focus on effects produced when female subjects are studied.

The last study to be cited of the effects of order on nominal and real groups is that by Dillon *et al.* (1972), who, it will be recalled, compared nominal and real groups when both groups worked on a "hot" problem. In this study, before subjects participated in either individual (nominal group) or (real) group conditions, they were exposed to videotape training and practice conditions. The effects of these conditions will be discussed more fully later (pages 105-106), but at this point it should be indicated that the practice condition took place in a group for 10 minutes, and then the subjects, depending on their assigned experimental condition, continued with 25 more minutes of individual or 25 more minutes of group work. The results of this study revealed that "there was a tendency for practice to facilitate individual brainstorming more than group brainstorming [Dillon *et al.*, 1972, p. 490] ." Which supports the Dunnette *et al.* (1963) study.

Opinion Data

The only investigator who gathered opinion data from subjects in studies in this area was Bouchard (1969). His investigation covered a number of issues. Included among them was some opinion data collected from subjects in real and nominal brainstorming groups as well as from groups of subjects who worked on problems through critical problem solving. Subjects were asked how they would feel if they were told that they did not do a good job. There was no significant difference in ratings obtained from subjects in real and nominal groups—although subjects in the real groups said they would feel worse. Both nominal and real groups said they would feel significantly worse than groups who worked on the problem through critical problem solving.

ATTEMPTS TO INCREASE THE EFFECTIVENESS OF BRAINSTORMING

While attempts are underway to understand the various factors that may affect the brainstorming process, there are also attempts underway to improve it. Several attempts in this direction have occurred with the goal of increasing brainstorming's effectiveness (measured in terms of number and/or quality of ideas) over and above that occurring in nominal groups. Then there is work on the relative effectiveness of brainstorming (almost) alone as compared to brainstorming plus other added procedures oriented to improve it.

Real over Nominal Groups

Let us turn first to those studies that have tried to increase the effectiveness of real over nominal groups. We have seen in the studies previously discussed (pages 80-104) that the thrust of accumulated evidence is that nominal groups are probably better than real groups at least for quantity of ideas. Relative to quantity of ideas the evidence for better quality in nominal groups is weaker. During the time that evidence for the superiority of real groups over nominal groups was collected, studies were also conducted to determine whether it was possible to increase a real group's effectiveness over and above that obtained with a nominal group. The practical reason for this is that in real-life situations one is very likely to work with real rather than nominal groups. Therefore, it would be of practical significance if the effectiveness of such real groups could be raised. In doing so the following procedures were used: (1) Practice by itself. (2) Practice and experience in watching a videotape of a very polished brainstorming group working on a problem. (3) Practice and a monetary reward as a motivator. (4) Sequencing—a procedure developed by Bouchard (1972a) in which a subject has a designated opportunity to respond.

Practice

In the Dillon *et al.* (1972) study referred to previously (page 104) the effects of practice, among other factors on the effectiveness of real and nominal groups, were investigated. Practice, in this study, involved working on the task problem for 10 minutes. Subjects would then stop and work on the problem for 25 minutes during which time subjects could utilize ideas they had thought of during the 10 minute practice period.

The result of this study was that practice had no effect. However, although it was not statistically significant, "there was a tendency for practice to facilitate individual brainstorming more than group brainstorming [Dillon *et al.*, 1972, p. 490]."

Practice and Observing a Videotape of Brainstorming

Bouchard (1969) suggested that a real group's performance would improve more with training than would a nominal group's. Dillon *et al.* (1972) picked up this suggestion for further study. As a training device the investigators used a 10-minute videotape of a 4-man group working on the people problem in a very smooth manner which generated ideas very rapidly.

Following such exposure some subjects brainstormed the task problem individually (later to be combined into nominal groups) and some brainstormed the task problem in real groups. As reported previously the investigators also studied the effects of practice.

One of the results of this study has already been reported: nominal groups performed better than real groups in terms of number of ideas—the only criterion used. But there were also two additional results: (1) there was a significant interaction between videotape training and practice; and (2) there was a significant interaction between videotape training and individual versus group brainstorming. With regard to the first result, it was found that practice was more effective if it was *not* preceded by videotape training, and also, that videotape training had no effect on real groups and actually diminished the effectiveness of nominal groups.

The authors conclude that "a videotape training session in which individuals and groups were given an example of a smoothly functioning rapidly idea-generating brainstorming group inhibited performance [Dillon *et al.*, 1972, p. 489]." One of the reasons for this according to the authors may be the nature of the group watched. The group on the videotape was a "perfect" group. It did not violate any of the brainstorming rules. Subjects working individually were more inhibited than groups because they might have felt that it was "inappropriate" to work alone after seeing an effective group in action.

It was further reported that practice was more effective for both nominal and real groups when it was *not* preceded by videotape training. One possibility according to the investigators was that when practice followed videotape training subjects "may have felt that their performance in the practice session did not come close to the level of performance they had seen in the videotape just prior to practice [Dillon *et al.*, 1972, p. 490]." When no videotape was used and subjects only practiced, they had no way of knowing whether their practice was good or bad.

One of the problems in the study, as the investigators suggest, may have been that the group on the videotape was so perfect. Possibly if the videotape group made mistakes that were then discussed, the videotape training might have been more effective.

In conclusion then, this technique of videotape training was not effective in improving real-group performance above that obtained from nominal groups.

Practice and Monetary Reward as a Motivator

Practice and a monetary reward as a motivator were two variables studied by Bouchard (1972a), but before describing how these two variables were utilized it is necessary to discuss two other aspects of the study—a process called sequencing and the personality characteristics of the subjects.

Bouchard (1969) suggested that one of the possible factors that may have had a negative effect on the behavior of real groups was that real groups did not manage their time effectively. In a real group some persons could monopolize the group's time to present their own ideas or to elaborate unnecessarily on their ideas. Other persons who might have had something significant to say would not necessarily get a chance to say it. Therefore he devised a procedure called "sequencing" in which each person, in turn, has an opportunity to offer his ideas, and if he does not wish to avail himself of the turn he "passes" to the next person. This procedure was used for all real groups.

Subjects in this study were equated for personality characteristics. Previously we discussed a study by Bouchard (1969) in which he had administered various personality tests to his subjects. He found that individuals scoring high on a personality factor called interpersonal effectiveness (using the California Psychological Inventory) performed better than individuals who scored low. In the study to be described now, Bouchard (1972a) studied nominal and real groups both of whose subjects were *low* on interpersonal effectiveness. In other words all persons in this study were similar in terms of this personality characteristic—they were low on interpersonal effectiveness, and in terms of previous data were not expected to have any particular advantage in terms of personality characteristics favoring problem-solving behavior.

The practice conditions (which Bouchard calls "training" in his paper) consisted of working on three problems *prior* to working on the task problem.

For the motivation condition Bouchard used money. In the "high" motivation condition for individuals, subjects were told they were competing against three other persons and that the best person would receive $15. (Real) groups were told that they would compete against one other group and if they were best they would receive $40 which they could divide among themselves. Previous data collected from the subjects indicated that they regarded a $15 reward for a person working in the individual session as equal to $10 for an individual working in the real group.

To summarize then, this study is based on subjects all of who scored low on interpersonal effectiveness. If a subject was assigned to a nominal group he might also be in the practice condition. If he was in the practice condition then he practiced on three problems before working on the experimental task. Then, too, before working on the experimental task, and whether or not he had had practice, he could be placed in one of two additional subgroups—one of high motivation (a potential $15 reward) or low motivation (no reward).

If an individual was assigned to a real group and if he was assigned to the training condition his group would practice on three problems before working on the experimental task. However, some of the real groups might have no practice at all. Regardless of the practice condition to which he was assigned a subject could then also be assigned to the high-motivation or low-motivation condition. When real groups worked on their test problems they used brainstorming plus sequencing.

Analysis of the data indicated that for total number of ideas the only significant result was that nominal groups performed better than real groups. And this effect was found for two out of the three problems used (thinking up brand names for a toothpaste and thinking up uses for an old tire but not for the thumbs problem). And nominal groups were superior to real groups when all three problems were considered together.

Turning to the quality criterion, the number of good ideas, the only significant result was that nominal groups performed better than real groups. This time significant results were obtained for the toothpaste and thumbs problems and for all three problems (including the tire problem) together. On the tire problem real groups almost outperformed nominal groups at a significant level.

Thus we find that practice and motivation did not help the real groups in this study where both real and nominal groups were composed of subjects low on interpersonal effectiveness.

Sequencing

In the study just described sequencing was used and Bouchard (1972a) believes that it had an important effect on the real groups because the difference between the nominal and real groups was smaller than that reported in other experiments.

As evidence Bouchard points out that, in two of his own experiments (Bouchard, 1969, 1972a) and in the experiment by Taylor *et al.* (1958) where the thumbs problem was used with real groups involved in brainstorming alone, typically "about 40 different ideas" were produced. However, in the experiment with a real group in which he (Bouchard, 1972a) used brainstorming plus sequencing for the same problem, an average of 75.75 ideas were produced. In the first two Bouchard (1969, 1972a) experiments and in the experiment of Taylor *et al.* (1958), nominal groups produced an average of 70.60. And, if the criterion was quality of ideas in this last experiment Bouchard believed that the trend in the results would similarly favor the sequencing procedure.

It will be recalled that this study is based on individuals low on interpersonal effectiveness, and Bouchard thinks better results would have been obtained if subjects who scored high on interpersonal effectiveness (I-E) had been used. High interpersonal effectiveness is positively related to effective problem solving. Therefore, combining this personality characteristic with sequencing may have resulted in a still better performance.

In summary then, aside from sequencing there is little that has been suggested that might help increase the effectiveness of real groups over nominal groups.

Real Groups with Variations

In the previous section studies were reviewed in which attempts were made to increase a real group's effectiveness by comparing its output when it used brainstorming plus some other technique with the output obtained from a nominal group in which its constituent members worked on a problem using only brainstorming. In these experiments that which was produced by nominal groups was regarded as a baseline.

In this subsection the experimental design is different. Here the comparison is made between real groups using brainstorming and other real groups that also used brainstorming plus some other procedure.

Practice, Motivation, and Personality

Bouchard undertook a study in which he investigated the effects of three variables on the effectiveness of real groups that went about working on their problems with brainstorming plus sequencing. The three variables were: (1) Practice (called training in this study)—which consisted of practice or no practice on three problems before proceeding to the test problem. (2) Motivation—which consisted of "low"- and "high"-motivation conditions. In the low condition subjects were simply given the standard instructions. In the high condition subjects in a group were told that they were competing against another group and whichever did best would receive $40. (3) Personality characteristics—which consisted of either a high or low score on the interpersonal effectiveness factor of the California Psychological Inventory (Gough, 1957). A sum of the first five scales (dominance, capacity for status, sociability, social-presence, and self-acceptance) were utilized for separating the two groups. Those subjects who scored higher than 146 were high on the interpersonal-effectiveness factor and those who scored lower were in the low condition. The experimental design was such that the effects of all three variables—training, motivation, and personality characteristics could be determined.

The test problems consisted of thinking up brand names for a toothpaste, thinking up uses for an old tire, and thinking up the consequences that might occur if everyone had an extra thumb (thumbs problem). A group's productions were scored for total number of ideas, and for each of the three problems there was a different quality measure. For the toothpaste problem the criterion was the number of good ideas with goodness rated on a 5-point scale. Ideas that had a score above 4 for ratings obtained from two raters were considered "good." For the tire problem the criterion was a number of unusual ideas. Ratings were made on a 3-point scale, and those that had a summed score above 3 were considered "unusual." For the thumbs problem a 5-point scale of practicality-importance was used. Here a summed score above 5 for ratings was necessary for an idea to be considered "important."

The hypothesis was that the group using brainstorming plus sequencing and which had trained subjects who were motivated and high on interpersonal effectiveness would score higher on the criteria than any of the other groups.

The major conclusion of this study is that subjects who scored high on the interpersonal-effectiveness variable responded in a more differentiated manner to both practice and motivation than did the subjects who scored low on interpersonal effectiveness. No effects are manifest with subjects low on interpersonal effectiveness. When subjects who are high on interpersonal effectiveness are not given any practice, they respond positively to high motivation and very poorly to the low-motivation condition. On the other hand, these same kinds of subjects respond differently to motivation when they are trained. When they are trained they respond poorly to high motivation but quite well to low motivation.

To account for these results with regard to number of ideas produced Bouchard (1972a) suggests that subjects who are high on interpersonal effectiveness, who do not have practice, and who are in the low-motivation condition may be described as playful, outgoing, and independent. When they do have experience in practice (or what Bouchard calls training) their social skills, their verbal fluency, and their outgoingness are integrated and channeled and they do produce. They are not under pressure to produce since they are also in the low-motivation condition. However if one also introduces a high motivator to their personality characteristics and practice experience, then their productivity is disrupted.

Similarly a high motivator without practice experience can also channel and integrate the skills of a subject high on interpersonal effectiveness. Apparently for such a person either the motivation or the practice is sufficient to produce the end result. Both combined will disrupt this kind of subject's effectiveness.

Insofar as the results are concerned for number of ideas with subjects low on interpersonal effectiveness, Bouchard suggests they were probably always working at the peak of their abilities and consequently practice and/or motivation made no difference. It should also be indicated that differences between kinds of subjects were best revealed with the thumbs problem.

Insofar as quality of ideas is concerned, Bouchard (1972a) suggests that the only effect found (significant at the 0.05 level) was that subjects high on interpersonal effectiveness produced better quality ideas on the thumbs problem than did those who were low on interpersonal effectiveness. There was a trend for the reverse to be true with the toothpaste problem.

Brainstorming Plus Sequencing with or without Personal Analogy

One of the reasons why sequencing may be effective, according to Bouchard, is that it does a better job of involving subjects in problem solving than does brainstorming alone. Bouchard therefore reasoned that if he could use other techniques to involve a group he would similarly increase their problem-solving effectiveness. To this end he selected personal analogy, one of the techniques used in synectics.

Synectics will be discussed in Chapter XV but at this point it is necessary, in terms of background information, to say that one set of the techniques it makes use of consists of various metaphors and analogies. Among the analogies recommended by Gordon (1961), the originator of synectics, is the use of personal analogy. In so doing it is suggested to the individual that if he wants to increase the number of ideas available to him he should try to feel like parts of the problem under consideration or try to feel like some of the objects involved in the problem. For example, if a coil of spring is involved in the problem then feeling like the coil when it is expanded and/or when it is under pressure might stimulate ideas.

As used in synectics it is usually sufficient for a problem solver to think of what it would feel like to be an object under consideration. There is nothing in the synectics procedure to prevent a person from also "acting out" what it would feel like to be the object under consideration. It was this "acting out" pattern that Bouchard used because, as we said, he felt it would be to a group's advantage if its members could be involved more in the problem-solving process, and "acting out" was to help in this regard. For example, one problem in this study involved developing brand names for a cigar. When a subject used personal analogy he was instructed to play the part of a cigar for 1 minute (Bouchard, 1972a). During this minute he would, while he was the cigar, as his turn came up in the sequencing procedure, verbalize his ideas.

To put the use of personal analogy into the context of Bouchard's experimental design, the procedure was as follows. The control group had practice and used brainstorming with the sequencing procedure. When the control group of four people was presented with the task problem, it had a set time during which to work on its problem (the time varied with the problem). During this time each person, in turn, could come up with his idea. If he had nothing to say he would "pass" and the next person would have his turn.

When personal analogy was used groups of four people were also involved and the time available to them also varied with the problem as was true of the control groups. They also had experience in practice. However, these experimental groups proceeded as follows: At any point in time one member of the group would verbalize his ideas using personal analogy—behaving like the object under consideration—while the others verbalized their ideas following only the brainstorming instructions that all groups were given. After the time allotted to one person was used up, another person would then have his turn using personal analogy to work on the same problem. And, so each person in the group had a chance to use personal analogy on the same problem.

The whole experiment was carried out over three sessions with a total of nine different problems. In addition, in both experimental and control groups there were groups of subjects who were either high or low on interpersonal effectiveness.

The results of this study indicated that on all nine problems used those subjects who used brainstorming-sequencing plus personal analogy were superior (in terms of number of ideas, the only criterion used) to those who used only brainstorming-sequencing. Statistically significant differences were obtained on four of these problems.

Bouchard correctly points out in discussing this result that it cannot be directly related to the use of personal analogy. It is conceivable, as Bouchard says, that the uniqueness of the procedure may have motivated the group or it may have involved it more (Bouchard, 1972b). While this may be true, it should also be noted that both control and experimental groups had the same amount of clock time to work on their problems. In actuality the experimental groups had less time to work on their problems since it did take time to change roles as subjects moved into and out of the use of personal analogy. This, as Bouchard points out, makes the superiority of the experimental groups over the control groups even more noteworthy.

In this study Bouchard also had data on the personality characteristics of his subjects—they were high and low on interpersonal effectiveness. While the data showed there were no statistically significant effects for the interaction of personality factors and experimental procedure, the evidence obtained favored the use of personal analogy plus brainstorming-sequencing with persons high on interpersonal effectiveness.

In conclusion then, a real group's effectiveness when using brainstorming with sequencing may be increased if the group also used personal analogy. It would be interesting to know if such groups would also increase their effectiveness if they used other techniques that are also part of the synectics program.

Summarizing the results of studies of nominal and real groups it is apparent that the evidence favors nominal groups for number of ideas produced. Consequently, if one wishes to use brainstorming with several individuals to obtain creative solutions to problems the practical suggestion is that he ask each of them to work alone and then to collect their ideas. Such a nominal group produces more ideas than a (real) group of individuals working together. Nominal groups also produce more better quality ideas than do real groups.

The superiority of the nominal groups in quality of ideas, is most likely attributable to the fact that nominal groups produce more ideas than real groups do. If number of ideas is equated for them there is no major difference between nominal and real groups. However, in a practical sense, the statistical "average quality" measure may not be satisfactory. Since one does not know before hand which of a number of ideas will be selected, used, and proven the most creative it may be desirable to obtain the largest number of possible ideas. This would then, in a practical situation, swing the balance in favor of using nominal groups.

However, in so doing one may lose out on the potential values of a group working together—group cohesiveness, group morale, etc. To achieve some of these group advantages and yet lessen the possibility of missing a creative idea because the total number was curtailed one may wish to consider either of two possibilities.

(a) Establish a real group of persons who will speak out their ideas using brainstorming's principles together with Bouchard's sequencing method and the use of personal analogy from synectics. It would most likely be of value to have the groups consist of persons high on interpersonal effectiveness as measured by the California Psychological Inventory.

(b) Use a combination of both individual and group work. A series of suggestions along these lines comes from Dunnette (1964) who is rather skeptical about the value of solving problems in group meetings. He thinks that group meetings should be used to share information and not for purposes of arriving at solutions.

(1) A memo should be sent to persons in the organization asking them for whatever *information* about the problem under consideration that they might have. A broad statement of the problem should be presented to them together with a statement of the specific areas of information which might be relevant and which the recipients of the memo should gather and be ready to present.

(2) A brief meeting of 30-40 minutes should be held during which information collected is shared. Solutions should be avoided. Another write-up restating the problem is then prepared.

(3) The participants then work alone in their offices for about an hour preparing solutions to the problem. Some might speak their solutions into a tape-recorder while others, as they prefer, might write them out.

(4) The solutions are reviewed by whoever called the meeting and the best elements in each of the suggested solutions are selected into a final solution.

(5) A final brief meeting of 10-15 minutes is then called during which the results of the problem-solving efforts are summarized and communicated to all participants [pp. 16, 29].

"TRAINING"

Studies of training have taken place primarily in the laboratory. This means that there are no studies, to our knowledge, in which persons have been trained in brainstorming and whose effectiveness on real-life problems was compared with that of a control group that had no training. There are studies in the literature where companies have reported that their employees were involved in brainstorming and certain of their achievements were then related to their training. Unfortunately the training procedures are not described and we cannot tell whether training was limited solely to brainstorming (the two principles and four rules etc.) or whether or not other techniques to stimulate creativity were also used. Because it is not clear just how much of the effects could be traced to training, we presented these studies previously (cf. pages 52-70) as studies of "outcomes" rather than as studies of training.

A similar problem occurred with other studies that also involved training. One such problem occurred with the Meadow and Parnes (1959) study in which "trained" subjects were used. Indeed they were trained but in creative problem-solving and *not* in brainstorming. As shall be pointed out in the next chapter, brainstorming is a part of creative problem-solving. Creative problem-solving, however, includes training both in brainstorming *and* other procedures. A person so trained might solve a problem creatively using any one of a number of different procedures. Therefore, this study was not included in this chapter. This is not an attempt to limit the laurels of brainstorming but rather to be careful in presenting the reader with studies where, insofar as possible, we can determine what the nature of the subjects' experiences was as related to creative results.

There are other studies in the literature in which investigators use the word training to describe their subjects' experiences [e.g., Bouchard (1972a); Dillon *et al.* (1972)] but which we do not include in this section. We have referred to the experience provided in these studies on previous pages (105-106) as "practice." We do not feel that this is merely a semantic issue or a matter of word preference. The subjects in these experiments worked on one or more problems using brainstorming before they worked on a test problem. Or, the subjects were shown a videotape of a brainstorming group in action. We feel that word "practice" is more appropriate to these procedures than "training."

Studies in this section also fall short of the training mark. They too do not present the subject with a specific schedule or program to be followed, they do not provide the subjects with feedback, they do not show subjects how to improve in their performance, etc. What they do do is provide the subject with more opportunity to practice specific procedures and in some instances methods are employed that we would regard as closer to training than practice. Because these studies also do not meet all of the requirements of training, the title of this section is in quotes—"training."

It should also be noted that studies in this section do not focus on the total brainstorming process. Rather they focus on a specific technique—the production of different associations to a stimulus word so as to arrive at more original and uncommon responses. And to the extent that such behavior is involved in brainstorming's goal—the production of quantity and quality of ideas—these studies cast light on the brainstorming process.

MALTZMAN'S BASIC PROCEDURE

What Parnes is to the study of brainstorming's principles and rules, what Taylor is to the study of the relative effectiveness of real and nominal groups, Maltzman (1960; Maltzman *et al.* 1958a, b, 1960, 1964) is to the study of training in this section.

His basic procedure is this: Subjects are presented with a list of twenty-five words and as each word in the list is presented to them they are asked to respond with the first association that occurs to them. Then the same list is presented five more times and each time a word appears a subject is asked for an association that is *different* from the association he gave to the same word on the previous occasion(s). The hypothesis or expectation is that more associations on the *last* repetition of the list, or a larger proportion of these associations, will be uncommon than was true on preceding trials with the same list. Also, a group so "trained"—that is a group that responds with different associations to the list—will produce more uncommon associations on the last trial than will a control group—a group that responded to the same list only once.

In addition to the basic procedure which is limited to the training list of words, Maltzman has also evaluated the results of training by determining whether trained subjects when presented with a new list of words will give more uncommon associations to its words than control subjects. Such a procedure, as we said, may be regarded as a test of training. It may also be a means of determining whether training effects transfer or carry over from one experience (the training list) to another (the test list).

Other transfer studies were also undertaken by Maltzman and his associates to determine whether there was a carry over of training effects to open-ended problems and problems with only one correct solution.

In Maltzman's procedure the criterion is uncommonness of response. It assumes that one of the requirements to be creative is to be able to produce responses that are uncommon or infrequently produced. Others have used the same criterion and called it "uniqueness." Whatever the name, this is a statistical definition; it is also frequently referred to as "originality." But original responses are not necessarily creative responses, for a creative response may need to be both original and relevant to the problem. Although Maltzman is not unaware of the importance of relevance, his primary focus was on uncommon responses.

The theoretical underpinings of Maltzman's procedure for producing un-common responses stem from operant conditioning. He reasons that when one is presented with a problem the first response he gives to it

> is the one which is dominant in the response hierarchy elicitable by that stimulus. . . . Responses that are uncommon or original must be lower in the response hierarchy. . . . If, therefore, a situation could be arranged in which *S* is induced to give responses low in his hierarchy, there would be an increase in the originality of his response. Training of this nature might then produce a disposition to give uncommon responses in other situations [Maltzman *et al.* 1958a, p. 392].

Studies that have been carried out within this framework have concerned themselves with the effects of training, the transfer of training, the effects of instructions, reinforcement, the character of the stimuli, etc. We now turn to these.

Effects of Training

The studies by Maltzman and his co-workers and those who followed them are rather complex. The problems they are interested in are relatively simple but to answer them they use complex experimental designs with several variables. To attempt to describe each of these studies would only involve us in a morass of unnecessary detail, therefore, we shall more or less limit ourselves to references to experimental and control groups with whom a specific variable has been studied. For more knowledge of the experimental design and the statistical techniques used to ferret out the results readers should consult the original articles.

As we have previously noted, to study the effects of training Maltzman *et al.* (1958a) presented his control subjects with a list of twenty-five words and asked them to respond with the first association that came to mind. The same procedure was used with the experimental group but, they were also given five more repetitions of the same list, and on each occasion they were asked for a different association to each word than they had given previously.

It was hypothesized that by the last repetition subjects would be giving more uncommon associations to the word than did a control group with the one trial. And, indeed, this was the case. Maltzman *et al.* (1958a) report that on the last repetition of the training list 75% of the responses were unique. The experimental group produced three times as many unique or uncommon responses on the last trial as they had produced on the first trial. This result was supported by some other investigators but not always at the same level of magnitude as that just reported. Caron, Unger, and Parloff (1963) reported 83% more uncommon responses and Rosenbaum, Arenson, and Panman (1964) reported 29%. One study, Gallup (1963), did not support these or Maltzman's findings.

With Reinforcement

In conditioning experiments it is assumed that reinforcing or rewarding an act will result in its repetition. Presumably, then, using reinforcement together with training might add to the effect of training. Maltzman *et al.* studied this problem using a partial reinforcement schedule—for every fifth uncommon response a subject gave the experimenter said "good."

The result of the study was that this reinforcement had no effect. Reinforced subjects did no better than nonreinforced subjects on the last repetition of the training list.

The effects that were found were attributed solely to training in the giving of different associations.

On an overall basis results of studies in this area support Maltzman's data that more uncommon responses are produced on the last trial with the training list. As a consequence, there are then more important questions that arose—were the effects of training transferable and what could account for training's effects.

Transfer of Training

Transfer of training refers to the extent to which produced effects carry over from a training experience to a new task. We have seen that training in the giving of different responses to the same list of words results in an increasing number of uncommon words on the last trial. This result is based on the use of the same list of words. The question now to be considered is whether the same result will be obtained using a different list, that is, will the training be transferable to other materials.

Studies have been conducted on the transfer of training to: (1) similar materials, (2) dissimilar materials—open-ended and one-solution problems, and (3) real-life problems. The first two categories of problems are strictly laboratory problems, while other problems that have also been studied in the laboratory were taken from real-life situations.

Similar Materials

To answer the question whether training is transferable to similar materials we turn again to Maltzman *et al.* (1958a). In this study a twenty-five word training list is administered to a control group which is subsequently asked to give its associations to a new test list of twenty-five words. The experimental group on the other hand is given five repetitions of the training list and then it is given the new test list.

If training is transferable then the experimental group should do better—produce more uncommon responses—than the control group on the new list of words. The results of this experiment indicated that the experimental group did indeed produce significantly more uncommon responses than the control group.

With reinforcement. In the Maltzman *et al.* (1958a) study there was one control group who, as previously described, had one training trial and one trial on the new list. There were two experimental groups. Both had the five repetitions of the training list but one group was reinforced as previously described and the other was not. Did this reinforcement have any effect on transfer to similar materials over and above training?

No. The group that had the training and was reinforced did produce significantly more uncommon responses than the control group, but it did not produce significantly more uncommon responses than the other group that had the training but not the reinforcement. (This latter group was also significantly better than the control group.)

With instructions to be original. Prior to the administration of the test list, Maltzman *et al.* (1958a) asked some of the subjects to be as original as possible in associating to the test list. Thus, there was one group that had the training to give uncommon responses plus the instruction to be original. This was also a group that was reinforced. Then there was another group who had the training for uncommon responses but was not reinforced, and this group was also instructed to be original. And, finally, there was a control group which, after one trial with the training list, was presented with the test list. This group had no originality training and no reinforcement, but before being given the test list, was instructed to be as original as possible.

The results were that both reinforced and nonreinforced groups with instruction to be original were not significantly different from each other in their production of uncommon responses. However, each differed from the control group in this regard. Thus, while reinforcement was not critical for the trained groups, the effect of the instruction to be original was. This result is similar to studies reported previously in which subjects also behaved in accord with their instructions.

Maltzman *et al.* (1958a) presented the instruction to be original *after* training and just *before* the test list. Rosenbaum *et al.* (1964) also studied the effects of the instruction *throughout* training.

Rosenbaum *et al.* first had their subjects respond to an "equating" list of words so that it could be established that the four groups were equal in ability at the start. Then the same training and test lists were used as were used by Maltzman *et al.* (1958a). These were administered to four experimental groups: (1) trained and no instructions to be original; (2) not trained and no instructions to be original; (3) trained and instructions to be original at each of the training trials; (4) not trained and instructions to be original.

When subjects were presented with the test list, none of them was given an instruction to be original. All of them were instructed simply to give their associations as they came to mind.

To study the immediate effects of instructions to be original, the subjects' associations to the first exposure to the training list were studied. The only significant effect could be attributed to the instructions—those instructed to be original obtained significantly lower originality scores. No differences in the results could be attributed to training.

Now, turning to the effects of training and instructions on the test list it was found that each alone affected the originality scores but no such effects could be attributed to the interaction between training and instruction to be original. Maltzman's results regarding effectiveness of training are supported. Thus despite variations in experimental procedure, Rosenbaum's study replicates Maltzman's work and supports his results.

Order of presenting training and test lists. The results of Maltzman's training procedure presented thus far are rather positive. And, to be sure more such results are to be presented. However, even before Maltzman's side of the story is completed a note should be injected to indicate that all do not agree with him as to the reason for his results.

Maltzman attributes his results to the effects of his training procedure. Gallup (1963), however, points out that Maltzman *et al.* (1960) did not counterbalance their study. Maltzman *et al.* first presented the subjects with a training list and then a test list. Since they did not also reverse the order by giving the test list first and the training list second they could not learn, as Gallup suggests, whether or not whichever list came second would produce the more uncommon responses or whether or not their results have anything to do with the training that asks for different associations.

Four groups of subjects participated in Gallup's study. Two of his groups used the Maltzman training list first. (For one group the order of the words within a list was exactly as Maltzman had it. For the second group this order was reversed.) These groups were then tested with Maltzman's test list.

To the third and fourth groups Gallup presented Maltzman's test list first. (Again, two orders of words within the list were used as before.) This list was then followed by the training list. The result of this experiment was that which-ever list order subjects had they "were more original on the second list than on a first list [Gallup, 1963, p. 924]."

Persistence of transfer effects. That transfer does occur to a list of words, a task similar to that used in training, is supported by the studies cited and other studies. While this is important it is also critical that these results should last. To learn whether they do, Maltzman *et al.* (1960, p. 14, Experiment V) undertook the following study.

Two control groups were used in this study. To each of them there was a single presentation of the training list. Then *1 hour* later the test list (as well as the Unusual Uses Test to be considered later, page 120) was administered to one group. During the hour of waiting this control group worked on ten paper and pencil problems. The second control group was dismissed after it responded to the training list and it returned *48 hours* later to take the other tests.

Two experimental groups were used and each of them had the usual training procedure with five repetitions of the training list. One waited 1 hour and the other waited 48 hours before responding to the test lists.

The results of this study indicated that transfer of training did occur and that it was related to the use of the training procedure. Moreover, the effects of training last for 1 hour as well as for 48 hours. There was something of a drop at 48 hours which Maltzman *et al.* regard as a manifestation of learning, and, in-deed, is something they would expect in terms of the learning theory they were working with.

In summary then, the results support the idea that the effects of Maltzman's training procedure is transferable to materials similar to those used in training (another list of words) and these effects last for 1 hour and for 48 hours. The question now is whether the effects of training will also transfer to tasks that are not similar to those used in training.

Dissimilar Materials

Transfer of training to two dissimilar tasks has been investigated. The two are: The Unusual Uses Test (Guilford, 1967) and the Remote Associates Test (RAT) (Mednick, 1962b). The former is an open-ended test in that there are several responses or several solutions to the problems it contains while for the latter there is one solution.

Open-ended problem. In the open-ended Unusual Uses Test a subject is asked to give as many uses as he can think of, within a 10 minute period, for an automobile, a tire, a key, a safety pin, a watch, a button, and eyeglasses. This test provides measures of fluency and originality. The fluency measure is based on the total number of different uses a subject produces and the measure of originality is based on the frequency with which a use is mentioned by a population of subjects. There are various adaptations of this approach but they are all based on the frequency of response.

In the Maltzman *et al.* study (1958a) two originality measures were used. For the first, the frequency of relevant uses was determined. Then a subject's originality score was the sum of the weighted uses (based on frequency) divided by total number of uses he gave. After some results were analyzed, a second scoring system was utilized which involved giving more weight to the less common uses. It was based on the number of uses given 10% of the time or less. This measure is an *ad hoc* measure. It capitalizes on chance and must therefore be regarded cautiously.

In the Maltzman *et al.* (1958a) study the Unusual Uses Test was administered to the control group after it had its one and only experience with the training list and after it had its one experience with the test list. For the experimental group it was administered after its five repetitions with the training list and one trial with the test list.

In this experiment Maltzman *et al.* studied the effects of training, reinforcement, and instructions. For the instructions condition subjects were instructed to be original just before they took the Unusual Uses Test. The results of the effects of these variables are presented both for fluency and originality. For *fluency* the only significant effect was the combination of training plus the instruction to be original. But this resulted in a decrease in the number of unusual uses offered. There is, however, a tendency for training without the instruction to be original to increase fluency of response. Maltzman *et al.* (1958a) suggest that, for certain statistical reasons this latter result should be regarded cautiously. However, we have noted that in previous studies where subjects are instructed to raise their standards (e.g., when they are instructed to be original) they do less well in the number of responses they produce. A larger number of responses is produced without the instruction to be original.

For *originality*, defined as a weighted score, the procedures used, including training, provided no significant results. However when another criterion of originality was used the results were different. This criterion was based only on those uses given 10% of the time or less. Using this criterion the results indicated that without the instruction to be original the training method produced an increase in originality. But originality training with instructions to be original and no reinforcement produced a decrement in originality. Furthermore, instructions to be original alone and no training also helped in the production of original uses. It should be carefully noted that the results just mentioned, although significant, capitalize on *chance* and should be regarded quite cautiously.

At best, Maltzman *et al.* (1958a) regard the effects of training and instructions on the Unusual Uses Test as rather ambiguous and as matters that require more research.

In 1960, Maltzman *et al.* reported better results for their training procedure when the originality criteria were changed once again. Rather than using the weighted criterion or the 10% or less criterion, in this study the originality score was based on number of unique responses. Any response was unique which was given only once to a test item. And, the measure of fluency was the number of nonunique responses.

Results of this study indicated that none of the experimental or control groups differed from each other in fluency. However, the training experience that involved giving different responses on each of five repetitions to the training list, yielded significantly higher originality scores than either of the two other control conditions or either of the two other experimental conditions in this study.

One of the two other control conditions was the same as that used in the Maltzman *et al.* (1958a) experiment in which subjects had one trial with the training list and one trial with the test list before they were given the Unusual Uses Test.

A second control group in this experiment had five repetitions of the training list but each time it had to give the *same* response to each stimulus word. Then the test list and Unusual Uses list were presented.

Among the two experimental groups was one that had one trial with the twenty-five word training list and was then given a list of one-hundred and twenty-five high-frequency (common) words. To each of these the group gave one association, so that like some of the other groups, it gave one-hundred and twenty-five associations. There was another experimental group that also had the twenty-five word training list, but after this list, it was asked for its associations to a list of one-hundred and twenty-five low-frequency (uncommon) words. Both these experimental groups had the test list and the Unusual Uses Test after the one-hundred and twenty-five word list.

The last experimental group had the usual training period with the twenty-five word association list, followed by five repetitions of the same list giving a different response at each repetition. Then the test list and the Unusual Uses Test were administered.

As was said previously, the Maltzman training experience was superior to all the other experimental and control conditions for originality. Why were the same results not obtained in the (1958a) study?

Maltzman *et al.* (1960) suggest that the differences could be accounted for by the larger sample size in the second experiment. Also there was a change from individual administration to group administration of the test in the second study. This too may have stimulated more responses.

We believe an additional factor was the change in criterion. That a criteron different from the one used in the 1958a study could have effects is reflected in a study by Rosenbaum *et al.* (1964).

Rosenbaum *et al.* (1964, p. 55) found that "Training, but not instructions, resulted in significantly more unique, common and total responses on the Unusual Uses Test." The Rosenbaum *et al.* criteria were different from those used by Maltzman *et al.* (1958a) and the same as those used by Maltzman *et al.* (1960). An original response was a response that occurred only once for an object for the whole population studied. A common use occurred two or more times.

Training produced original effects according to Rosenbaum *et al.* because during training there is a greater demand for productivity and therefore there is a carry over to greater productivity on the Unusual Uses Test. A secondary effect of this greater productivity is an increase in the number of unique responses.

In summary, the results regarding transfer of training to a dissimilar task which is open-ended (Unusual Uses Test) are rather inconsistent. Other studies to be reported later are more positive. Therefore, we are inclined to suggest that transfer of training does occur but more support for this finding would be desirable.

Just as with transfer of training with similar tasks, here too the question can be raised whether or not the effects of training do persist. In the same experiment that was referred to for the persistence of effects with similar tasks (Maltzman *et al.*, 1960, p. 14, Experiment V) there is also data for dissimilar tasks. It will be recalled that in this experiment there were two control groups. For the first, 1 hour elapsed between the training list and the Unusual Uses Test (during this time the group worked on ten paper and pencil problems) and for the second 48 hours elapsed between the training list and the Unusual Uses Test.

There were also two experimental groups both of whom had the five repetitions of the training list and were asked to give different associations to the words in the list on each occasion. After this training experience one experimental group waited 1 hour and the other group waited 48 hours before responding to the Unusual Uses Test.

The result of this study indicated that the transfer effects did not last. For the fluency measure, the number of different uses suggested, neither training nor delay effects were found. For originality, a training effect was found but no effect was found for the delay.

In sum then while there does appear to be some evidence, albeit not very strongly supported, that transfer of training does occur with a dissimilar openended task the effects do not seem to last long.

One-solution problem. The second category of dissimilar task that has been studied is the one-solution problem. The test around which the research centers is the Remote Associates Test (RAT) (Mednick, 1962b). In this test a subject is presented with three words and asked to come up with a word, a solution, that relates to all three. For example, he is presented with: "bitter," "sixteen," and "heart." The correct response is "sweet" because it is associated with all three words as in "bittersweet," "sweet sixteen," and "sweetheart." Associations to the test word may be forward as in "sweet sixteen" or backward as in "bittersweet." Any one form of the RAT may allow for either one or both types of associates. It should be emphasized, as Caron *et al.* (1963) point out, that this test involves only "associative relevance" and not "conceptual or logical relevance."

[The RAT is not the only test used to study the transfer of training to one-solution problems. The two-string problem of Maier (1930) was also used (Maltzman *et al.*, 1964). Since more extensive work was carried out with the RAT, only this is considered here.]

After conducting a series of experiments with the RAT, Maltzman *et al.* (1964, p. 20) concluded "that performance on the problems employed which have only one correct solution cannot be facilitated by the originality-training procedures employed with tasks having no one correct solution."

Caron *et al.* (1963) obviously had no knowledge of Maltzman's work and found less ambiguity and less value in the use of Maltzman's training procedure with the RAT. They raised the question whether Maltzman's training technique produced uncommon responses that are largely *irrelevant* rather than *relevant* to the problem studied. It is obvious that for creative problem solving one wants not only an uncommon response but one that is relevant to the problem under consideration or else the association is worthless for any effective work.

Three training procedures were used in their experiment: (1) originality training—which asks for different responses from the subject and is the procedure used by Maltzman *et al.* (1958a) in their initial work; (2) repetition training in which each subject again has five repetitions of the stimulus words but is now asked to give the *same* association to each word on each repetition—this technique was also used by Maltzman *et al.* (1960); (3) control conditions in which there is only one presentation of the word list.

The subjects in this study were ninety high school juniors both males and females all of who had tested IQ's of 119 or higher. They were distributed into twelve groups (due to conditions beyond the experimenters' control the groups were of unequal size). The groups were equated for total IQ, language IQ, and a measure of test anxiety (Mandler & Cowen, 1958).

These twelve groups were distributed (four each) into each of the three previously mentioned training conditions. Two of the four groups were male and two were female. After the groups had their respective training experiences they were divided into two larger groups of six groups each—one male and one female group from each training condition. To one of these sets a twelve item form of the RAT was administered. This form allowed for both forward and backward associations. In this sense it was easier than the twenty item RAT administered to the second group in which only forward associates were correct ones.

To summarize then: subjects were trained with the same training-list words used by Maltzman *et al.* (1958a) and then, as the experimental condition required it, subjects were presented with the RAT test.

Turning to the results of this experiment it first needs to be pointed out that Caron *et al.* replicated part of the Maltzman *et al.* (1958a) study. Training in the giving of different responses does result in a larger proportion of uncommon responses on the last repetition of the training list than is true for a control group. Caron *et al.* found this to be 83% which compares rather well with the 72% figure reported by Maltzman *et al.* (1958a).

To study subjects' responses to the RAT three measures were used: (1) number of items responded to correctly, (2) a measure that gave more weight to the difficult items, (3) a measure of irrelevance which "involved a response which was of questionable relevance [Caron *et al.*, 1963, p. 439] ."

The results of this study indicated that the group that had the Maltzman originality-training procedure did not solve *more* items in the RAT than either of the other two groups in the study. And the *weighted measure* also did not yield significant results.

With regard to errors of commission the group with repetitive (same) training produced significantly more errors of commission (irrelevant responses) than did the control group. Subjects with Maltzman's originality-training also produced more errors of commission than the control group but this difference was not signficant. Therefore, Caron *et al.* (1963, p. 441) say that both the repetitive training group and Maltzman's originality-training group, "but particularly the former, committed more errors of commission than the Control *S*s." Consequently these authors conclude (Caron *et al.*, 1963, p. 442) "No facilitative effect was demonstrated on either of two forms of the Remote Associates Test as a consequence of originality training, nor was a decremental effect found as a consequence of Maltzman's repetitive-training control procedure." [It will be recalled that in the Maltzman *et al.* (1960) study the same repetitive procedure did produce a decrement in number of uncommon responses.]

Maltzman's originality-training procedure obviously does not apply to one-solution problems like the RAT. But why? A study by Freedman (1965) casts light on this problem. In this study Freedman suggests that successful performance "on the RAT depends upon the production of many associations in a short time [p. 89]" and that a correct response to the RAT is usually a *commonly* associated word. Maltzman's technique on the other hand, is designed to produce uncommon responses, and therefore, it is not likely to be as effective with a technique for which common associations are required. In their 1964 study, in which Maltzman *et al.* used the RAT rather extensively, they believed uncommon responses were necessary for the RAT for they said [p. 1] they were investigating "problems having a unique solution, where only one uncommon response is correct, or at best a small number of responses meet the criterion." The Freedman and Maltzman *et al.* approaches therefore were quite different.

To test these hypotheses Freedman studied ninety college students who were divided between two main experimental conditions and one control group. In one experimental condition, called *facilitation*, there was a group consisting of forty subjects, twenty males and twenty females. To each of these subjects a list of ten words was presented and subjects were asked to produce associations to each of these words as presented for 30 seconds. This was the group that was to satisfy the previously stated condition of having associations available to it.

The control group consisted of ten males each of whom was paired with one male in the facilitation group. A control subject was presented with a stimulus list of words but rather than giving his own association he responded with the association given by the subject in the facilitation group with whom he was paired. Thus both the facilitation and control group members *said* the same associations but the former originated them and hence actively participated in developing them while the latter did not.

The second experimental group consisted also of twenty males and twenty females who were also presented with the same list of ten stimulus words but their task was to *define* and *not associate* to each word. This group was the *nonfacilitation* group. This group was exposed to the same stimulus words as was the facilitation group but it did not experience the development of associations. It should also be indicated that the words in the stimulus list given to the subjects were so selected that neither the words themselves or the associations to them were related to the correct responses to the RAT.

The RAT used consisted of thirty items and took 40 minutes to administer. It was divided into two equal parts and before each part, the experiences of the experimental conditions described above were repeated.

The results of this study indicated that facilitation groups of both sexes produced significantly higher scores than the nonfacilitation group. (This effect was stronger for males than females.)

It might be argued that associations of the facilitation group might have been similar to or related to the words in the RAT. The facilitation group's success could be related to this if it were true. Therefore, it was necessary to study the behavior of the control group who read the facilitation group's words as responses to the stimulus words. Although they didn't initially produce these words they were at least aware of them and to that extent were not at a disadvantage with regard to the RAT. Therefore, if availability of association was critical, the facilitation and control groups should do equally well on the RAT; "if the act of associating were critical, the control group should score less high and should not differ from the nonfacilitation group [Freedman, 1965, p. 91]." The data are in line with the second possibility. The control group performed less well than the facilitation group with which it was compared, and it was not different from the nonfacilitation group. "Thus, it appears that the actual act of associating is the critical factor which facilitated performance on the RAT [Freedman, 1965, p. 91]."

To account for his results, which are better than Maltzman's for the RAT, Freedman suggests two possibilities. One, that the Freedman free-association procedure requires the subjects to associate to several different words as they must do in the RAT. In Maltzman's procedure the subject has more training in giving different responses to the same stimulus.

Two, the free-association procedure used by Freedman requires the subjects to produce a number of responses in a short period of time and this is one of the necessary conditions for successful performance on the RAT. Maltzman's procedure provides training in producing one association at a time.

In addition to the finding that Freedman's procedure works with the RAT, this study should be regarded as an example of what we have referred to in the previous studies reviewed—that some training procedures will be better than others for certain kinds of problems.

In summary then it appears that the Maltzman originality-training procedure is not very effective with problems that are dissimilar to those used in training and which are one-solution problems.

Considering all of what has been presented regarding the transfer of Maltzman's originality-training procedure it may be said that a curve of its effectiveness slopes downward as one moves away from the kind of material covered during training. We have yet to consider one other kind of problem and then the study of the transfer of training issue will be complete.

Real-life problem. From a practical point of view the value of a technique such as Maltzman's is whether the effects of the training it provides is transferable to real-life situations. We come close to such a goal in a study by Hyman (1960) in which he studied the effects of Maltzman's standard procedure, with some variations, on an industrial problem. The problem is called the automatic warehousing problem, and as its title indicates, it is concerned with the automatic warehousing of industrial materials. The problem was not an existing one but stemmed from industrial experience. It was presented to engineers at General Electric during the course of their creativity training.

In Maltzman's work described thus far he used a twenty-five-word training and twenty-five-word test list. As we shall see later (cf. page 132) Maltzman also experimented with other lists—a twenty-four-word training list and a ten-word test list. Hyman used the ten-word test list and six repetitions of the twenty-five-word training list. The sequence therefore was: training list, test list, automatic warehousing problem, and then a decision-making test used to study another matter reported later (cf. page 132). This is Experiment VII in Hyman (1960). In addition to this design, which is the same as Maltzman's, Hyman also gathered other interesting data which we shall also present.

The training group in this study with Maltzman's procedure was called the positive training group, for it was involved in giving different associations to the stimulus words which lead to more uncommon responses. This group's behavior was contrasted with a negative training group's behavior which was to give the same association on six repetitions of the training list. Such a procedure had been used by Maltzman *et al.* (1960) and was found to inhibit the production of uncommon responses.

As shall be reported later, (cf. pages 132-133) Hyman found, in agreement with Maltzman findings, that the positive training group produced more uncommon responses to the test list than did the negative training group. However, results obtained with the automatic warehousing problem were another matter.

First, in terms of number of solutions produced to the automatic warehousing problem, Hyman found that the negative training group produced just a bit (not significantly) more responses. It produced a median number 6.0 solutions as against 5.4 solutions for the positive training group. There was greater variability (variance) in the number of solutions produced by the negative training group.

Hyman then divided the subjects' suggested solutions into "common" and "uncommon" categories and found that the positive training group produced a slightly larger number of uncommon responses than did the negative training group. This trend was in agreement with Maltzman's data but it was not significant. Turning to *common* responses it was found that the positive training group produced a significantly *smaller* number. [This finding is congruent with Freedman's study (1965) reported previously (cf. pages 125-126) in which it was also found that Maltzman's procedure produces uncommon responses and that a usual free-association procedure may produce common responses.]

Hyman then also weighted subjects' solutions for originality and found no difference between the two training procedures. Thus far Hyman's study is very like Maltzman's in terms of type of data gathered (but not in results). Hyman, however, gathered additional data.

Each subject selected his one best solution and it was evaluated by judges. The results were in favor of the negative training group. It produced somewhat (but not significantly) more better ideas than did the positive training group.

Hyman also told his subjects to indicate how well satisfied they were with their solutions. And, here his data indicated that members of the positive training group, the group that had Maltzman's training procedure were significantly less satisfied with their solutions than were members of the negative training group. In discussing this finding Hyman raises the possibility, to be investigated in future research, that possibly the positive training group has its standards raised and therefore becomes less satisfied with its solutions.

Summarizing the effects of positive and negative training groups in Hyman's study we may say: The positive training group avoids the common or obvious solutions and experiences greater dissatisfaction with their performance. The negative training group produces greater variability in the subjects. Some presumably get bored and withdraw from the problems; for others the repetition results in more stimulation and effort. And there is a suggestion in the data, according to Hyman that this training procedure may produce better solutions.

Exploring Reasons for Training's Effectiveness

Maltzman *et al.* (1960), feeling quite convinced of the value of their training procedure, proceeded to conduct a series of experiments in which they sought to investigate the potential effects of a variety of variables. Those they considered and their experimental effects are now presented.

Evocation of Different Responses

The Maltzman training procedure, as we have pointed out, is based on the theory that individuals can be trained to produce uncommon responses. If this is so, is the training effective because it calls upon subjects to produce different responses? Does the character of the stimuli matter? Is the training effective because different responses are produced to the same stimuli, or, would simply producing different responses to different stimuli be sufficient?

To answer these and other questions Maltzman *et al.* (1960, Experiment I) conducted an experiment in which there were the following groups: (1) the standard control group which associated only once to the twenty-five-word training list, (2) another control group in which subjects engaged in five repetitions of the same responses to the twenty-five-word training list, (3) the standard training group which gave different responses to each of the five repetitions of the twenty-five-word training list, (4) a group that responded once to each word in a one-hundred and twenty-five-word list of frequently used (common) words, and (5) a group that responded once to each word in a one-hundred and twenty-five-word-list of infrequently used (uncommon) words.

First, the results indicate that the second control (the same-repetitive) group gave significantly fewer uncommon responses to the test list than did the experimental groups which indicated to the investigators that results could not be attributed to the number of responses given "or to habituation factors." The three experimental groups which performed significantly better emitted the same number of responses during training. "The differences obtained must be due to the uncommonness of responses per se emitted by the experimental groups or the uncommonness of responses emitted to the given stimulus words [Maltzman *et al.*, 1960, p. 5]."

On the Unusual Uses Test the control group that repeated the same response gave significantly fewer unique responses than the standard control group. Since the first response one gives to a stimulus word is most likely a common response the same-repetition group then is practising repeating a common response and this would increase their tendency to give common responses in the test situation. These data, therefore, say something specifically about the importance in the Maltzman technique of giving uncommon responses.

However, is it only the evocation of different uncommon responses that produces the obtained results or is it the repeated production of uncommon responses to the *same stimuli* that leads to the final effect?

To answer these questions Maltzman *et al.* (1960) studied effects produced by the usual training group and the other two experimental groups—those that were presented with the one-hundred and twenty-five-word lists.

The two one-hundred and twenty-five-word lists were used on the assumption that if different responses are evoked in training they are also likely to be evoked in the test situation. That this does happen is attested to by the fact that these two experimental groups produce more uncommon responses to the test list than do the two control groups. And, both training groups do as well as the group that had the standard training approach.

However, Maltzman *et al.* (1960) argue that results with the originality score on the Unusual Uses Test suggest that what is happening is more than the mere production of many responses. It will be recalled that the Maltzman training group outperformed all other groups on the originality measure for the Unusual Uses Test. And, it will be recalled that these results are limited to the production of uncommon responses since no significant effects were found for the fluency score on the Unusual Uses test. Therefore, Maltzman *et al.* (1960, p. 5) say, "These results indicate that the procedure of repeated evocation of different responses to the same stimulus words produces a more general disposition to produce uncommon responses than the procedure of evoking different responses to different stimuli."

In another experiment (Experiment II in Maltzman *et al.*, 1960) the authors again find support for their precise training procedure. In this study among the groups studied there were the usual control group, the usual training group and two other experimental groups. Both these experimental groups read uncommon associations to the stimulus word and were used "to determine whether emission of uncommon responses by S is a necessary condition of the originality training procedure [Maltzman *et al.*, 1960, p. 5]." To one of these experimental groups one-hundred and twenty-five pairs of items were presented and the subject was to indicate which word in each pair went with the stimulus word (a word in the training list). To the second experimental group only the one-hundred and twenty-five-word pairs were administered. The stimulus word was not and the subjects were asked to underline which of the two words in a pair was more familiar to them.

Results of this study indicated that the standard training procedure yielded more uncommon responses to the test list than did any of the control or other experimental groups and it yielded more original responses than they to the Unusual Uses Test. On fluency the standard procedure and the two experimental procedures were superior to the control group. On the basis of these results Maltzman *et al.* (1960, p. 8) say "These results show that with the stimulus materials employed, uncommon responses must be evoked as intraverbal responses by the stimuli if there is to be an increase in originality in the test situations."

These studies by Maltzman and his co-workers therefore support both the use of different words as stimuli in the training and the procedure of asking subjects to give different responses to them. Maltzman's training procedure as it has been used appears to be the desired one.

Emphasis on Difference of Response and Nature of Interpolated Task

Each time Maltzman's experimental group was presented with a repetition of the training list it was asked to give a "different response." Gallup (1963) questioned whether uncommon responses on the test list could be attributed to the instruction to give a separate response and so the subject developed a set to give different responses or whether just giving different responses without the instruction to be different could produce the same effects.

Another question asked by Gallup concerned the nature of the interpolated task. Maltzman's experimental subjects had a 10-minute delay between the training list and the test list. Gallup used this same time interval to give a nonverbal task to his subjects. Gallup used Maltzman's technique for scoring uncommonness as well as his scoring technique for measuring relevance.

Five groups of subjects participated in this study. There were three experimental groups and two control groups. For all groups a list of nouns was presented and to each noun subjects were asked to give a verb. This was their training list experience. And, as indicated, instead of being told to give a different response, they did, in fact, give different responses just because they were asked to give verbs in response to nouns. On the test list subjects were presented with another list of nouns and again asked for verbs.

Between their experience with the training list and the test list subjects had other experiences. Two experimental groups had the same training list twice more and on the first occasion they were asked for adjectives and on the second occasion they were asked for other nouns. These experiences were then followed by the test list.

The third experimental group was asked to take a difficult vocabulary test and thus was also exposed to uncommon words. The two control groups had 10 minutes on an arithmetic test.

No differences on originality were obtained between groups. The only significant effect obtained was that originality was greater on the test list as compared to the training list regardless of the interpolated activity.

This study led Gallup to question Maltzman's results and therefore he decided to replicate Maltzman's work more precisely. Eight groups participated in this other study. Groups 1 and 2 had the Maltzman instructions exactly. They were presented with a list for five repetitions and each time were asked for a different response. Two other groups served as control groups in that right after the training list they went to the test list. A third pair of groups worked on arithmetic tests between their training and their tests. The amount of time they took on the arithmetic tests equalled that taken by the first pair of groups giving different responses. The last pair of groups spent time, on the same basis, on a vocabulary test.

One group of each pair had one of Maltzman's lists as the training list and the other as the test list. For the other pair the sequence was reversed.

Again the results of this study indicated that whichever list of words came second it received a higher originality score. And due to the lack of significance of the other variables Gallup says that "The conclusion must be drawn here that originality as reported by Maltzman and his colleagues had not been demonstrated to be advantageous over having Ss work on arithmetic problems, vocabulary tests, or simply doing nothing between trials [Gallup, 1963, p. 927]."

Alternative Stimuli and Lists for Facilitating Originality

Maltzman *et al.* (1960) asked whether there were not alternative methods to training for originality that did not require the use of list of words to which different responses would be given on five different occasions. In one experiment (Maltzman *et al.* 1960 Experiment II), they used as stimuli in one experimental condition, the six items from the Unusual Uses Test. Five repetitions to each of these items were used. The effects of this experience were compared to the effects of the standard training experience with a list of words. The criterion was the number of uncommon words associated to a list of words. The results indicated that the usual training procedure was significantly superior to the new one.

Another experiment, (Maltzman *et al.*, 1960 Experiment III) was conducted in which more unusual use items were used and the number of repetitions were increased. Again, no change in frequency of uncommon responses to the test list was produced.

Still another experiment was conducted (Maltzman *et al.*, 1960 Experiment IV) in which the investigators used still other test stimuli.

For this experiment the investigators selected a twenty-four-word training and a ten-word test list. The words in both lists were selected because they tended to evoke opposite associations. The net effect of this was that the words would evoke relatively few different responses—associations would have high communality.

A control group was used in which the twenty-four-item word list was presented once and after its associations were obtained it was presented with the ten-item test, then the Unusual Uses Test was administered. (Another control group was used to ascertain whether giving opposites on the training list would yield more opposites on the test list. This was not found to be the case.) In addition to the control group there were three experimental groups. They had one, five, and ten repetitions, respectively, of the twenty-four-item training list before the test list and the Unusual Uses Test were administered.

The results indicated that on the test list the experimental groups that had five and ten repetitions did not differ from each other in the number of uncommon responses they gave to the test list. They both were significantly different in number of uncommon responses from that produced by the control group and the group that had only one repetition of the twenty-four-item training list.

On the originality measure for the Unusual Uses Test each of the three experimental groups gave more unique responses than did the control group. On the fluency measure, number of common responses, the group that had five repetitions of the training list had a higher fluency measure (gave more common responses) than each of the other two experimental groups or the control group. No other significant differences were found.

On the basis of these data Maltzman *et al.* (1960, p. 13) say "The data obtained show that reliable changes in free-association originality may be produced by varying the amount of training in the standard experimental procedure. The particular form of the trend, however, is no doubt a function of the length of the training list as well as the number of its repetitions."

Hyman (1960) in two experiments (VII and VIII) with General Electric engineers used both the twenty-four-word list for training and the ten-word list as a test list. These studies deviated in the following ways from the usual experimental design in a Maltzman study. Subjects were divided into two groups. One was called the positive training group, whose training was like that which Maltzman gave his subjects. They had five repetitions of the training list and on each occasion had to come up with different associations to the stimuli. The second group of subjects in the primary experiment (VII) made up a negative training group. This was a group that followed a procedure previously used by Maltzman *et al.* (1960) in which subjects gave the same association to each of the stimuli on each of the repetitions.

In the first of the two experiments the experimental sequence was: training list, test list, automatic warehousing problem (how to warehouse things automatically), then a decision-making test used to check out some ideas on the process involved in Maltzman's procedure and which will be considered later (cf. pages 134-135). In Experiment VIII, an Unusual Uses Test was substituted for the automatic warehousing problem. Here our concern is only with results obtained for the test list and the Unusual Uses Test.

The results that Hyman (1960) obtained for the test list replicated Maltzman's findings. The positive training group did produce more uncommon problems to the test list than did the negative training group. However, Maltzman's results with the Unusual Uses Test were not replicated. The positive training group did not give more unique responses to the problems than did the controls. (Hyman does not report data on fluency.)

Summarizing the material presented for the reasons why some have found Maltzman's technique to be effective, as well as summarizing the studies of variations in training stimuli, we are left with the need for more replicated studies. The position here is such that if Maltzman and his co-workers run a study it supports their orientation. If they do not conduct the study the support is shaky and even questionable.

An Alternative Explanation for the Effectiveness of Training

Maltzman based his training technique on the theory that after the first association (which is usually a common response) is given to a stimulus word that the instruction to give different associations to the same stimulus directs the subject to seek these different responses, which are most likely to be uncommon responses. In this process the subject becomes practiced and reinforced in the development of uncommon responses so that when they are presented with a new stimulus list they are more likely to come up with uncommon responses than would a group untrained in such emphasis.

Hyman (1960) has advanced another orientation. This orientation does not predict different behavior on a test list from that predicted by Maltzman but it does predict whether after training a subject would select an easy or a difficult task to work on. Maltzman's theoretical orientation does not say anything about the ease or difficulty of the selected task.

According to Hyman the Maltzman training procedure requires the subject to come up with more and more uncommon responses, but in so doing he has to suppress those associations which he has already given, and which are the dominant ones, before he can come up with a new one. Therefore, as the subject goes along producing more and more uncommon responses he has to devote more energy to suppress the interference from the responses he has already given, and he has to exert more and more energy "to go deeper" and come up with more uncommon responses.

Briefly, according to the Maltzman view there is a change in the dominance among the response tendencies. The uncommon responses which were initially weak become stronger with the continued training experience. According to Hyman there is no change in the dominance of associations but there is a change in how deeply the subject must dig in the response hierarchy available to him before he comes up with an acceptable response.

Since the difference between the two orientations is such that they do not differ in the prediction of number of different responses given but only in the level of difficulty of task selected for solution, the issue is to utilize a series of problems that are graded for difficulty and to present them to the subjects after training. If subjects differ in the difficulty of the problems they select to work on then the evidence would be in favor of Hyman's orientation. On the other hand, if choice of task is not affected and only the responses to the task are affected then the results favor Maltzman's explanation.

The experiment that is germane to this point is one that has already been presented. But in this instance there is an addition that has not yet been mentioned. The experiment is the one in which positive and negative training groups were established. The former was trained with Maltzman's originality-training procedure and the latter gave the same response on repeated presentation of the stimulus words. The training list consisted of twenty-four words. The sequence in the study was training list, test list, and automatic warehousing problem. Then to gather data on ease or difficulty of test selected for further solution a decision-making test was used.

The decision-making test used was one developed by Meyer and Litwin for their study of relating need achievement to risktaking. This test consists of four problems, and each of these problems consists of four tasks which are graded in terms of difficulty. The subject has 15 seconds to investigate the tasks and to select the one he wants to work on. The credit (or score) the subject receives depends on the difficulty of the task he selects and solves. If he does not solve the problem in the task in 1 minute he receives no credit.

These initial results did not support Hyman's view. The positive training group did in fact select the more difficult problems than the negative training group. However, inspection of the range of difficulty levels selected by subjects in each training group indicated that subjects of the positive training group limited themselves to problems in the middle range and subjects in the negative training group selected problems throughout the difficulty range and also had the greater variance.

It appears then, according to Hyman, that the negative training experience is not simply the opposite of the positive training experience but that its effect probably varies with the subject. For some subjects the monotony of the negative training experience affects them so that they do not put forth much effort or they withdraw from the task. On the other hand other subjects find the monotony of the task drive arousing. They approach new tasks with renewed vigor.

To try to pinpoint whether task difficulty and effort are related, Hyman correlated the number of solutions suggested by subjects to the automatic warehousing problem with the difficulty of the problem selected. The correlation was .54 which was statistically significant indicating that people who give more solutions and who implicity expend more effort are more likely to be those who select the difficult tasks.

There is more evidence in favor of Hyman's hypothesis. The previous data in favor of the positive training group was based on a comparison of this group with the negative training group. For this comparison Hyman assumed that the negative training group was the opposite of the positive training group. This is obviously not the case. He therefore conducted another experiment (Hyman, 1960, Experiment VIII) in which he reran the basic format of his experiment only this time he compared the positive training group with a standard control group. The results of this study did indeed indicate that, in accord with Hyman's hypothesis the positive training group did select more difficult test problems than the standard control group.

This study, which runs counter to predictions that one would make from Maltzman's theorizing, while very interesting, should be regarded cautiously. It needs support through further replication.

Summarizing the results of studies surveyed in this section we may say: Maltzman investigated the effects of a procedure in which subjects were asked to give different associations to the same training list of stimulus words on the number of uncommon or unique words that subjects would give to other stimuli. In essence the work of Maltzman, his colleagues and others, indicates that the further one moves away from similarity with the training list (to open-ended and to one-solution problems) the less evident are the effects. The evidence presented by Maltzman and his co-workers, in a series of papers, for transfer to similar and open-ended tasks, and for the persistence of effects is quite good. However, the data presented by others is not wholly supportive.

Maltzman and his co-workers also utilized a technique in which subjects repeated the same response to a stimulus list and thus presumably became satiated. They found that such a procedure produced a decrement in the number of uncommon responses for an open-ended test. Studies of others suggest, however, that not all persons respond similarly to repetitive training. Some persons may become satiated and withdraw from the situation and give common responses while others become stimulated and respond with renewed effort and uncommon responses.

Maltzman's theoretical rationale for the effects he found is based on the idea that initial associations to a stimulus list are common associations while later ones are more uncommon and unique. Consequently, requesting subjects to give different responses to a training list would get them to give uncommon responses to a test list. While Maltzman *et al.* have pursued their point of view, an alternative viewpoint by another investigator in this area, Hyman, pursued another hypothesis. This hypothesis does not say anything about the nature of the outcome on a test list after experience in giving different responses to a test list. But it does say that after Maltzman's training procedure subjects should select rather difficult tasks. Maltzman's theoretical orientation says nothing about the nature of the difficulty of the selected task. The results of this study when Hyman compared the level of risk selected by subjects who were trained in Maltzman's procedure, and those selected by a control group, supported his hypothesis.

This type of work and other efforts need to be carried out to help clarify further the nature of effects produced by the Maltzman procedure and other procedures designed to study training. In pursuing such efforts investigators would do well to consult Cramer's (1968) book entitled *Word Association*. In this work she has a number of comments relevant to the work reviewed in this section. For summary purposes we list them here.

(1) When subjects are asked to give different responses to a stimulus list "the complexity of the verbal context" is increased and unless the stimuli are chosen to produce a specific effect "the results of increasing contextual complexity is to decrease response commonality and to increase response variability. Looked at in this way, it is not surprising that the originality-training techniques increase both idiosyncrasy and variability of response [Cramer, 1968, p. 112]."

(2) Effects produced by Maltzman's training procedure may result from interpolated tasks and not from practice in giving different responses.

(3) Training in giving the same response may have a negative effect on the giving of original responses because a set to giving common responses may be established.

(4) Transfer effects may be quite transitory.

(5) A question may be raised when responses obtained to test lists are indeed original. Cramer (1968, p. 113) says, "the best interpretation of the word-association results of originality training studies. . .is that such training increases the number of idiosyncratic responses, which may or may not also be original responses."

(6) Satiation may account for part of the effect produced by Maltzman's originality-training procedure.

(7) And, finally Cramer (1968, p. 114) concludes that caution be exercised in interpreting results in originality-training studies that emphasize giving different responses. Caution is especially necessary if one focuses on "originality" and use of "this term is meant to imply some phenomenon distinct from statistical infrequency."

SUMMARY

Brainstorming is both an individual and group procedure for stimulating creativity. It arose out of dissatisfaction with the results produced by conventional business conferences which suffer from the rigidifying effects of too much evaluation. The goal of brainstorming is to produce a checklist of ideas which may then be evaluated and which may then serve as a source for creative solutions.

This goal may be achieved by following two major principles: *deferment of judgment* and *quantity breeds quality*, and four major rules: (1) *criticism is ruled out*, (2) *freewheeling is welcomed*, (3) *quantity is wanted*, and (4) *combination and improvement are sought*.

Because brainstorming is a cognitive approach based on associationism and because many psychologists have been schooled in this and related matters (conditioning and learning theory) it has been subjected to many more research studies of its assumptions, outcomes, process, and training possibilities than any other technique for stimulating creativity. As we summarize these research findings it is necessary to bear in mind that, as in other areas of psychological research, here too there is the need for replication of the studies and extension of these in such a manner that they will help answer the critical question of what kind of person should use what kind of creative problem-solving procedure with what kind of problem.

The research indicates that deferring judgment, as suggested by the proponents of brainstorming, does result in a larger *number* of ideas than do other procedures that emphasize evaluation. Deferring judgment, however, does not necessarily result in more better quality ideas than a procedure that asks people specifically to produce ideas of quality. Stress on quantity does not produce better *average* quality of response.

One of the reasons why the number of ideas produced with brainstorming is larger than that produced with more evaluative procedures may be that subjects' standards of evaluation are possibly lowered under the brainstorming conditions. It also appears that it may not be as necessary *to defer* judgment as it is to separate idea judgment or idea evaluation from idea generation. One can think up criteria for evaluation and this can *precede* or *follow* the generation of ideas without any negative effects. It is only when idea generation and idea evaluation come together that negative effects are obtained.

Much research effort has been devoted to answering the question whether it is better for individuals to work separately and to have their ideas collated as if they had worked together (therefore they are called "nominal" groups) than it is to have them work together as *real* groups. The results of these efforts indicate that nominal groups do produce more ideas than real groups but that when one turns to the quality of ideas produced (especially, the average quality of ideas) then sometimes the evidence favors nominal and sometimes it favors real groups.

To achieve the advantages of a real group (group-cohesiveness, group morale, etc.) together with the advantage of number of ideas obtained from a nominal group, it may be of help in a practical situation to alter the usual brainstorming procedure to include sequencing. In so doing each individual has a turn to offer his ideas or suggestions. Individuals in the group are not free to respond at will since under such conditions some persons may speak up little or none of the time while others monopolize the brainstorming session.

To this sequencing procedure suggested by Bouchard, one would do well to add a technique called personal analogy which Bouchard borrowed from synectics, another procedure for stimulating creativity described in Chapter XV. In this technique an individual behaves "like" or "acts out" an object or ideas involved in the problem under consideration and so is stimulated to think of a potentially creative solution.

And there is evidence to suggest that preselecting groups so that they consist of individuals who score high on interpersonal effectiveness is also likely to improve the probability of getting better results.

Another approach suggested by Dunnette, which utilizes both individual and group efforts is to limit the use of the group to sharing *information* about the problem and to have the individuals work separately from each other on solutions. When they have completed their efforts their ideas are collated and evaluated.

Studies of the effectiveness of training in brainstorming have occurred primarily in the laboratory where attention has focused on the effects of training persons in the production of different ideas and associations in the the hope that such training will increase the production of uncommon ideas. The results of such research indicates that the effects of such training are most manifest with techniques that are similar to the training materials. Transfer is less effective when the tasks are dissimilar or when they are real-life problems. It has also been suggested that training in giving the same response to a stimulus list of words may also be quite an effective training technique for some persons, however, more research effort on this matter is necessary.

Actually, little if any effort has been expended in the study and evaluation of training in brainstorming alone. Such work has usually occurred when brainstorming has been included in another procedure that has included other techniques to stimulate creativity as in *creative problem-solving*, a procedure described in the next chapter.

With regard to the effectiveness of brainstorming in the production of creative solutions to real-life problems there are numerous testimonials and anecdotal reports attesting to its value and significance, and no reports of its failures which may or may not occur. What is needed is more effort devoted to systematic and careful reporting of the circumstances under which brainstorming is used, how it is used, and how effective it proves to be. Such research, as well as research devoted to replicating studies reported in this chapter and research focusing on the assumptions, processes, and effectiveness with a variety of problems, would go far to helping us further understand and better evaluate brainstorming as a method for stimulating creativity.

By way of concluding this chapter, several comments are in order as to the character of research on brainstorming and as to some ideas about the direction it might take in the future. Our comments are focused on brainstorming with full knowledge that future research is more likely to concern itself with brainstorming as part of some other more encompassing procedure for stimulating creativity rather than with brainstorming by itself. Nevertheless the suggestions we make here about brainstorming very likely also apply to the conduct of research with other creativity-stimulating techniques.

Research on brainstorming has generally involved a test of the hypothesis that deferred judgment will result in more ideas and more better quality ideas than will some other problem-solving technique that obviously involves evaluation and critical judgment. Sometimes experimenters assume they induce the deferred-judgment state by instructing subjects to solve a problem without the use of judgment or in some other way assume that this state has been induced. Another method of choice is to use the more lengthy instructions which involve communicating to the subjects the two principles and four rules. And, by the same token, whatever the technique with which brainstorming is compared, deferred judgment is also assumed to be induced either with some direct instruction to be nonevaluative or something more elaborate.

It is indeed surprising that experimenters, regardless of the results they obtain, seem to believe that subjects who have probably never before used brainstorming in a deliberate manner for creative problem-solving can be induced to do so with either a simple or even with a more elaborate instruction, and, if they are induced to so behave that the induction is "deep enough" so that the subjects, at the time of the experiment, can be regarded as good representatives of the creative problem-solving technique they presumably have used in the experiment. In other words without much, if any, prior experience or training the instructed subjects are regarded as being capable of fulfilling the requirements of the technique they purportedly follow. We are aware of the fact that it is not uncommon that in psychological experiments subjects are regarded as "set" after they have been instructed, but, if they are so set is it permissible to take the next (big) step to say that when they are set they are behaving as the technique demands. For example, in psychoanalysis patients are asked to free associate. At the beginning of the therapeutic experience patients behave as if they are free associating but it takes some time before they really do so.

It would seem that experimenters take too much for granted, or else they believe in the magic of instructions if they regard their instructions as setting their subjects as good representatives of a problem-solving technique. It would seem that the technique is better represented by subjects who are practiced and experienced in using it. This holds for brainstorming, critical problem solving, or whatever. It may be difficult finding and/or training such groups. However, one would have fewer questions than now as to whether a technique is properly represented in an experiment. Whether a trained group is available or not, it is incumbent upon experimenters to provide some evidence that their instructions "have taken." If this cannot be done with some indirect method then a questionnaire may be of value. The questionnaire should elicit from the subjects whether they have indeed followed the instructions and have been involved in the processes they used. If they have done neither or both their data should be excluded from the data analysis.

It seems rather on the naive side to assume that subjects not involved and not trained in a procedure can represent it well. At best the data they yield are minimal data, and this holds whether the focus is on brainstorming, critical problem solving, or what have you.

Just as the representatives (subjects in the experiments) of the problem solving techniques leave much to be desired, the same is true of the problems used in the experiments. The problems, to a large extent, are simple, naive, funny, "real" or "unreal." From some experimenters' points of view they are used "because they have been used before." But because one does not know the characteristics of the problem or because a very limited range of problems is used in any one experiment there is little one can do with the data obtained in any experiment insofar as knowing as to what kinds of future problems to apply any technique. This point has been rather fully discussed in the text and no further elaboration is necessary at this point.

It is unlikely that to any great extent real problems will be used in experiments or that subjects will be permitted to build real models to test their ideas. This might be desirable if one really is interested in studying how creative the produced ideas really are. It is more likely that raters will have to be used to evaluate the ideas produced. If so, it would be well to utilize raters of known characteristics, either in terms of their personality and/or their attitudes toward novelty. Raters, because of their own value systems, do not, as has been indicated in some experiments, all follow the same frame of reference. It is better to specify that frame of reference than to leave it as an unknown. In that manner a better evaluation of the results will be possible.

It would also be of interest to learn what the nature of the results would be if one conducted experiments under conditions where subjects did and did not know the criteria that raters used.

Finally, future research would do well to bring the problem solver back into the problem-solving situation. By and large, most studies have been conducted without any knowledge of the subjects' personality characteristics. A few other studies have pointed out that the effectiveness of a technique may well depend on the characteristics of the subjects involved.

All of these suggestions come to the fore in the chapter on brainstorming because brainstorming, steeped as it is in associationism, has lent itself to more experimentation than other techniques for stimulating creativity. Experimenters have devised numerous experiments on one or more aspects of brainstorming and, in some instances, felt they were talking about the total process. Other complex techniques for stimulating creativity probably do not allow themselves to be so easily fractionated, and consequently, they will not spawn such a proliferation of research.

Therefore, because so much work has taken place with brainstorming we say here, at the risk of being much too repetitious and with full knowledge that it also applies to other techniques for stimulating creativity, that in studying these techniques we need to learn more about which of them will be most effective with what kinds of problems as used by different kinds of persons.

Chapter **XIV**

Creative Problem-Solving

While brainstorming has become one of the best known procedures for stimulating creativity, it is only one of many suggested by Osborn. All of these, plus suggestions of his own, his associates, and others in the field have been organized by Dr. Sidney J. Parnes into a Creative Problem-Solving* training program.

Dr. Parnes is president of the Creative Education Foundation and Professor of Creative Studies at the State University College at Buffalo, New York. He has presented his basic training program in a *Creative Behavior Guidebook*† (Parnes, 1967a) and a *Creative Behavior Workbook* (Parnes, 1967b). These can be used

---

*We feel it is rather unfortunate that the training programs and institutes are known as Creative Problem-Solving Programs and Institutes for there are other programs such as those described in this book that also focus on creative problem solving. The phrase is generally applicable and should not have been appropriated for any one program. Hopefully such usage will not result in confusion or in the belief that only this program provides an opportunity for creative problem solving. It should also be noted that when we use the term generically we do not hyphenate "problem solving." Only when it refers to the name of Parnes' program do we do so since such is his customary usage.

†In addition to containing a description of the training program the *Guidebook* is an excellent source for bibliography and a listing of available audio-visual aids that may be incorporated into any program to stimulate creativity.

by persons working alone, or in a group with the help of an instructor. This basic training program plays a central role in Parnes' college program, entitled the Creative Studies Project, at the State University College at Buffalo. The project is described in a series of four articles in the *Journal of Creative Behavior* (Parnes & Noller, 1972a,b, 1973; Noller & Parnes, 1972). In addition, Parnes' contributions serve as the foundation for *Creative Problem-Solving Institutes* that are held periodically in various parts of the United States. They are described in various brochures announcing when they will take place.

Each of these three programs will be described following presentation of the theoretical rationale underlying them. Should more information be desired than what is presented here or which is already available in other published sources, it may be obtained by writing to: Creative Education Foundation, Inc., State University College at Buffalo, Chase Hall, 1300 Elmwood Avenue, Buffalo, New York, 14222.

THEORY

For Parnes (1967a, p. 36) the creative problem solving process involves "observation," "manipulation," and "evaluation." And creative behavior includes both "uniqueness *and* value in its product [Parnes, 1967a, p.6]." To be creative an individual has to be sensitive to problems around him. As first encountered the problem is a "mess" and must be refined, clarified, and worked on through the following stages—*fact finding, problem finding, idea finding, solution finding*, and *acceptance finding*.

Parnes is quite eclectic in his theoretical approach. In addition to Osborn's (1963) work, he draws upon a variety of work from theorists and writers and selects from their contributions that which will illuminate some aspect of the creative process as he views it. Within this broad theoretical framework, Maslow and Guilford occupy central positions.

Maslow (1954) hypothesized that a person has five basic needs—physiological, safety, love, affection and belongingness, esteem and self-actualization. Theoretically speaking, these needs are arranged hierarchically. Needs lower in the hierarchy have to be satisfied before those above them are satisfied. Satisfaction of the four basic needs therefore precedes self-actualization or self-fulfillment— when an individual can become "everything he is capable of becoming. 'What man *can* be, he *must* be,' says Maslow [Parnes, 1967a, p.4]."

To maximize the development of his potential an individual requires an optimum environment. And so Parnes orients his training program: "To present the best possible environment for the full development of creative potential, to offer a well-balanced, nutritional diet for creative growth...[Parnes, 1967a, p.5]."

While Maslow provided Parnes with the concepts of a need hierarchy and self-actualization, Guilford (1967) provided him with a factor structure of the intellect and numerous tests of cognitive abilities. These are used to study the effects of the parts or of the total creativity training program.

The primary thrust of Parnes' effort is to effect the cognitive characteristics involved in the creative process. He is aware of the role that personality characteristics play in creativity, and he acknowledges the function of nonconscious factors but he does not spend much time focusing directly on these. Rather he assumes that appropriate personality changes will occur primarily as a result of successful experiences with the cognitive aspects of creative problem-solving.

TRAINING PROGRAMS

The training program described by Parnes in his *Guidebook* and *Workbook* is basic to his other programs. To differentiate it from the others it will be referred to as *The Training Program* for purposes of this presentation. It will be described first and then we shall turn to the college project and the regional institutes.

The Training Program

From 1956 to 1963 the material used in the training program was developed, tested, and reused. It was studied and researched to establish the best order of presenting it. In its current form it is so organized that it may be taken by persons working alone or by not more than twenty-five persons in classes led by instructors. Instructor-led classes are regarded as more effective than self-study programs.

The training program as presented in the *Guidebook* consists of sixteen sessions which can be covered in approximately 22-24 class hours or in 3 days. It may be expanded or shortened, and Parnes suggests ways to do either. If the program is shortened then, depending on what is omitted, a student may lose out on one of the four creative problem-solving sessions which constitute an experience cycle provided by the course.

The experience cycle is rather interesting. In each of the sessions that make it up the individual practices the total creative problem-solving process. But the cycle is so arranged that the individual only gradually gets to be on his own. In the first experience-cycle session the student observes the instructor at work. He then works with groups and programmed worksheets. For the third session of the experience cycle he works with one other person and with less-structured and programmed materials. And, finally, the trainee works complete on his own.

The material covered in each training session is presented very carefully and systematically. Together with materials and suggestions to facilitate creativity, the sessions include quotations from creative persons or from research studies of creativity which are designed to inspire and encourage the individual in his creative effort.

The overall goal of the program is to teach individuals to apply "deliberate creative effort." This means that use is made of various methods, including brainstorming or deferred judgment, that have been found useful for creativity. Another goal of the program is to provide training not only for group participants but also for group leaders. The program aims "to help nurture creative ability in an individual as well as to help do so in those he supervises or teaches. It therefore is designed to do much more than to prepare one to lead a brainstorming session; however, those who complete such a program should have the necessary knowledge, skills, and abilities to be effective brainstorming leaders [Parnes, 1972, personal communication]."

Objectives

Within this general orientation the training course aims to help the student become:

1. confident in his ability to be creative deliberately;
2. highly motivated to be creative;
3. open-minded to others' ideas;
4. more curious about life's challenges;
5. more aware of the importance of creativity in all areas in life;
6. more aware of the problems around him and to want to solve and improve them;
7. better at producing ideas of high quality and original ideas that will help solve problems creatively.

Training instructors try to develop a nonevaluative, warm, and optimistic atmosphere in the training program. For his part the student or participant is expected

> to provide the 'internal climate' most conducive to best results. This will involve, on your part, a willingness and commitment to look openmindedly at every phase of the course, as well as a willingness to re-evaluate some of the opinions, attitudes and habits that you have cultivated throughout your life [Parnes, 1967b, p. 2].

Specifics

There are sixteen training sessions and by the time the trainee or participant has completed the first six he has had experience with various methods and techniques designed to increase his sensitivity to problems, and to become more effective in *fact finding, problem finding, idea finding, solution finding,* and *acceptance finding.*

Starting with the seventh session the sessions vary in their emphasis. Sessions 7, 9, 12, and 14 constitute the experience cycle in which, as has already been mentioned, the trainee practices what is known about the creative problem-solving process and gradually moves from the first step in which he observes the instructor to the final step where he works by himself on his own problems.

Interpolated among these four sessions are sessions devoted to further training and practice with techniques that are designed to increase trainees' effectiveness in the different stages of the total problem-solving process. Two sessions are devoted to additional training in sharpening one's powers of observation. Toward this end two methods are presented: (1) the use of the descriptive categories (Session 8) and (2) the use of manipulative categories (Session 10). Session 8 is also designed to help the trainee in *fact finding*, and Session 10 is designed to keep the trainee in *idea finding*.

Session 11 is devoted to the use of evaluative criteria and the value they may have for developing additional ideas. Thus, it also contributes to *solution finding*. And, Session 13 focuses on how to gain acceptance for an idea and how to stimulate creativity in others.

The last two sessions of the training program are devoted to how to make rapid use of what has been learned (Session 15) and a review of the total program (Session 16).

At various parts of the training program participants are encouraged to defer judgment and to strive for quantity of ideas and so receive training in brainstorming. At practically every major point of the creative problem-solving process trainees are also presented with checklists. These checklists contain words or brief phrases which serve as "idea-spurrers" when used alone or in conjunction with already available problems, ideas, or objects.

Another common procedure in the training program is "forced relationships." This procedure has been described previously (cf. Volume I, pages 217-219) and consists in forcing a relationship or in forcing one to come up with an idea that combines two or more available disparate ideas.

With these general statements in mind let us turn to some highlights of each of the individual sessions.

Session 1. At the beginning of the first session participants are introduced to each other and to the idea that *"a problem* (is) *a challenge* [Parnes, 1967a, p. 119]." A person's habits and attitudes may prevent him from seeing problems and challenges. Therefore, this session is devoted to training in *problem sensitivity* or how to become aware of problems that can be worked on creatively.

As an aid in this regard the participant is presented with two lists of words. One list consists of such words as "friends," "family," "neighbors," "church," "house," etc. These words are "stimulators" and associations to them may evoke "challenges" or problems from the participant.

To evoke still more responses the participant makes use of a second list of words. This list contains such words as "improvements," "happiness and comfort," "misunderstandings," "complications," etc. By combining a word from the first list with a word from the second list and by forcing a relationship between the two, still more ideas or "challenges" may occur to the participant. "For example, the word 'house' in the left column, when related to the word 'complications' in the right column, might suggest the challenge, 'How to speed up the amortization of my mortgage' [Parnes, 1967b, p. 4]."

Although this session is devoted to sensing problems and not to the specifics of solving problems, the participant is asked to tell what suggestions he may have for solving any one of the problems he has come up with. And, so, this session comes to a close.

Session 2. The state of affairs at the time the problem is first come upon is a "mess." the problem is "fuzzy" and ill defined. It must undergo a process of problem definition, and the subject is presented in this session with various ways of so doing.

One of these ways is to redefine the problem by asking, "Why?" To clarify a problem and so find the *real* problem the individual has to ask "What is my basic objective,–what am I really trying to accomplish?" This question may lead to a proper definition of the real problem and facilitate finding a solution. The "mess" may also be clarified by breaking it down into its subproblems.

An illustrative example given by Parnes (1967b, p. 124) is that of the speaker who, before giving a talk, noticed that he had no stand for his lecture. The challenge as he saw it was how to get a lectern. He then asked himself why he needed a lectern and concluded that he was uncomfortable unless he had a place for his notes. After arriving at this statement of the problem, the speaker realized he did not have to search for a lectern but could use a basket that was nearby on which he could place his notes and proceed with his lecture.

In addition to asking "why" about the "mess" a second way to redefine the problem according to Parnes is to change the verb in the statement of the problem. Thus the problem as first stated may be how to toast bread? But "to brown and dehydrate" may be substituted for the verb to toast and new and different methods for toasting bread may be found.

A third method recommended by Parnes is to word the problem in such "a way that is conducive to idea-finding [Parnes, 1967b, p. 130]." Thus, if one has problems with a subordinate and asks, "Should I or shouldn't I fire him?", he is confronted with a question that doesn't lead to many ideas. The word "should" is not helpful because the supervisor is obviously not satisfied with either alternative in the question or else he would have already done something about it.

To arrive at a better statement of the problem the individual needs to ask himself why he wants to fire his subordinate? When he answers for example, that the subordinate is not productive, indifferent, etc., he is now working with a better statement of the problem. Also by expanding these statements, for example, by asking himself how the job might be done still better without the specific worker in mind, the trainee has arrived at a still broader statement of the problem. With such a broad statement of the problem at hand the problem solver is now in a better position than he previously was to come up with many more ideas from which he may select the best to help him solve the problem creatively.

Session 3. In this session the participant begins his first contact with deferred judgment or brainstorming. The session starts with a discussion of how our habits dictate stereotypic and rigid responses to situations. Habits lead us to overlook potential novel and creative responses. After exposure to this line of reasoning, trainees participate in several exercises designed to demonstrate and make recognizable the negative effects of habit. With such experiences as a base trainees are told that it is important to make deliberate use of their imagination if they are to overcome these negative effects.

Two exercises are particularly interesting in this regard. One is to think of someone of whom one is fond and then to think of other than habitual ways of demonstrating this fondness. In the second exercise participants are asked if they can think of twenty varieties of birds. As Parnes says, most people would say they cannot think of or recognize this many birds. However, Parnes then goes ahead and lists twenty-five varieties of birds all of which are quite common and all of which are probably recognizable by most people. This second exercise also reveals how our habitual ways of thinking about ourselves or the knowledge we possess can effect our orientation to problems. The exercise reflects the importance of not staying with the first idea that occurs to us and the importance of exerting effort to make manifest our potential for creativity.

The discussion and experience with all these points set the groundwork for presenting trainees with the four brainstorming principles: (1) criticism is ruled out, (2) free-wheeling is welcomed, (3) quantity is wanted, and (4) combination and improvements are sought.

The importance of separating imagination from judgment is stressed and the importance of deferring judgment about ideas generated is emphasized. Trainees practice using the principles on problems of different content as they work in small groups each with its own leader and recording secretary.

In addition, all along the way attention is focused on stimulating trainees' motivational levels. To spur them on to higher levels of aspiration trainees are told how many ideas others have produced at this point in the training program. They are also told how research data support the value of their efforts.

Session 4. In this session trainees are taught another technique for overcoming fixed ways of thinking and for stimulating creativity—forced relationships (cf.

Volume 1, page 217). This technique emphasizes the importance of forcing a relationship or combining two quite unrelated objects or ideas. The resulting relationship or combination may appear quite ridiculous but Parnes cautions it is important to defer judgment, for some of these seemingly ludicrous ideas may lead to or result in valuable creative ideas.

The *Guidebook* (Parnes, 1967a; pp. 159-165) describes several kinds of forced relationships. One of these involves the combination of two objects which on the surface are quite unrelated. To illustrate such usage Parnes (1967a p. 160) combines a *shoe* and a *pillow*. This combination was initiated by the task of trying to find ways of improving shoes. As an individual thinks of the characteristics of a shoe and a pillow it might occur to him that one function of a shoe is "to cushion the feet against the impact of floors or pavement [Parnes, 1967a, p. 160]." Then the individual might wonder about the possibility of walking on pillows.

By combining the idea about cushioning the feet and walking on pillows, Parnes suggests that one could come up with several captions for an advertising campaign for shoes, for example, "like walking on air," "the comfort of walking on feathers," etc.

A second use of forced relationships involves the use of nouns and verbs. The individual may, according to Parnes (1967a, p. 162) start with two nouns—paper and soap. One of them is converted into a verb—soap into soaps. And, a relationship is forced between the noun "paper" and the verb "soaps." The resulting forced relationship or combination is "paper that soaps." This, according to Parnes could then lead to the following useful innovations—paper impregnated with soap for washing and labels made of soap that can easily be removed from jars, etc.

The effective use of forced relationships may frequently depend on how well a person observes everyday objects around him and uses them in various combinations for the problems that confront him. For example, an individual may have the problem of improving an automobile or its parts. Looking at the heels of his shoes he may try to force a relationship between them and his problem and come up with a rubber dashboard.

The importance of carefully observing one's environment and the significance of using all of one's senses are stressed in this and other sessions in the training program.

Session 5. This session focuses on evaluation. Some critics of brainstorming frequently argue that it results in ideas some of which are and some of which are not useful, and furthermore, that ideas generated are not evaluated. This obviously is not true, and one of the facts that attests to the invalidity of such statements is what transpires in this training session.

During this session the trainee is specifically told that there comes a time in the creative problem-solving process when it is important to stop generating ideas, if only temporarily, and to evaluate them. To do so it is important to generate as many evaluative criteria as possible using deferred judgment. The more criteria one has the better off one is because one thereby diminishes the probability of finding something wrong later. Evaluative criteria also help in anticipating the future consequences of the use of creative products. Ideas may then be stimulated to cope with these consequences.

After evaluation criteria have been developed, each idea that has been generated is then evaluated in terms of each of them. A rating of 1 is then assigned to an idea rated "poor" on a criterion, 2 is "fair," and 3 is "good." One may also use letters "G" for "Good," etc. After all ideas are so rated on each of the criteria the ratings for each idea are surveyed. Parnes suggests that for future work it is probably wisest to select those ideas that get most 2's and 3's.

Session 6.   The goal of this session is to learn how to get acceptance for one's solutions. Needless to say, ideas selected to go through this part of the process are still to be regarded with some degree of tentativeness for changes in them can still occur. Therefore, the trainee is cautioned not to feel locked into any one idea and to stubbornly pursue its use without modification. At each step of the creative problem-solving process it may be necessary to generate new ideas and defer judgment.

An aid to finding acceptance for a solution is an "implementation checklist." As recommended by Parnes it consists of the following categories and sample questions:

Acceptance   What advantages does the idea have and how can it be portrayed?
Anticipation   What objections might be raised about the idea and what is the best preparation to answer the criticism?
Assistance   How can other persons be of help in implementing the idea?
Location   What is the best place for putting the idea into operation?
Timing   Is there some specific time that is best for putting the idea into use?
Precautions   How may the selected idea be pretested?

Reviewing the selected idea or ideas with this checklist in mind no doubt raises many possibilities that will likely faciliate its acceptance.

Another recommended checklist for solution acceptance consists of: "*Who, what, where, when, why, how.*"

For example, as pointed out by Parnes (1967b, p. 179), as one considers the use to which an idea may be put he might ask: Who is likely to raise objections to the idea? What will they say? How might it (their objection) be prevented? Where and when might something be done about it? Such key words stimulate questions and help one anticipate "trouble spots."

Still another suggestion for acceptance finding is to use " 'protective' thinking"—to think up ways of protecting one's ideas. After using any or all of these suggestions, the most promising way or ways of implementing the idea is selected and a plan of action is developed.

Throughout this session, as in previous ones, the trainee is cautioned not to jump to conclusions about the value of his ideas. He is cautioned constantly to defer judgment and encouraged to strive for more and more ideas and to force relationships between them.

Session 7. This session is devoted to a demonstration by the instructor of the total creative problem-solving process as covered in the preceding sessions. In this effort the following problem suggested by Osborn is used.

A school bus driver must deliver his passengers to where they are going no matter how badly they behave in contrast to a public bus driver who can always get rid of people creating distrubances. On one such bus a boy started a fight and the whole bus was in an uproar. The driver almost had several accidents. The boy would not stop his bad behavior and when the other children complained, the principal tried to punish him by keeping him at recess. This did not afffect the boy nor did appeals to his parents. The boy, according to the driver, was as bad as ever. The driver was told by the principal that anyone who spanked the boy was liable for legal suit and prosecution.

The question is: What should the bus driver do? The training instructor demonstrates how to answer this question by going through each of the stages of the creative problem-solving process. In so doing he also illustrates techniques to facilitate development of each of the stages. For purposes of our own review let us briefly survey the instructor's demonstration.

The instructor begins by demonstrating a technique for becoming more effective in *fact finding*—the finding out of more information about a problem than one has at the start. The technique consists in dividing a sheet of paper into three equal columns. In the first column the facts one wants are listed in the form of questions so stated that they are oriented to fact finding. They are not judgmental in character. "Should" in a question often reflects a judgmental question. Thus, "What is the cost of a piece of apparatus?" is a fact-finding question. But, "Should I buy this apparatus?" is a judgmental question. The latter can be made into a fact-finding question by asking "When will I need this piece of apparatus?" "What can I use it for?" etc. It is critical to list all questions about the information or facts one wants and not to concern oneself with whether the information will be available.

In the second column all possible sources for the desired information are listed. And then when the information is obtained it is placed in the third column on the same line as the starting question and as a response to it.

To illustrate the use of the three columns in answer to the bus drivers' dilemma, Parnes suggests as one fact-finding question for the first column—Does the boy have personal or family problems? As possible sources of information for the second column parents, teachers, principal, etc. are listed. And finally, to conclude the example the third column contains the statement that when appropriate sources were contacted they revealed that the boy had no serious personal problems.

For the second major stage of the creative problem-solving process, *problem finding*, the fuzziness of the stated problem has to be clarified. Toward this end the trainer illustrates the importance of seeking creative-type questions. These questions focus on subproblems or challenges that are derived from the broader, fuzzy problems. When stated they are in the following forms: "How might I. . .?" "What ways might I. . .?" Again, in the bus driver's situation they are in the forms of: "How might I settle this boy down?" "What might I do to obtain a better understanding of the boy?"

Fact-finding and judicial-type questions should be avoided in this stage. And, if they do occur Parnes recommends restating them as creative-type questions by asking "How might I find out. . .," or "How might I decide. . .?"

When each of these questions are listed the trainee asks "why" of each of them. He asks himself why he wants to do this and why he wants to do that. In response to each question the trainee tries to restate and to broaden the problem and so allow for the largest possible number of alternatives and ideas that may help solve it. As other aids, it is suggested that the trainer try to paraphrase the questions, change the verbs in the questions, etc.

Once again in terms of the bus driver's situation, illustrations of broad questions are: "How might I maintain order on the bus?" "How might I achieve peace on the bus?"

From the list of questions so obtained the trainer selects the question he regards as most promising for creative attack. In so doing he tries to select that question with the largest number of possibilities for later exploration. It may be a statement of the problem that is so broad that it includes a number of the other problems or it may be a narrow statement of the problem that may be at the heart of the matter. In any case, the problem-finding stage is concluded when the trainer selects that problem for further work that he regards as most significant.

The one selected in the bus driver's example is "How might I achieve peace on the bus?"

With a clear and succinct statement of the problem before him the instructor starts to fulfill the third stage of the creative problem-solving process, *idea finding*, through the use of *deferred judgment*. All the ideas so arrived at are listed. Some of these, in cases where the first statement of the problem is very broad, are really statements of subproblems. Each subproblem is then treated separately as if it were a problem in its own right. In other cases one continues to work directly with the list of ideas generated. When it is complete, those ideas in the list which are judged to have "the best potential" are encircled to signify they will be worked on further. Among the ideas generated for the bus driver's problem were: (1) to keep the troublemaker and the other children separated, (2) to have all children decide what to do with troublemakers, and (3) to have the boy causing the trouble serve as a monitor. Of these three, in the example given by Parnes (1967b, p. 43), the first two are encircled indicating their potential for further work.

We come now to the fourth stage—*solution finding*. This is the stage in which criteria are developed to evaluate each of the previously generated ideas regarded as potentially valuable.

The capacity to select proper criteria according to Parnes is a reflection of the problem solver's "sensitivity to problems." That is, it is a reflection of the problem solver's awareness of the "effect, repercussions, (and) consequences" that may occur if the selected idea is utilized.

Once again, use is made of a worksheet divided into two major columns. The first is headed "criteria" and beneath it are separate columns one for each of the suggested criteria. Some of the criteria in the bus driver's situation were: "effect on objective," "effect on boy," and "school policies and laws."

Then each idea is evaluated on each criterion using a rating scale in which "G" is for "good," "F" is for "fair," "P" is for "poor," and "DP" is for "doesn't pertain."

The second major vertical division on the worksheet is utilized for the decision arrived at after studying the evaluations that each idea is given. The titles for each subcolumn could be as indicated in the example given by Parnes (1967b, p. 44) "Use Now," "Hold," "Reject," or "Modify" (below each heading space is allowed for suggested modifications.)

To illustrate the use of the criteria and the worksheet let us return to the bus driver's situation. It will be recalled that two of the ideas selected for further work were: to have the troublemaker and the other children separated, and to have all the children decide what to do with troublemakers.

Three of the suggested criteria were: effect on objective, effect on boy, and effect on children. The first idea was rated fair, poor, and good, respectively, on each of the three criteria. And the decision was to "hold" this idea and then to consider modifying it by establishing a seating plan in which the boy is least likely to get into trouble.

Using the three criteria with the second idea, having all the children participate in arriving at a decision, it was rated good on all three of them. It was therefore decided to use this idea right away and to consider a modification in it. Its modification involved combining this idea with another previously evaluated one (not presented in this discussion) that involved punishment for misbehaving. This resulted in a new idea—to get all the children motivated "to squelch the troublemaker [Parnes, 1967b, p. 44] ."

After evaluating all ideas, those whose ratings and decisions (or modifications) reflected most potential are then concentrated on for the last step of the creative problem-solving process—*acceptance finding*. The one selected from the bus-driver example was how to get the other children to squelch the troublemaker.

As with the other stages of the creative problem-solving process so also for acceptance finding use is made of a worksheet divided into three parts. The first consists of "Ways of implementing, carrying out, accomplishing, gaining acceptance for, insuring effectiveness of, improving, etc. [Parnes, 1967b, p. 45]" the selected idea. Answers to all questions are again arrived at through deferred judgment.

After all implementation ideas are listed, the best ones are selected for further work. This additional work consists of answering the questions "Who, when and/or where?" in the second column and "How and/or why?" (how to get others to accept ideas enthusiastically) in the third column.

Returning to the bus-driver example let us illustrate this part of the procedure with the first of the implementation ideas, to stop the bus when trouble starts and to start up only when things have settled down. In answer to the questions "who and when and/or where," the responses were on returning home, on a hot day, and next to a policeman. For the last column's questions "how," and "why," the responses were without warning and to start suddenly to read a magazine.

The second implementation idea was to have the children come up with an idea for an activity during the bus ride. Responses to the "who and when and/or where" questions were to have a school contest and to conduct a brainstorming session with the children. Finally, for the last column, responses to the "how and/or why" questions, were to have children bring a tape recorder to record ideas or to put up a suggestion box in which to collect students' ideas.

Of the two ideas considered the first, to stop the bus until the trouble stops, was selected for use and according to Parnes it worked well to solve the bus driver's problem. Parnes points out (1967b, p. 45) that in a problem such as the one considered here, which involves a constantly changing human situation, it is best to have several ways of implementing an idea, whereas in a problem involving mechanical objects one way of implementing the solution may be sufficient.

This seventh session is the first of four sessions which together constitute an experience cycle for the participants. In this first session of the cycle, as we have seen, participants observed the instructor at work demonstrating the total creative problem-solving process. In the remaining three sessions of the experience cycle (in sessions 9, 12, and 14) the participant moves from working with groups to working alone on a problem selected by himself.

Session 8. This eighth session is one of four (the others are 10, 11, and 13) sessions interpolated between sessions devoted to the experience cycle for the total creative problem-solving process. Each of these four sessions provides additional suggestions for and practice in becoming more effective in each of the stages of creative problem-solving.

Observation and sensitivity to problems, as well as the characteristics of objects with which one works, are critically involved in the creative problem-solving process. Therefore, training Sessions 8 and 10 are devoted to improving observation and to two techniques that may be helpful in this regard—the use of descriptive and manipulation categories. Thus, the individual gets further help with *fact finding* and *idea finding*. The eleventh training session is devoted to further work with criteria and solution-finding. Then, in the thirteenth session there is still further training in the use of forced relationships for the selling of an idea to others, so the trainee has more work with *acceptance finding*.

Considering the eighth session by itself we find that in it use is made of several visual stimuli that have traditionally been used by psychologists to illustrate various perceptual effects. As used in this training session these stimuli serve as illustrations or as analogies to what goes on in many of one's own experiences in creative problem-solving. And, so, they highlight and provide the trainee with insight into his habitual behavior patterns which could negatively effect his creative behavior.

Among the visual patterns used are those which are known among psychologists as hidden figures, illusions, and reversible figures. The first consists of complicated drawings in which, if he looks carefully at them, one will find figures or shapes that were not visible at first glance. The second pattern, an illusion, is a visual figure which makes us see things that are not there, and, the third, a reversible figure, is one that consists of a drawing which is so constructed that if the viewer concentrates on what is called "the figure" he will see one thing and when he focuses on "the ground" (or background) he will see another.

These three types of visual stimuli serve to illustrate how past experience and perceptual habits block out the full use of the variety of available visual stimuli and limit the range of one's responses. Exercises with different visual stimuli also serve to illustrate these effects and provide an opportunity to practice ways of overcoming them.

The effects of an illusion may be overcome by deferring judgment. The number of perceptions one comes away with from observing an array of hidden figures would be a function, in part, of the effort devoted to searching them out. And, the capacity to reverse figures and the frequency with which one can do this is a function of the flexibility of one's own thought processes.

The visual figures are used not only for their relationship to thought processes but also for their relevance to social relationships. For example, what one sees in a reversible figure depends on whether one focuses on the figure or the ground in the stimulus. This is then used by the trainer to illustrate how the same inter-personal event may be viewed differently by two people involved in it. Each person might focus on a different aspect of the event and so come away from it with a different viewpoint.*

To summarize, at least two points are involved in the use of these visual stimuli. First, as the trainee works with the stimuli he learns how his perceptions are effected not only by the method, time, and place of his observation but also by his purposes, attitudes, and past experiences. He learns the critical function of observation, flexibility in perception, and how his own characteristics as well as those of the visual stimulus effect his perceptions, ideas, and behavior.

In addition to the foregoing, participants are also helped to improve their powers of observation during this training session. For example, they are asked to state the characteristics of a common object such as a pencil. After they have done what they can, they are encouraged to strive for unusual responses and for more responses. To help him in his efforts, the participant is trained in the use of descriptive categories. These are contained in a checklist consisting of the following words: "function, structure, substance, color, shape, texture, odor, sound, taste, magnitude, time, and space." Each word is to serve as an idea-spurrer or stimulus to thinking up more usual and unusual ideas. For situations rather than objects the checklist of idea-spurrers consists of "who, what, where, why, and how."

This eighth training session then tries to help the participant improve in observation and fact-finding ability by making him aware both of the effects of certain of his habits and how these can be overcome through the practice of selected techniques. In this training session an attempt is also made to make the trainee more sensitive to the challenges and problems around him by focusing on their component characteristics.

Session 9. Once again as in Session 7 the trainee practices the total creative problem-solving process using a practice problem. This time, however, the participant works in a small group and experiences what it is like to work with others as he tries to find creative solutions to problems.

Session 10. This is another of the sessions devoted to improving one's skills in another phase of the creative problem-solving process—*idea finding.* While Session 8 was devoted to improving fact finding through the use of a checklist of descriptive categories, this session is devoted to improving idea finding through the use of manipulation categories.

Manipulation categories, according to Parnes (1967a, p. 215) are extensions

---

*In Chapter XVI another training program is presented in which other visual stimuli are used for a variety of other analogies to processes and factors involved in creativity.

of three manipulative verbs—magnify, minify, and rearrange. The idea-spurring questions in the checklist are: "Put to other uses? Adapt? Modify? Magnify? Minify? Substitute? Rearrange? Reverse? and Combine? (Parnes, 1967b, insert)."

Each of these questions may be applied to objects. For example, minifying automobiles could result in building miniature racing cars. They could also be used in forced relationships with other ideas already suggested. For example, if the idea is to use dogs to protect a store against burglars then to use magnification in forced relationship with this idea could result in amplifying the dog's bark. And, finally, the manipulation categories can themselves be combined to spur an idea. For example, minification and rearrangement are manifest in the development of contact lenses. These lenses are made small (minification) and put into a new arrangement by placing them over the eye rather than in frames (rearrangement).

Session 11. This session is devoted to perfecting a participant's skill in the third phase of the creative problem-solving process—*solution finding.* It is divided into two parts with the first focusing on the use of what may initially appear to the trainee to be wild ideas as a means of arriving at creative solutions. The second part is devoted to the use of an evaluative criterion by itself as a stimulus to developing ideas.

The use of manipulative verbs for purposes of idea finding sometimes results in silly or strange ideas. But terms as "silly" and "strange" are evaluational terms. If such judgments are deferred then ideas that result in rather useful solutions may be obtained. For example, as Parnes (1967a, p. 225) points out in his *Workbook* a minified drinking cup may be used as an egg holder or an eye cup. In another example given by Parnes, another suggestion that appeared ridiculous led to a useful solution. This suggestion was to blindfold workers in a manufacturing plant so they would not slow up the work as they read the newspapers in which the manufactured objects were wrapped. Indeed blindfolding the workers was a ridiculous idea but it was the basis for a rather useful idea—to hire blind people to do the packaging.

In this eleventh training session, participants engage in a variety of interesting exercises to improve their creativity. One of these involves making something entertaining for a child from the following materials: a rubber band, two paper reinforcements, a label, a piece of cardboard, two paper clips, and two pipe cleaners. Other exercises involve thinking up ideas for improving a glove and ideas for improving a scarf.

The second half of the eleventh session is devoted to work with criteria. To help in developing various criteria Parnes (1967b, p. 231) suggests responding to the following question, "How to enrich your personal life through greater use of creative imagination?" Responses to this question Parnes suggests would likely be similar to the following checklist of idea-spurring questions [p. 232] for criteria:

(1) Effects on objective? (2) Individuals and/or groups affected? (3) Costs involved? (4) Tangibles involved (materials, equipment, etc.)? (5) Moral or legal implications? (6) Intangibles involved (opinions, attitudes, feelings, aesthetic values, etc.)? (7) New problems caused? (8) Difficulties of implementation and follow-up? (9) Repercussions of failure? (10) Timeliness? etc.

The primary use of criteria is to evaluate ideas and suggestions, but they might also be used as stimuli for additonal ideas. For example, ideas are evaluated by rating them as good, fair, or poor, or 3, 2, 1 on each of the criteria. It could occur that an idea although rated highly on most criteria is, however, rated poorly on one of them. By using what Parnes calls "creative evaluation" the trainee asks himself how his poorly rated idea might be improved so that it will receive a higher rating on the criterion involved. By so doing, another potentially valuable idea may come to light.

Session 12. This is the third of the four sessions in the experience cycle devoted to the practice of the total creative problem-solving process. In this training session participants work alone, as well as in two-man teams and in larger groups. This way they learn something about the advantages and disadvantages of each of the three types of work situations. Within the group situations participants have experience in being leaders, as well as experience in serving as recording secretaries and group members.

During the twelfth session participants are also given the opportunity to experience the effect of incubation. Participants describe a particular challenge or "fuzzy problem" that they have selected for creative attack. The participants then take an overnight break. When they return to the training site the next morning they are asked what ideas if any, have been produced after the period allowed for incubation. If participants wish to change their problem they are permitted to do so. Whatever problem they select, participants then work on it using what they learned about the creative problem-solving process. Should they encounter difficulties the trainer is available for help.

Session 13. This session focuses on helping an individual sharpen his ability with *acceptance finding.* Within this context it provides further training in the use of forced relationships for selling an idea.

The main exercise in this session is one in which participants assume they "*see possibilities* in the *creative problem-solving approaches* (they have learned) and would like to '*sell' the ideas to other persons or groups back home* [Parnes, 1967a, p. 248]." Participants use the checklist consisting of the words "who, what, when, where, why, and how." Assuming that the "who" and "why" are clear the participant is asked to come up with as many ideas as he can for "what," "where and when," and "how." In generating ideas participants defer judgment, listing ideas as they occur. Then within each of the three lists participants circle those they think have greatest potential. An idea is selected from each column and relationships are forced among the three to attain a new idea. This process is repeated for all ideas in the three columns. As Parnes points out (1967a, p. 250) if a trainee generated twenty ideas under each of the three categories ("what," "where and when," and "how") and relationships were forced among them then 8,000 possibilities would be available. Among them there will be some, no doubt, that are not very useful, but there will also be others that provide a good basis for developing further creative plans.

Session 14. This is the last session in the experience cycle for the practice of the creative problem-solving process. The trainee now works on a problem of his own choosing and without guidance. After participants have completed their work they discuss each other's efforts. The training instructor then reviews and summarizes all that has transpired.

Session 15. Trainees, in this session, practice the use of creative problem-solving procedures in the making of rapid, "on the spot" decisions. Several problems that require immediate attention and action are worked on. One of these involves a long and important business letter that is about to be mailed but is soiled accidentally. A rush is on to mail it before the last mail pickup which is due momentarily.

The trainee tries to decide what to do by going through the problem-solving process very rapidly. At each stage of the process, the trainee gives the first response that occurs to him and some few additional ones. He does not strive to think up all possible alternatives as would be the case if he had more time.

Session 16. In this, the last session of the training program, trainees and instructor review the whole program. The instructor answers whatever questions trainees have. He also discusses with them his experiences with other groups. Trainees discuss their experiences in the program and also talk about their future plans.

This then is a condensed version of the sixteen sessions of the creative problem-solving course presented by Parnes in his *Creative Behavior Guidebook* and *Creative Behavior Workbook*. In summary, the individual is provided with a series of individual and group experiences in which he learns various procedures for becoming more effective in creative problem-solving. Featured among these procedures are deferred judgment and brainstorming, various checklists, and the method of forced relationships.

Throughout the training sessions trainees are encouraged to make full use of their creative potential in an environment that is accepting, encouraging, and stimulating.

The Creative Studies Project

The program for training in creative problem-solving just presented is at the basis of Parnes' work in other endeavors. One of these is the Creative Studies Project he directs at the State University College at Buffalo. This is an interdisciplinary training program at the college level based on the research and experiences of Parnes and his associates who are central to the work at the Creative Education Foundation.

This project has several goals: to help college students apply creatively their knowledge of academic subjects; to help them become more creative in the nonacademic areas of their lives, and to improve in personality characteristics, mental abilities, problem-solving behavior, and job performance behavior which are all regarded as significantly related to creativity.

At the time of this writing the project is described in a series of four articles in the *Journal of Creative Behavior* (Parnes & Noller, 1972a, b, 1973; and Noller & Parnes, 1972). A "mini-book" entitled *Toward Supersanity: Channeled Freedom* and supplements have also been announced (Parnes & Noller, 1973). They will be published by D.O.K. Publishers, Inc., 771 East Delavan Avenue, Buffalo, N.Y. 14215. The material to be presented is based on the four articles in the *Journal of Creative Behavior*.

After a year (1969-1970) of pilot study the Creative Studies Project was begun with one-hundred and fifty students in the 1970 entering class at the State University College at Buffalo. Students were divided into groups of fifteen each. The project lasted for 15 weeks over a period of four semesters (two academic years). Classes were held twice a week for a total of 3 hours a week (1 day there were two 1-hour classes and on the other there was only a one class hour).

The curriculum was based on Parnes' *Creative Behavior Guidebook* (Parnes, 1967a) and Parnes' *Creative Behavior Workbook* (Parnes, 1967b). Other books, films, and materials were also utilized. During the first semester some of the content to which the students were exposed included: films to illustrate various aspects of nonverbal awareness, work with puzzles and problems that required new viewpoints for their solution, exercises in developing evaluational criteria, "creative experience in dance," a lab in group interrelationships, exercise in creating things from discarded materials, work in general semantics, exercise in selling an idea, etc.

During the second semester students had experience with: synectics (Gordon, 1971), bionics (Bionics, 1968) work with clay, experience in group and individual problem solving, exercises in creative writing, and various other projects in which students applied what they learned in the Creative Studies Project to their academic courses, to college life, or to life outside of college.

Students also had periodic meetings with instructors during the course of the project, and they participated in determining the levels of accomplishment that had to be achieved for specific grades.

During the two semesters of the second year emphasis was placed on creative leadership. Classes met twice weekly for 75 minutes for each class. Students again worked on various exercises in the *Guidebook* and *Workbook* and discussed and practiced problems in group relations. They also worked on sensory awareness, synectics, their own projects, etc. During the last semester of the second and final year, students among other things had experience in relaxation, sensory experience, and problem solving. The main goal of the second year was to provide students with the opportunity to lead others in the kinds of experiences they themselves had during the first year. For this experience students in the project worked with seventh, ninth, and twelfth graders from The Campus School for one 45-minute period per week.

Curricular plans for the third and fourth years were not completely formulated at the time the Creative Studies Project was started. Such plans were to depend on an evaluation of the programs' first and second years' experience. From available material it appears that these plans were never put into use. Among the projected plans for the third year there were those that involved concentration on college and community matters. Together with appropriate faculty, students were to get involved in experimental classes for practice teaching and leadership. There were also to be experiences in the use of creativity-development activities in traditional teaching programs.

The projected fourth year of the program was to include a teaching internship and research assistantship in creativity-related areas. And, then there were projected plans that involved an additional nine years of graduate study.

The Creative Studies Project is quite diversified in the approaches and materials it covers. It is based on Parnes' *Guidebook* and *Workbook* and is enriched by the inclusion of many varied experiences. Parnes and Noller tell us the elaboration of the specifics of the curriculum will be presented in future publications. At that time we will know much more about what transpired. From what is currently available it is apparent that the offerings were rich and the plans were far-reaching. It appears, however, that the evaluation of the program was not as fulsome as one might have hoped.

The Institutes

A third kind of experience in creative problem solving is the Creative Problem-Solving Institutes. Initially they were conducted only at the State University College at Buffalo. Now a series of regional programs have been developed which cover beginning and comprehensive advanced programs in creative problem-solving. In addition to the Institutes at the State University College at Buffalo there are, at this writing, West Coast, and New England

programs. In 1975 the fee for attending a Creative Problem-Solving Institute was
$225. This covered instruction, textbooks, and learning materials (for use at the
institute and also for those sent to the participant throughout the year). Room
and board were extra. For further information about these Institutes write to:
Creative Education Foundation, Inc., State University College at Buffalo, Chase
Hall, 1300 Elmwood Avenue, Buffalo, New York 14222.

The material presented here was obtained from the brochure announcing
institutes to be held during June, July, and August of 1973. The institutes run
for 6 days starting on Sunday morning and closing after 2:30 p.m. the next
Friday.

One kind of institute is a basic or beginning institute for people who have had
little or no experience in creative problem-solving. This program is described in
the brochure announcing it as a condensed version of the Creative Studies
Project (cf. pages 160-161) and other similar college programs. The goal of the
beginning program is to "assist participants in becoming more aware of their
own creative processes, in nurturing their personal creativity, and in better understanding how they may help to nurture it in others. Participants are encouraged to express creative decisions while processing problems of their own choosing [Nineteenth Annual Creative Problem-Solving Institute and Regional Exten-
tions, 1973, p. 5]."

About two-thirds of the sessions in the beginning program are devoted to the
creative problem-solving course in Parnes' *Guidebook* and *Workbook*. In addition participants may select from four elective areas: (1) creative technique,
(2) leading creative problem-solving sessions, (3) human-potential development,
and (4) introduction to advanced offerings.

The advanced programs are to help participants apply the principles and
procedures of creative problem-solving to their own professional fields. Hopefully participants in the advanced program would return to their jobs with plans
for the application of creative processes to at least one area of their work. By
repeated attendance at various advanced institutes an individual covers a variety
of areas that may be of use to him in his daily work.

There is a whole host of topics available for the advanced institutes. They
include: "organizational innovation," "experiences in heightened awareness and
spontaneity in the creative process," "developments in creative education," etc.
The potential richness of the program is reflected in the variety of tentatively
planned sessions for the 1975 institutes. Among them were: "Creative Engineering Design," "Hints for Adults to Develop Creativity," "How to Sell
Creativity," "Basic Sensitivity Training," "A Glimpse into the 'Psyhic
Dimension,'" etc.

Advisement is available at each of the institutes to help place the participant
into an appropriate study program. There are evening and special sessions. There
is a large faculty available for teaching and guidance. And there is a family

program, costing $125 per person, which is a condensed version of the Institutes' beginning program, that participants' families may attend while they are at the Institute.

It is also possible to receive college credit for participating in an Institute. Details regarding college credit are available from the Creative Education Foundation.

EVALUATION STUDIES

There are studies in the literature evaluating the effects of the training course and the Creative Studies Project, but there are no studies of the Institutes.

Of the Course

Several studies will be presented in this section which some readers might have expected to find in the previous chapter on brainstorming. These studies are presented in the literature as if they concerned themselves solely with the effects of brainstorming. That is, one group of subjects is instructed to work on problems with brainstorming instructions and a control group is not so instructed. However since some of the groups had been through a course in creative problem-solving these studies are regarded as investigations of the effects of brainstorming instructions *with* subjects previously trained in creative problem-solving. Although the experimental setup did not allow the subject to make physical use of checklists and such we cannot be certain just how many of the techniques the subjects learned in training they did actually use. Consequently, we regard these as experimental studies of the effects of brainstorming instructions *with* subjects who did or did not have previous training in creative problem-solving.

Meadow and Parnes (1959) evaluated a 30-hour training course in creative problem-solving. The subjects were fifty-four students who had attended three different sections of a Creative Problem-Solving course at the State University College at Buffalo. All of these experimental subjects were tested before and after training with both ability and personality tests. Differences in their pre- and posttraining test scores were obtained and compared with variations in test scores for two control groups. One control group had ability tests and the other control group had personality tests. Each member of the experimental group was matched with one subject in each of the two control groups for age, sex, and intelligence.

The instructions to the subjects before and after training were simply those associated with the tests. No specific reference was made to brainstorming. The subjects, were told, however, in the posttest session that they were participants in an experiment designed to measure changes that might have occurred in their thought processes.

It was hypothesized that course effects would be manifest in an increase in quantity and quality of ideas as well as changes in three personality variables—need achievement, need dominance, and self-control.

For measures of quantity of ideas the Other Uses Test (only the wirecoat hanger problem) of the AC Test of Creative Ability and Guilford's Plot Titles-Low Test were used. For measures of quality the following tests were used: Unusual Uses, Apparatus Test, the Other Uses Test of the AC Test of Creative Ability, Plot Titles-High, and a specially developed originality measure based on stories to pictures from the Thematic Apperception Test (TAT).

For personality measures the authors used a need achievement measure based on stories from the Thematic Apperception Test (TAT)* and two scales from the California Psychological Inventory (Gough, 1957)—that for need dominance and that for self-control.

The results of the study indicated that students who had been in the Creative Problem-Solving course produced significantly better quality ideas on the Other Uses Test of the AC Test of Creative Ability, the Guilford Plot Titles-High Test and TAT originality scores.

The differences on two tests of quality (Other Uses Test of the AC Test of Creative Ability and Guilford Unusual Uses Tests) need to be regarded cautiously for students who had the Creative Problem-Solving course had practice on the *type* of problem (but not the same problem) included in these tests.

Meadow and Parnes suggest that the significant differences between their experimental and control groups suggests that the former used the methods they learned in the Creative Problem-Solving course even though they were not asked to do so explicitly.

Insofar as measures of the three personality variables (achievement, dominance, and self-control) are concerned, the experimental group scored significantly higher than the control group on only one of them—need dominance of the California Psychological Inventory (Gough, 1957). In line with Gough's (1957) interpretation of the meaning of this scale, it would appear that those students who had the training course became more self-reliant, independent, verbally fluent, aggressive, and confident than did the control group.

Although the experiment just cited produced differences between trained and untrained subjects the results for the number and quality of ideas must be regarded with extreme caution, as was previously pointed out since the experiment was biased in favor of the trained subjects—there were problems used in the training program that were similar to those used to evaluate the program.

*This measure followed that suggested by McClelland *et al*. (1953) and Gough (1957).

Parnes and Meadow were aware of this defect and therefore undertook another study with Reese (Meadow *et al.*, 1959). In this study only trained subjects were used. Implicitly it was assumed that if differences in results were obtained they could not be ascribed to differences in prior training experiences.

Two problems were used in this study and attention focused only on quality of solutions produced. Subjects were asked for their ideas after being given two types of instruction—those that involved deferred judgment and those that contained an explicit request for good quality ideas as well as a penalty for bad quality ideas (and thus sought the actual use of judgment rather than its deferment).

The results of this study indicated that when trained subjects were instructed to use deferred judgment they produced higher quality ideas than when they did not. While the investigators in this study interpret this result as stemming from the freeing of the individual's thought processes through the use of brainstorming instructions, it is also conceivable that trained subjects when told not to use deferred judgment were at a disadvantage. These latter subjects were told during training of the advantages of deferred judgment. In the experiment, however, they were told, in one condition, not to use it. This could have interferred with their spontaneous behavior and produced negative effects. The discrepancy between training and instruction could also have diverted subjects' energies to suppressing something they wanted to do and which they were taught to do but which now they were not permitted to do.

Furthermore, trained subjects might well be emotionally invested in believing that deferred judgment is better than evaluated judgment. In the latter condition they might not have been very motivated to do their best. Therefore the non-brainstorming condition did not fare so well.

There is still a third study by Parnes and Meadow (1959) that evaluated the effects of training in creative problem-solving as well as the effects of using deferred judgment. In this study both trained and untrained subjects participated. The results were that more good quality ideas were produced when subjects were instructed to use deferred judgment than when they were instructed to use evaluative judgments. Furthermore, trained subjects, with the deferred judgment instructions, produced significantly more quality ideas than untrained subjects with the same instructions. On the basis of this finding as well as other data cited in the published study the experimenters claim that the "brainstorming instruction is an effective method for increasing the production of good ideas in a particular type of creative thinking problem, and that it is even more effective if preceded by extensive training in its use [Parnes & Meadow, 1959, p. 175]." This conclusion is not well based for this study is still subject to the same defects as the Meadow and Parnes (1959) study. Subjects with training in this study had worked on problems that were similar to those used to evaluate the course.

In the three studies by Parnes and his associates just reported the factor on which attention was focused was the use of deferred judgment by persons trained in creative problem-solving. However, as we have seen in the description of the training program, deferred judgment is only one, albeit a very important one, of the techniques that trainees are taught to use to be creative. It does not constitute the whole program. It would, therefore, be of value to have some evaluation of the other parts of the training program. Toward this end it would be interesting to compare quantity and quality of ideas produced by two groups of subjects both of whom work on problems with brainstorming or other instructions—but one group would be trained only in brainstorming and the other would have participated in a total creative problem-solving program. It might also be of interest in this experiment to compare the products of both these groups with one trained only in use of evaluative thinking or critical problem solving.

Parnes, together with Meadow (1960), focused their attention not only on the use of brainstorming instructions and deferred judgment with trained and untrained groups but also on how long the effects of a one-semester course in creative problem-solving last. As it turns out, not all the twenty-four subjects in this experiment took the same training course at the same time. The number of years that elapsed since training was variable. For ten subjects it was eight months; for fifteen subjects, one to two years; for four subjects, two to three years; and for three subjects, three to four years.

At the time this study was undertaken, nine of the subjects had registered for an advanced course in Creative Problem-Solving and fifteen had not. The scores of the nine and fifteen on the tests were not significantly different from each other and therefore one group of twenty-four was established.

Two control groups of twenty-four subjects each were selected from a group who were registered for, but had not yet taken an elementary Creative Problem-Solving course. Each control group person was matched with an experimental group person for intelligence as measured by the vocabulary scale of the Wechsler Adult Intelligence Scale.

Six of the test measures that were used by Meadow and Parnes (1959) were also used in this study (Parnes & Meadow, 1960). They were: the coat hanger problem of the AC Test of Creative Ability scored both for quantity and quality. The Guilford Plot Titles-Low Test scored only for quantity. Additional tests scored only for quality were: Guilford's Apparatus Test, Guilford's Plot Titles-High, and Unusual Uses Tests.

The results of this study were that the experimental group scored significantly higher than one of the control groups on all six tests and in four of the six it was significantly higher than the other control group. On balance then, it appears that the effects of training in creative problem-solving do last. The factors contributing to these effects would be more clear if data were available on whether the experimental subjects had used what they learned in the time that elapsed since they had had their training. It could well be that some of the obtained effects could be attributed to just amount of experience with problems.

One question about the effectiveness of all types of creativity training programs is whether they are effective for all kinds of problems or whether they are limited only to certain kinds. Collating the evidence available in the studies previously discussed we find that the coat hanger problem of the AC Test of Creative Ability (scored for quality and quantity) differentiates significantly between trained and untrained groups across the board. The Guilford Plot Title-Low, scored for quantity also produces consistent results. But Guilford's Apparatus Test, Unusual Uses Test, and Plot Titles-High Test do not produce consistent results.

Just why certain tests do produce consistent results and others do not is not clear from the studies cited. Hopefully future studies will elucidate on this problem.

In summary then studies of the effectiveness of the training program in creative problem-solving appear to provide evidence that when trained subjects are given instructions to defer judgment in working on a problem that they do better than other subjects with the same instruction but who are not trained. Trained subjects also seem to be more dominant after training than they were before training. Also, effects of training seem to persist. However, all these studies need to be replicated, and special attention should be paid to the degree of similarity between problems used to study effectiveness of training and problems used in the training program. In the studies reviewed some of the effects favoring trained subjects could be attributed to the similarity in problems used.

In future research it would also be desirable if the experimental design used to evaluate the effectiveness of training in creative problem-solving included the study of techniques other than brainstorming which are also part of the training program. It would also be wise to consider the amount of practice or use an individual has made of training in evaluating the persistence of training effects. Finally, it is to be hoped that the training course will be studied to determine whether it is equally effective with all kinds of problems or whether its effectiveness is more limited in scope. At present there is little data on this.

Of the Creative Studies Project

Turning now to the evaluation of the Creative Studies Project it should be said at the outset that our knowledge is limited to the information presented by Parnes and Noller (1972b, 1973). A more detailed account in a "mini-book" and supplements, have been announced (Parnes & Noller, 1973) which, no doubt, will contain much more material than we have available at the time of this writing.

Various data were collected to evaluate the Creative Studies Project. This project, it will be recalled, lasted for a period of 2 years. Evaluational data consist of data on student enrollment, the judgment of the college administration, the results of psychological tests, and an opinion questionnaire administered to the students.

Considering student enrollment we find that 60% of those who started the program completed the first year and 25% of those who started the program completed both years. It is rather difficult to evaluate this datum. This is a unique course and there is no information on what might have occurred in similar courses for a college population with which comparisons could be made. Furthermore, numerous factors might effect student enrollment which could be other than the quality of the course itself.

The article by Parnes and Noller (1973) contains a description of some of the characteristics of students who dropped out of the program. On the basis of Parnes and Nollers' discussion and our own evaluation of these considerations, there is the strong possibility that many students registering for the course were not prepared for the rigors and discipline involved in a program to stimulate creativity. Many individuals think of such programs as opportunities to "open up" and "let loose." They give little consideration to the effort involved in generating ideas. They think little of the discipline involved in evaluating and testing ideas and the frustration tolerance necessary during the acceptance and other stages of the creative process. These "demands" of the creative process are given relatively little publicity, and students who are attracted to "creativity" out of some romantic notions let themselves in for a fair amount of disappointment. Consequently, it is not surprising that there should be some sort of drop-out rate. It could be that the obtained figure is higher than desired or expected. Only when the more complete report of the project is available will we know how to better evaluate this datum about student enrollment. At the moment, while we mull over these considerations, let us keep in mind that in addition to overall enrollment figures Parnes and Noller (1973) also report that several students who completed the two-year program continued their interests in independent advanced study.

The second evaluational datum available is the decision of the administration of the State University College at Buffalo. Projected plans for the Creative Studies Project included not only the two-year program but also opportunities for a third and fourth year and a graduate program. This might have been a bit optimistic since what the administration decided upon and what is now avaialble is a two-year program, four semesters, of elective courses.

Once again, it is difficult to evaluate this outcome until the more complete work describing the program is available.

Turning to the results of the mental ability tests administered to the students, Parnes and Noller (1972b, pp. 164-165) report the following:

(1) Compared to data obtained from a group of control students, i.e., students who did not participate in the Creative Studies Project, those that did showed significantly greater improvement after participating in the project by scoring higher on "real-life" situational tests including the production of ideas, their development, and evaluation. (2) Students who participated in the Creative Studies Project (experimental students) did better than a control group in applying their creative abilities in special tests given in English courses. (3) The experimental students outperformed control students in those of Guilford's cognitive tests used to measure divergent and convergent thinking. However, there were no statistically significant differences between the two groups in Guilford's test measures of symbolic and figural factors nor in his tests of memory or evaluation.

Reports obtained from students also contain results favorable to the Creative Studies Project. Students who participated in the project reported " 'large gains' " in their productive and creative behavior and regarded the course as helpful to their work in other courses and in their daily lives. A significantly larger percentage of students in the second year of the program than in the first reported that they were better able to cope with problems and to actively participate in their class discussions. Also, although not statistically significant, data reported by students participating in the project showed a growing trend to greater productivity in nonacademic areas that called for creativity than was true of those students who did not participate in the project.

Finally, Parnes and Noller (1973) also report results of personality data collected. To collect these data the following tests were used: the Stony Brook Coping Problems test (Goldfried and D'Zurilla, 1972), the Adjective Check List (Gough and Heilbrun, 1965), the Alpha Biographical Inventory (IBRIC, 1968), the Myers-Briggs Type Indicator (Myers, 1962), the Minnesota Multiphasic Inventory (Hathaway & McKinely, 1951), the Strong Vocational Interest Blank (Strong, 1943), and attitudinal questionnaires that were specially prepared for the experimental subjects.

No statistically significant differences were obtained between personality data collected from those who did and those who did not participate in the Creative Studies Project. However, "more positive movements [Parnes & Noller, 1973, p. 29]" were shown by those who did participate in the program.

It is unfortunate that the California Psychological Inventory was not used in this program. It will be recalled (page 164) that it was used by Meadow and Parnes (1959) in their study of the Training Program and they found that the need-dominance measure of the CPI did increase significantly as a result of participating in a 30-hour course. Either the need-dominance measure is particularly sensitive to picking up effects of training in creative problem-solving or it was just a chance result in the first study. Another alternative is that need dominance was actually a manifestation of a change in verbal fluency since Gough (1957) reports that his measures of dominance are related to verbal fluency, and this study of the effects of a two-year program also reports effects on verbal tests but not on personality tests. It might have been clearer which of these alternatives was correct if the CPI had been used in the two-year study.

In summarizing the data evaluating the two-year Creative Studies Project it appears that it results in changes in tests of cognitive abilities but not in tests of personality characteristics. Positive effects on students participating in the program were also manifest in their work in academic and nonacademic areas. While only 25% of the students who started the program lasted through the two-year period of the project, and while projected plans for larger courses of study were not fulfilled it is difficult to evaluate these two bits of data properly, and one must wait the more lengthy report on the project which is forthcoming. From what is available the program appears promising.

SUMMARY

Creative Problem-Solving is a program for stimulating creativity based on Osborn's formulations and suggestions. It assigns a central role to deferred judgment and brainstorming and concentrates on the use of checklists and forced relationships. Parnes, who has been most central to the development of Creative Problem-Solving also uses it as the basis for college courses and regional institutes. It is specifically designed to help stimulate creativity. These programs are quite eclectic including a wide variety of procedures and techniques not originally suggested by Osborn but which have been developed by others and found useful for stimulating creativity.

Studies evaluating Creative Problem-Solving are limited to the efforts of Parnes and his co-workers. Some of these studies are restricted to the effectiveness of the use of the instruction to defer judgment by people trained and untrained in Creative Problem-Solving. The studies show that the former do better than the latter in the quality and, at times, in the number of ideas produced. However, these studies need to be replicated. It would be especially desirable if they would be so designed as not to favor trained individuals who had practice with problems also used to evaluate effects of training. It would also be desirable if these studies took into account the amount of use individuals made of their training in evaluating how long training effects last. And, then too, it would be desirable if these studies did not limit themselves to focusing on the use of brainstorming or deferred judgment instructions but broadened their scope to evaluate the usefulness of the other procedures and techniques used also in creative problem-solving.

Parnes' work is the basis for regional Institutes in Creative Problem-Solving and the more eclectic Creative Studies Projects. The latter was studied at the State University at Buffalo for a two-year period and is currently available in a series of electives. It appears to have many interesting features. There are no published reports of the systematic study of the effects of the Institutes and further consideration of the effects of the promising Creative Studies Projects awaits the publication of a more complete report by the project's directors.

Chapter XV

Synectics

Synectics, "the joining together of different and apparently irrelevant elements," originated with Gordon (1961). It is based on the use of metaphors and analogies within a systematic framework to achieve creative results. It is central to synectics that we can attain better comprehension of a problem that is strange or unfamiliar to us by thinking of an analogy or metaphor that makes it more familiar and hence more amenable to a creative solution. On the other hand, there are problems with which we have difficulty because we are too familiar with them. We feel we are "too close" to them. We cannot see the forest for the trees. Under these circumstances, once again an appropriate metaphor or analogy provides us with necessary distance so that we can get a better view of the problem and move on to a creative solution.

In synectics, then, the problem as one is presented with it initially has to be restated and looked at in various ways through the use of metaphors or analogies. During the course of this process the individual goes on what synectics people call an "excursion" and as a result of such a trip creative solutions are attained. Just how different kinds of analogies and metaphors may be used, what the purpose and function of an excursion is, and related matters are all part of synectics training.

Synectics began about 1944 when Gordon undertook an intensive study of individual and group processes in creativity. This was followed with systematic exploration of his ideas in 1948 with a group of artists in what Gordon refers to as the Rock Pool Experiment. Gordon later formed a subgroup within the consulting firm of Arthur D. Little & Co., and went on to set up synectics groups in several companies. He left Arthur D. Little in 1960, and together with G. M. Prince, whom he had met there in 1958, set up Synectics, Inc. in Cambridge, Massachusetts, to provide training facilities and training personnel for those interested in learning his technique to stimulate creativity. He then left Synectics, Inc. to start another organization, Synectics Education Systems (SES), which "is involved with all forms of problem-solving and education based on the metaphorical approach [Gordon, 1972]." Synectics Education Systems works both with groups and individuals. It is not limited to groups "because such learning experience makes people group-bound and unable to function alone [Gordon, 1972, personal communication]."

Synectics, Inc. is presently headed by George M. Prince, a former advertising and marketing executive who had been experimenting since 1951 on how new ideas could be generated.

Gordon's views of the creative process and how to stimulate it are set forth in his first book, *Synectics* (Gordon, 1961). This book contains the basic information on what Gordon called psychological states and the operational mechanisms, both of which will be discussed at greater length. *Synectics* also contains descriptions of how synectics has been used systematically in various situations, as well as Gordon's thoughts on how a synectics group might be set up within an industrial organization. Gordon's later book, *The Metaphorical Way* (Gordon, 1971, but first published in 1966), is devoted to the central concept in his system—the metaphor. He discusses its use in education, learning, the inventive process, and psychological processes. *The Metaphorical Way* also contains an interesting section on the variations in the use of the metaphor in synectics in which Gordon also brings synectics up to date from his point of view.* Gordon's primary involvement, therefore, is with what he calls the operational mechanisms—what we would regard as the mental procedures and techniques for unlocking the psychological processes involved in creativity.

Although Prince also makes use of metaphor in his work, his major interest is in how group processes can be used to stimulate more creative contributions. His

---

The Metaphorical Way is sold by SES for $5.00 without supplements. If supplements are desired the cost is $12.50. At present two supplements are available: Supplement No. 1, *What Color Is Sleep*, and Supplement No. 2, a new workbook, *Strange and Familiar*. Other publications available from SES for training purposes are presented on page 177. Unless otherwise indicated the books and materials are available from Synectics Education Systems, 121 Brattle Street, Cambridge, Massachusetts 02138. Before purchases are made, prices should be checked with SES. SES will send those who desire it a catalog of its publications free of charge.

book, *The Practice of Creativity* (Prince, 1970a), contains new insights into the procedures for stimulating creativity, and elaborations and extensions of previous ideas, as well as some excellent discussions about the dynamics of meetings, the roles of the leader, participant, and client-expert. Of special value are transcripts of actual synectics sessions with Prince's comments on them. All of this is well subsumed under the subtitle of his book, *A Manual for Dynamic Group Problem Solving.* The Gordon (1961, 1971) and Prince (1970a) books are the primary sources for what follows.

The terminology used in synectics has undergone various changes over time. Some of this has come about simply because synectics is a developing system. But there is another factor. Although there is a good deal of overlap of terms and concepts used by Gordon and Prince, they have also separated and established their unique emphases. The disparate terminology that has resulted makes it somewhat difficult to present a very precise and accurate statement that would satisfy Gordon, Prince, the reader, and the author. To cope with this dilemma it must be explicitly stated at this point that we assume responsibility for indicating similarities and differences between the two approaches. This will be most apparent when we discuss the different kinds of metaphors where, on several occasions, we have grouped several kinds of metaphors together. We are fully aware that there may be differences in nuance, although we tried to avoid such differences even on broader matters. If we have not succeeded, we hope that the fine points will become more clear to the reader with further study of Gordon's and Prince's work.

SYNECTICS, INC. TRAINING PROGRAMS

Synectics, Inc.* currently provides the following services [Synectics (no date)], some of which will be discussed later:

1. New Product Service

Synectics, Inc. will take responsibility for putting new concepts into practice.

2. Synectics Problem Laboratory

This is a "closed" or confidential laboratory organized for a client's specific needs. Essentially, a client puts forth a problem in the hope of finding one or more solutions that may be used or tested further. Involved in such a lab are Synectics staff members as well as experts from the client's staff who have information relevant to the problem. A Problem Lab generally consists of three

*Synectics, Inc., 28 Church Street, Cambridge, Massachusetts 02138.

phases: about ½ day for preplanning, 3 days for problem solving, and ½ day for a postlab meeting. The lab is held in Cambridge and the cost is in the neighborhood of $1700 per day (Prince, 1970b).*

3. Synectics Training Courses

A. Synectics Creative Problem Solving Course

This is the primary course for training in synectics. It lasts for 5 days and costs $700 per person. In "open sessions" which include individuals from different organizations, each participant is asked to bring with him a current company problem of which he is knowledgeable. These problems are used for training. In "closed sessions," limited to members of a single organization, confidential exploration of the client company's problems is carried out.

B. Workshop

The purpose of the workshop is to provide participants with direct experience in the use of synectics processes, training, and research. It consists of two phases. Phase I is a 3½ hour session devoted to an analysis of problem-solving meetings as well as an analysis of a videotape of the group's behavior. Phase II includes a presentation and discussion of the major elements of synectics together with some sessions devoted to practice in their use.

The workshop is conducted on the client's grounds. Although the synectics staff has worked with one synectics trainer to 16 participants, it prefers working with a ratio of 8 participants to 1 trainer.

The cost for the first phase of the workshop is a minimum of $500 for one trainer/leader. The cost for a full day, including Phase II, is $800.

C. Teambuilding

This course (Synectics, 1971) consists of nine 3-hour units. It is designed for top level managers and executives and their immediate groups. Before starting the course, the group may take advantage of a 3-hour diagnostic teamwork evaluation in which the manager and no fewer than 4 nor more than 7 individuals participate. In addition to the participants, the only other physical requirements are two easel pads and closed circuit television. During the course of the 3 hours, the Synectics staff conducts an experiment which they believe has diagnostic significance for the manager and his team. The participants may stop at the end of his diagnostic session and retain and use what they have learned or they can proceed with the rest of the course.

Two to 4 weeks after this first unit is completed, units 2 through 7 are begun

---

*This fee is based on data available in 1971. All fees and costs should be checked before applying for any service described here.

and held at the offices of Synectics, Inc. for a 3-day period. The last two units of the course are conducted at the client's location about 1 to 3 months after the completion of unit 7. During the last 2 units participants are helped to adapt what they have learned to their own situation.

If the first diagnostic unit is conducted at the client's location the cost is $750 plus expenses and if it is conducted in Cambridge, Massachusetts, the fee is $500. If video equipment has to be supplied by Synectics, Inc. at the client's location the cost is an additional $200. The fee for units 2 through 9 is $4750 for up to 8 participants. Charges for the initial diagnostic unit are credited to this fee.

During the teambuilding course, real problems confronting the client are worked on. Work accomplished on these problems is used as a measure of how well the group is progressing toward the goal of the course. The course has four objectives: (1) to solve the problems brought to the course; (2) to make salient the strengths of each participant and to help participants and the group make use of these strengths; (3) to provide further training in procedures and skills, so that participants can make fuller use of their creative potential; and (4) to obtain further understanding of how to use self-observation as a means of further development.

The group's interactions are videotaped at each session, and then examined and interpreted by the Synectics staff members. Thus, information accumulates on the dynamics involved in the group—teamwork and problem-solving ability. Experience in the group and comments about individuals' behavior that have been taped provide the participants with basic skills and knowledge. With continued practice both the group as a whole and the individual participants become more expert in teambuilding and problem solving.

In addition to the foregoing, the Synectics staff can provide edited versions of the videotapes, which then can be used as model tapes by the managers for teaching purposes. There is an extra charge for the edited model tapes.

D. Synectics Advanced Applications Course

This course is limited to persons who have graduated (January 1969 to present) from the Synectics Creative Problem Solving Course (cf. page 175) or its equivalent. Those whose experience with the contents of this course is prior to 1969 can take a one day review session to qualify for the advanced course discussed here.

The advanced applications course is divided into two phases. Phase I lasts for 4 days and consists of synectics review and practice sessions as well as training in the application of synectics techniques to real problems. Sessions are conducted in teams of 5 participants under the guidance and supervision of Synectics staff members. There is also opportunity for intensive personal coaching.

The cost for Phase I is $500 per person. If one continues the optional 2 days of Phase II the total cost (for both Phase I and Phase II) is $750 per person.

For the first day of Phase II, participants decide their own plan of action and use the Synectics, Inc. staff as resource personnel. The second day of Phase II is devoted to the application of synectics to rather difficult problems.

4. Special Training Services

In addition to the Synectics offerings already outlined, some special services are available, such as a training and problem-solving program for retail employees; self-instructional programs; training in leadership for educational seminars; and training in synectics for use with high-conflict groups—political, labor-management, inner city, etc.

5. Other Materials and Services

Synectics, Inc. also makes available demonstration materials for graduates of training courses; a college counseling service that teaches the use of synectics for more effective learning in problem-solving courses; and a speaker's service, generally involving the demonstration of synectics procedures. Staff members can work with executives and managers on the conduct of meetings.

SYNECTICS EDUCATION SYSTEMS TRAINING PROGRAMS

Synectics Education Systems (SES) provides the following services from which its emphasis on the individual is apparent.

IA. The Basic Course—Invention-Problem-Solving

This is a programmed course for the individual to take at home. It is a practical sequel to the theoretical material in the book, *Synectics* (Gordon, 1961). The cost is $29.50 per course.

IB. The Basic Course—Special

This contains the same material included in the basic course, but also includes special problems that should be of interest to the client. The cost is $50.00.

II. The Basic Course with Monitoring Service

This includes the special basic course but in addition the client may send his written exercises to SES for criticism. The cost is $300.00 per course.

III. The Monitored Course with Follow-Up Service

This group course includes the basic course with monitoring plus one of two follow-up activities: (1) When a client group containing 10 or more participants returns the first written exercise to SES for criticism it will be visited by the senior training officer who will conduct the whole synectics process with the group. After the sixth written exercise has been sent to SES, the senior training officer makes two other 2-day visits to the client's group. The cost for this is $375.00 per course plus expenses. (2) Clients can visit the SES laboratories in Cambridge for further training and consultation. This alternative is available after the client's group has completed its written course. The cost for this course is $350.00.

IV. The Intensive Problem Solving Workshop

These courses are developed for special groups. Costs are negotiated.

A *Sensitivity Course* and a *Communications Course* are in preparation.

For teachers and for educational purposes SES has the following courses.

1. Teacher-Training Course

A teacher working by himself can go through a programmed course entitled *Teaching Is Learning to Listen* that introduces him to the theory and practice which form the basis of synectics teaching techniques and learning materials. The cost of this course is $29.50.

There is also a *Teacher-Training Course—Special* which includes the material just described plus special practice problems suited to the individual teacher's area of interest. With large groups there are follow-up visits. The cost of this course is $50.00.

2. Sample Exercises

Synectics Education Systems has developed programmed written exercises in the fields of general science, systems/unified learning, social studies, creative thinking, and vocational/shop for use by the teacher in the classroom. These programmed exercises are designed to be carried out in less than the usual class hour. The teacher acts as a consultant. The following sample exercises are available.

(a) *Facts and Guesses* in the general science area for grades 3 through 9. These exercises are designed to help students get beneath the surface of what they learned in class by helping them develop their own personal metaphors for the scientific principles they were taught.

(b) *The Art of the Possible* in the social science area for grades 7 through 10. These exercises help the student concretize the abstract ideas he has heard in the social science class. The student is invited to speculate about the origin of human feelings and how complex objects were invented.

(c) *Making It Whole* in the area of systems/unified learning for grades 4 through 10. The exercises here are designed to demonstrate to the student how material covered in one subject may be understood with the metaphors and analogies of another subject. In this manner the different subjects are moved closer to integration.

(d) *Invent-O-Rama* for shop-invention for grades 4 through 12. These exercises are designed to replace the ubiquitous ash tray in shop work. Students are led through the steps of conceiving of an idea for an innovation (e.g., a safety-pin) and then they make a model of it in the shop. Students are also taught how to make use of teachers as consultants when they need help.

3. Workbooks

(a) *Strange and Familiar* for training in creative thinking for children in kindergarten through 10th grade. Five dollars for a single workbook.

(b) *Making It Strange* for training in the language arts. Five dollars for a single workbook.

4. Customized Materials

Synectics Education Systems will develop special texts and programmed materials, as requested. Costs are negotiated.

SYNECTICS IN COMPARISON WITH OTHER GROUP TECHNIQUES

In common with others who have used group techniques for stimulating creativity, the synectics people believe that the group process in creativity is analogous to the individual process; that the creative process can be understood, described, and taught; and that individuals can increase their creativity if they understand and use the process. They also believe that creativity in the arts is analogous to creativity in the sciences and that emotional and intellectual, rational and nonrational components are involved in creativity. One of the differences between Gordon and Prince concerns the relative emphases they place on, for example, the rational and nonrational components of creativity. Gordon* believes that in the creative process the emotional is more important

---

*Gordon's emphasis is much more apparent in his first book (1961) than in his second (1971).

than the intellectual, and the nonrational more important than the rational; therefore, if creativity is to be increased, the emotional and nonrational elements must be understood. For Prince, however, the emotional is as important as the intellectual and the nonrational as important as the rational.

Metaphors

Awareness of the importance of nonrational processes and the attempt to engage them through the purposeful use of metaphors probably reflects the uniqueness of the synectics approach. Many individuals have theorized about the roles of the preconscious and unconscious in the creative process, but no one has so systematically tried to engage these sources of creative possibilities as have the synectics people. However, rational and logical processes are also used in synectics. They too are valued, encouraged, and enhanced in a group atmosphere that is free, easy-going, and accepting. Furthermore, regardless of the emphasis placed on nonrational factors, the whole synectics process occurs within a framework that has very practical goals.

There are many factors that shaped the processes used in synectics. Gordon's and Prince's reading, thinking, and theorizing, as well as their observations of the problem-solving behavior of the groups with which they worked were no doubt very important considerations. Gordon (1971) cites several instances from pure and applied sciences where he believes metaphorical thinking played a critical role. Commenting about his own thought processes, Einstein is said to have reported that he used visual and muscular "signs" and "images." The Wright brothers based their work on turning and stabilizing the airplane on observations of buzzards keeping their balance in flight. James Clerk Maxwell is said to have used balls and cylinders in working out his electromagnetic wave theory. Darwin's work was based on several earlier developments; one was Lyell's demonstration of the earth's age and his refutation of the notion of catastrophic extinction of animals. Lamarck described evolutionary continuity. What Darwin lacked for his theory was how animal adaptations occurred. Gordon reports that Darwin based his work on the efforts of husbandrymen who could selectively breed animals to make them more valuable. Thus, he developed the thesis that there was a naturally occurring selection process among wild animals similar to that used by husbandrymen with domesticated animals.

Laplace is also mentioned by Gordon for his use of the self-healing process of the body in the development of his theory that the status of the solar system is continually restored despite derangements that are radical and temporary.

Schrödinger talked about living organisms sucking in negative entropy when eating and breathing, for his critique of the second law of thermodynamics. Brunel developed the concept of the caisson on the basis of observations of the boring capacity of the toredo, a shipworm.

Bell used the function of the inner ear bones as one of the bases on which he built the telephone receiver; and Kekulé, imagining a snake swallowing its tail, thought of carbon atoms in a ring rather than in a linear chain. Pasteur used the analogy of "safe attack" for his work on hydrophobia, and Cajal the analogy of "protoplasmic kiss" for his work on the manner in which nerves transmit impulses.

An Early Synectics Group

Another important factor in the development of synectics was the number of years in which Gordon worked very closely with a group of six men who came from diverse fields—physics, mechanics, biology, geology, marketing, and chemistry. The values of the group, the nature of their interaction, the regard they had for each other, and the confidence they had in synectics facilitated their efforts to remove inhibitions and restrictions that might have interfered with the utilization of thoughts and feelings that need to be expressed if the creative process is to be carried out successfully.

In order to illustrate the characteristics of this group and provide some sense of what can occur in a synectics session, let us quote from Gordon's own work with this group. Here, they were working on a vapor-proof *closure* for space suits. Some of the operational mechanisms for stimulating creativity will be introduced in what follows. They are presented in parentheses at appropriate places.

The approach to the problem started with the question, "How do we in our wildest fantasies desire the closure to operate?" [Gordon, 1961, pp. 49-51] and this is an excerpt of what followed (G is the leader):

> **G:** Okay. That's over. Now what we need here is a crazy way to look at this mess. A real insane viewpoint . . . a whole new room with a viewpoint!
>
> **T:** Let's imagine you could will the suit closed . . . and it would do just as you wanted by wishing . . . (Fantasy Analogy mechanism).
>
> **G:** "Wishing will make it so . . . "
>
> **F:** Shh, Okay. Wish fulfillment. Childhood dream . . . you wish it closed, and invisible microbes, working for you, cross hands across the opening and *pull* it tight. . . .
>
> **B:** A zipper is kind of a mechanical bug. (Direct Analogy mechanism). But not air tight . . . or strong enough. . . .
>
> **G:** How do we build a psychological model of "will-it-to-be-closed"?
>
> **R:** What are you talking about?
>
> **B:** He means if we could conceive of how "willing-it-to-be-closed" might happen in an actual model—then we. . . .

R: There are two days left to produce a working model—and you guys are talking about childhood dreams! Let's make a list of all the ways there are of closing things.

F: I hate lists. It goes back to my childhood and buying groceries. . . .

R: F, I can understand your oblique approach when we have time, but now, with this deadline . . . and you still talking about wish fulfillment.

G: All the crappy solutions in the world have been rationalized by deadlines.

T: Trained insects?

D: What?

B: You mean, train insects to close and open on orders? 1-2-3 Open! Hup! 1-2-3 Close!

F: Have two lines of insects, one on each side of the closure—on the order to close they all clasp hands . . . or fingers . . . or claws . . . whatever they have . . . and then closure closes tight. . . .

G: I feel like a kind of Coast Guard Insect (Personal Analogy mechanism).

D: Don't mind me. Keep talking . . .

G: You know the story . . . worst storm of the winter—vessel on the rocks . . . can't use lifeboats . . . some impatient hero grabs the line in his teeth and swims out . . .

B: I get you. You've got an insect running up and down the closure, manipulating the little latches . . .

G: And I'm looking for a demon to do the closing for me. When I will it to be closed (Fantasy Analogy mechanism), Presto! It's closed!

B: Find the insect—he'd do the closing for you!

R: If you used a spider . . . he could spin a thread . . . and sew it up (Direct Analogy mechanism).

T: Spider makes thread . . . gives it to a flea . . . Little holes in the closure . . . flea runs in and out of the holes closing as he goes. . . .

G: Okay. But those insects reflect a low order of power . . . When the Army tests this thing, they'll grab each lip in a vise one inch wide and they'll pull 150 pounds on it . . . Those idiot insects of yours will have to pull steel wires behind them in order . . . They'd have to stitch with steel. *Steel* (Symbolic Analogy mechanism).

B: I can see one way of doing that. Take the example of that insect pulling a thread up through the holes . . . You could do it mechanically . . . Same insect . . . put holes in like so . . . and twist a spring like this . . . through the holes all the way up to the damn closure . . . twist, twist, twist, . . . Oh, crap! It would take hours! And twist your damn arm off!

G: Don't give up yet. Maybe there's another way of stitching with steel . . .

B: Listen . . . I have a picture of another type of stitching . . . That spring of yours . . . take two of them . . . let's say you had a long demon that forced its way up . . . like this. . . .

R: I see what he's driving at. . . .

B: If that skinny demon were a wire, I could poke it up to where, if it got a start, it could pull the whole thing together . . . the springs would be pulled together closing the mouth. . . . Just push it up . . . push—and it will pull the rubber lips together. . . . Imbed the springs in rubber . . . and then you've got it stitched with steel!

Some of the psychological states and operational mechanisms that will be discussed later are manifest in this excerpt. This group was observed and described by Bruner (1962). One of the things that impressed him about this group was its "commitment." According to Bruner, none of these men was creative on his own. As individuals, each did not regard himself as very creative. The group was also committed to the importance of its operation. This commitment Bruner felt made "for a certain preciousness, a certain overly-long lingering on body imagery and organic metaphor." The group provided an atmosphere as well as relationships for the men so that they could experience a wide range of identities, which then enabled them to come up with many hypotheses.

Bruner carefully observed the group's behavior and noticed that there existed "an interlocking set of identities." For example, one of the individuals, flamboyant, paraded his "wild ideas" before another who he hoped was acting that day as a "tamer" and who would therefore bring his ideas under control. In another twosome, one person was concerned with the comfort and convenience of a product and the other with how difficult production would be. Although these individual behavioral differences existed, "all the members share[d] in a community where elegance and generality are a standard."

Experiences such as the one reflected in the excerpt just presented reinforced the synectics advocates' belief in the importance of nonrational factors in the creative process and in the value of the operational mechanisms to achieve their goals. It may be asked whether the nature of the relationships manifest in the group just described was crucial to the creative process. The way in which this group functioned was undoubtedly the only way in which it could have achieved the desired solution. But other synectics groups can arrive at creative solutions by using interaction patterns that may be entirely different from those illustrated. Later (pages 203-204) an excerpt will be presented of another synectics group session to show how they may be so.

Before going further let us consider some differences between synectics and brainstorming.

Differences between Synectics and Brainstorming

Both synectics and brainstorming involve the generation of ideas under conditions in which criticism, evaluation, and other characteristics of critical problem-solving behavior are deferred or suspended. (Synectics shares much more with creative problem-solving since the latter is so eclectic and has begun to absorb some of synectics' methods.) However, they differ from each other in rather significant ways.

Brainstorming urges the individual to defer judgment and to produce quantity of ideas. And, as quantity is produced, quality follows. As aids in achieving these goals, the individual is presented with and encouraged to follow the two basic principles and four rules. In synectics the goal is also to arrive at a creative solution to a problem but more direction and structure are provided than in brainstorming. The structure comes to the subjects in the instruction to direct their thoughts along the lines set forth by explicit operational mechanisms—analogies and metaphors. It is through the use of these mechanisms that subjects in synectics free up their thought processes.

In both synectics and brainstorming participants go on a "trip" following their thoughts wherever they lead. Indeed in synectics this trip is called an "excursion" for which the roadway is charted through the use of a variety of guideposts—analogies, metaphors, force fit, viewpoint, etc. until a tenable or workable solution to the problem is attained. Such guideposts are lacking in brainstorming for it puts its faith in deferment of judgment and the principle that as one strives for quantity, the proper quality will be produced. Then from all that has been produced, one makes necessary selections of ideas that may indeed be the creative solutions.

Interaction between group members in brainstorming is generally calm, pleasantly warm, good-natured, supportive, devoid of anger, and emotionally low-keyed. The leader in a brainstorming group functions as an overseer who tries to ensure that the formal aspects of the brainstorming technique are not overlooked. There are actually two types of synectics groups: those run according to Gordon's technique and those run according to Prince's. Gordon's groups are very intimate; they are good humored, but also sarcastic; thus a generally active atmosphere can, on occasion, become quite charged with emotion, expressed as joy, anger, irritation, or enthusiasm. With Gordon as leader of the group the leadership role is very influential, and his charisma can affect not only the group process but also its success or failure. While this behavior and atmosphere is most likely to be characteristic of a Gordon-run group, the style, is, without doubt, adapted to the needs of a group especially if Gordon's techniques are used with children.

The climate or emotional tone of groups run by Prince falls somewhere between that found in brainstorming and that found in Gordon's groups. The sarcasm, aggression, and hostility expressed in Gordon-conducted groups would be much more controlled in groups conducted by Prince. In Prince's groups leadership is critical. He has rules of leadership (to be presented later), and in his groups the leadership role is rotated among the group members.

With these comparisons between synectics and brainstorming and with some references to Gordon's and Prince's approaches in mind, let us now turn to more specific matters in the theory and technique of synectics.

THEORY AND TECHNIQUE OF SYNECTICS

Psychological States

Among the various factors that play important roles in the theory and technique underlying synectics are four "oscillating" psychological states involved in the creative process and one other state that is not so oscillating—the hedonic response.* These states are induced by several operational mechanisms to be discussed later.

The four psychological states are:

(1) *Involvement and Detachment*—This state refers to the relationship between the individual and the problem on which he is working. Involvement refers to understanding and interacting with the elements of the problem. In involvement there is a feeling for and resonance with the problem. However, the creative process also involves the capacity to detach from and become distant from the problem—to view it objectively.

(2) *Deferment*—There is a danger in quick and immediate solutions to a problem: Experience has shown they are likely to be premature and superficial. Deferment refers to the capacity of both the individual and the group to defer these quick solutions until they have arrived at the best one.

(3) *Speculation*—The group and its individual members need to be able to let their minds run free so that they can come up with ideas, hypotheses, and solutions. Speculation refers to this type of thinking.

(4) *Autonomy of Object*—As the creative process proceeds and a solution is approached, there is a feeling that the solution has an entity and demand quality of its own. The individual or group must be willing and free enough to allow this feeling to develop and to follow it. (These four psychological states have much in common with the creative process, discussed in Volume 1, Chapter II.)

---

*In his later work Gordon (1971) lists this as a psychological state and it is presented as such here.

(5) *Hedonic Response**—Synectics involves, among other factors, play with "apparent irrelevancies." This play is used to generate energy for problem solving and to evoke new views of problems. One of these irrelevancies is an emotional factor called "hedonic response," which serves as an "irrelevance filter." The feeling involved in the hedonic response is very subtle. It is similar to the inspiration or intuition that is sensed prior to achieving the solution to a problem (Gordon, 1971). It is the pleasurable sensation that accompanies the feeling of being right about a hypothesis or a solution before it has been proven correct. There are both aesthetic and pleasurable elements in hedonic response. Gordon has been unable to develop an operational mechanism to bring it about. It is obviously of tremendous importance, and if an individual could learn how to recognize it, then he would probably not waste so much time and energy in the creative process; the individual would have that "feeling"—aesthetic or otherwise—that would "tell" him when to follow up a hypothesis and when to pursue a tentative idea to solution. Most techniques for stimulating creativity have one or more procedures for stimulating ideas and possibilities that may result in manifest creativity. None of them has much to say about how to go about selecting from what one has thought of. The hedonic response may be a clue to what might be helpful in this regard. To learn more about it and enable us to make better use of this response, Gordon suggests† that tape recordings of synectics sessions be reviewed and that special attention be paid to those points at which an individual achieved a breakthrough in the problem-solving process. Such study may lead to a knowledge of those cues that alert an individual to the fact that he is coming upon something quite significant. It is important that this point be recognized because, once a solution is articulated, it becomes autonomous and develops a life—a "being"—of its own.

Operational Mechanisms

The aforementioned psychological states are induced by operational mechanisms. There are four such mechanisms: (1) *personal analogy*; (2) *direct analogy* or *example*‡; (3) *symbolic analogy or book title*‡ or *essential paradox*‡ or *compressed conflict*; (4) *fantasy analogy*. When working on a problem what one actually utilizes are these operational mechanisms, and if they operate ef-

---

*The *hedonic response* is analogous to experiences that accompany inspiration, intuition, and the recognition of leads to be followed up or solutions or conclusions to be accepted.

†From the point of view of developing more data on how to be cognizant of the hedonic response, it is unfortunate that there is not more material in Prince's (1970a) or in Gordon's later work (1971) than in the earlier one (Gordon, 1961).

‡The marked items are the terms used by Prince. Although Prince's and Gordon's terms are presented for each mechanism, one may well find that there are subtle shades of difference.

fectively, then the psychological states function very quietly and "take care of themselves." The operational mechanisms do not make up the whole problem solving process, but they are a most important part of it.

One of the functions of the operational mechanisms is to *make the familiar strange*.* In so doing, one of the important psychological functions that is accomplished is to increase the "distance" between the individual and the problem. This increased distance enables the individual to avoid becoming stuck with what he already knows about a problem and being limited to it. As we shall see, the degree of distance achieved between individual and problem varies as a function of the operational mechanisms used. The four operational mechanisms are:

1. Personal Analogy

The individual imagines himself to be the object with which he is working. He "becomes" the spring in the apparatus and feels its tension, or he "becomes" the pane of glass and allows himself to "feel" like the molecules in it as they push and pull against each other. The rigid and controlled individual finds this hard to do, for it stirs too much anxiety and insecurity. To use this mechanism effectively involves the capacity to "lose" oneself.

As a result of his work with this mechanism, Gordon (1971) believes that the critical element in *personal analogy* is *empathic identification* and not mere role playing. Role playing as a means of arriving at *personal analogy* is rather useless when working on a problem with a sociological or psychological base—a people problem. For this kind of problem, role playing, instead of making the familiar strange, makes the strange familiar because it does come up with enough strangeness.

Together with *compressed conflict* (pages 189-190) this operational mechanism is regarded as an auxiliary operational mechanism [direct analogy (pages 188-189) is the basic operational mechanism]. A *personal analogy* has more freedom and breadth than does a *direct analogy*, and the former yields more understanding than the latter.

Four degrees of involvement in *personal analogy* have been described (Synectics, Inc., 1968). They are as follows:

(1) *First-person description of facts.* This is very shallow and involves a mere statement or listing of facts. Thus, in the Synectics *Teacher's Manual* the example is given of someone who is asked to imagine he is a fiddler crab and he says that he would have a hard outside and a soft inside, etc.

(2) *First-person description of emotions.* This level represents "the lowest

---

*Among other things, this phrase is to differentiate it from another aspect of the synectics problem-solving process—to make the strange familiar—in which one tries to become very well acquainted with the problem and its various parts.

order of identification [Synectics, Inc., 1968, p. 13]." The content of this analogy, although better than the previous form is too general to yield any very valuable insight about that which the analogy was developed. For example, when asked to imagine himself as a fiddler crab, a person responded that he was busily involved in getting food for himself and had to watch out that he did not become food for a bigger fish. Such an analogy yields no added insight into the fiddler crab since all animals are confronted with the problem of eating or being eaten.

(3) *Empathic identification with a living thing.* This is regarded as "true" personal analogy. It represents both kinesthetic and emotional involvement with the object. Again, while imagining to be a fiddler crab, a person might say that his big claw is rather burdensome and useless. When he waves it nobody is frightened and it is quite heavy to carry around.

(4) *Empathic identification with a nonliving object.* This is the most sophisticated kind of empathy. Relatively speaking, it may be easy to attribute human emotions to living objects as in level (3) but it is much more difficult to do so with nonliving objects. For example, when asked to imagine that he was the mud in which the fiddler crab lives, a person said that he felt that no one cared about him. The crabs do not thank him and he would like to make them do so.

Prince describes only three levels of involvement in personal analogy—the first two are the same as the first two just described, and the third combines the third and fourth just described. Prince feels that the use of personal analogy can help a group become more cohesive. After members of a group have produced good personal analogies, Prince feels they can work together more effectively.

2. Direct Analogy or Example

Here facts, knowledge, or technology from one field are used in another (e.g., a shipworm tunneling into wood serves as an analogy to solve problems in underwater construction). Biology, Gordon believes, is one of the most fruitful areas for direct analogies in solving technical problems. Knowing how certain goals and activities are accomplished in biological organisms serves as a good basis for developing ideas in technology and other areas. Emphasis on biology does not preclude interest in other areas. Whatever other information an individual has at his disposal may be helpful to him in direct analogy.

Experience has shown Gordon (1971) that organic direct analogies used for inorganic problems, or inorganic direct analogies used for organic problems, are more effective than organic for organic or inorganic for inorganic.

Gordon (1971) makes an intriguing statement about the relationship between "constructive strain" that is introduced "by the distance on the analogy" and the "level of inventive elegance [p. 235]." He says that analogies with small psychological distance from the problem can be effective for problems being worked on for the first time; but for problems that have been worked on a great deal, analogies that reflect great psychological distance—those that are rather remote from the individual's experience—are required.

Prince (1970a) says that the more strange the example (his term for the direct analogy), the greater the logical distance between subject and example. And the less the seeming relevance to the example, the greater is the chance that it will be meaningful and helpful in the problem-solving process. He points out that two examples of *closure* are *door* and *mental block*. The latter is more likely to enable an individual to look at a problem in a new way than is the former because it is logically more distant from the subject and it is less immediately relevant.

These are very intriguing statements which beg further elaboration, and indeed it would be especially helpful if experimental or research data could also be presented. Mention is made in a footnote in *The Metaphorical Way* (Gordon, 1971) that research on direct analogy has been conducted at the China Lake Naval Station. However, no data that would allow for independent evaluation of the direct analogy mechanism are presented.

Direct analogy is the basic mechanism by which an individual tries to see problems in new contexts. A direct analogy is clear and straightforward. It produces immediate results and "its process can be reproduced [p. 239]."

3. Symbolic Analogy, also Called Book Title, Essential Paradox, and Compressed Conflict

This form of analogy "uses objective and impersonal images to describe the problem." An individual effectively uses symbolic analogy in terms of poetic response; he summons up an image which, though technologically inaccurate, is aesthetically satisfying. It is a compressed description of the function or elements of the problem as he views it (e.g., one synectics group used the Indian rope trick as a basis for developing a new jacking mechanism).

Although direct analogy is the basic operational technique, compressed conflict and personal analogy are used together with it to increase the conceptual distance between the individual and the problem. In a compressed conflict there is direct analogy with built-in "conceptual strain"; there is both a modifier and a noun; the noun reflects the direct analogy, and the modifier produces strain or conflict, e.g., " 'structured freedom' " or " 'wax cloud' [Gordon, 1971, p. 239]."

Prince, in whose system *book title* bears many similarities to symbolic analogy and compressed conflict, says that in a book title there is "both an essence of and a paradox involved in a particular set of feelings [1970a, p. 80]." The function of book title is to generalize about some specific matter and to use the generalization to suggest a direct analogy. According to Prince, the technique helps people who stay close to the problem to get away from it.

Prince cites a group working on a problem involving a ratchet and, when asked to develop something paradoxical, contradictory, or opposed to one of the ratchet's characteristics—dependability—the group came up with *dependable intermittency, directed permissiveness,* and *permissive one-wayness.*

4. Fantasy Analogy

This is based on Freud's idea that creative work represents wish fulfillment. The individual states a problem in terms of how he wishes the world would be. For example, the synectics group that was working on a vapor proof closure for space suits, asked the question, "How do we in our wildest fantasies desire the closure to operate?" This form of analogy is said to be very effective if used early in the process of making the familiar strange. Gordon regards it as an excellent bridge between problem stating and problem solving because it also tends to evoke the use of the other mechanisms.

In the early days of synectics, it had become apparent that fantasy analogy was getting mixed up with the other mechanisms. It seemed to be part of the other mechanisms. Between 1961 and 1965 it was not used because it did not seem necessary. Fantasy analogies were usually offered by group members while they were using the other analogies. Synectics sessions in which fantasy analogy is used become productive very quickly but can also become dry very quickly. It is a very efficient operational mechanism but also a very limited one according to Gordon's (1971) experience.

Synectics thus tries, in the course of problem solving situations, to make the familiar strange and to make the strange familiar through the use of the different types of analogies just described. These analogies enable the individual to look at problems in new ways, and thereby hopefully gain new insight into the problems.

Also by means of the operational mechanisms, synectics attempts to make conscious what goes on in the unconscious. It is also through the use of the operational mechanisms that the psychological states of involvement, detachment, deferment, speculation, and commonplaceness are induced. These states create the psychological climate necessary for creative activity. it is assumed that all people have experienced and utilized these analogies. Hence, when group members are asked to use them in synectics sessions, they do not feel they are being manipulated. They claim that their natural creative potential is increased rather than decreased.

It is apparent from the descriptions of the operational mechanisms that they are simple. However, it does take a great deal of energy to apply and use them. Synectics, therefore, does not make creative work easier but "rather is a technique by which people can work harder." At the end of a synectics session, participants may emerge quite fatigued, because they move into areas that appear irrelevant and expend a good deal of mental energy developing their analogies and trying to determine how well those analogies help to solve the problem. Although sometimes exhausting, the synectics session is often profitable and mentally fulfilling.

The material presented on psychological states and operational mechanisms contains much of the required theory for understanding the basics of synectics. For these basics to be of use in creative problem solving more is required than what has been said thus far. Before considering the characteristics of the problem-solving process or how a synectics session is conducted, let us look at the characteristics of its constituent members—the leader, the participants, and the client-expert.

THE PARTICIPANTS IN A SYNECTICS MEETING

In addition to their experience in coming up with new ideas and the time they have spent analyzing the creative process in groups, synectics workers have also had much experience in the conduct of group meetings and have learned how to utilize group dynamics so as to facilitate the creative process.

The "typical" (i.e., nonsynectics) meeting, Prince (1970a) points out, reflects confusion in purpose or confusion in organization. While the function of meetings is generally described as solving problems, people participating in them usually find their creativity and speculations discouraged. An antagonistic attitude toward ideas is evident, and group leaders use their power unwisely. Group leaders usually feel more important than group members and hence there is not much open and free communication in the group.

Prince sees a meeting as consisting of offering information, asking for information, and accepting or rejecting information. He believes that in the traditional meeting, each person sees the situation as capable of being won or lost. For Prince, group participants manifest combinations of such opposing characteristics as sensitivity and aggression. Sensitivity dictates that the individual take advantage of opportunities and manifest his creativity. However, when responding in terms of aggression the individual displays poor conduct. Thus such an individual may put forth a creative idea in an aggressive way. This may elicit aggressive criticism and the individual must spend a good deal of time defending his ideas and/or repairing his image. Therefore, the sensitive-aggressive individual appears to be constantly on the defensive. Prince tries to counteract such negative aspects of behavior in groups. He believes that the information involved in a negative situation can be conveyed to an individual without evaluation or rejection, and that everyone in a group does have a contribution to make and no one needs to lose or to feel he is losing something.

Prince has developed a variety of methods, some of which he admits are "mechanistic," to help keep a group at a high level of effectiveness. One of those developed to cope with negative features in a group is called the *spectrum policy*.

At a meeting there is a spectrum of ideas or suggestions. All of the ideas may be good or parts of the ideas offered are good and acceptable and other parts are unacceptable. Prince believes that people tend to emphasize the unacceptable characteristics. In doing so, however, they impede the development of solutions. In the early stages of problem solving, no member of the group can tell whether or not an idea or any part of it may indeed prove quite valuable at some time during the problem solving process. Consequently, it is unwise to concentrate on the bad characteristics. Group members should build on what is worthwhile, and try to overcome the faults in an idea. One of the problems that people have in applying the spectrum policy is that they simply do not listen to each other. Prince solves this problem by suggesting that if someone cannot find something good in what another has said, he should keep the other person talking until he can apply the spectrum policy—comment on what he does not like but also comment on what is good in the idea.

Another technique that Prince uses effectively involves videotaping the group's sessions. The tapes are played back to the group so that the participants can observe and discuss their own, each other's, and the total group's inter-action.

The other important factor that Prince emphasizes is a clear perception of the roles that all persons—the leader, the participants and the client-expert—play in the group sessions. In a traditional meeting, these roles can be comingled, but in synectics they are separated and clarified to avoid confusion. The role prescriptions will be spelled out on the following pages, but as a general overview in a single, concise statement, it can be said that for Prince (1970a) the leader is servant of the group, the group is servant of the problem, and the client-expert is the problem's representative. The client-expert's opinions are honored solely with respect to the problem and not with regard to the conduct of the group or its behavior. Let us now turn to what Prince has to say about each of the roles.

Leader's Role and Principles of Leadership

It is important that the leader structure his role according to the following principles (Prince, 1970a):

1. *"Never Go into Competition with Your Team"*

This is a very difficult principle for leaders to accept, since everyone feels he has ideas to offer. However, it is important that this principle be accepted, since leaders are likely to favor their own suggestions. If this were to happen participants would become discouraged and not participate fully in the meeting.

There are times when the leader can contribute his ideas in a synectics group—when early possible solutions are sought (*suggestions*) and during a stage called *force fit* (both will be described later on pages 198 and 200-204, respectively). Even on these occasions the leader offers his only when no others are offered. Should someone else have an idea, it has precedence over the leader's. The leader supports members' ideas and if possible he should build or add to a member's idea to strengthen it.

2. *"Be a 200 Percent Listener to Your Team Members"*

The leader's job is to understand participants' points of view. He should be sure he understands a participant's point of view, and to achieve this goal he might well try to paraphrase what he hears. He should *not* evaluate what he hears. In this manner, the leader fosters an atmosphere in which everyone's idea is worthy of consideration. In his book, Prince (1970a) presents a list of phrases to be used by leaders for "intervening without manipulation" and to generate nondefensiveness.

3. *"Do Not Permit Anyone to Be Put on the Defensive"*

The leader operates with the belief that there is value in whatever a participant offers, and his job is to find that value. The leader never asks for justification of a metaphor; he accepts opposing points of view, and if a member starts by looking for negatives he asks him to tell what he likes about what he heard (*spectrum policy*); when an idea looks like it may falter he tries to keep it alive by generalizing from it; he sees to it that ideas are never completely condemned, they are only put aside; he sees to it that no participant is pinned down, pressured, or put on the defensive.

Laughter should be looked into because it may be stirred by an elegant idea that is just beginning to emerge and no one may be consciously aware that this is so.

4. *"Keep the Energy Level High"*

The leader's intensity, interest, and alertness can spread through the group. It is therefore of help for him to move around and underscore points by using body movements. He should select areas of interest to himself, and keep the meeting moving quickly; he should be humorous or encourage humor in others; he should ask challenging questions; and use the element of surprise.

5. *"Use Every Member of Your Team"*

All group participants are to be used and encouraged to respond. Quiet and/or shy persons may need to be brought out or handled quite tactfully. Prince suggests that verbose members be thanked rather quickly after a response; their eyes should be avoided when the leader asks for a response; and the leader should hold his hand up and look at someone else to stop the compulsive talker.

If none of these techniques works, a frank talk or the suggestion that the compulsive talker listen to the tape of the session may be worthwhile.

6. *"Do Not Manipulate Your Team"*

The purpose of the group is to come up with new solutions. A group is generally manipulated if the leader already has a solution in mind and his goal is to get the group to accept it. The leader's authority and responsibility is to "aim the members' minds in a specific direction" [Prince, 1970a, p. 53] ." He keeps them informed as to where they are in the synectics process, but he does not push for a specific solution.

7. *"Keep Your Eye on the Expert"*

The final goal of a meeting is to provide the expert with as many potential solutions or *"viewpoints"* as possible. It is therefore very important that the leader keep his eyes on he expert. When the expert seems to be interested in something, the leader keeps going at it and works with the group to come up with more viewpoints, and if the expert gets very involved with a possible solution the leader should even encourage him to take over. When an expert responds to something, the leader should be careful to note that the spectrum policy is followed. Positive statements, what the expert likes about something, should be included with negative ones.

8. *"Keep in Mind That You Are Not Permanent"*

Assuming that traditional leaders can enjoy too much the exercise of power and authority, and also assuming that everyone wants to be a leader, Prince suggests that the leadership role be rotated. Thus, everyone can be motivated to participate more fully. If one can be both participant and leader he can learn the relative advantages and disadvantages of either role.

In summary, then while Prince (1970a) regards the leader in the traditional meeting as "self-serving and manipulative," he sees the leader in the synectics meeting as serving others. The leader must use his power and capacity to control a group very carefully, for he becomes a model for the group members for the time when they will become leaders, as well as affecting their behavior directly when he is leader. The leader watches, records, and stays with a plan as the group moves freely and imaginatively along. He emphasizes imagination and flexibility and tests all kinds of ideas for their usefulness. He maintains a constructive viewpoint constantly by keeping open communication lines between participants, he does not allow fear of being wrong to be a deterrent to participation, and he tries to see to it that experts' objections are also used constructively.

The leader gives priority to avoiding damage to anyone's image; to directing aggression against the problem and not the people; and to showing that through effective participation no one loses and everybody wins.

The Participant's Role

The participant's role is to give all of himself to the problem. In so doing, he will manifest his uniqueness and individuality, and thus every participant in a group ends up looking at a problem in his own way. The participant uses his own sensitivity to offer ideas and speculations about the problem at hand. He need not concern himself with whether or not a suggestion or idea is helpful. In this sense, synectics also removes evaluation as one of the participants' responsibilites. The participant should try to overcome his habitual tendency to spot weaknesses in ideas and try to expose them. It is better if he seeks ways to overcome the weaknesses he spots. In the process of being a participant the individual also learns about leadership patterns by observing his leader, and he can profit from this as well as from his own reactions to these patterns since he too will have to assume the leadership role at some point.

Client-Expert's Role

The third role in a group is that of the expert. He is the individual with the most factual understanding of the problem. He is generally the client's representative and within the client's organization is the person who is responsible for solving the problem. Consequently, in most traditional meetings the expert is likely to be put on the defensive. Having the responsibility for solving a problem, he may not relish the idea of having someone else solve it. For effective participation in a synectics group he must strive to overcome this attitude. He must become both participant and expert. By freely speculating about ideas during the course of a meeting he sets an example for the participants to follow. In his responses to participants' ideas and suggestions he follows the spectrum policy in which he tries to strengthen the positive in their ideas and point out weaknesses. In this fashion he encourages the group to build on that which is positive. In so doing, his intent is not to be polite but rather to be thorough. His is a difficult role since he supports ideas, but he must also be realistic and voice realistic concern as he moves along.

The expert tries to demonstrate to the group that he is there to find workable ideas. He is not to build himself up at others' expense. He points out acceptable directions. He shows the group he is willing to listen to their ideas. He builds on their suggestions when possible, and he helps the group understand as much as necessary about the problem. He counts on the group, since he is the one who will most likely make use of potential solutions.

The leader checks the goals that the group is working toward with the expert. The leader also checks with the expert to make sure that possible solutions and viewpoints are clearly understood.

Composition of a Synectics Group

A synectics group is never larger than seven individuals; it is better to have six than seven and ideal to have only five (Prince, 1968). The group includes the leader, the client-expert and the participants. If the group is run within a company, Leek of Remington Arms, who has used synectics in his company (Garcha, 1969), recommends that some of the group represent the department directly involved in the problem and the remainder come from different departments. One should try to ensure a "good mix" and bring together different personalities. Leek suggests that the men's boss should not be the group leader, and if possible he should be kept out of the group.

The group's meeting place is important. It needs to be quiet and have no distractions. It is therefore important to protect the group from interruptions by secretaries, telephones, etc. Leek held his meetings close to nature, in a fishing club in the woods and a stable of an old mansion owned by his company. He has also held meetings in a local theater club, a motel room, and home basement.

As indicated previously, meetings should be taped, and the tapes should be available to the group members for review of their processes and behavior. A synectics session requires the expenditure of a fair amount of energy; it is recommended, therefore, that no session go longer than an hour without a break.

SYNECTICS' PROBLEM-SOLVING PROCESS

We have covered the psychological states, the operational mechanisms, the various individuals who make up a synectics group, and the roles they play. These constitute almost all the basic ingredients for a synectics problem-solving session and almost all the critical jargon and terminology. There are still several other terms, such as *problem as given*, *purge*, *suggestion*, *force fitting*, and *viewpoint*. All of these and several others will be noted in their proper places, defined, and discussed as we present the synectics problem-solving process. Again, Gordon's and Prince's approaches will be combined, and where differences exist they will be pointed out.

The synectics problem-solving process consists of three major segments. The first is devoted to defining, elaborating, analyzing, and understanding the problem. The second is devoted to applying the different operational mechanisms, the metaphors and analogies, to the problem. When this is completed the group tries to *force a fit* between what they have arrived at as a result of applying the operational mechanisms and the problem on which the group was working. Hopefully, the result of the force fit is such that it either is a solution to the problem, a suggestion that can lead to a solution, or an idea that results in a better understanding or better approach to the problem. Under the last circumstance, the whole process is now begun again bearing in mind the new view of the problem. The process may be repeated as many times as necessary until a solution is found.

Because a synectics session can become quite free flowing, discipline and structure have been introduced by the synectics people by way of a flow chart. The place of the group in terms of the flow chart may be written on a blackboard or on a flip-chart placed on an easel by the leader so that the members of the group will know where in the process they are. The material that follows will be presented in the form of a flow chart.

1. Problem as Given (PAG)

For both Gordon and Prince* the character of this step is denoted in its title. The problem may be posed by an outside source or by an individual in the group.

Prince adds an interesting emphasis. He suggests that the word "problem" may connote, for some individuals, obstacles or difficulties which might serve to block an individual in his efforts. Prince recommends substituting for the word *problem* the word *opportunity*, which can serve as a positive signal for solving the problem.

2. Short Analysis of the PAG; Analysis

Essentially these first two steps constitute attempts at analyzing and defining the problem. The first step is a statement of the problem as presented by the client. Another technique has also been used by Gordon. In this procedure the problem or goal is actually hidden from the group and in its place the group is asked to discuss a matter central to the goal. For example, in one problem the group was to come up with a new can opener. It was not told, however, that the goal was a can opener. Actually, problem-solving activity began with a discussion of what "opening" meant to the group.

Whatever approach is used for the group's activity the first two steps in the process are to "make the strange familiar," as Gordon puts it. The group tries to understand the problem and to make still unrevealed elements in the problem better known. One of the dangers of this phase of the problem-solving task is to become too engrossed in details.

Prince puts greater emphasis on the client-expert and at this point in the process calls on him to present an analysis of the problem in sufficient detail

---

*If Gordon and Prince use different words for what is apparently the same stage, Gordon's terms precede the semicolon and Prince's follow it. Where a significant change has occurred in Gordon's terminology those terms used in *The Metaphorical Way* (Gordon, 1971) will be selected.

that everyone has a good understanding of it. Of course, no one need have as complete an understanding as the expert.

An example of what transpires thus far in the process comes from Prince's book (1970a) in which the *problem as given*, is to "Devise an ice tray that releases ice without effort." The expert starts by explaining the problem in sufficient detail that the group has a common understanding. Since the expert is also a participant, he does not need to reveal all the minute details of the problem. These can all come out later during the session. For example, in the ice tray problem, the expert's contribution consisted of the following statement: "The ice tray must be superior to anything on the market and must not cost any more than those already available."

3. Purge; Immediate Suggestions

During the time that the group is clarifying the problem it is likely that individuals will think of suggestions or solutions. Such solutions are not likely to be valuable; they should, however, be verbalized. By doing so, individuals and the group can rid themselves of superficial ideas and be forced to turn to more innovative possibilities. Solutions at this point of the process serve another function. It will be recalled that the expert also participates in the problem-solving process. Therefore, early solutions can be criticized by the expert, resulting in further clarification of the problem as a by-product.

4. Problem as Understood (PAU); Goals as Understood (GAU)

Some element or aspect of the problem as given is selected for work and solution. This element is called the *problem as understood*. It is stated as clearly as possible, and members of the group focus on it.

Prince suggests that, at this step, each participant be called upon to come up with his personal way of seeing the problem and his dream or wishful solution. These are written down by the leader. Prince feels that engaging in such personal ways of looking at the problem at this point is important for the following reasons: (1) Each participant can make the problem his own. He can preserve his own individuality and need not be forced into a shared consensus. (2) Giving each person an opportunity to state the problem as he sees it takes advantage of the diversity in the group. (3) Allowing oneself to engage in wishful thinking at this point enables the participant to broaden his perspective and not restrict himself to limiting conditions. (4) By analyzing the goals as understood, the goals can be broken down into parts of problems that can be dealt with separately, thereby eliminating the need to cope with a large, unmanageable problem.

Continuing with the ice tray problem, the following two goals as understood were arrived at: "1. How can we make an ice tray disappear after ice is made? 2. How [can we] teach an ice tray to release instantly on signal." (The last goal is not as wishful nor as far-fetched as it may appear, for if an ice tray is suspended it will make icicles which when they reach a certain size can be "used" to signal the release.)

After checking with the expert, the leader selects one of the goals as understood to work on. He then asks the group to put the problem out of its mind and to concentrate on what he asks. Essentially, he now starts to take the group on a mental excursion.

5. Excursion

At this point a rather extended stage of the problem-solving process follows, which, for Prince, is like taking an "artificial vacation" or "a holiday from the problem." He makes a point of asking the participants to put the problem out of their minds. He is aware that if they are capable of doing so, they will put it out of their conscious minds while continuing to work on it in their preconscious minds.

It is during this stage of the process that the different operational mechanisms—the different kinds of analogies—are used. Essentially, it is during the excursion that the group tries to "make the familiar strange." The leader questions the members and tries to evoke responses to his requests for different kinds of analogies.

Prince adds further elaboration of this step. He suggests that after analogies are produced that the leader select one of them for further *examination*. The example is selected on the basis of these criteria: (1) The leader finds it interesting. (2) The example seems strange and irrelevant to the problem. (3) He thinks the group has some information about the example or analogy.

The example is examined to produce "factual and associatory material" which enables the participants to view the problem in a new way. The facts produced during an examination are differentiated by Prince as "simple descriptive facts" and "superfacts," which are more speculative and "more associatory." These are more interesting and useful than descriptive facts.

Prince points out that a good deal of self-discipline is involved in the examination since the participant must not think back to the problem unless he is asked to do so by the leader. Thus, "each step in the excursion closes the door on the previous step . . . ." In so doing, Prince believes that the probability of diversity in thinking is increased.

Thus, both Gordon and Prince conclude the excursion in essentially the same way. In Gordon's terms the direct analogy is analyzed for further understanding, and for Prince the example is examined.

To summarize what has been presented thus far in terms of a flow chart, we find the following steps have been covered:

GORDON–PRINCE

Problem as Given (PAG)

Analysis of PAG–Analysis and Explanation by Expert
Purge–Immediate Suggestions
Problem as Understood (PAU)–Generation of Goals as
Understood (GAU)
–Choice of Goal as Understood (GAU)
Evocative Question: Direct Analogy (EQ:DA)–Leader's Question (LQ)
for Example (Ex)
Direct Analogy (DA)–Choice of Example
–Examination of Example
Evocative Question: Personal Analogy (EQ:PA)–Leader's Question (LQ) for Personal
Analogy (PA)
Personal Analogy–Choice of Personal Analogy
–Examination of Personal Analogy
Evocative Question: Compressed Conflict (EQ:CC)–Choice of Book Title
–Examination of Book Title
Evocative Question: Direct Analogy (EQ:DA)–Leader's Question (LQ)
for Example (Ex)
–Choice of Example
Direct Analogy (DA)–Examination of Example

6. Fantasy Force Fit (FFF)–(Gordon)

At this point it is necessary to separate our presentation of Gordon's and
Prince's approaches. For Gordon, there are two steps here; Prince uses only one,
but covers the same material.

For Gordon an attempt is now made to force a fit between the analogy and
the problem as understood. In forcing a fit a very obvious attempt is made to
make effective use of the last analogy to solve the problem. Gordon calls this
stage fantasy force fit because fantasy provides the individual with greater
license and freedom for response.

7. Practical Force Fit (PFF)–(Gordon)

The next step is then to come up with a practical application of the analogy
to the problem.

To illustrate these two steps in Gordon's approach, consider a problem he
deals with in which a better mousetrap is to be invented. The participants in this
problem-solving session are working with the analogy "Trojan Horse." In fantasy
force fitting this analogy, the idea of "leaving something about which mice will
covet so much that they will pull it into their nests" is suggested.

The next step is to take the fantasy out of this force fit and to make it
practical (practical force fit). Under these conditions lint which mice can use for
nest building is left around for the mice. This lint is so treated that when
warmed by the mice in the nest it gives off a painless but lethal gas.

6. Force Fit (FF)–(Prince)

The goal of this step is the same for Prince as it is for Gordon. Among the techniques suggested by Prince to help the participant are the following:

(a) "Happening"

When told that the group is to force fit someone comes up with an association, thinks it will be helpful, and starts the ball rolling. This initial association is called a *happening.*

(b) Return to Material

If no one in the group comes up with an association, the leader returns to material that came up as a result of examination and tries to find something himself. However, he is constantly alert to the participants, and as soon as one of them has an idea he drops his own and supports the participant.

(c) Forced Metaphor

There are four steps to this: (1) Consciously consider the element that the group is trying to force fit; (2) Try to make a dynamic connection; (3) Try to get the group to speculate widly—for example, by asking them if they had all the money and power how they would get the idea to work; (4) Find some way of making the idea work.

(d) Get-Fired Technique

Since many people freeze up during force fit, the purpose of this technique is to loosen them up. The emphasis is on dreaming and associative thinking.

To help in this process, Prince recommends that the individual write his own force fit. But whatever he comes up with must be outrageous and a violation of common sense. It should be an idea that would cause the individual to be fired if his boss heard about it. Then, gradually, reality is brought into the association.

8. Viewpoint or New Problem as Understood (Gordon); 7. Viewpoint (Prince)

The problem-solving process ends either in a viewpoint that could be used for the solution, or in a new problem as understood, and the problem-solving process begins all over again.

Prince emphasizes that a viewpoint remains a possibility until leads to a possible solution are developed. It stays "possible" until it has been implemented and found workable. Implementation is obviously quite difficult; a solution that actually works may be several times removed from any one viewpoint.

Care must be exercised in selecting a viewpoint. At this point, Prince involves the expert and suggests that a viewpoint be selected that the expert believes has new elements and is promising. The expert must know what steps to take with the viewpoint to arrive at a solution. It is best to give the expert several viewpoints, so that if one does not work he can chose from the others.

Either the client-expert or the group will start work on a practical model. During the early days of synectics, Gordon used the group to develop the model.

Let us now summarize what has been said in diagrammatic terms to continue the flow chart started earlier.

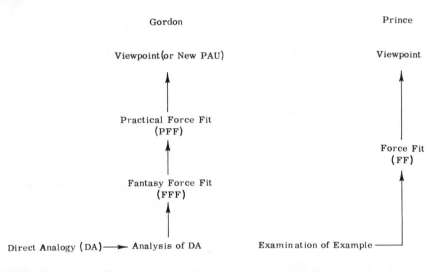

In conclusion, it should be emphasized that, for heuristic purposes, the synectics problem-solving process has been presented in a rigid fashion. In actuality when the process operates smoothly all of the steps are quite unobtrusive.

SYNECTICS IN ACTION

What follows is an illustration of how synectics was used to solve a problem. This excerpt comes from Prince's (1970a) work. Other examples can be found in both Prince's (1970a) and Gordon's (1961, 1971 books). Comparing this excerpt with that taken from Gordon's work quoted previously (pages 181-183), we can see that intense intimate group relationships and the charismatic role of the leader need not be characteristic of all synectics groups. Groups can be conducted in various styles, and each is effective.

The excerpt that follows comes from a large case study entitled *The car wheels leaked*, which appears in Prince's (1970a) book. The problem as given was to develop quick and inexpensive methods of detecting leaks in car wheels during final stages of production. For the goals as understood phase, there were three goals and the one selected by the leader was "How can we make leakers cure themselves?"

An excerpt [Prince, 1970a, pp. 147-150] of what happened then follows:

> **Leader**: ... In the world of psychology think of an example of healing itself.
>
> **Ron**: Forgetting.
>
> **Leader**: Yes... would you say a little more?
>
> **Ron**: I think forgetting a painful experience may be a healing of yourself.
>
> **Leader**: If I understand, rather than continually being upset over something you forget it?
>
> **Ron**: That's it.
>
> **Horace**: A prejudice. [Horace is the expert.]
>
> **Leader**: A prejudice, yes. . . .
>
> **Horace**: I think a prejudice is most often formed to allow a person to tolerate ... or perhaps cope with a feeling, anxiety, or insecurity. I am not sure of that.
>
> **Leader**: That doesn't matter. Are you saying that I have a feeling of discomfort with a black person—so to heal that unease I form a prejudice? ... Let's take this prejudice idea. Take twenty seconds and I want you to turn yourself into a prejudice. Then tell me how it feels to be a prejudice . . . .
>
> **Dick**: I feel invincible and a little contempt for the person I am in. He never questioned my credentials, and in his hierarchy of prejudices I am just as important as his don't-jump-out-of-the-window prejudice. I've got it made . . . .
>
> **Al**: I feel very grateful to my host because if he didn't nourish me and keep me, where would I be? I try to serve him and come to his mind often to keep that anxiety away . . . .
>
> **Leader**: OK, let's take this material on prejudice and make some book titles—capture the essence but include a paradox.
>
> **Horace**: Impulsive Care.
>
> **Ron**: Anxious Contempt.
>
> **Horace**: Insecure Invincibility.
>
> **Al**: Malignant Gratefulness.
>
> **Leader**: Good. Let's go to the world of modern tribal customs—can you give me an example of anxious contempt?
>
> **Dick**: Speeding—we customarily break the speed laws and so we are showing contempt but there is nearly always, at least in me, a little anxiety about it . . . .

Leader: OK, let's examine speeding. What does this speeding idea bring to mind?

Ron: There is an exhilaration about speeding that is very sensual. It is, in a way, almost as exciting as sex . . . .

Horace: I wonder if that is a male thing or do girls feel the same way? . . . .

Leader: Let's go back to our problem: How can we make leakers cure themselves? How can we use this speeding idea—any of them—to help us?

Al: I think of a cop speeding to the scene of . . . of a leak? . . .

Ron: He pulls his gun and fills the hole with lead . . . .

Leader: We could fill his gun with thumbs . . . but what is this saying?

Horace: I like the cop idea because we can do that—our dye speeds to the scene of the crime, but then it just lies there.

Ron: You know, on the side where you look for leaks with black light?

Horace: Yes.

Ron: Could you shoot lead or something wherever you see dye coming through?

Horace: You know, we have never thought of making a repair at that point. We were so obsessed with detecting we haven't thought of that. That is a good thought, but lead bothers me.

Leader: What concerns you, Horace?

Horace: These holes are really small—like pores, really. Black light shows you a stain, but that only tells the general area. We would have to have a very thin, dye-like lead that would stay molten until we knew it had filled the pore.

Al: Horace, could you use two different dyes—boy-girl type dyes? That turn thick?

Horace: Yes, I like two components . . . like an epoxy. A slow curing one . . . . But we have to make it really penetrate somehow.

Dick: I thought Al meant boy on one side, girl on the other.

Horace: That is it! A two-component epoxy, both thin as dye. Spray one on the outside, the other on the inside . . . they meet and react in the hole.

Other Applications of Synectics

This procedure resulted in a program that was implemented and utilized on the production line. Prince tells us that it resulted in substantial savings for the client. Other problems with which synectics has been used effectively include a car safety device, a gasoline pump that dispenses a variety of octanes, and to cope with the shortage of psychiatrists a free-form meeting in a waiting room was suggested; for a major facial tissue manufacturer the idea was conceived of pressing much of the air out of the box so that a smaller box can be used for the same number of tissues. Hence there is saving on paper board, shipping costs, and warehouse space.

Among the new hardware-like product problems on which synectics groups have worked, there were developing a more efficient fuel cell; making profitable use of a waste by-product; and making an easier way of applying paint. Among business-oriented process problems they have worked on devising a marketing strategy for a dying brand; developing an educational program that will keep employees of a company alert and interested; and developing an idea-incentive program. Finally, in the area of people-oriented process problems, they have worked on helping reduce an individual's prejudices and on the question of how those in power in the church can pass their power down to those lower in the power hierarchy.

SETTING UP A SYNECTICS GROUP WITHIN AN ORGANIZATION

As described earlier (pages 173, 181-183), one of the original groups that Gordon worked with was within Arthur D. Little & Co., a Cambridge, Massachusetts, consulting firm. Other groups from which the examples cited in this chapter were culled are described in Prince's (1970a) book. These groups were also members of consulting firms. However, it is also possible to establish a synectics group within any company, and Gordon (1961) and Leek (Garcha, 1969) have done so. In his book Gordon presents several specific ideas on the selection, training, and reintegration of a group chosen for synectics training and whose goal would be product improvement and product development within a company. These suggestions are probably not very workable in most situations. They are presented here only to stimulate further thinking about various possibilities on the part of individuals who might want such a group within their own organization. The purpose of "stimulation only" needs to be emphasized, since several groups that have been established in various companies have not survived. The reasons for this fact are neither all clear nor all available. It may well be, for example, that being involved in synectics is not a full-time job. But whatever the reasons, what follows might be of help to those who want to start such groups.

Selection of Participants

Eight criteria for selecting participants for an in-house synectics group are suggested by Gordon.

(1) **Representation**—the group, consisting of five to seven members, should be representative of the company's total operation.

(2) **Energy Level**—a group member should have a high energy level.

(3) **Age**—members should be over 25 and under 40 to maximize the probability of selecting flexible individuals and individuals with experience. These age limits also allow for more homogeneity in salary levels and status.

(4) **Administrative Potential**—individuals with administrative potential have the ability to generalize, and furthermore, since these individuals are likely to rise in the organization, starting with them increases the probability that synectics techniques will later be introduced at higher levels of management.

(5) **Entrepreneurship**—the group must be able to accept the responsibility for the success and failure of its operation regardless of management's sanction. The group should feel apart from the company since if it is too close to it, it may feel and/or actually be controlled by the company.

(6) **Job Background**—diversity in experience allows for a broad base of knowledge of the company.

(7) **Education**—the selectee should have a history of having shifted major fields of interest. Broad interests will help increase his "metaphoric potential."

(8) **The "Almost" Individual**—experience has shown that there are individuals who have characteristics of productive people but whose own work remains mediocre. These persons may have their abilities "liberated" by a synectics program.

Each potential participant then goes through further selection in meetings with the "Synectors," members of Gordon's staff, to determine if he possesses the following characteristics: metaphoric capacity, attitude of assistance, kinesthetic coordination, enjoyment of risks and what kinds of risks, emotional maturity, capacity to generalize, commitment, nonstatus orientation, and "complementary aspect." Of course, each person in the group cannot be expected to have all desirable characteristics to an equal degree. Deficiencies in one person should therefore be compensated for by characteristics of the others, and the last characteristic mentioned, complementary aspect, refers to whether a person's characteristics complement those of others in the group and whether theirs complement his.

The group, as finally composed, thus represents a wide variety of skills, knowledge, and interests. One of the most important criteria in selecting group members is their "emotional constitution"—the way in which they go about solving problems. For example, is the individual amused at himself when he is wrong, does he use his energy effectively or does he become passive at crucial moments. The synectics group should be composed of individuals with a variety of emotional constitutions. Thus, if there were a choice between two individuals of similar intellectual background and emotional orientation, only one should be chosen; but two individuals with the same intellectual backgrounds and different emotional orientations might both be included. Emotional and experiential diversity helps the group tolerate different approaches to a problem with depth.

Since no group of five to seven people can have all the technical competence to determine the technical feasibility of a solution, experts can be called in as needed. The expert either plays the role of encyclopedia or devil's advocate. He is a resource person who provides technical advice or isolates weakness in a concept or solution.

The leader of the group, the person who will become the group's administrative head when the group is reintegrated into the company, is to be selected on the basis of observations made of the group during the course of his training. He needs:

(1) *extreme optimism*—reflected in believing that anything is possible;

(2) *total grasp*—involving experience in life and in industry that would enable him to integrate and interpret what comes up in the group;

(3) *synectics grasp*—a deep understanding of synectics; and

(4) *psychical distance*—a capacity to maintain proper control over his personal involvement with others so that sessions can be steered constructively.

Course of Training

The selected group, Gordon suggests, should have a place in the company that is separate from others so that high morale can be built. It undergoes training for 1 week a month for 12 months. Training begins with having the members read books that are selected to help them increase their metaphoric potential. These are books in the life sciences, because they yield the best metaphors, and "books of trauma"—for example, those which describe polar expeditions, exploration in general, and disasters at sea. The books serve to increase bonds between group members and to alert them to many basic life situations for which creative ideas and inventions are necessary. There are discussions with the group as to how their industry fits into the American economy and how they fit into their company's value system.

With this as groundwork, the group selects one of the problems presented to it by the company for solution—trainers help it apply synectic mechanisms either by demonstrating the mechanisms or by replaying tape recordings of the sessions to correct the errors that the group may have made and to alert them to appropriate uses.

Throughout the year the group is in training, each of the individual members tries to develop an understanding of the work activities of the other members. In this manner the group becomes better integrated. The group is also made to feel it must move faster than similar groups in existing traditional large corporations.

There are certain reactions that need to be guarded against during the early experiences of the group. One is the feeling of guilt. Although the group works hard and long, its members may nevertheless be vulnerable to guilt feelings; members may find the work not onerous but enjoyable. Selectees also suppose that they are expected to conform to certain roles; it takes them time to learn that they are expected to behave as they wish. Finally, during the early days of training, selectees are cynical until there is some successful experience.

Gradually, the trainers become less and less important to the success of the group, until finally the group works independently of them. Independent sessions, however, are tape recorded for later evaluation by the trainers. Since the group works on company problems, management is in a position to pace and during the training program, rate the quality and quantity of the group's accomplishments.

Reintegration into the Company

After a year of training, the group is ready to be reintegrated into the company. During the course of training, the men carry both their training and their company responsibilities. But after training, Gordon suggests they should be set up as a synectics group within the company. One of the problems that almost all management training programs and creativity programs face on reintegration is that they tend to lose their effectiveness because members frequently must return to the roles that they had left. Therefore the effectiveness of the synectics procedure is inhibited. Hence, it is rather important to note several suggestions that Gordon has on this point.

Since the group is likely to be envied by others, Gordon recommends that their quarters be separate from theirs. Having its own quarters allows for freedom from censure and possible ridicule and makes their space always available and accessible. The group may be set up in the corner of the research and development department so long as it is separate, but if there are academic institutions nearby, Gordon believes it is a worthwhile idea to set the group up near them. They also should not have any of the company's status symbols; their tools and equipment should be secondhand but serviceable.

To foster the group's autonomy, as well as to cope with some problems of dealing with the company's comptroller, the group should be set up with its own budget to be calculated by multiplying each man's salary with the company's usual overhead figure. With this budget the group should pay salaries, buy its equipment, and pay for consulting help.

The group should present its solutions both in terms of the end product and the processes used to arrive at it, so that management can better understand the synectics process and become part of it. Although there is often a problem in assigning credits for patents achieved by a group, Gordon suggests that patents resulting from a synectics group be processed according to traditional procedures. All members can sign an invention record following the conception of an idea. Those responsible for preliminary reduction to practice can sign these records and, finally, the formal application can be signed by those who, through experimentation and model building, proved the validity of the concept.

Rewards for the group, it is suggested, should be based on bonuses for specific performance rather than on overall company performance. Of course, the effectiveness of the group can be constantly evaluated in terms of its accomplishments compared to other groups within the company.

These, then, are Gordon's suggestions as to how a group can be set up within a company. It is apparent that there is much that is involved and for some situations a group may be unrealistic, while in other situations some worthwhile adaptations of Gordon's suggestions can be made.

SYNECTICS GROUPS IN REAL COMPANY SITUATIONS

As has been pointed out previously, Wayne E. Leek, Manager of Firearms Research and Design of Remington Arms Company, Inc., in Ilion, New York, used synectics in his company. His company had a problem with little studs that held gun stocks on a conveyor belt. According to the published report of Leek's experience (Garcha, 1969), process engineers had spent over 100 man hours on the problem. Then Leek put a group of six people to work on the problem, and in a 30-minute session had more than one solution. To solve the problem, the group used an analogy from nature. One of the participants in relation to his prior experiences said, " 'A hole! What lives in a hole that cannot be easily pulled out?' " The group focused on the earthworm which can be safe in its hole and then creep out at will. The earthworm can do this because it "is covered with a lot of tiny brushlike spines that give it an inverse grip on the hole." This was the springboard for four devices: "expanding rubber, file or fish barbs, rifle brush and gravity activated hook" that could be used on the conveyor. All four were "based on the inverse grip principle."

Leek has also used synectics for other design and production innovations—e.g., a new kind of magazine latch for rifles, a new box magazine to hold cartridges, a new recoil reducing device. These are now standard features on some Remington guns (Garcha, 1969). In view of the results he has achieved, it is not surprising that Leek has had all of his design group take a synectics course and stay abreast of developments in the synectics field. Needless to say, synectics does not work at every session; when it does not, the group returns to the problem in another session. For rather serious problems requiring immediate solutions, Leek uses two or more groups, has them work in different geographical areas, and selects whichever ideas appeal to him. Leek also used synectics before making presentations to management. His group discussed every phase of the problem so that he was not found wanting when he made his presentation.

One use of Prince's synectics procedure occurred in a department store, and is described in a little brochure (Synectics Casebook, no date a). According to this brochure the Synectics staff was called upon by a department store to help ease racial tension among some of the employees.

In undertaking this work, the Synectics staff taught their problem-solving techniques to eight groups of employees. Each group contained six people—some black, some white—taken together, the participants covered a wide range of jobs in the store. Each of the participants brought in a problem from his own job and experience, one for which the participant was responsible. For example, one man's problem was that he was bored; a woman complained that another worker in the shift before hers never replaced the merchandise. All groups received six 3-hour training sessions. Some of the groups, for control purposes, were asked during the initial phase to try to solve their problems without any synectics training.

The sessions were taped on closed circuit television and observed by a trained observer. In the sessions conducted before synectics training was given, hostility, unrelated to racial differences, soon appeared. Cooperation was rare. However, during the course of training, each person learned how to understand the elements of a problem, to speculate about different approaches, and to build on the contributions of others. This was cooperative problem-solving, and the group enjoyed it. When hostility occurred it was a problem the group had to deal with, and participants had to use their skills to solve it. Thus, there was an increase in cooperative problem-solving and a reduction in hostility; there was also an increase in the understanding and appreciation of everyone's problem-solving ability. Underlying all of this was the reinforcement of the concept that cooperation could be learned and that it was productive and satisfying. It is pointed out in the brochure that one of the biggest changes was that some persons gained appreciation of their own ability to identify and solve their own problems and thus feel that they had greater control over their environments. According to the brochure there are three full-time synectics trainers in the department store. Their job is to expose as many individuals as possible to the synectics experience.

Another example of the use of synectics comes from the casebook brochure entitled *The Metropolitan Hospital Experiment* (Synectics Casebook, no date b). The problem in this instance was that the number of individuals applying for out-patient psychiatric help was outpacing the number of individuals available to supply such help. In undertaking their work with individuals who came for such help, the synectics staff felt that if individuals could learn to problem solve more effectively, this very experience might serve as a catalyst, or hasten their progress in individual or group therapy.

The synectics problem-solving techniques were taught to a group consisting of two young men and four young women. Each person had a chance to offer up his problem while the others tried to help him develop solutions. The group met for 2 hours twice a week for a total of 6 weeks. The group was observed over closed circuit television by a psychiatrist, a Ph.D. researcher, and a research assistant from the hospital. Data were also collected from postcourse interviews and observations in traditional therapeutic settings.

The results indicated that all of the six participants did change to some degree. Their self-images changed from helplessness to seeing themselves as able to solve their problems. Four of the participants undertook specific actions to change their life situations. Three of the participants were in psychotherapy at the time of their synectics experience, and their doctors reported that they showed more rapid progress and greater willingness to recognize and deal with the problems that motivated them to seek psychiatric help. The results are quite promising, because it seems that training in problem solving together with psychiatric help may well speed up the therapeutic process. Additional work in this area is planned.

A third procedure for use in research and development organizations has been suggested by Bujake (1969) who believes that a programmed effort can be made to increase the creative output of these organizations. Toward this goal he developed a four-step process in which synectics plays a critical role in the fourth step, which is devoted to "concept development." A more complete description of Bujake's approach and the role of synectics in it will be presented in Chapter XVII.

SYNECTICS FOR EDUCATION*

Before evaluating synectics for purposes of stimulating creativity, we shall consider Gordon's use of synectics in learning situations.

Gordon believes that the learning process is very similar to the creative process. Consequently, the following points hold: (1) Knowledge of psychological processes by which people learn will help them increase their learning efficiency. (2) Emotional components and intellectual components, rational and nonrational components, are all equally important in the learning process. (3) For successful learning the emotional and nonrational elements must be directly involved in the learning process.

Gordon's belief and its consequent points have served as background rationale for synectics programs that have been used in schools in West Roxbury, Brookline, and Holyoke, Massachusetts; New York City; Sacramento; Philadelphia; and New Haven. In *The Metaphorical Way* there is mention or discussion of various programs that have used synectics. These include several mathematics, science, and visual arts courses at Phillips Andover Academy; the

---

*Gordon's (1971) book, *The Metaphorical Way*, contains descriptions of a number of uses of synectics in school situations.

general education courses at Franconia College; an abnormal psychology course at Harvard University; a science program in the Harvard Freshman Seminar Program; Harvard Graduate School of Business Administration, in which synectics and T-group activities were compared.

Various teaching materials and techniques have been developed to make the use of synectics more effective in school situations. One of these, a workbook in the area of social studies at the junior high-school level, is entitled *The art of the possible*. It involves teaching social studies explicitly and language skills implicitly. The first section, *Cultural Inventions*, encourages students to guess and talk about how simple human feelings and ideas started and then how more complex things were invented. The object is to demonstrate how the commonplace can lead to new ideas. The second section, *Individual Inventions and Defeats*, presents material on how some individuals had to invent their way out of their "private prisons." For example, the experiences of Helen Keller in overcoming her handicaps are discussed. The third section contains programmed exercises in which students are taken through the process of changing attitudes about such concepts as *freedom* and *pleasure*.

Another developed text is *Invent-O-Rama* for use in the area of invention. The exercises in this text are designed to help the student develop the attitude that all problems are solvable. There are two forms of inquiry included:

(1) *Problem-solving inquiry*—the goal is for students to learn a problem-solving technique that will give them increased confidence in going "beyond" what they have available.

(2) *Substantive inquiry*—the goal is for students to learn the need for more data. Essentially, the purpose is to indicate the importance of a "knowledge bank" for the development of metaphors.

For example, students are encouraged to guess about how some commonplace things were invented. In all instances the students are told to pick things readily available to the inventor. Thus, as a warm up, the student is asked which animal an African chief might use to help him invent the vacuum cleaner? (Elephant.) And what animal would give an Australian bushman the idea for a knapsack? (Kangaroo.) These warm-up exercises are followed by such problems as inventing a new bridge that can be built more quickly and cost less than existing bridges. And, in the course of the problem-solving process the student is encouraged to think of insects that form "bridges in some way," such as the inchworm, and then to use this as a base for building the bridge.

The material in the texts is quite interesting, and it is easy to see how students are stimulated by it. What is not so apparent from the material in *The Metaphorical Way* is that a good deal of thinking had to go into the development and presentation of available procedures. For example, as Gordon points out, in synectics jargon, when an individual learns substantive material, he is essentially *making the strange familiar,* whereas in situations that require innovation he is *making the familiar strange.* What is more critical is Gordon's additional remark that when working with substantive material, a student's learning processes can be inhibited if the metaphors used introduce "too much conceptual distance" between the student and the subject matter. But when dealing with innovative matters, the more distance, the better. These intriguing ideas have many possibilities for teaching purposes.

In general, the material used in the text is commonplace and purposely so. Everyday objects and experiences are highlighted through the use of synectics and the metaphor so that they can be most effectively used for a variety of purposes.

Some of the educational situations in which synectics has been used and the types of effects that have been obtained, as reported by Gordon (1971), are as follows.

Richard Hindley, Dean of Faculty at Franconia College, has been using Gordon's approach with his general education courses. *The Metaphorical Way* contains material on how he used metaphorical thinking with an unmotivated group of sophomores in a discussion of Socrates. An excerpt of this discussion follows.

Teacher: We started out with the question: "How was Socrates viewed by his culture?" We have been developing some metaphorical distance as a means of producing a fresh context for looking at the situation. What do our metaphors tell us about the question?

Dave: Raw because it is exposed.

Teacher: How did it get exposed?

Betsy: Socrates came along as a combination of heavy winds and violent rains . . . .

Jim: . . . a relentless bastard . . . .

Betsy: Shut up, Jim . . . and washed away the nice greenness of his society.

Jon: Green like naiveté?

Betsy: Well, perhaps. At any rate, like Adam and Eve in the garden after being devastated by the apple. The Athenians saw their nakedness and felt guilty. More than that, they were angered—left bare, raw, exposed. It hurt.

Dave: Tradition was pulled up by the roots, huh?

Betsy: Yes. And only Socrates didn't care about being exposed because it was his big idea. To rub it in further, he drank the hemlock and put Athens in such a fix it never recovered.

Jim: Huh? Why?

Betsy: Hey, look, stupid! The society was faulty—planned wrong.

Jim: Oh, bad five-year plan [pp. 35–36].

Hindley found that as a result of synectics the unmotivated students in his class became more motivated, found learning to be fun, and had a widened scope of understanding. Apparently, the students became more motivated because there was greater emphasis on their own experiences and contributions.

This last point is probably quite crucial to the successful use of synectics not only with unmotivated students but also with culturally deprived students. Ghetto students, who are frightened and suspicious of their teachers, find that by using the metaphorical approach their private worlds and experiences become quite important. With the metaphorical approach such students can build on their personal experiences. For example, Gordon might ask a ghetto student what in his experience reminds him of a river cutting through a bank of clay. The answer might be explaining something to his brother in which he has to repeat something over and over again until his brother understands it.

Ghetto students may find some teaching experiences very irritating. Thus, Gordon says that teachers who tried to work with ghetto students using a recognition of housing discrimination and the ghetto experience found that open discussion of the problem only stirred bitterness. But use of the metaphorical approach allows the student to put conceptual distance between himself and the material and to cope with the material better. Analogously, Gordon presents interesting material in dealing with prejudice.

The synectics approach has also been tried with both achievers and under-achievers in school. Probably because they were initially low in achievement, the underachievers are reported to have shown the most improvement. To account for this improvement Gordon assumes that the metaphorical approach demands that the teacher listen to the students, which implicitly denotes the teacher's respect for the student and care for his ideas, feelings, and experiences.

An Evaluation of Synectics' Educational Use

The Invent-O-Rama material referred to previously was integrated into an industrial arts program in a Pennsylvania vocational school with 50 ninth-grade boys who had an average IQ of 101. One form of the Torrance Tests of Creative Thinking was administered before the course and an equated test was administered afterward. Although this was not a well-controlled study, the results do have value as pilot information. They indicated that two of the test factors, fluency and flexibility, did not change significantly. And two test factors, originality and elaboration, did change significantly.

Gordon himself taught a basic synectics course in problem solving in the Harvard Freshman Seminar Program. He quotes from the report of the students' evaluations of the program:

(1) All 25 freshmen who participated in the program thought the synectics program "powerful" and "successful" in accomplishing what it set out to do.

(2) They could apply the metaphor approach to technical problems and pure problems.

(3) The students reported that they had improved their ability to comprehend and communicate complex concepts.

(4) They solved problems.

(5) They "frequently" developed an interest in science and "sometimes" in psychology and the arts.

(6) They felt the course was "liberating and instructive" and "as distinctly the most profitable of their freshman courses."

On a rating scale that ranged from 1 for "extraordinarily valuable" to 5 for "a waste of time," the students "consistently checked ... extraordinarily valuable."

In addition to reported "side effects" of being respected and cared for, Gordon says that the students, after training and experience with the metaphoric approach in class, begin to speculate spontaneously about the world around them. Those in a science course, for example, saw the interconnections among the sciences and how science was related to their personal lives, personal feelings, and the humanities.

If these effects are substantiated and supported in other independent studies and evaluations, then it goes without saying that synectics might well be another very important technique for stimulating creativity in the classroom.

EVALUATION

Evaluative data—some anecdotal and some more systematic—on the effectiveness of synectics as a creativity stimulating technique come from a variety of sources in the literature of the past several years. In the summer months of 1948 when Gordon was exploring possibilities that culminated in synectics, he set up a group of between 12 and 20 artists in Lisbon, New Hampshire, called the "Rock Pool Experiment." In this experiment a climate was developed in which artists could live together and trade ideas about their creativity. Regarding the effectiveness of this experiment, Gordon (1961) reports that participants won many prizes, including the Tiffany prize for painting, several graphic arts prizes, and numerous awards for silver work, sculpture, and ceramics. With the exception of one participant, all have gone on and become well known in their various fields. But it should be noted, as Gordon himself points out, that there is no hard evidence that the awards and future careers of the participants could not necessarily be attributed directly or solely to the participants' experiences in the Rock Pool Experiment. They obviously had other experiences that could also have been significant in this regard.

Gordon (1961) reports that operating groups were established at Kimberly-Clark, Singer Sewing Machine Co., Johns-Mansville, and RCA-Whirlpool. Prince (Synectics, no date) presents a list of 36 companies that have participated in synectics programs.

Bruner (1962) who studied the synectics group at Arthur D. Little that was under Gordon's leadership reports that nothing revolutionary was produced, but what was produced was more than usually imaginative. Although Bruner was unable to talk about specific achievements, because of their confidential nature, he did say that the group's work on mechanical axes did contribute significantly to foresting operations; a suit was designed that reduced missile loading hazards; a draftproof sleeping bag was designed; and a method for reducing the price of delivered gas was also produced. In concluding this statement of the group's contributions, Bruner adds a sentence that might well be applied not only to synectics but to all other techniques for stimulating creativity: ". . . we cannot judge the pragmatic excellence of an effective surprise in any deep sense at its moment of emergence."

Turning to more recent anecdotal material, there is a letter from the Director of the Tire and Textiles Division of Monsanto Company, C. E. Anagnostopoulos, who wrote to Prince (1970c), saying:

> As you know, I have been involved with Synectics since 1964. I myself have participated in communications sessions; I made it an important tool of my Research Department with demonstrated results; my managers and I have used it to develop better management techniques; I taught it to a group of high school students who used it in solving such problems as better teaching methods, efficient utilization of school facilities, and meaningful grading procedures; the same group of youngsters used it to develop the scenario for a movie on sex education and one on "nature and men"; finally, I worked with a group of teachers and ended up using Synectics to arrive at long-range plans for improving the educational system of the school.

In addition to collecting anecdotal material for evaluation purposes, Synectics, Inc. has been undertaking more systematic evaluation efforts. A study of the reactions and evaluations of individuals who have participated in synectics has been undertaken by Mrs. Stephanie Hughes, a sociologist at Boston University and an employee of Synectics, Inc. Her study involves a survey of over 500 individuals who represented 36 companies in synectics courses over a 10-year period. In 1970 a pilot study (Hughes, 1970a) based on data obtained from 49 Problem Lab participants who filled out a questionnaire, 17 individuals who were interviewed by the research team, and three Synectics Development Corporation staff members was undertaken.

Some of the findings are as follows:

(1)   Individuals who participated in the Problem Labs did so on the basis of personal contact with associates and supervisors.

(2)   About a third of those surveyed involved others in synectics. This may well be regarded as a positive evaluation of their own experiences.

(3)   One of the reasons that the participants turned to synectics was for a number of possible solutions to their problems. These solutions were obtained.

(4)   They learned skills for their own use.

(5)   As might be expected the number of solutions reflected in a used/discarded ratio was a function of the problem tackled and the objectives of the organizations or sponsors of the participants. It should be noted specifically that the ratio was higher in the marketing area than in technical areas, where fewer ideas were produced but a higher percentage was used.

(6)   Generally, those surveyed pointed to more likes than dislikes about the labs. They liked the approach and techniques, the stimulating atmosphere, the detailed listing of the final report and the background material. On the negative side participants felt the problem they worked on was not well defined and follow-up was insufficient. One interpretation of these data was that they wanted the synectics group to become more involved in implementing the suggested ideas for solutions.

(7)   Positive reactions to the Problem Labs are a function of the length of experience that a company has had with the labs and also a function of how good the techniques for conducting the problem labs are.

(8)   More than half of the respondents said they used listening and the spectrum policy with their associates, subordinates, and superiors as well as with their families.

(9)   When the participants returned to their jobs there were some factors in their organizations that made it difficult for them to apply their synectics experiences effectively. These included time pressures, formality of organizational atosphere, absence of mutual intent, and the lack of trained leaders.

(10)   When solutions were arrived at in the Problem Labs, the participants said they not only wanted to implement them but also to follow-up on them. The participants in Hughes' survey found that one of their frustrations on returning to their companies was the mobility of people within the company. This mobility complicated the possibility of follow-up as well as the possibility of implementing long-range solutions.

(11)   The respondents also wanted more follow-up assistance from the Synectics people and more cooperation between the Synectics people and the company staff in summarizing tentative solutions and in presenting the logic of the ideas and their relevant analyses. They also wanted more follow-up sessions to handle problems and difficulties as they arose. They wanted assistance in reporting to management, and help from the Synectics people in gathering data from consumers on the solutions that were arrived at.

Some may see this last point as a possible reflection of the dependence of the participants on the Synectics staff. This may be so. Only further analysis of the people, the problem and the organization involved can tell us whether it is so or not. However, consideration also must be given to the possibility that what the participants said did not necessarily involve dependency but interest in more training and experience in what we have called the communication phase of the creative process.

It thus appears that the Problem Labs, and possibly also the other synectic experiences, provide the participant with the satisfaction of what Hughes (1970b) has referred to as manifest and latent functions. On the manifest side, the pilot data suggest that participants do come to solve problems and go away satisfied with solutions to their problems. But they also fulfill more "latent" functions—the enhancement of professional growth as reflected in having learned techniques for their own use and the enhancement of personal growth as manifested in learning skills for working with others.

There are hardly any studies that compare different techniques for their effectiveness in stimulating creativity. One of the rare ones is a laboratory study by Bouchard (1972b) presented previously (cf. pages 106-108). It will be recalled that in this study Bouchard used as his basic technique brainstorming-plus-sequencing. Sequencing is Bouchard's innovation in which each subject in a brainstorming group has his turn to offer his suggestion or idea. This approach avoids the possibility of having one or more subjects monopolize the brainstorming session.

Bouchard compared this basic technique of brainstorming-plus-sequencing with brainstorming-plus-sequencing plus personal analogy. Personal analogy was adapted from synectics and involves asking a subject to take the role of an object in this instance. As the subject does so it is assumed that the process of coming up with an idea is facilitated.

Both groups of subjects were asked to come up with brand names for a cigar within a 5-minute period. In the brainstorming-plus-sequencing condition each subject had his turn to say what he wanted. If he had nothing to say he "passed" to the next person who then had his turn. In the other condition each person had his turn at using personal analogy. The first person would assume the position of a cigar and offer his ideas. The next person would offer his ideas sitting up and so it would continue around the group for one minute. Then the second person in the group would assume the position of the cigar and offer his ideas and so it would go till all persons had their turn.

All groups worked on nine problems. The results of the study indicated that personal characteristics made no difference in the results. The groups using brainstorming-plus-sequencing plus personal analogy from synectics were superior to brainstorming-plus-sequencing on all nine problems and on four of them the differences were statistically significant.

To account for his results Bouchard offers some tentative suggestions. The physical acting out of the personal analogy, he believes, might have involved the participants more in the problem and its solution. Also, the difference between the two procedures may have arisen from the fact that the synectics procedure was novel for the group. While brainstorming does not focus on an individual's thoughts, since it is a free-associative procedure, the use of personal analogy, according to Bouchard, makes the individual's thoughts and suggestions more focused and more relevant to the problem. He also believes that individuals find it easy to understand the personal analogy procedure and fun to apply.

Bouchard believes that adding the personal analogy procedure to brainstorming will have most value for groups. It is unlikely, he believes, that individuals using it will benefit as much relative to brainstorming individuals as synectics groups will benefit from it relative to brainstorming groups.

Finally, Bouchard (1971) believes that the use of personal analogy will bring real brainstorming groups up to the level achieved by nominal brainstorming groups and that the use of personal analogy helps generate "that elusive creative atmosphere or set of special circumstances that enables one to be creative in groups."

Bouchard's combined method has much to recommend it. Certainly it demonstrates the value of overcoming any rigidities in approach that may stem from a partisan attitude in favor of or against any specific procedure for stimulating creativity. The point is not to stick literally to any one procedure but to adapt a procedure to suit the needs of the person using it and the requirements of the problem and the situation or conditions in which it is to be solved creatively.

While Bouchard has carried the work through the laboratory stage, it is to be hoped that more published reports will become available when others have the opportunity to compare the various techniques for stimulating creativity both in laboratory studies and real life situations.

SUMMARY

Considering synectics within the context of all else that is known or theorized about creativity, there is much in Gordon's and Prince's reports that is worthy of attention and consideration. The psychological states that they speak of are congruent with those that others have also observed in studying the creative process. It might be argued that the states do not cover all aspects of the process in all its details, but it does cover its essentials. The operational mechanisms, the use of analogies and metaphors, and suggestions about increasing metaphoric potential by reading in a wide range of areas are suggestions that many individuals could find useful in overcoming problems of "functional fixedness" (cf. Volume 1) that may interfere with their creativity. Analogies and metaphors also help to increase the associative range of responses so that new combinations of associations may be arrived at. Another important factor highlighted in Gordon's discussion is the awareness of what he calls the hedonic response that is aroused in the individual as a solution to a problem is approached. Whether an individual plays back tapes to sensitize himself to this state or whether he relies upon his memory and recall, the critical point is that a certain aesthetic state or hedonic tone may be a significant guidepost in deciding when to pursue a particular course of action.

The discussion on the training and integration of a synectics group into a company's activities merits further attention by those responsible for creative developments in some situations. Obviously, they need not go along with all of what Gordon said, but certain parts could be very helpful. Prince's case studies also indicate synectics may be used with company groups on specific problems on the job, and synectics can also be used together with other techniques for stimulating creativity.

Groups can be established within companies either by selecting individuals who presumably possess "metaphoric potential" or by allowing all employees to participate. It might be a good idea to experiment with and gather data on both procedures, for frequently the assumption is made that all individuals can profit maximally from all techniques. We do not yet know what techniques are most appropriate for what individuals, and until the techniques have been used with a sufficiently large number of different persons there will be no research data on which to base suggestions. Until data do become available, however, all that an individual can do is to try to discern what the requirements and demands of the techniques are and select those persons who seem to have the potential to meet these conditions. Gordon emphasizes the need for diversity in the group, and research data appear to support the need for such diversity.

Probably the most difficult role and function to fulfill in any group will be that of the leader. He obviously has to be a very insightful and understanding person, but he also has to be very well trained and capable of making suggestions at critical points in the group's deliberations. If consideration is given to the total group as reflecting characteristics and processes that occur within individual creativity, then it could be said that the leader serves a variety of "ego functions." He focuses the efforts of the group and, in a sense, is involved in making judgments not only on the relevance of ideas, but also on the nature of group processes. It is conceivable that there can be both a group with one leader and others with rotating leaders. If difficulty in finding a leader for a group exists, it might be helpful to observe a training group and then select the individual who seems to have most potential for this complex role. It is also possible to discover potential leaders when the leadership role is rotated. Of course this method also allows for the training of a number of leaders. Prince's and Gordon's suggestions for the leadership role can benefit both experienced and inexperienced leaders.

Probably no group can function with maximal effectiveness unless it has good communication with and acceptance by its superiors. Synectics and other group techniques for stimulating creativity are relatively new, and often represent departures from traditional management procedures. If an organization is to profit from the time and money invested in creativity training, then its management has to be sufficiently flexible to adapt to the processes and conditions that maximize the probability of the group's effectiveness. Hence, one of the requirements is that management have some knowledge and awareness of the group's processes. If members of management have not participated in the training procedure, they need to be educated as to how their subordinates operate and gain some appreciation and acceptance of the processes.

What is certainly of utmost importance is the potential significance of synectics with school children. Should enough evidence in support of its use with school children be compiled, then it would be worthy of wider use and from these efforts much of value and significance would accrue to us in the future. Finally, it would be most desirable if more systematic research efforts were devoted to the test of synectics' assumptions, to a clarification of its dynamics and to an evaluation of its results.

Chapter XVI

A Study of Cognitive and Personality-Insight Approaches

As was stated earlier, techniques to stimulate creativity can be divided into two major groups—those that make use of cognitive factors and those that make use of personality factors.

In the three preceding chapters three group techniques for stimulating creativity were presented. Two of them, brainstorming and creative problem-solving are concerned largely, if not completely, with cognitive factors. Synectics, on the other hand, although it does not deal directly with personality factors, does deal with the nonrational aspects of creativity, and hence involves personality factors indirectly. Since the question sometimes arises as to the relative contribution of both cognitive and personality factors to the creative process, a study of the matter would be worthwhile. The study presented in this chapter involves both sets of factors, but they are used differently than in previously presented programs. Nevertheless it represents the kind of study that should be undertaken for such an evaluation.

The study contains several novel aspects that may be of help in the development of new techniques for stimulating creativity. It is of further interest because it contains significant variables of sufficient diversity and range that should be included in any study devoted to an evaluation of the effects that follow attempts to stimulate creativity. For example, it includes a measure of the environment in which the men worked which is based on the men's perceptions of their environments. As a result we learn that what an individual gains from a program to stimulate his creativity will depend somewhat on the kind of working environment he comes from and the kind of program he goes into.

The study to be discussed was undertaken by James *et al.* (1962) at the University of Chicago. As indicated, the purpose of the study was to compare cognitive and personality approaches to stimulating creativity. The participants in the study were administrators of federal programs.

Cognitive training in this study involved teaching the individual how to cope with cognitive problems. In addition, this training was used as an analogy for interpersonal problems encountered by the administrators in their real-life working situations.

Some readers, possibly those involved in the arts and sciences, may feel that creativity cannot be involved in administration. Others disagree, believing that creativity can occur in all areas of work and life. Our involvement in this argument is unnecessary at this point; more important are the data on the relative effectiveness of the two procedures involved in this study, the techniques used, and the experimental design insofar as all this information may be useful in other situations and other studies.

THEORY OF THE CREATIVE PROCESS IN THIS STUDY

In this study the creative process is conceived of as consisting of "phasic alternation between (1) *Opening (idea generation), in which the mind is receptive and searching for novel ideas,* and (2) *Closing (idea selection), in which the mind strives to inspect and evaluate the novel ideas, either retaining them for further elaboration or tentatively rejecting them* [James & Libby, 1962, p. 2]." Both phases are necessary for the creative process and they oscillate through the following stages:

1. Initial sensing of a problem, requiring an interest in, and critical attitude toward some aspect of one's environment.
2. Problem definition. This entails development of general criteria for accepting or rejecting solutions.
3. Solution searching, usually involving nonconscious "incubation" or intuition.
4. Solution development, involving conscious elaboration of possible solutions with the help of critical judgment.
5. Final solution selection. Generally one solution must be at least tentatively adopted for testing, though often there is little or no chance for testing.

6. Convincing others of the merit of the solution, i.e., "selling the solution."

7. Solution implementation or application [pp. 2-3].

Brainstorming, according to these authors, confines the group to stage three, while synectics, they say, carries the group well into stage four.

THE TWO APPROACHES

Two experimental programs were used in this study: (1) *cognitive skills training approach* and (2) *personality-insight approach*. The goals in both courses were to help stimulate participants' creativity by giving them training and experience in a variety of techniques and to increase their awareness and appreciation of creativity as it develops and appears in others.

Cognitive Skills Training Approach

The cognitive skills training approach "was based upon the postulate that creativity is a complex of cognitive skills and that innovative behavior can be maximized by providing the participant with opportunity for practice of such skills [James & Libby, 1962, p. 5]." Practice in the skills was provided at four levels: (1) simple perceptual problems, (2) simple verbal problems, (3) simple exercises involving the human context, and (4) complex exercises involving the human organization. At all levels, but especially at the simpler ones, the trainers utilized the problems not only for their intrinsic value, but also for their metaphoric value; i.e., analogies were drawn between simple perceptual factors and processes and experiences involving more complex thinking and real-life situations. The analogies exercises ran throughout the training program. An illustrative example follows.

One of the exercises with simple perceptual problems was called *Sticks*. In this exercise participants were given six colored sticks of equal length and were asked to make first one triangle, then two, three, four, five, six, seven, and eight triangles.

This simple device illustrates two points: (1) any meaningful pattern is formed from a set of elements—here artificially limited to six sticks—and the possible patterns are limited only by the range of elements; and (2) given a set of elements, the number of meaningful patterns that can be generated is larger than immediately evident [James & Libby, 1962, p. 7].

In drawing an analogy from this problem to administrative behavior it was pointed out to the participants that the range of information available affects the solution to a problem. Furthermore, the kind of solution obtained depends on the individual's capacity to assemble the available information into meaningful patterns. These patterns can be broken up and rearranged into a variety of alternatives from which a solution may then be selected. The value and meaningfulness of these analogies is dependent upon the capability of the instructor.

Another example from the area of perceptual problems is the *Embedded Figures Test* (Witkin *et al.*, 1971). In this test a participant identifies a simple meaningful pattern hidden in a larger more complex one. This problem is analogous to the administrative situation in which awareness of a problem occurs because a meaningful pattern of relationships exists in an administrator's mind. A less innovative executive faced with the same kind of data or information might see it only as a jumble of information. James *et al.* (1962) present other techniques utilized and the situations to which they are analogous.

The second training area was *simple language devices*. This was regarded as one step "higher in the metaphoric transition from the simple perceptual level of thought to the complex decision problem of innovative administration [and] involves the presentation of information in the form of single words or 'concepts' [James & Libby, 1962, p. 10]." One of the devices used here was the *Remote Associates Test* (RAT) (Mednick, 1962a). It was used to help clarify the potential value of intuition and nonconscious thinking processes. Solutions to RAT problems generally do not come at once but only after some time has passed in which the subject was still working on the problem consciously or unconsciously. Experience with this technique illustrated that the mind was still working on the problem while the person was doing other things. A second technique in this area was called *Word Finding*. This is the same as the embedded figure problem (which involves designs), except that it involves words and, being of verbal content, it brings the participant one step closer to problems of an administrative nature which are also largely verbal in character.

Content Devices make up the third area of training. One device, called *Cartoon Apperception*, involved completing the captions in the balloons of comic strips. This exercise gave the participant practice in both reaching a decision on partial information and in changing the decision as more information became available. The second technique was called *Executive Apperception* in which a picture of an executive situation is presented and the participant is asked for his interpretation. This interpretation is then reported to the class for their reaction. "The goal is to indicate the wide range of interpretations which can follow from the same cue information [James & Libby, 1962, pp. 14-15]."

The fourth area involved *complex human content devices* and they demonstrated problem solving under conditions that approximated actual organizational life. Three devices were used: (1) *Categorization of Organization*

Stereotypes in which participants were given a set of small cards, each containing the name of an organizational stereotype—the "grind," the "apple-polisher," the "play-boy," etc. The participant is asked to identify each stereotype with someone in his experience and to collate or categorize the stereotypes into as many groups as possible according to their similarities and differences. They are asked to strive for quantity and variety of categories, and in the sorting process they are also asked to strive for common characteristics among superficially different people. Through this experience of repeated categorization of the same cards, participants purportedly obtained an understanding of the tentative nature of seemingly meaningful patterns as well as of the variety of viewpoints through which innovation in problem solving may be approached. (2) *Brief Situations*, consisting of brief statements of typical administrative situations, e.g., "Your boss has asked you for ideas on a new problem. He never accepted any of your ideas yet [James & Libby, 1962, p. 15]." The analogy between these scenes and simple perceptual experiences is discussed and participants are asked to use fluent-flexible thinking in defining the problems involved; in imagining the sequence of events and the context in which the problem arose; and in producing alternatives that might solve the problem. From the alternatives, they select the most promising. First the participants do this individually and then they work as a group to help increase their repertoire of responses. (3) *Administrative Cases*, in which fictional cases were designed to elicit innovative thinking on policy questions.

In each of the 15 sessions devoted to the cognitive skills training approach it was not possible to deal with all four levels of complexity, but some balance was sought between simple pictorial representation and complex administrative reality. Emphasis was placed on the use of analogies to relate the relatively simple materials to complex problems of organizational life.

The role of the trainer in this approach was primarily to administer the practice devices. Those who taught in this approach felt that a "stripped down" cognitive skills approach was dehumanized, and that it produced anxiety and resistance in the participants. "Skills-practice alone produces a somewhat threatening test atmosphere in which some invidious comparison and defensive behavior develops. The steady methodical pacing of such courses has its own characteristic fatigue concomitants [James & Libby, 1962, p. 20]."

Personality-Insight Approach

The second training approach assumed that stimulating innovative behavior is a function of understanding the nature of the creative process and how it relates to the innovator's personality. This course begins with an intensive discussion of how the individual, from a psychological viewpoint, is composed of unique characteristics as well as "a repertory of 'roles' which are played in accord with social expectations [James & Libby, 1962, p. 17]." These roles might be used to fulfill the individual's own purposes, or in giving up individuality and going through life with "a series of social masks [p. 17]"; or both uses can blend creatively in living. Within this context the conflict between the self and what the organization expects of the individual is discussed and two themes are stressed: "(1) adjustment, adaptation, and change of the organization in its environment and self fulfillment in this setting; and (2) the intuitive, nonconscious, and 'nonrational' aspects of innovative behavior [p. 17]."

The theory of creativity, including the works of the social scientists upon which it is based, is discussed with the participants. The cognitive skills devices, described previously, were also presented, but in this program, only to give the group members insight into and understanding of the creative process. They were *not* practiced as they were in the cognitive skills approach.

In addition, three new devices were introduced [James & Libby, 1962]: (1) *Heuristics: Tools for Discovery of Problems and Their Solutions* [p. 18]: A 39-page booklet was presented to the participants; it outlined the basic nature of problem solving and various approaches to solving problems. These were discussed in order to give the participants insight into the variety of approaches available and their relationships to the personalities of the problem solvers and the characteristics of the institutions in which they worked. (2) *Fixed Role Play—('Innovative Steve')* [p. 18]: Participants were asked to study a description of an ideal innovative executive and to model their behavior after him during the last 2 weeks of the course in situations where the participants would be free of criticism. As the participants became accustomed to their new behavior style, they were asked to try out their new behavior patterns in more familiar situations. (3) *Progressive Concept Refinement* [p. 19]: Since a word may be taken as a symbol, its meaning in any one context may be understood from the ways in which it is similar to or differs from other words with which it is associated. In this device, a word is presented with other words, and then the participant is asked to say how the word resembled and differed from all preceding words. For example, this sequence of words was used: horn, bell, radio, newspaper, book, painting, education, and confusion.

The course began with a discussion of the phasic alternation of the creative process. The instructor started by conducting the sessions on a fairly directive basis. Gradually, control was relaxed so that flexibility and fluency were emphasized in the interpretation of personality and insight factors. Direct teaching style was then resumed, brief lectures were introduced; these were followed by permissiveness intended to emphasize fluent-flexible responses. By contrast with the cognitive skills approach, the trainer in this program was rather deeply involved in his work and consequently found this experience more rewarding. The group included only 12 participants.

Control Group

In addition to the two experimental programs just described, a control seminar was held. It was designed to be similar in content to courses usually offered in management development. In this course, attention was paid to "human relations and administration," and to "organization and administration [Forehand & Libby, 1962, p. 1]."

PARTICIPANTS

The participants in this study were men who held administrative positions in federal agencies. A total of 10 agencies, all located in the Chicago area, were represented. One hundred and sixty administrators registered for the program in which attendance was voluntary; 127 completed the program and provided data on which the results are based.

Instructors in the program participated in both the design and conduct of the seminars. Each instructor taught both the experimental and control seminars, and the results for each type of seminar are combined for both instructors.

Environmental Questionnaire

Prior to the start of the experimental sessions the participants were given a questionnaire that provided data on the kinds of working environments from which they came. Specifically, by dividing their scores at the median the participants were differentiated in terms of whether they saw themselves as working in "group-centered" and hence, more "democratic" organizations or whether they saw themselves as working in "rule-centered," more "bureaucratic" organizations. Individuals who said they came from both kinds of organizations were studied in each type of seminar. With proper statistical analysis it is possible to differentiate not only between the overall effects and significance for each type of seminar but also to determine whether there is any specific effect of seminar on type of organization.

The 127 administrators completing the program were distributed as follows: Thirty-six participated in the cognitive skills programs; 21 said they came from group-centered and 15 said they came from rule-centered organizations. Forty participated in the personality-insight seminars; 22 said they came from group-centered and 18 from rule-centered organizations. Finally, 51 made up the control group; 26 said they came from group-centered and 25 from rule-centered organizations.

The Experimental Design and Evaluation Technique

One week before the experimental seminars were to begin the participants met and listened to a brief orientation lecture. Following the lecture, the nature of the research was described, and the participants took pretests and responded to the environmental questionnaire.

The tests used to evaluate the effects of the seminar were as follows:

(1) *Organizational Performance Questionnaire: Innovative Rating Scale*—which consisted of ten 7-point rating scales on which subjects could be rated by their peers and superiors on innovative behavior.

(2) *Organizational Performance Questionnaire: Innovative Forced Choice Scale*—which asked superiors and peers to select from pairs of adjectives, the one that best described the subject. One adjective referred to innovativeness and the other to noninnovativeness.

(3) *Organizational Performance Questionnaire: Global Rating Scale*—in which superiors and peers were presented with three 7-point rating scales that they were to use in rating the subjects on matters of general administrative effectiveness.

(4) *Apparatus Test*—designed to measure sensitivity to problems.* In this test the participant was asked to suggest two improvements for common appliances.

(5) *Social Institutions*—used as a measure of sensitivity to problems and penetration. Here the participant was asked to suggest two improvements for a social institution.

(6) *Similarities*—used as a measure of penetration. The participant was asked to write six ways in which a pair of common objects is alike.

(7) *Object Synthesis*—used as a measure of semantic redefinition. The participant names an object that could be made by combining two specified objects.

(8) *Brick Uses*—used as a measure of spontaneous flexibility and ideational fluency in which the participant is asked to write as many uses as he can think of for a brick.

(9) *D-Scale*—This is a scale developed by Rokeach (1960) as a measure of dogmatic attitudes. At one extreme the subject is regarded as a closed system and unresponsive or unopen to experience; at the other he is more responsive and more open to experience.

(10) *Remote Associates Test* (Mednick, 1962b)—This is a test of the individual's ability to make remote associations. The subject's task is to supply a word that can be associated to each of three other words which, on the surface, appear to be unrelated.

Immediately after the close of the last session final test data were collected. On all tests, except *Brick Uses* and the *D-Scale*, subjects took different forms of

---

*The terms for the psychological characteristics measured by these tests come from Guilford (1967).

the test in pre- and posttraining sessions. *Social Institutions, Apparatus, Object Synthesis,* and *Similarities* tests each have two halves; one was given before the training session and the other after it, as a measure of the program's effectiveness. All took Part A of the *Remote Associates Test* on pretest and Part B on posttest.

Before the men participated in the experimental course, ratings on their administrative effectiveness were obtained by mailed questionnaires from their superiors and peers. Two to three months after the courses, ratings were obtained from the same sources to determine whether any changes occurred which could be attributed to either of the two programs' effectiveness.

RESULTS

Two major variables were studied: the kind of training seminar the administrator attended and the kind of organization he said he worked in, whether it was "rule-centered" (bureaucratic) or "group-centered" (democratic) [Forehand & Libby, 1962, p. 8]. Hence, in recounting the results we will be interested in learning not only the effects of the training programs but also which kinds of environments seem most conducive to their success.

Among the dependent variables in this study were a series of psychological tests (including both cognitive and personality variables) and rating scale evaluations from the participants' superiors and peers, all of which were already described. From the results, we hope to learn whether the programs affected cognitive and/or personality characteristics. And, as a means of evaluating the programs we are also interested in the ratings participants received from their superiors and peers 2 to 3 months after they returned to their jobs.

Let us start by considering the effects of the courses on the cognitive tests, and then turn to the other instruments that were used to measure training program effectiveness.

Cognitive Tests

The only cognitive test on which a significant difference was obtained was *Brick Uses*, designed to measure spontaneous flexibility and ideational fluency. The obtained difference was between the two experimental seminars and the control seminar. Those who attended the cognitive skills seminar did no better on this test than did those who attended the personality-insight seminar, but both of them did better than those who attended the control seminar.

The other result obtained with this test was that men who came from rule-centered environments (bureaucratic) did better on this test than did men who came from group-centered environments (democratic). In other words, men who said they worked in environments that were more authoritarian in attitude did better on this test as a result of their training experiences than did those who came from what they perceived to be more democratic environments.

Both of these findings are especially interesting when considered in the light of the material presented with regard to brainstorming. In one of the favorite tests for measuring the effects of brainstorming the subject is asked to give as many uses as he can think of for a coat hanger. The *brick uses* test is very similar to the *coat hanger* test [although it should be pointed out that not all object uses tests yield the same result—witness the experiment by Parnes and Meadow (1959) in which uses for a broom did not yield encouraging results for brainstorming]. If the brick uses problem and the coat hanger problem are similar, then it is conceivable that the positive results obtained with brainstorming may be a function of the rigidifying experiences that the participants had in the bureaucratic environments from which they came. It is possible that for such persons brainstorming may have a liberating and "loosening" effect. Is it possible that with participants from environments in which individuals might have more experience with freedom of expression brainstorming would not be so effective? Thus, in future studies of brainstorming it would be worthwhile to obtain measures of the participants' environments and background experiences.

Personality Tests

The one measure of any personality change that might have been an outcome of training was that obtained on the dogmatism scale developed by Rokeach. This is a measure of how dogmatic an individual is in his belief systems. The hypothesized relationship between dogmatism and creativity is that individuals high on dogmatic values are likely to be closed to new experiences and hence less creative than those who are low on dogmatic values and hence more responsive to new stimuli and therefore more creative. The results of the James *et al.*, (1962) study were that as a result of participating in the personality-insight seminar there was a *decrease* in dogmatism, but as a result of participating in the cognitive skills seminar there was an *increase* in dogmatism. Those individuals who participated in the control seminar showed only a slight increase in dogmatism. Thus, the two experimental seminars affect dogmatism in opposite directions.

The other effects obtained with the dogmatism scale were that those men from rule-centered organizations *decreased* in dogmatism, and those from group-centered organizations *increased* in dogmatism, regardless of the type of experimental program they participated in. Second, there was an interaction effect that seems to be due to the group who perceived their organizations as rule-centered. Those of the participants who came from rule-centered organizations and who participated in the personality-insight approach showed a very large *decrease* in dogmatism. This again shows that the success of a creativity training program may well be related to the organizational environment from which the participant comes.

Turning now to the ratings that the men received from their colleagues and superiors for administrative effectiveness, we learn that differences in course content had no significant effect on the ratings the men received. There was evidence for a slight degree of superiority for those men who were in the control group. The mean change (a "+" indicating improvement and "−" indicating a loss) in administrative effectiveness score before and after the courses was +1.0 for the control group, +.07 for the personality-insight group, and −.08 for the cognitive group. These results, the authors say, might have been expected, since the control group was designed to produce increased general effectiveness, as different from innovativeness. Since the insight course produced a nearly equal increase to the control group, it suggests that the insight course might have a bearing on general administrative effectiveness. These results are similar to those Guetzkow *et al.* (1962) found for similarly designed but longer studies.

Superiors also rated the men on innovation. Here we find that the rule-centered group gained more in their ratings but not significantly more than did the group-centered group. Both groups started off with different levels of ratings, and the rule-centered group had more room for improvement than did the group-centered group. (It might well be that the rule-centered group started off at a lower level because they were kept down by the values in the bureaucratic environments in which they worked.)

That the training programs did *not* have demonstrable effects is consistent with the evaluations other training programs have received. Training programs may have subtle effects, to which raters are too insensitive. Other studies (Guetzkow *et al.*, 1962) have shown that there are two circumstances which must obtain before changes in ratings can be demonstrated. First, programs that are most effective generally run for longer than the 15 hours spent in the programs described here. Second, superiors in the organization, essentially those in power positions, must deliberately encourage and support attempts to utilize the course material. In other words, the environmental value system must be congruent with the techniques and values that have been taught in the courses.

SUMMARY

In summarizing their findings, Forehand and Libby (1962) point out that the cognitive skills approach alone did not produce the kinds of effects for which such programs are presumably designed. Only on one of the cognitive tests did this approach produce any significant effects, and here the insight approach was equally effective. The insight approach also produced less dogmatism than did the cognitive or control approaches, and it was also almost as effective as the more generalized control seminar in producing improvement in general administrative effectiveness. They also point out "that the changes that occurred take the form of changes in attitude or set rather than in cognitive aptitudes or skills [p. 7]." Since other programs which combine skill and insight have produced changes in skills, they suggest further that attitude changes produced by the insight approach are needed to produce changes in problem-solving skills.

Two ways in which such an effect might operate are (a) providing motivation for the acquisition of skills, and (b) providing a context for generalizing and applying the skills attained. Thus, an educational program that combines our two curriculum elements might produce improvement in skills that the skills-oriented approach alone did not. In summary, it may be suggested that the insight approach can have effects independently of the skills approach; a skills approach in isolation is less likely to have impact, but might be effective in conjunction with a greater emphasis upon insight into innovative processes [Forehand & Libby (1962), p. 7].

The results of this study, although still to be regarded with caution until replicated, nevertheless indicate the potential importance of attending to two critical factors when considering the possibility of sending a company employee or other individual to a creativity training program. Whether or not an individual will profit from such an experience will depend on his personality and cognitive characteristics as well as on the nature of the program. In addition, the kind of organization in which the individual works should also be taken into account. As the investigators of this study suggest,

. . . individuals whose personal need systems already emphasize individual, 'go-it-alone' tendencies (e.g., autonomy, aggression) might be expected to profit most from a cognitive skill oriented program, while those whose need systems suggest tendencies toward interpersonal dependency (e.g., succorance, affiliation, abasement) might profit more from a personality-insight program [Forehand, 1962, p. 5].

PART VI

OTHER PROGRAMS

The four previous chapters were devoted to: brainstorming and creative problem-solving, which emphasize cognitive factors in creativity; synectics, which makes use of a series of operational mechanisms that try to make the non-rational aspects of the creative process more effective; and a study concerned with an evaluation of cognitive and personality-insight approaches. These techniques, in addition to those considered in the individual procedures sections of this book, constitute an array of techniques from which the reader can choose directly or in which he can find the tools with which he can develop his own techniques. Selection of stimulating techniques should not be haphazard. They should be made in terms of the kind of problem, kind of people, and kind of situation in which the creative work is to be undertaken.

To further increase the range of available techniques for the reader, we present in Chapter XVII, a variety of programs used in different companies. We do not know whether or not they are still in use. We felt that this was not critical since the programs themselves are interesting enough in their own right to warrant utilizing them as illustrations of various training possibilities. Where evaluation data are available they are presented. The names of the companies associated with the different programs are presented primarily for identification purposes.

Chapter XVII

Diverse Organizational and Company Programs

A number of organizations and companies have developed their own programs for stimulating the creativity of their personnel to meet specific organizational needs and requirements. Others have pieced together parts of existing programs; and still others send their personnel to existing seminars and programs or retain consultants to help them.

The material presented does not pretend to be all-inclusive. Rather, its purpose is to reflect a range of various attempts to stimulate creativity. From this material as well as from what was presented previously the reader can pick and choose whatever suits his needs best.

In all likelihood there are systematic evaluations of the procedures described in this chapter by the organizations that used them. If they exist they are not always available or published in as much detail as we would like. Consequently we are limited in the amount of evaluational data we can present.

One study that cuts across organizatons was published by Edwards (1966). In this study he surveyed various organizations and gathered data and opinions about the programs they used. Hopefully, in the future, organizations might consider providing more systematic information about their programs and more information about their evaluational criteria so that we would all be in a better position to know under what kinds of conditions different programs for stimulating creativity would be most effective.

DESCRIPTION OF PROGRAMS

To concretize several of the programs that have been used, several examples have been culled from the literature and are presented below. These are intended only to be examples of the variety of techniques used. Furthermore, no effort has been made to ascertain whether the programs described are currently in use or currently endorsed where they were used. Therefore the name of a company or organization which is presented in conjunction with a program is so presented solely as a means of identification. Where evaluations are available, they too are presented.

Stanford Research Institute

Edwards (1966) reports that an eclectic course was developed at the Stanford Research Institute (SRI). A special notebook based largely on Parnes's (1967b) *Creative Behavior Workbook* was prepared for it. A number of specific techniques including brainstorming and synectics were explained and practiced. And, to overcome whatever inhibiting factors the participants may have experienced in terms of their creativity, there was emphasis "on the three-fold principle of alternation—i.e., alternating between thinking up and judging ideas, between individual and team or group work, and between intense commitment to and involvement in a problem and detachment from it, in order to invite incubation and illumination or insight [Edwards, 1966, pp. 15-16] ."

Fourteen researchers at SRI (including three women) plus three individuals from other companies completed the course (one of these had been an instructor in a creative problem-solving course). The average age of the members in the group was 38. The course ran for 34 hours, involving one 2-hour session per week for 17 weeks. Half the sessions were run after working hours. The 34 hours included time allotted for group and individual work on problems, discussion and demonstration of principles to be used, films and tapes devoted to course content, discussion of personal projects, guest speakers, and "before" and "after" tests for evaluation purposes. Because of conflicts with job pressures, there were many interruptions, and most participants attended only about two-thirds of the training sessions. These conflicts also interfered with another technique used in the class—that of keeping a journal of ideas, problems, blocks to the free use of imagination, observations, insights, etc.

To evaluate the course, an experimental group of 16 was compared with a control group of 16 staff members who did not participate in the course. Four tests were used: *AC Test of Creative Ability*: abbreviated test, and three of the Guilford (1967) tests—Making Objects, Associational Fluency, and Consequences (Obvious and Remote).

Those who participated in the class did better on three out of the five tests than did the control group. The class improved more on the *AC Test of Creative*

Ability and Guilford's tests of *Associational Fluency* and *Consequences Remote*, while the control group did better on Guilford's *Making Objects* and *Consequences Obvious*. None of the differences, however, were statistically significant.

The lack of statistical significance might be accounted for by the fact that relatively few individuals participated in the study and that most of them scored so high on the tests used to measure the effectiveness of the program that there was insufficient room or "ceiling" for the men to show how much they gained after the training program (if such gains did in fact exist). Nevertheless, Edwards (1966) believes that "most members of the class made slight to good gains at least in verbal idea fluency (and probably the related items of flexibility and uniqueness of ideas), but not in nonverbal skills. Confirmation of this, as well as mention of other non-measured gains is found in the subjective reports of the participants [p. 20]."

A questionnaire was used to determine what the men's perceptions were of their experiences as a result of the training program. Five out of 17 subjects reported "no change" in their self-ratings on creativity, and all except one of the remaining 12 who reported indicated either "some" or "considerable" changes in abilities or attitudes related to creativity. Eleven of the participants reported "some" gain in two to eight abilities, and six reported "considerable" gains in one to six abilities. The abilities that were mentioned most frequently were as follows: "sensitivity to problems, fluency, flexibility, open-mindedness toward the ideas of others, effectiveness in attacking and solving problems, curiosity and interest in a wide spectrum of fields and areas, confidence, originality, and motivation to carry out ideas [Edwards, 1966, p. 20]."

When asked what was the "most helpful" part of the program, "new methodologies, approaches, and/or techniques were mentioned most frequently." Also mentioned were "identification of what is creativity, 'open-minded' problems, guest lecturers, brainstorming, new outlook toward group idea-finding and class exercises in problem solving [Edwards, 1960, p. 20]."

There was no clear-cut attitude on the amount of time spent in the course. Four of the participants felt that the amount of time was right, two felt that it should have been longer, and three felt that it should have been shorter. Apparently, the time of the day when the training sessions were held did bother some of the participants.

Four participants felt that if the program were to be continued at SRI, it would be "useful"; and six said that it would be "highly desirable." Two others did not express such positive feelings.

There did not seem to be any relationship between gains that a participant made as measured by test scores and either class attendance or the amount of homework reported. All but three of the participants missed four or more sessions, and Edwards suggests that if there were better attendance or better utilization of the available time, the total amount of time used for training could have been reduced by about a third. Finally, Edwards suggests that both self-evaluation questionnaires and before and after tests be used in evaluating such training programs, since frequently striking discrepancies between the data collected with both measures can occur.

Edwards concludes his report by suggesting to the Stanford Research Institute that it should adopt a continuing program that would, among other things, be "aimed at (1) adding to the level of knowledge about creativity and its development, and (2) the enhancement of the creative abilities of its staff, . . . [Edwards, 1966, p. 5] ."

General Electric

The Creative Engineering Program at General Electric has gone through a series of stages since its development in 1937. According to Bittel (1956) it began as a two-stage process involving concentration on problem and solution of it; in 1950 it became a four-stage process, including "define, search, evaluate, solution (p. 102)" and in 1955 it became an eight-stage process including "recognize, define, search, evaluate, select, preliminary design, demonstration, follow-through [p. 102] ." At the time of Bittel's description of this program in 1956, some 19 years after the program was started, about 400 engineers had gone through the program, and its graduates produced patents at about three times the rate of nonparticipant engineers, and the results are equally good for both older and younger men.

The approach followed at General Electric draws on brainstorming and includes it in various phases, but it is best described as a "patterned approach." It includes orientation, training in the various duties and responsibilities within the company, as well as specific training in creative problem-solving techniques.

About 15 to 30 men each year go through this program. They are selected primarily through a combination of extensive interviews and tests, including one to measure knowledge of physics, a second to identify design curiosity which purportedly tests the power of observation, and a third to test ability to generalize and apply experience from one field to another.

The course consists of two phases, and extends for a period of 18 months. The first phase, Creative Engineering Program-I, CEP-I, aims at developing ideas and runs for the first 6 months. The second phase, CEP-II, lasts for 12 months and bridges the gap between idea-gathering and practical application. The class is supervised by recent graduates of the program, and supplementary instruction is supplied by company executives, inventors, engineers, and other guest speakers.

CEP-I consists of ten elements: *Orientation*—in which course administration, history, policy, salary procedures, and facilities are discussed. *Creative Philosophy*—in which participants read Alex Osborn's *Applied Imagination*, hear lectures on creativity, and read other materials in the field. During this element they see, hear, and practice idea-building. *Engineering Fundamentals*—which is essentially self-explanatory. This section places emphasis on engineering principles, equations, electronics, control systems, and measurements. *Unusual Materials and Processes*—in which participants are told about new and unusual materials, which can be included in their ideas. *Useful Basic Components and Devices*—in which participants are taught how certain devices work so that such devices could, if necessary, be incorporated in their ideas. *Company Services and Organization*—in which the participant is told how he can make use of various departments of the company (patent, purchasing, traffic, etc.) *Presentation of Ideas*—in which the participant is given training in how to communicate his ideas in writing or oral presentation. *Human Relations*—in which the participant is given training in uderstanding human relationships and is taught how to deal with people.

In addition to the aforementioned sessions, the participants spend about 15 to 20 hours a week on *Homework Problems* in which they try to get at least eight workable solutions to the problems presented, and then there is a 5-week *Model-building Project* which, in its own way, is at the level of a thesis for a master's degree.

The second part of the General Electric Creative Engineering Program is designed to help the participants convert their ideas to action. They learn to reduce ideas to a "packaged product having technical superiority, optimum manufacturing cost, and functional qualities that win public acceptance [Bittel, 1956, p. 103]." Students spend about 34 hours per week in class, and 15 to 20 hours at home on homework assignments. This second part of the course consists of six elements, which can be described as follows: *Project Engineering*—which includes presentation of techniques for organizing, planning, and scheduling projects. It also involves presentation of cost-estimation of group efforts. *Design for Manufacture*—in which there are discussions of the effect of design on manufacturing costs, including inventory control, materials handling, quality control, packing and shipping, and plant layout. *Creative Stimuli*—in which participants submit one new product idea a week, and participate in leading the group in brainstorming. *Technical Topics*—in which the participants' backgrounds are increased by discussions concerning a variety of technical areas; computers, microwaves, etc. *Problem Discussion*—which consists of two 8-week projects and one 5-week project in which plant layouts are made for prototypes designed earlier. *Rotating Engineering Assignments*—throughout the 18-month period of the training program each participant works on five or six assignments under the guidance of an experienced engineer.

As can be seen, then, the program at General Electric is not simply a creative engineering program. Rather, it is a training program in which many of the various aspects of the creative process are included. In addition, the engineer is provided with an orientation to the company and educated in which of its resources are available to him and how he might go about using them effectively. During training, he is constantly learning through lectures and discussions of new materials and ideas. He is given experience not only in the generation of ideas, but also in the building of practical models. He is also provided with training in the communication of ideas and in the "selling" of products produced.

Hotpoint

Bittel (1956) also describes a program which was instituted by A. C. Studt of Hotpoint and which runs for five 1½-hour sessions. A variety of techniques that can be helpful in stimulating ideas are used in this program. One, called the *garbage can method*, is designed to help students develop a sensitivity to problems. For example, students are told about waste products of various operations and are asked what the company itself or other companies can use them for. The class brainstorms this problem. To stimulate creative thinking an involved story is told to the group at each session, but it is interrupted before completion, and the class is told to complete it. Several of the more unusual completions are then read in class.

Another technique was called the *tear-down method* in which two men brainstorm some operating practice. The role of Man 1 is to find everything wrong with the present practice, and to suggest a different (but not necessarily better) way of doing it. Man 2 cannot agree with him and must suggest still another way. Man 1 then disagrees, and still another way is suggested. This procedure continues until the two men hit upon an idea that they think will work. A second method in which two individuals again participate is called the *and-also method*. Under the rules of this method one participant must make a suggestion and the other must add to it. So, after the first participant suggests an idea, the second says that it is a good idea "and-also it can be improved by . . . [Bittel, 1956, p. 104]." A third technique is the *17-solutions method* (17 was selected arbitrarily, thus any number can be substituted for it). Before a meeting is called to discuss a problem, the problem is sent to all concerned. To be admitted to the meeting, participants must come with a list of solutions. Duplicates are discarded and the group tries to ferret out the good ideas and develop them.

AC Spark Plug

At AC Spark Plug, Harris and Simberg set up a seminar in creative thinking (Bittel, 1956) that consisted of 12 2-hour sessions attended by 12 to 15 persons. The sessions were conducted seminar fashion to allow free expression of ideas. The ideas were recorded by the participants, who took turns at being secretary. Osborn's (1963) book was used as a source of stimulation and for the exercises it contains. Each session contained the following five steps: *Warm-up Exercise*—in which the group brainstormed the use of some object. *Illustrated Lecture*—in which charts were used to summarize the reading assignments in Osborn's book.

Recital of Assignment—in which several of the participants showed how they solved a homework problem. *Problem Solving*—which involved working on some hypothetical or specific problem. The greatest share of time was alloted to this phase. *Homework*—participants were given problems to solve at home.

The 12 sessions covered the following subject material:

1. History and objectives.
2. Judicial *vs.* creative thinking.
3. Factors affecting creativity.
4. Factors promoting or inhibiting creativity.
5. Training the mind to think.
6. Gathering data and developing hypotheses.
7. Restating the problem and rectifying.
8. Effect of effort, motivation.
9. Values in self-questioning.
10. Supervising creative people.
11. Review.
12. Re-test with new questions [Bittel, 1956, p. 105].

Among the results of this kind of program are greater sensitivity to problems, greater tendency for teamwork, decreased negative thinking, willingness to try new methods, and increase in number of ideas (Bittel, 1956).

Coca-Cola

Dr. J. E. Bujake, Jr. (1969), at the time of his article, Development Associate for the Coca-Cola Company Foods Division, pulled together a variety of procedures into a four-step process: "(1) opportunity search, (2) form evolution, (3) concept expansion, and (4) concept development (Bujake, 1969, p. 279)." In each of these steps various techniques, most of which have been described earlier are used.

Opportunity Search

The purpose of this step is to identify areas having potential for new products. To aid in this process, attribute analysis is used. All desirable and undesirable attributes of existing products in a specified area are discussed and analyzed. The attributes are listed in a very general manner to provide for greater flexibility.

Bujake uses a new breakfast food for illustrative purposes and points out that it might combine some of the following attributes: "nutrition, aroma, multiple flavors, and textures with convenient preparation, compactness, and texture retention [Bujake, 1969, p. 280]."

In addition to attribute analysis, systems analysis can also be used for ideas about new products. "In this technique all the inputs and outputs of a physical system that involve the product area of interest are examined. Attempts are then made to improve the efficiency of the system by developing new product concepts [Bujake, 1969, p. 280]."

For packaged breakfast foods some of the concepts included: "(1) minimize or eliminate preparation step by developing a ready-to-eat room temperature product, (2) eliminate serving by having a product that is prepared by each individual, and (3) eliminate clean-up by using disposables or having individual servings in edible containers [Bujake, 1969, p. 281]."

Form Evolution

This involves taking the material generated in the previous step and developing a unique form with it. Here Bujake makes use of morphological analysis (cf. Volume 1, pages 94, 200, 211–214). After establishing a matrix for purposes of morphological analysis the following suggestions for the breakfast food were developed:

> a foamed-flake product, highly porous and having a large surface area to give a light crisp texture; a breakfast drink concentrate in aerosol form; a breakfast product containing an encapsulated liquid to enhance aroma; a frozen liquid breakfast concentrate; a low calorie frozen foamed breakfast food; and a product, possibly foamed, in a toaster envelope, such as a soufflé [Bujake, 1969, p. 281].

Concept Expansion

This step involves generation of alternatives. Brainstorming techniques are used for this. Another possible aid are trigger sessions* (a technique developed by G. H. Muller of Ford Motor Co.). This technique adds competition to group procedures. After a problem is defined and analytically stated the group is given a list of words relevant to the problem. The members of the group are then given 10 minutes to build and develop their own

---

*The trigger sessions involve the combination of competition with group attempts at idea generation. When the problem is defined, each group member takes some minutes to prepare an initial list of key words relevant to the problem. The group then has some 10 minutes to build and develop further the key words and add any additional ideas. The trigger session starts with each person in the group presenting his list of ideas. An idea that is presented must then be deleted if it occurs on someone else's list. The group notes additional concepts that are triggered in them, and, after the first list for everyone is completed, a second list is developed by each participant, and the process just described repeats itself. A group that is experienced in this procedure can apparently go through some four or five cycles at a session. This technique was developed, according to Bujake (1969) by Geroge H. Muller of the Ford Motor Co., Dearborn, Michigan.

key words and ideas. The trigger session starts by moving from one person to another to have them state their ideas. Once an idea is presented it must be deleted from everyone else's list. In the first go-around about 50% of the ideas that the group has are dropped.

Additional ideas or concepts as they occur are then noted on a second list. After everybody has had a chance to present his ideas a second cycle is started. Experienced groups go through four or five cycles. By using the trigger session for concept expansion on the concept of foamed flakes as a breakfast food, Bujake's groups suggested:

(1) micro-sized, porous foamed flakes containing encapsulated liquids and aromatic flavors,

(2) a large foamed flake with a filling in an open-celled matrix,

(3) small foamed spherical particles or flakes added to liquid to give flavor and texture,

(4) a toaster product consisting of a filling encased in a foamed shell, and

(5) large multi-layered sandwich-like foamed structure containing spun or textured protein in breakfast flavor combinations, e.g., bacon and eggs [Bujake, 1969, p. 283].

If an unfeasible concept is selected the process is continued with another concept.

Concept Development

This is the last and most critical step. Its goal is a solution of the problem. Synectics is used for this. The concept worked on in this example was: How can a foamed multitextured sandwich-like structure be made? An example of a viewpoint obtained as a result of using synectics was (Bujake, 1969), " 'the use of a high pressure extrusion of a starch-water-protein mixture to produce a foamed sandwich-like multi-textured structure that can be filled or impregnated with flavors and aroma' [p. 285]."

Bujake points out that four or five highly trained people are needed for this approach and that its effectiveness is related to product area and group experience. Practice is required, and to produce meaningful concepts, critical evaluation is also necessary. The ideas have to be tried out and evaluated before they are implemented.

The procedure fosters more cooperation between individuals, greater interaction between groups, and since people with different backgrounds in the company are involved (the procedure works best under this condition) it facilitates communication between different groups, and instills "open-minded and positive attitudes [Bujake, 1969, p. 286]." Bujake regards the approach as useful "to develop unique approaches in administrative, marketing, financial, and manufacturing efforts [Bujake, 1969, p. 286]." It can be used for both long- and short-range planning, and "Perhaps, most importantly, a group using this method can instill a more creative atmosphere that will permeate the entire corporation and help motivate it in the achievement of the corporate goals [p. 286]."

Additional Sources for Information and Assistance

One of the pioneers in the field of programs to stimulate creativity is Charles H. Clark (1958) who currently heads his own *Idea Laboratory*. He has conducted creativity stimulation programs for government, industry, schools and professional associations. For industry, he has conducted creativity programs for personnel in research organizations and managerial personnel in supermarkets and oil companies in the U.S. and abroad.

Clark's programs can be tailored to suit various needs and those referred to above included programs that consisted of 3 3-hour sessions, and 1-day and 2-day seminars.

One of the procedures that is basic to Clark's training program is a morphological matrix in which he utilizes several of Guilford's (1967) concepts across the top and on the left are elements of an idea tool kit that he has developed.

Clark may be contacted by writing him at Idea Laboratory, 1236 Star Ridge Drive, Pittsburgh, Pa., 15241.

We would have liked to describe efforts of other consultants too, but we could not because this work is not intended as such a directory. Clark's work is cited as an illustration of what is available on a consultative basis. It is also cited because he is a pioneer in the field and because one of his techniques is a combination of techniques and variables described in these two volumes. Nevertheless, we should like to point out that a number of people have written articles and books on creativity, e.g. De Bono (1970), Goldner (1962), Von Fange (1959) and others. One might wish to consider inviting these authors or other persons who have written about creativity as speakers, consultants and/or directors for a creativity stimulating program.

Personal programs can be conducted by using Osborn's book as a text in conjunction with Parnes' *Creative Behavior Guidebook* (1967a). The Creative Education Foundation, Buffalo, New York, has available a set of 44 color training slides that can be rented or purchased. The rental price is $10 a week and the purchase price is $30 (January of 1974).

Some colleges and universities conduct courses in which individuals can enroll for further training. *The Center for Creative Leadership*, Smith Richardson Building, 5000 Laurinda Drive, P.O. Box P-1, Greensboro, North Carolina

27402, conducts a program for identifying and developing creative leaders. It also engages in research on the creative process. A technique developed at this center called *Simultaneous Sensory Stimulation* will be discussed in the next chapter (p. 258). Further information about such outside help is available from the Creative Education Foundation, 1300 Elmwood Ave., Buffalo, New York 14222.

Parnes's *Creative Behavior Guidebook* (1967a) contains an excellent list of bibliographical readings, a listing of audio-visual aids, sources from which they can be obtained, and a sampling of references to methods and programs for stimulating creativity.

Finally, current information on new courses, techniques, and programs can be obtained from at least three major publications: *Journal of Applied Behavioral Science*, published by the National Training Laboratories, P.O. Box 9155 Rosslyn Station, Arlington, Virginia 22209; *The Journal of Creative Behavior*, published by Creative Education Foundation, and the *Training and Development Journal*, P. O. Box 5307, Madison, Wisconsin 53705.

EVALUATION OF SOME EXISTING PROGRAMS

Unfortunately, there is no systematic program in which the same procedures and criteria are utilized to evaluate the effectiveness of all creativity programs. Such programs are needed if we are to have a better understanding of the relative effectiveness of existing programs. A study that is a step in the right direction was conducted by Edwards (1966), who asked 30* organizations to evaluate their creativity courses and programs. These 30 organizations included 15 industrial corporations, 1 government agency, 1 research organization, 4 consulting firms, and 9 colleges and universities. Since some of the larger companies having creativity programs were not involved in this survey, the sample is far from complete, and may not even be representative. Nevertheless it gives us some idea of how some programs are evaluated.

The creativity courses involved were directed at various levels of management, engineering, research and development personnel, salesmen, etc. In most cases the courses took place during job hours, they ranged from 6 to 80 hours each, with most of them in the 25- to 40-hour range. The size of the average class was between 16 to 30 persons. Courses conducted in companies ran from 4 to 10 weeks; those in colleges and universities usually lasted one semester.

The content of the courses was quite varied. They included discussions and

*The questionnaire was sent to 43 organizations. Thirty-four replied and, of these, 30 provided information on the courses or programs in which they were involved.

involvement exercises. In some instances stress was placed on specific techniques such as synectics, sensitivity and awareness training, and brainstorming. Insofar as costs were concerned, those companies that conducted their courses on their own time had as their major cost the cost of the participants' time. In addition, if an outside instructor or consultant was used then the cost increased from $75 to $100 a person. All these cost figures, it should be carefully noted, come from Edwards' report published in 1966. New costs should always be checked.

In most instances, some means of evaluation was used. They included questionnaires, test administered before and after training (e.g., *AC Test of Creative Ability*, Guilford's tests, Barron-Welsh *Figure Preference* Test, the Barron *Complexity Scale*) and more concrete and practical measures, such as increases in patent applications, problems solved, money saved on processes or products, improvement in products or processes, increased profits, increases in participation and in amount of awards in suggestion systems, positive evaluation by management, new innovations and/or inventions, and increases in bonus awards given.

Edwards received a variety of positive reports and statements regarding the usefulness and value of the different programs. In evaluating these statements it must be kept in mind that the satisfied client is most likely to send a positive testimonial. Thus there may be an overrepresentation of positive statements. There is no way of knowing how many programs were started and abandoned or how many were completed with unimpressive results. The following evaluations should therefore be regarded with caution.

Among the positive results Edwards (1966, Appendix B) reports that the B. F. Goodrich Company experienced a "39% increase in improvement projects (estimated financially beneficial)"; Southern Bell Telephone Company had a "120 percent . . . increase"—on the *AC Test of Creative Ability*. Sylvania Electric Products Inc., and General Telephone and Electronics Corporation "Doubled profit; [had] 2100 new products; beat competition on 2 new products; increased patent applications five-fold; [and] saved $22 million." The U.S. Army Management School also used the *AC Test of Creative Ability* for evaluation purposes and reported, "26% average improvement." Reactions obtained to questionnaires were also favorable.

Other reports include such statements as, " '. . . proven savings have reached in the millions plus immeasurable intangibles,' 'one company [saved] $75,000 on inventory work,' 'ten new patent applications from [a] class of 26,' " and another reported that as a result of application of principles learned $4 million was saved.

According to Edwards, several factors were noted as important for success:

(a) establishing a psychologically secure atmosphere where all ideas are welcome;

(b) leading participants out of " 'mental ruts,' " thereby enabling them to see problems in a different light;

(c) stimulating participants to recognize and circumvent the individual inhibiting factors or blocks to the free play of their imagination;

(d) involving students intellectually by working on something of interest to them and learning by self-demonstration;

(e) encouraging "cross-fertilization" of ideas;

(f) gaining self-confidence and skills by actually solving problems of progressively greater difficulty; and

(g) challenging students to be "open to experience" constantly and to stretch their imagination as far as they can.

SUMMARY

In this chapter various creativity programs that have been used or are currently in use in different companies and organizations were presented. Obviously these are applicable to the applied or engineering areas, but aside from education programs, there have not been such concentrated approaches for creativity in the arts and humanities.

Various sources for materials that can be of help to a creativity training program were mentioned. And, for the reader who wishes to remain informed about contemporary research in the area of creativity as well as important related materials, names of journals that can fulfill these needs were also presented.

By using these different resources as well as materials, procedures and ideas mentioned throughout this book, the reader should be able to develop a creativity training program either for others or himself.

Hopefully, in the future, more effort will be devoted to systematic evaluation of all programs such as those described in this chapter. Such data would enable us to better understand the process of stimulating creativity. They would also enable us to select correctly from what is available to fulfill our plans to further stimulate creativity.

PART VII

CONCLUSION

This is the last part of this two-volume work. It contains one concluding chapter rather than a chapter of conclusions. As such it has a twofold purpose. First, it summarizes the individual and group procedures for stimulating creativity together with the research testing their underlying assumptions and effectiveness.

Second, this chapter takes a look at the future and discusses some of the problems that are still in need of further study. Hopefully all future work will contribute not only to specific substantive issues but also to two major goals that were frequently stated in this work. One is to further understanding of the effects on the creative process of the transactional relationships between the individual and his immediate environment and between the individual and the society in which he lives. The other goal is to attain such knowledge and understanding that will better enable us to know what kinds of creativity stimulating techniques and procedures to select for different kinds of people when they work with various kinds of problems under diverse conditions.

Chapter XVIII

A Summary and a View toward the Future

This work was organized around the following definition and assumptions. Creativity is a process that results in a novel product or idea which is accepted as useful, tenable, or satisfying by a significant group of others at some point in time (Stein 1962, 1963, 1967). It occurs within both individual and social contexts and is affected by both *intra*personal and *inter*personal processes.

It consists of three overlapping stages—hypothesis formation, hypothesis testing, and the communication of results. A preparatory stage also exists but since it is used largely for educational purposes it is not regarded here as uniquely part of the creative process.

The creative process is not the only process through which novelty may be achieved. Novelty may be achieved through trial and error, insightful problem solving, serendipity, discovery, etc. None of these involves the broad, integrating "jump" that is characteristic of creativity. In any one case the creative process could involve the other processes. Consequently, by orienting ourselves to the creative process, benefits of the other processes would also be derived.

Each of the stages of the creative process has its own set of participants, goals, demands, and requirements. Creative individuals possess the psychological characteristics necessary to fulfill all of these. Therefore the characteristics of the creative process and the creative individual are set up as requirements to be fulfilled and goals to be achieved by various individual and group techniques for attaining creative novelty. Hopefully through the successful use of the various techniques, people could come closer and closer to the way in which the creative individual behaves as he seeks and finds creative solutions.

The individual techniques for stimulating creativity discussed in this work concerned themselves with what a person could do for himself and by himself to overcome blocks to creativity and to proceed in more effective ways to fulfill the requirements of the creative process. As aids in this regard, attention was focused on those positive personality factors that facilitate the creative process as well as on what might be done to cope with some of the personality characteristics that obstruct its smooth development. And, since an individual is more than just a composite of his personality characteristics, we were also concerned with what might be done to stimulate the cognitive factors (how he perceives his environment, how he thinks about what he extracts from his environment, how he goes about solving the problems he sees in his environment, etc.) that have also been found to affect creativity.

In addition to what an individual can do by and for himself to become more creative, there are also things he can do in working with others. Indeed, there are persons who are more responsive to group procedures than to individual ones. Consequently, a major portion of this work was devoted to discussing a variety of group procedures. Although we separated the individual from the group procedures, we hope that no one will feel constricted by this division and will make his choice of the techniques that suit him best, from any part of the work.

In this concluding chapter we wish to call attention to some of the more critical features of both individual and group techniques for stimulating creativity and to call attention to areas that require work in the future.

INDIVIDUAL TECHNIQUES

There are individual techniques that focus on the person, his personality, and cognitive characteristics, and there are individual techniques that focus on the stages of the creative process. These are simply two different ways of looking at the same coin and we shall discuss both sets of procedures.

Affecting Personality Characteristics

A basic assumption underlying the various techniques for stimulating creativity is that change is possible and that whatever has blocked, distorted, or inhibited the creative process for the individual can be dealt with and reversed. They can be removed or cleared up so that an individual can begin or continue to make significant contributions.

Three procedures were discussed: role playing, hypnosis, and psychotherapy. Role playing in this instance essentially involves "making believe" that a person is creative and by taking on this role, will behave more like a creative person. There are no systematic studies of how role playing affects creativity in real-life situations but there is research evidence that it produces positive results as measured by psychological tests of creativity. In other words, a rather simple technique like role playing, in which a person behaves as if he were creative, may help overcome blocks to creativity. Such behavior may indeed produce creative results.

Hypnosis has been used in a variety of situations to help people cope with their difficulties and blocks in various life situations. In all likelihood the same difficulties that interfere with an individual's effectiveness in these different areas could also cause problems in creativity. There are anecdotal reports, case studies, or individual "stories" of how hypnosis has helped creativity but reports of systematic attempts to investigate the effects of hypnosis on creativity in real-life situations is lacking.

Anecdotal reports of the effects of psychotherapy on creativity are also available. A book has been written about creative persons who were on the couch (Freeman, 1971)—Graham Greene, Hermann Hesse, Tennessee Williams, etc. However, there is no systematic research of the effects of psychotherapy on creativity. What is available is a research study by Wispé and Parloff (1965) on the relationship between psychotherapy and productivity. One of the findings of this study was that psychologists who had had psychotherapy and who said they were satisfied with the effects of their therapy also said they produced works of good quality and quantity. No statistically significant relationship, however, was found between an individual's rating of his satisfaction with his therapy and a rating of his publications by others.

In these two findings we find some of the problems involved in evaluating the effects of therapy on creativity. Specifically, who is the more important judge of the value of psychotherapy for the individual—he himself or someone else. Those who favor psychotherapy generally might argue that the person himself is the best judge. Others might argue that this is not necessarily so for a person who has been in therapy has a great deal at stake in believing that his therapy has been helpful and worthwhile. It is obvious that this is an important problem that will have to be solved in future work.

Another finding of importance on the relationship between psychotherapy and productivity is that psychotherapy probably helps those who are productive maintain the level of their productivity while their colleagues, who have not had the benefit of psychotherapy, witness a decline in their productivity. Would similar results occur if creativity were involved? Some anecdotal material suggests that we should anticipate a positive answer to this question. It is to be hoped that persons in therapy and their psychotherapists would be motivated

toward this goal of gathering data on this matter so that we should be better able
to answer the question of the effects of therapy on creativity.

Affecting Cognitive Processes

Cognitive processes refer to an individual's way of knowing, understanding,
perceiving, learning, problem solving, etc. A creative individual sees, approaches,
thinks about, and deals with his materials differently than a less creative person.
The question then is, is there some way to affect an individual's cognitive
characteristics so that he can behave more creatively?

One approach is to try to alter a person's state of consciousness. His
consciousness may be too narrow and constricted to allow many ideas to come
to the fore, or, the ideas that first come to consciousness are commonplace ones
that have to be verbalized and "gotten rid of" to allow more unusual and more
creative ones to come forward. If a person's consciousness is not shaken up in
some way he may be quite pedestrian in how he solves his problems.

A variety of methods used to alter consciousness have been considered:
relaxation-reflection; dreams; alcohol; caffeine; and mind-expanding drugs
including marijuana, morphine, the amphetamines, LSD, mescaline, and
psilocybin. Accumulated evidence suggests that there is no simple way or simple
"pill" for stimulating one's creativity. Caffeine has a stimulating effect on
certain psychological functions involved in creativity and alcohol in too large
doses can have a debilitating effect. A study of creative persons' drinking habits
indicates that they do not drink to be more creative but to help them relax from
the tensions they experience while working creatively.

Subjective reports on the effects of mind-expanding drugs indicates that they
improve creativity. But more objective studies indicate that while drugs facilitate
the use of some of the psychological processes involved in creativity, they affect
other processes negatively.

There are numerous problems involved in studying the effects of mind-
expanding drugs. Some persons find it hard to accept the results of drug studies
since they believe that obtained results could, in large measure, be attributed to
such nondrug factors as a subject's attitude, psychological state, relationship
with experimenter, and the social atmosphere in which the experiment was
conducted. Others, like Harman *et al.* (1969) are not bothered by such criticism.
They argue, essentially, that taking the drug may involve a unique set of conditions, and that it is probably impossible to disentangle their individual effects—
so why try to do so. Why not focus instead on the total condition and the
combined or total effect produced. Therefore, they did just this in their study of
the effects of mescaline on individuals who were employed in academic and
industrial situations and who were counted on to come up with creative solutions to problems. The results of this study did indeed indicate positive

relationships between the drug and creativity measured by tests, questionnaires, and reports of accomplishments in real-life situations.

The methodology in this study strikes us as quite interesting but like other experiments it requires further study and replication. If the original results are supported in future work then society would have to reexamine its attitudes and values about the use of drugs under various conditions. On the other hand, we must bear in mind that the final word is yet to be heard on the short- and long-term effects of drugs on a person's health and biology. When these data are in they will also have to be evaluated in terms of situations where the use of drugs to help stimulate creativity is considered.

In writing this work we have tried to be reasonably thorough in the number and kinds of techniques covered. However, the field of stimulating creativity tends to be a very active one, and new techniques are always being developed. Sometimes techniques are developed to deal with a specific problem in the creativity area and sometimes techniques which have proven interesting and useful in other areas of psychological research are adapted for use in the creativity area. Consequently, any work such as this has a hard time staying up to date with each and every type of technique.

There are two techniques that have come to our attention since we called a halt on the investigation for this work. We shall present them briefly since they are quite different from techniques covered elsewhere in the work and extend the range of procedures available for stimulating creativity. The first makes use of biofeedback and the second focuses on a person's various senses.

Biofeedback is a rather recently developed technique in which an individual learns how to use various cues to maintain voluntary control over his internal states. By becoming increasingly aware of the physiological correlates of a psychological state an individual learns to determine when he has arrived at a desired psychological state and then to maintain it.

In using biofeedback, brain waves, which can be recorded and made recognizable to subjects, have been "fedback" to the subjects, i.e., the subjects have been made aware of the characteristics of their brain waves when they were in the midst of certain psychological states. In an experiment by Green *et al.* (1971) the desired state to be maintained was that of reverie-hypnagogic activity. And this state was to be brought to an individual's attention by making him aware of the frequencies of brain waves related to this state.

Specifically, Green *et al.* reasoned as follows: some creative individuals reported using reverie-hypnagogic activity in their creative work. Kekulé's observation that some organic compounds occurred in closed rings had its origin in a series of reveries in which he observed that atoms took the form of a snake and that the snake had caught hold of its own tail.

To the use of reverie-hypnagogic activity by creative individuals, Green *et al.* added the fact that certain brain waves—theta waves, and low-frequency alpha waves (between 4-8 waves/second)—have been associated with the production of reverie-hypnagogic images—images that come to mind "full-blown." They, therefore, argued that if individuals could be made aware of when they were having theta waves and low alpha waves they might be exposed to the proper cues for knowing when they were in a condition or state for having reveries that could then be used for creative work. Green *et al.* did not train persons to produce creative work but they did suggest studies for the further investigation of the potential value of their procedure.

While Green *et al.* concerned themselves with how internal stimuli may affect external stimuli, I. A. Taylor reversed the direction of influence and tried to affect internal states through the manipulation of external stimuli. Taylor presented his subjects with a variety of "simultaneous sensory stimulation" that in one study (Taylor, 1970, p. 48) included "a high frequency signal from an oscillator, a phosphorescent Archimides spiral wheel, pungent incense, a floor vibrator, a loud percussion-type music." (Tactile stimulation and visual stimulation through the use of ceiling lights were omitted in this study but used in others.) Subjects were exposed to these stimuli for as long as 20 minutes at a time (Taylor & Knapp, 1971) over a period of weeks. The number of weeks varied in different studies. Before and after subjects were exposed to the stimulation they were tested for various psychological functions. They were also asked to make still life drawings as a measure of their creativity.

The results of these experiments are interesting. In one study with very bright young adults (Taylor, 1970) and in another study with chronic schizophrenics (Taylor and Knapp, 1971), improved creativity was reported after sensory stimulation.* In a third study (Taylor, 1972) with college students, divergent thinking (a psychological characteristic that is regarded by some psychologists as related to creativity) improved after exposure to the simultaneous sensory stimulation, while convergent thinking (a psychological characteristic regarded as not related to creativity or even standing in the way of creativity) was not affected at all. Whether people in real-life situations would use sensory inputs such as those used by Taylor and just what effects these would have on creativity are intriguing questions for further investigation.

---

*It is interesting to compare the effects of sensory stimulation with those obtained from sensory deprivation. Taylor (1970) cites a study by Fuerst and Zubek (1968) in which they reported some of the effects of sensory and perceptual deprivation on some of Guilford's tests of psychological functions related to creativity. These tests were administered before and after 3 days of either sensory deprivation or perceptual deprivation. The deprived subjects, when data from several studies were combined, were found to have performed significantly less well than control subjects only on Ideational Fluency. Within experiments there were no differences between experimental and control subjects on the various cognitive measures that were used.

The Stages of the Creative Process

Just as there are techniques and procedures that focus on the person, his personality and cognitive characteristics, so there are individual techniques that focus on each of the stages that make up the creative process—hypothesis formation, hypothesis testing, and the communication of results. These three stages are preceded by a preparatory stage which also has broader educational purposes. According to the tack taken in this book we do not regard the preparatory stage as an integral part of the creative process. However, because it obviously does have important effects it is important that techniques which can facilitate its contributions to the creative process be considered. Consequently, we start with the preparatory stage before turning to the others.

Preparatory (Educational) Stage

The preparatory stage of the creative process includes all formal and informal educational experiences which provide an individual with the information, training, and experience necessary for the work he will do in his chosen field. Experience during this stage of the creative process may have a marked effect on the person's attitudes and values for creativity.

Because it was obviously impossible to concern ourselves with all the relevant aspects of the learning situation, we limited ourselves to a presentation of critical aspects of relationships with classmates and teachers, teaching techniques, and the school or teaching environment. Social relationships with classmates and teachers most usually (but fortunately not always) emphasize conformity. There are frequently pressures in these relationships that try to keep the person from becoming and being his own unique self—a self who can explore various ways of manifesting his originality and creativity. Unfortunately encouragement for development in the creative direction is frequently lacking. It would be a very important step forward if ways could be found wherein classmates and teachers would value, encourage, and reward the creativity of the students with whom they come into contact.

To stimulate further creativity in a school environment attention should be paid not only to the teaching techniques used but also to matters associated with them. Specifically, attention should be paid to the following: (1) Notation should be made that emphasis on evaluation and criticism while learning new information focuses a student's attention on these matters and can so constrict the student that his capacity to integrate what he has learned is impaired. Under these conditions a student also becomes handicapped in his ability to develop newer and more creative combinations from what he has been taught and from what he has learned. (2) Newer and newer techniques are being developed for teaching and some of these focus directly on creativity. One of the newer developments involves the use of computers and programmed learning and another technique which is especially noteworthy is one developed by Gordon (1971) in which use is made of the metaphor.

The school system needs to be regarded as a social organization and as any such organization it too affects creativity. To help affect the characteristics of such an organization special attention might be paid to the following: (1) the use of diagnostic surveys should be designed specifically to highlight the organization's assets and liabilities for creativity. (2) Selection of school administrators and principals who value creativity in their teachers and students should be stressed. Unless such values exist "at the top" it is unlikely that the creative behaviors of those "down below" will be reinforced and encouraged. (3) Teachers who are creative in their own right could serve as models for their students who in emulating their teachers' behaviors become more creative in their own right. (4) More complete diagnostic information is necessary about students' personality and cognitive characteristics so that they can benefit from proper guidance procedures. (5) Specially trained counselors who understand the problems of creative students can be of much value in the school system. (6) More basic research is necessary on the nature of the creative process and the factors that affect it throughout the course of the school years. Such research should be part of the on-going experience during the school years so that courses and teaching techniques can be periodically assessed and improved.

Stimulating creativity through educational practices should not be limited only to pupils in school. Such opportunities and procedures should also be made available to adults. Similarly the concept of education should not be limited to the school system. The young student as well as the adult student should be exposed to the educational values of traveling, visiting museums and galleries, listening to poetry readings, going to concerts, etc. All can help foster creativity. Also, to further help foster creative accomplishments, a person's storehouse of information should constantly be increased so he is not simply limited to a tiny specialized area of knowledge. Depending on the area of work, ideas that may be of help in future endeavors may come from books on animal behavior, science fiction, catalogs, etc.

In all of these learning activities, it is important to emphasize that what an individual learns is important but that the attitudes and values associated with the learned content are also important.

Hypothesis Formation

The process that results in a creative end product is set in motion by an individual who has been receptive to the "gaps," the questions, and the problems that exist in his environment. The process may also be set into motion by an individual with a "thorn in his side" who pokes around seeking incongruities in his environment. If he doesn't find them he creates them. He takes an existing order, puts it into some disorder and then reestablishes an order that is better than that which previously existed. Needless to say not all individuals are capable of such behavior. They are afraid to deviate from the status quo. They suppress questions about that which exists for to do otherwise would only disrupt an existing structure and provoke anxiety.

The creative individual also has the capacity to view his environment as if it were animated, in flux and constantly in a state of becoming or evolving. He is not afraid to toy and play with the objects and ideas around him. In so doing he behaves in a childlike but not in a childish manner. He can as the occasion demands turn such behavior off and become "adult"—formal and logical. While the less creative individual may be capable of one behavior pattern or the other, the creative person is capable of moving back and forth through a range of behaviors and psychological processes and so is capable of raising more questions and providing more ideas which help him develop creative solutions to his questions. A person who tries to overcome his rigidities and strives to emulate the patterns just described may go a long way in furthering his own creativity.

Asking *the* question or *a* question (for the question itself may change as the process develops) only starts the creative process. After it has begun the individual has to acquaint himself with the question's components. He has to immerse himself into its various characteristics. As Gordon (1961) says in discussing the first stage of his synetics procedure for stimulating creativity—it is necessary in the early stages of the creative process to make the strange familiar. But once this has been accomplished the individual has to start coming up with ideas to help solve the problem. It could happen that once a person has a good statement of the problem and has become familiar with it he may have an instantaneous creative thought. If so, all to the good. In most instances the first ideas that come to mind are not likely to provide the creative solution. The question remains a question. At this point in the creative process the lesser creative individual may give up. However his more creative counterpart calls upon a more flexible approach to both inner resources and external stimuli.

To help others overcome the effects of obstructing blocks and constricting rigidities, a series of techniques were presented designed to help persons come closer to emulating the behavior of creative persons and to develop a variety of hypotheses that may help answer the original question or solve the initial problem. The techniques presented were essentially cognitive in character. All of them are designed to stimulate thought processes and idea generation through the concretization and externalization of what presumably goes on in the mind and work of the creative individual.

Some of these techniques instruct the individual to defer judgment and to put away evaluation as he strives for ideas. Other techniques provide a person with questions he should ask himself about his materials or his ideas. And, still others provide him with some simple techniques and guidelines for manipulating the basic variables that make up his materials. In doing so he is relatively unencumbered by the fact that he does not have to keep them all in his mind at the same time. And, as this person tries to carry out the suggested manipulations he picks from the array of permutations and combinations that appear before him that one or that number which he believes will lead to a fruitful result at the end of the creative process.

While the self-help procedures reviewed facilitate the development of ideas, there is little, if anything, that has been recommended which is techniquelike in character and which can be of help in selecting from available ideas that one which will result in the creative work. What can be of help, short of a testing procedure, is becoming aware of an "aesthetic" feel, an awareness of something that feels good, and then developing confidence in it so that it may serve as a guide in making fruitful selections from the array of available ideas.

The process of hypothesis formation can be extremely frustrating and irritating. Some individuals give up at this point in the creative process; others stubbornly avoid the hard work involved as they wait to be struck by intuitions and inspirations. Both intuitions and inspirations do occur but they neither strike like lightening or light up like bulbs. They occur to individuals who have worked hard on their problems and who are prepared to accept and acknowledge the value of their intuitions and their inspirations.

The self-help techniques presented as aids to hypothesis formation are, as we said, primarily cognitive in character. Their value depends not only on their characteristics but also on the motivation, perseverance, confidence, and the other related personality characteristics of the persons using them.

Hypothesis Testing

An idea once generated requires testing. It has to be checked and evaluated to determine whether it provides a creative solution to the problem that set the process in motion. And, as each stage of the creative process changes so does the role of the creative individual. During the previous stage, hypothesis formation, the creative person may have been more passive—allowing ideas to come to mind without evaluation. But during hypothesis testing the creative individual becomes more active—testing and evaluating those ideas which have occurred to him.

During hypothesis testing the creative individual carries on a dialog with his environment and that problem on which he is working. He becomes both creator and critic. He alternates between these roles utilizing his knowledge and training in actualizing his ideas.

While intuition, inspiration, and the "aesthetic feel" are all part of the mystique of the hypothesis-formation stage of the creative process, "feeling with" the stresses and strains of a problem and following these to a creative solution constitute some of the mystique of the hypothesis-testing stage of the creative process. Another part of the mystique is recognizing when the work is completed.

As a person works his way through the hypothesis-testing stage of the creative process he may experience self-doubt, depression, anxiety, etc., in his attempts to shape his ideas so that they meet the demands of the problems confronting him. The intensity of these feelings need to be kept under control lest they become insurmountable blocks to creativity. Keeping in mind that they are "natural" reactions to a process with intense demands may help a person keep his reactions in perspective so that his creativity moves along constructively. Should the individual have difficulty overcoming some of these reactions by himself, it would be of value to his creativity if those around him—teachers, supervisors, administrators, family, or friends—are cognizant of the effects of the psychological state he is experiencing. Then, rather than adding their criticism to the negative effects of his self-doubt they might provide the individual with the emotional support necessary as he works his way through the difficulty of the creative process.

Serendipity, discovery, trial and error, insightful problem solving are all ways in which persons may find answers during the hypothesis-testing stage of the creative process. These techniques vary in the extent to which they involve rational and nonrational factors. Not all of them are equally applicable to all problems and all fields of endeavor. And, not all individuals are capable of using them.

Throughout the creative process, and during hypothesis testing specifically, it is important to keep in mind that there are various types of people who may develop various types of solutions to various kinds of problems. To facilitate the workings of the creative process the following may be of help: to know oneself and the hypothesis-testing procedures that one feels most comfortable with; to maintain one's motivation at an optimal level—a level that does not allow one's drive to override the demands of the situation or that is so low as not to make for a sensitive response to external stimuli; to learn different and newer ways of solving problems; to learn how to make use of analogies and metaphors by using materials from fields other than the one in which one works; to allow oneself to explore freely various leads and ideas even though they take him right out of the narrow confines dictated by the problem; to avoid "excess stimuli" and "mental dazzle"; to try to overcome "functional fixity"; to breakdown embeddedness; to allow oneself the opportunity to play with the spatial arrangements of stimuli and not be stuck in a time set; to avoid the carry-over of blocks that stem from previously applied conventional ways of solving problems; to increase psychological distance between oneself and one's problem, and so, in all these ways, adapt his behavior to the needs and demands of the problem worked on so that a creative solution may be found.

Communication of Results

The last stage in the creative process is that stage in which the person communicates the results of his labors to others. Not all treatments of creativity concern themselves with this stage of the creative process. Some limit themselves to what goes on within the creative individual and do not consider what goes on between the creative individual and others from the time he has completed his work to when others have accepted it.

Just as many theoretical treatments do not include the communication stage as part of the creative process so too many creative individuals are not happy with the inclusion of this stage as part of the process. They frequently resist carrying it out because of their difficulties in dealing with others and because their experience with others may have deprived them of recognition for their creative works. Rather than acknowledging these experiences for what they are, these persons may diminish the significance of the communication stage of the creative process by arguing that it relates more to the commercial than to the creative aspects of the creative process, and that when one turns to the communication stage one is dealing more with popularity than creativity.

When we turn to the communication stage we find that the participants in it include the creative person, one or more people whom we call "intermediaries," and finally the audience or public that is the final target of the creative communication. Sometimes as one surveys the history of creative developments one may have the impression that the creative person is more likely than not to be the victim of others' reactions. However, there is evidence that creative persons sometimes also have to bear the responsibility for the unhappy experiences they have during this stage of the creative process. By virtue of their own behavior and personalities they may have created situations that make others' support of their future creative efforts rather difficult. Just as the creative person's personality may facilitate the course of the creative process so it may complicate or frustrate it. Nowhere is this better indicated than at the communication stage of the creative process.

One of the constraints imposed on the creative individual during the communication stage of the creative process lies in the nature of the roles he is expected to fulfill. These roles vary according to the creative person's field of work and in terms of their own diversity and clarity. Hopefully by explicating them in this book as we have done for the case of researchers in industry, we may have been able to help others by providing a framework which would enable them to see more clearly the nature of the stresses and strains in which they themselves are involved so that these tensions might be somewhat reduced.

The intermediaries in the communication stage of the creative process have a position between the creative person and the audience or public whom they serve. They serve the creative person by providing him with emotional and financial support, and at times they serve as a "sounding board" for the creative person, providing him with criticism as he needs it in a nonthreatening environment. Intermediaries also serve the public or audience by providing reasoned judgments and evaluations of new works. Thus intermediaries serve as selective filters for the society. They are "gatekeepers" (Lewin, 1958) who exercise control over the various creative elements in the evolutionary development of the culture. Unfortunately little systematic effort has been devoted to elucidating the roles played by intermediaries as supporters, patrons, experts, and transmission agents. Hopefully more effort will be expended in this direction in the future.

The audience or public, in addition to the creative individual and the intermediaries, is the third major component of the communication stage of the creative process. Sooner or later it becomes the target of the creative work. The creative work gets to the audience or public through a series of stages, and, by the same token it is adopted by the audience or public through a series of stages. The first set of stages does not have any specific name, and work on it indicates that this set consists, in fact, of several steps rather than just one jump from creative person to audience or public. On the other hand, work devoted to understanding the nature of the adoption process through which members of the audience or public go indicates that the process has four functions: knowledge, persuasion, decision, and confirmation (Rogers and Shoemaker, 1971). This adoption process takes time, often much to the annoyance of the creative individual. Furthermore, not all of the persons who make up the public or audience are capable of fulfilling the requirements of the full adoption process. Some only become aware of the creative work and reject it. Others move from awareness to interest and some among these move from interest to a positive evaluation of the work and proceed to try it out. If this trial also ends positively, the work may be adopted.

The course and success of the adoption process are affected by the proper and effective use of available channels of communication for the presentation of creative works to the public and by the characteristics of the creative works themselves. If the communication process is to be maximally effective then, in addition to all else, one must attend not only to what different media may have to offer but also to the various ways in which available media differ from each other. This is necessary since effective communication requires the form and content of the message to be compatible. Creative persons themselves usually are not concerned with this aspect of the creative process and leave this work to others. However, when an objective outsider looks at what goes on in this part of the process he sees quite well that this too is part of the creative process. From the creative person's point of view this part of the process may not be as developed as one would like for all fields of creative endeavor.

For our purposes of elucidation we drew on the efforts of communication specialists, specifically those in the field of advertising. In presenting some of their information we did not assume that all points would be applicable to all fields of work. It was decided to present the information in total, nevertheless, first because of the intrinsic interest of the material and second because illustration of the kind of information available when there is an intensive effort to obtain desired data is useful. In this regard attention was called to McLuhan's (1964) differentiation between "hot" and "cold" media and Ogilvy's (1963) descriptions of the characteristics of various advertising media. Again, these were intended primarily as examples of factors that affect the communication process. No doubt there are other examples and works in the literature of equal value. The characteristics of the innovation or the creative work also play a critical role in the communication stage of the creative process. Here, as in so many other parts of the work, attention focused on primarily "applied" or technical innovations rather than on those "pure" contributions in the arts, humanities, and the sciences. These latter works had to be omitted because such matters as art and literary criticism, which deal with the nature of such contributions, are beyond the scope of this work.

In that light let us proceed to summarize these applied innovations in communication. We note that new products that come on the scene have an exceedingly high mortality rate. Consequently, effectiveness of the creative process may be improved if more attention is paid to such matters as the characteristics of these products that affect their acceptance by others, which, as pointed out by Rogers and Shoemaker (1971), are made up of categories such as compatibility, complexity, trialibility and observability—all of which can affect the product's acceptance.

The target of the communication, as we have said, is the audience or public. Both words were purposefully selected to differentiate between the number of persons involved. "Audience" was selected for the smaller groups such as those that gathered around Freud, Einstein, Picasso. "Public" is more properly used for the larger groups of people extending even to the whole society. Here again there is a difference in how much information is available about the characteristics of the audiences and publics who are accepting the novelty in the applied and pure areas. It is much greater in the former than in the latter. Much of what is known about these groups in the applied areas stems from the data gathered by advertising agencies who spend a great deal of time and money learning about the characteristics of responsive and accepting audiences and publics. Knowledge of such characteristics may function to facilitate the creative process in two ways: It may make explicit the characteristics of a public that facilitated its acceptance of a new product and could serve as a starting point from which ideas may be generated for new creative products.

Five ways of learning about and understanding the characteristics of the audience or public were discussed—adopter categories, typologies, psychographics, life-styles and benefit segmentation. Each of these techniques tries to describe subgroups within larger groups which differ from each other in terms of the rapidity with which they will adopt innovations or in the uses they will make of various innovations and the conditions under which they will use them. Each of the techniques spells out the characteristics of groups that resist, as well as the characteristic of groups that will accept, innovations and creative works.

Since all methods of breaking up the larger into smaller groups yield a subgroup that resists or refuses to accept innovations, some classical studies in the behavioral science literature designed to overcome resistances to innovation were discussed. An important point in these studies is that they call attention to the fact that a critical ingredient in helping people overcome their resistances to innovation is to allow them to participate actively and democratically in whether or not they wish to make changes in significant areas of their lives which would require them to give up some older and more traditional ways of doing things for newer and more creative ways of doing them.

Since the time that Lewin and his co-workers embarked on their studies there have been many other studies of social change and social influence far too numerous to be reviewed here. Since these studies contain much of interest, it is suggested that readers most interested in the communication stage of the creative process and in the type of data that these studies might contain seek out this literature.

With the presentation of the studies for overcoming resistance to change, we concluded the discussion of the various ways for stimulating creativity using the three stages of the creative process as our framework. This also concluded our presentation of the individual procedures for stimulating creativity. At this point we turned to the group techniques for accomplishing the same goal.

GROUP TECHNIQUES

In painting, literature, and science, creative works (with the exception of what transpires during the communication stage of the creative process) are produced essentially through the solitary efforts of creative individuals. On the other hand, it is more characteristic of the sciences and the technologies to involve group endeavors for achieving creativity since they have been so organized in institutes and academic and industrial organizations. Organizations in contemporary society are set up so that there are groups of administrative, scientific, and entrepreneurial personnel, all of whom are intimately involved in the decision making that affects their own creative processes as well as that of others. Whatever the nature and characteristics of these groups, the fact of the matter is that just as individuals produce creative works so do groups or individuals who are strongly affected by groups, and just as individuals have their problems, groups also encounter obtacles and difficulties in their creative endeavors. Groups have assets as well as liabilities for creative efforts as do individuals.

To make effective use of a group's efforts for creativity, it is important to be cognizant of various characteristics which may signal whether the group is or is not working creatively. In this regard we drew on the work of Pelz and Andrews (1966) who studied scientific groups. Their work illustrates how group climate, patterns of communication, the heterogeneous or homogeneous composition of the group, its age, etc. affected the level of the group's contribution and usefulness.

While organized groups in our society may be counted on primarily for creative contributions one should not overlook the potential contributions of leaderless groups. As Maier (1967) points out these groups have various assets and liabilities which we also discussed. Therefore, since both leaderless and organized groups may be called upon for creativity we presented a series of group techniques for stimulating creativity. While these techniques are presented as group techniques it is to be hoped that readers who seek individual procedures will not be put off by the section of the work in which these techniques are discussed. The group techniques discussed were: brainstorming, creative problem-solving, synectics, a research study evaluating personality-insight and cognitive programs for stimulating creativity, and various programs used by different industrial organizations.

Brainstorming

Brainstorming, a process for individual and group use for the generation of ideas, was originated and popularized by Osborn (1963) to replace the usual business conference with which he was dissatisfied.

Brainstorming is based on two principles. The first emphasizes deferment of judgment and the second stresses the ability to strive after many ideas so that ideas of better quality will be produced.

The first principle is based on the assumption that people produce both a small number of ideas and few ideas of good quality because they are fixated on evaluation. If people would not be so involved in evaluating their ideas then more ideas and better quality ideas would be produced. What should be stressed here is that evaluation is only deferred. Within the total process designed to achieve creative ideas, evaluation is not completely lacking. After ideas are generated then another group session is held to evaluate the ideas produced and to select those that should be followed up.

The second principle of brainstorming, that the more ideas produced the better the ideas produced, is based on the assumption that the first ideas one generates in answer to a problem are likely to be usual and commonplace. The more unique and potentially creative ideas are more likely to occur later in a chain of ideas, and they only can be arrived at by producing a quantity of ideas.

Brainstorming is a cognitive approach to creativity based on the theory of associationism. This approach and theory is quite congenial to many psychologists because they have been trained in this orientation. Consequently, more research has been carried out in the study of brainstorming's assumptions, outcomes, and training possibilities than is true of any other technique designed to stimulate creativity. However, at the same time research in brainstorming shares with other areas of investigation the lack of replicated studies. Therefore, all of the reported studies and their results must be regarded cautiously.

With this caution in mind the results of research efforts in this area may be summarized as follows: When subjects are asked in one way or another to defer judgment and to strive for quantity of ideas they do, in fact, produce more ideas than if they are instructed to allow themselves to be evaluative as they produce ideas. When quality of ideas is considered, however, then the instruction to defer judgment and to strive for quantity does *not* result in *more better quality* ideas or in a *better average quality* of ideas.

Some research suggests that the reason more ideas are produced under brainstorming than nonbrainstorming instructions stems from the possibility that under the former conditions persons lower their standards as they generate ideas. Another study suggests that for the effects of brainstorming to be manifest it may not be so necessary for judgment to be deferred as it is to separate idea-judgment or idea-evaluation from idea-generation.

One matter that has attracted a good deal of attention in the brainstorming literature is the method of how groups should be set up for the production of ideas. Should a group of individuals all work together as they produce ideas (called "real groups"), or should each of the persons in the group work by himself and should all of their ideas be collated as if they had worked together (called "nominal groups" which are really artificial groups)? Which of the two groups would produce more—the real or the nominal groups? The results of research designed to answer this question indicates that nominal groups produce more ideas than real groups but when quality of ideas (and, especially average quality) is considered as the major variable then sometimes the evidence favors nominal groups and sometimes it favors real groups.

Several studies have explored ways of increasing the value of brainstorming in real groups. One such study suggests that to retain some of the potential advantages of real groups (group cohesiveness, group morale, etc.) with the advantage of the larger number of ideas produced by nominal groups, it may be of value to add a process called "sequencing" (Bouchard, 1972a) to the usual brainstorming procedure. In the usual brainstorming procedure participants can speak out and offer their ideas any time they wish so long as no one else is talking. One possible effect of such a procedure is that one or more participants might monopolize the group's time and offer up their own ideas while others say nothing. To cope with this and similar problems and to help increase the number of ideas produced by real brainstorming groups, Bouchard (1972a) recommended the use of sequencing with brainstorming. When sequencing is used each participant has his turn to make his suggestion, and when he has done so, the next person can offer his idea and so on until every one has his turn. Then the cycle is begun again. If a person has nothing to say he says so but eventually he has another turn. In this manner no one can monopolize the group's time. Since everyone has his turn there may be more ideas generated and many more different ideas offered.

Another procedure suggested by Bouchard to help increase the effectiveness of real brainstorming groups is to add to sequencing another procedure called Personal Analogy. Personal Analogy is a technique that comes from another group procedure for the stimulation of creativity called Synectics (Gordon, 1961). In this technique, to help a person generate ideas he is asked to "behave like" or "act like" some aspect or some object that is part of the problem being worked on. In the procedure studied by Bouchard each person in a group has his turn using Personal Analogy or being like the object. While he generates his ideas in this manner, the other group members simply verbalize their ideas. When their turn comes in sequence they too use Personal Analogy. Bouchard's evidence seems to suggest that the combination of sequencing and Personal Analogy would be worthwhile pursuing in future work.

Still another way of improving brainstorming groups is to preselect participants in terms of personality characteristics (Bouchard, 1972). One such set of personality characteristics that has merit in this regard is Interpersonal Effectiveness as measured by the California Psychological Inventory. A group of persons scoring high on this variable is according to Bouchard's research more likely to be more productive in brainstorming a problem than a group that scores low on this measure.

While some investigators explored ways of increasing the effectiveness of real brainstorming groups, others (Dunnette, 1964) suggested that the use of brainstorming be limited to sharing information about a problem. After information has been shared, the group members should work separately from each other to arrive at possible solutions to the problem. When solutions to the problem have been generated they should then be collated and evaluated to determine which of them should be followed up for further use.

Training in brainstorming has also come under scrutiny in laboratory research designed to measure its effectiveness. As with all other laboratory studies these did not duplicate all brainstorming conditions but rather focused on specific aspects of the brainstorming procedure. Thus, attention was concentrated on the production of different associations to the same list of words. Each time a word in the stimulus list came up, the subject was asked for an association that was different from the one he offered previously. The results of this research indicated that training in the giving of different responses had a positive carry over effect with materials that were similar to the training materials. Transfer of training is, however, less likely to occur to dissimilar laboratory tasks or to real-life problems.

There are numerous anecdotal reports attesting to the value and effectiveness of brainstorming in real-life situations. There are no reports of failures, and therefore we do not know whether they do or do not occur. It would be most helpful for a well-based evaluation of the work in this area if more systematic efforts were devoted to investigating brainstorming's effectiveness in a variety of real-life situations. By the same token, more research on the effectiveness of brainstorming with a variety of laboratory and real-life problems would also be of much value in further understanding and evaluating brainstorming as a technique for stimulating creativity.

Creative Problem-Solving

Creative problem-solving consists of a series of procedures, including brainstorming, that were suggested by Osborn and added to by Parnes. A program of training in this eclectic approach is conducted under the auspices of the Creative Education Foundation, Buffalo, New York, of which Parnes is President.

The effectiveness of creative problem-solving has been studied in two types of investigations by Parnes and his associates. In one, a laboratory type of investigation, there are two groups of subjects one of which had and the other of which had not been trained in creative problem-solving. Both groups were then brought into the laboratory and asked to brainstorm a problem. The results of this kind of study indicated that the trained group did better than the untrained group when the criterion was quality of ideas, and at times the same result obtained when quantity of ideas was the criterion.

Parnes has also been responsible for an investigation of a two-year creative studies project at the University of Buffalo. In this project creative problem-solving played a critical role. A study of this program's effects indicates that it results in changes in the students' cognitive abilities but not in their personality characteristics. The program's positive effects were also manifest in both academic and nonacademic areas. Further evaluation of this project awaits a more complete report from the project's assessors.

Synectics

Synectics, a very sophisticated method for stimulating creativity, was originated by Gordon who has written about the use of the procedure with adults (Gordon, 1961) and with pupils in school (Gordon, 1971). Through his *Synectics Education Systems* in Cambridge, Massachusetts, Gordon provides training in synectics as well as consulting services associated with the use of his procedure.

Prince, a former associate of Gordon's, heads *Synectics, Inc.*, Cambridge, Massachusetts, which provides a variety of training opportunities and services involving the use of synectics. Prince's (1970a) emphasis, to differentiate it from Gordon's, focuses more on the nature of the group process and interaction among the participants while Gordon, although he obviously works with the group, concentrates more directly on the synectics process.

Synectics starts to work on a problem by "making the strange (i.e., the problem) familiar." This involves becoming acquainted with the problem and its various components. This start is then followed by a process of making that which has become familiar strange. In other words, once the problem's characteristics have become familiar the task is to move away from them, to get some distance from them, and thus allow the necessary conditions for the development of ideas that might result in creative solutions.

To help make the exploration of hypotheses and ideas more fruitful, subjects are trained in the use of what are called operational mechanisms. These are procedures for inducing in an individual a variety of psychological states which provide a fertile groundwork for the development of creative ideas. Included among the operational mechanisms are metaphors and analogies which are used to help the individual increase his associative range. The products of such associative experiences are then purposely fitted to the problem in a conscious attempt to arrive at a creative solution. During the course of this experience a trainee's attention is called to his affective or "hedonic" reactions that might be used as cues signaling responses or associations of creative import.

There are numerous reports in the creativity literature where some persons have indeed broken through to creative solutions to their problems by using metaphors. And there are also reports of the successful use of synectics by various groups in real-life situations. Some of these reports include excerpts of the transactions involved in the synectics process itself so that a reader may read and learn just how the process was used.

A previously mentioned laboratory study by Bouchard (1972b) explored the value of one kind of analogy that is part of synectics—Personal Analogy. This analogy plus sequencing seemed to be a more effective brainstorming procedure than was sequencing alone.

All of these reports are quite encouraging. Hopefully we shall find more systematic reports of laboratory and field investigations of the assumptions, use, and effectiveness of synectics in the future.

Cognitive and Personality-Insight Approaches

The third report in the section devoted to group techniques for the stimulation of creativity did not really involve a procedure that is available for the stimulation of creativity. Rather it is a report of a study of the relative effectiveness of two different types of techniques for the stimulation of creativity. This study was conducted by James *et al.* (1962) at the University of Chicago, and it involved administrators of federal agencies as subjects.

One of the approaches used in this study focused on improving a participants' cognitive behavior, and the other focused on his personality characteristics. The cognitive and personality characteristics selected for improvement were regarded as playing important roles in the creative process. For each of the areas studied the experimenters devised some rather interesting techniques. For example, when the focus was on cognitive training, subjects were presented with various cognitive exercises from which they could learn how cognitive factors influenced their working behavior. When the focus was on personality factors, subjects were similarly exposed to information as to how personality factors operate for and against creativity.

The cognitive and personality-insight approaches were not only compared with each other in this study but they were also compared with the effectiveness of a control group. The control group consisted of a group of participants who were very similar to the participants in the other two experimental conditions. They attended a seminar on general administrative effectiveness.

Before and after participants were trained in their respective procedures they were studied with a variety of tests, questionnaires, etc. Analysis of the data revealed that subjects who participated in the cognitive training program improved significantly on only one cognitive test. However, those who participated in the personality-insight program were equally effective on this same cognitive test. In other words although the personality-insight approach was not designed to effect cognitive factors, it nevertheless did so.

Turning to personality characteristics it was found that dogmatism, a personality variable that in previous studies was found to be negatively related to creativity, decreased more among those subjects who participated in the personality-insight approach than was true of both those who participated in the cognitive approach and those who participated in the control group administrative seminar. Furthermore, on a test of administration those who participated in the personality-insight approach performed equally as well as those who participated in the control seminar on administration.

The important changes that occurred in the participants in this study occurred in their attitudes rather than in their skills. The investigators in this study make the following rather interesting suggestion for those involved in the training for creativity. They believe that changes in attitude (such as those produced by the personality-insight approach) probably have to occur before changes in problem-solving skills occur. Consequently, a personality-insight approach might produce effects independent of a skills approach. A skills approach by itself, may not be very effective, but it could be effective if it were combined with a personality-insight approach. Consequently, to maximize the probability of increasing creativity, they would suggest that subjects participate in both personality-insight and cognitive programs.

Another very valuable outcome of this study is that it calls attention to the interaction between training programs and the working environments i.e., the kinds of federal agencies in which the participants worked. Participants in this study who saw their agency environments as authoritarian improved more, as a result of their training experience, on the cognitive tests than did the participants who said they worked in what has been called democratic environments. In other words, subjects who said they worked in authoritarian environments which could be expected to reinforce cognitive rigidity and so interfere with the creative process, profitted more from their training experience in that their cognitive behavior became less rigid. Such a decrease in rigidity might result in more flexibility which is more beneficial to creativity.

There is still another important relationship that this study underscored. Participants who were autonomous and independent were more likely to profit from training in cognitive skills than training in a personality-insight program. On the other hand, participants who were not inclined to be autonomous and independent in their social relationships were more likely to profit more from a personality-insight program.

These last two findings regarding the interaction between the participants' working environments and their personality characteristics are very interesting and important. One gains the impression from reading about training programs that their protagonists believe that such programs may be equally effective with all kinds of persons. This is yet to be demonstrated. And, until it is, it is safest to assume that training programs will be differentially effective with different kinds of persons. The study by James *et al.* (1962) does well to call attention to these matters. Hopefully more research efforts will be devoted to such matters in the future. If this should come to pass then both individuals and organizations will be provided with better bases for determining the kinds of training programs in which they should participate and which they would find most valuable in terms of their own skills and personalities.

Other Programs

In addition to brainstorming, creative problem-solving, and synectics, a series of diverse organizatonal and company programs for stimulating creativity were presented. These programs contain combinations of previously presented procedures as well as some new ideas. No attempt was made to determine whether or not the presented programs were still in existence. Our aim was to increase the range of available possibilities so that the reader could make appropriate selections to fulfill his needs.

Published reports on the effectiveness of these programs are generally quite favorable. However, the character of the published materials was rather incomplete. It is to be hoped that in the future various organizations and companies would engage in more cooperative efforts sharing both variables and experiences so that our knowledge and understanding of creativity stimulating procedures and their effectiveness would increase more rapidly.

Some Considerations before Embarking on a Creativity Stimulating Program

At this point with the advantage of an overview of both individual and group techniques for stimulating creativity, it is important to address ourselves to several crucial issues that arise when one considers the possibility of embarking upon a program for stimulating creativity. For whom are such programs? What considerations should one entertain before embarking on such a program? What kinds of information should an organization have before it sends its people to a program for stimulating creativity? What procedures should be established to evaluate the effects of creativity stimulating programs?

With the exception of the individual who is manifestly creative, all persons may benefit from exposure to and/or participation in individual or group techniques for stimulating creativity. The individual who was once manifestly creative, but whose creativity is now blocked for one reason or another, and the individual who has never been creative are candidates for these procedures. Hopefully, the former through use of these procedures would gain insight into either the personality or cognitive factors that hamper his work while at the same time learning some more effective way of proceeding along a creative course of action. Those who have never been creative might be encouraged and stimulated to try their hand at such efforts. Hopefully, they too will find the techniques profitable and will find creative effort less forbidding.

To become more manifestly creative is obviously a desired goal. However, if this is not achieved there is still much to be gained by persons who participate in these various programs, if it is only that they become better informed about what it is that transpires during and what it is that affects the creative process. Such persons could then become part of a more informed audience and public possessing greater appreciation and acceptance of other persons' creativity.

Creative individuals are frequently hampered in getting an opportunity at the start or during the conduct of their creative efforts because others are skeptical and even deprecatory. Hopefully, if these others participate in the various techniques for stimulating creativity, then, although they might not ever use what they learned for creative works directly, they might develop greater awareness and appreciation of what is involved in another person's work. Hence, they may become more positively disposed and more supportive financially, emotionally, and socially of the creative individual and his work.

What an individual will get out of experiences designed to stimulate creativity, as with other experiences in general, will depend on how prepared or ready he is to gain from them and how much effort he puts into the experience. In this regard, a prospective participant, before he embarks on joining a program designed to stimulate creativity, would do well to analyze and evaluate his history of experiences with creative endeavors. He should assess them with whatever objectivity he can muster to determine the nature of his problems and difficulties be they personality-wise, cognitive, social, information, technical, etc. At times others' opinions on these matters may also be of value.

In the course of this self-analysis a person should also try to decide just how important it is to him to be creative. There are many other happy and satisfying experiences in life. Some persons do have very romantic ideas about creativity based on misconceptions in which eurekalike fantasies color the total experience. These persons overlook the dedication, devotion, perseverance, and hard work involved in the creative process. They tend to focus only on the creative end product and those occasions in which fame and fortune are the rewards for creative work. In fact, creativity and success are not always positively correlated, and those who put a very high premium on success are likely to be disappointed if they expect it to follow easily from their creative efforts. Similarly, those who expect creativity to be a panacea for their difficulties and problems are not likely to find a direct and smooth parthway to happiness through their creativity.

Rather than satisfaction through derived goals, satisfaction must be sought largely in and through that which transpires in the creative process. A commitment in terms of time and energy must be made to creative pursuits, and within the total range of an individual's hierarchy of values they must be high on the list.

Having made the personal commitment, the work to straighten out personality problems and difficulties then needs to be undertaken because, as James *et al.* (1962) indicate, it is unlikely that learning skills will be effective unless there is some change in personal attitude. When personalities are more congruent with the requirements of the creative process, it is easier for the individual to learn, to absorb, and to make use of specific techniques and skills that could help foster his creativity.

Psychotherapeutic and counseling services available in many communities can be of enormous help in trying to overcome the personality difficulties and problems that stand in the way of creative work. For learning about creative skills there are books such as this one and the host of others that have been considered in the text that should be checked into for the variety of resources available. Some persons might find it easiest to try to use the various self-help procedures mentioned in this work while others, finding group participation more to their liking, might join a training program conducted by their universities, community agencies, or private consulting groups. In such a training program they could find not only the skills they seek but also the positive effects of group encouragement and cohesiveness that would enable them to be better able to cope with the trying periods that are apt to arise in the process of learning about the creative skills and applying them effectively.

Just as a person needs to assess his assets before embarking on a creativity program so too must an organization. The company, the school, the institute, etc. that wishes to stimulate the creativity of its members or employees needs to undertake a study of just what its potentialities and needs are insofar as creativity is concerned. In this regard, they can receive much help from a variety of existing diagnostic surveys (Stern, 1958; Stern and Pace, 1958; Pelz and Andrews 1966; Stein 1959 a-e), or special ones designed for the purposes of each specific situation may be developed to determine whether the organization is properly oriented to creativity.

What is probably of equal importance is the question of whether the problems could be more appropriately solved by other than creativity-training programs. Some organizations are much too quick to assert that it is the lack of their personnel's creativity which accounts for the organization's problems. The fact of the matter may well be that there are other difficulties that directly or indirectly affect how much creativity the organization is likely to have. The manifest lack of creativity may be symptomatic of organizational problems other than the personnel's level of creativity.

Diagnostic surveys conducted by in-house personnel or by consulting groups can frequently help make a proper determination of where some of the organization's difficulties lie. In doing so they would have to focus on an organization's value system, communication system, power structure, quality of all levels of personnel, quality of physical plant, etc., and determine the direct and indirect effects of these on creativity. Some specific questions in this survey might be: Does the organization and its personnel at different administrative levels value creativity or does it really want more efficient productivity? Does the organization reward creativity or other behavior and goals that make for success and which may or may not be correlated with creativity in the organization? How well qualified, technically, professionally, and administratively are all levels of personnel? How stressful is the nature of the role conflicts within the organization and especially among those individuals who are counted on for creative accomplishments.

In addition to such survey-type questions, more specific assessment might be made of the psychological characteristics—personality and cognitive—of the persons who are counted on for creativity or who may be involved in the total creative process. Since there are no hard and completely valid findings as yet as to what does or does not make for a creative individual, such psychological data would have to be evaluated cautiously to allow reasonable latitude for those making the assessment. When the assessments are made they should be followed up so that the benefits of past experiences are accumulated.

Sometimes the matters made salient by the surveys can be handled best and most easily by administrative decisions which break through the obstacles to creativity. Sometimes the organizational goals need to be made more congruent with creativity goals. Sometimes more channels of communication within the organization need to be opened up. Sometimes it is not that the internal channels need unclogging but that more channels to the outside need to be made available to the individuals who can really profit from the information they obtain through these outside channels. Sometimes it may be that the organization may not be able to do very much with available personnel but will have to go out into the marketplace and hire persons who have more of the characteristics necessary for creativity. And, finally, there is the possibility that the best course of action for an organization is to embark on a program designed to stimulate creativity.

If it is decided that the last course of action is the best then the diagnostic material collected can serve as baseline data which will later be compared with other data to evaluate the effectiveness of the training program. The training must and should be evaluated. Mere reliance on impression and stories is completely inadequate. Various systematic ways need to be developed and instituted for use in determining the value of the program. Therefore, after a reasonable number of persons have gone through a training program one should expect that certain organizational changes occur and be picked up by later surveys. A comparison between the data in these later surveys and the data in the earlier diagnostic surveys will make it apparent what changes, if any, have occurred and whether they have been desirable changes.

Data collected in the diagnostic survey also serve as a basis for determining what kind of program should be selected for one's organizational personnel. Obviously much more data are needed in this regard but suggestions are available in the material covered in this work. James *et al.* (1962), for example, pointed out, as we said, that a skills program can be most effective if the participants are unencumbered by personality problems. Therefore, we can see that there are some conditions under which participants might profit more from going to one type of program (cognitive or personality) rather than another. Within each category, decisions would probably have to be made on the basis of knowledge of the psychological characteristics of participants and the nature of the program itself. These could be discussed with those conducting the programs, previous participants or consultants so that rational and reasonable decisions could be made. Since there is an insufficient amount of information available which could be of help in making such determinations, it would also be of value for each organization to collect and evaluate its data periodically thus developing a data bank to be used for future decisions.

When considering the possible usefulness of a creativity stimulating program it is also important to have criteria of success. Often organizations send their personnel to such programs but do not develop a rational organized set of measurable criteria which could be used in determining whether they have found the program effective and valuable for their purposes. Again such criteria are necessary because without them one can only have recourse to impressions which then could become unsteady targets for criticism. When we speak of impressions we refer to unsystematic reports which do not contain all of the desired data. Impressions and subjectivity can be used together with rating scales provided that there is some systematic set of variables to provide guidelines as one looks for information.

Among the various criteria to be used there should be those that focus on concrete end products, as well as those that focus on a variety of intangible characteristics. When a list of the criteria is reviewed, it would also be necessary to try to come up with some determination as to the period of time in which one would anticipate or expect the criterion to be fulfilled. For example, if the criteria call for actual products then one should ask himself how much time might be involved. And, if one is asking for change in personality or some other characteristic he is confronted with a much more difficult question, but one might want to answer it by saying how long he is willing to wait for the change to occur or how much time he wishes to invest.

Evaluational criteria should be set up at the beginning before participants are sent to the training programs, otherwise one is exposed to the possibility of hearing later critics say "We could have done that without the creativity training." By checking the extent to which evaluational criteria have been fulfilled, it should be possible to make some rational decisions about whether participation in a program should be continued or not. The criteria might also serve as basis for determining who of the persons in the organization might attend the creativity program to greatest advantage. It can also be used to answer the question as to how good an investment the organization has made in terms of time and money.

RESEARCH CONSIDERATIONS

In a work such as this where we have covered a goodly number of research studies of a variety of problems in the area of creativity, it is only appropriate that several comments be made about the characteristics of the research in this area, as well as to point to the direction that future efforts might take. Before making these comments it is important to acknowledge the fact that many of the studies in this area are pioneering studies which have opened up difficult areas of research. Almost all of the studies have had to cope with difficult issues. Consequently, our remarks are not intended as criticism of that which has been done for we are fully aware of our debt to past efforts. They are intended to build on these past efforts so that we can profit from them in the design of future work and so ensure a continuous flow of valid and reliable data.

One of the problems in studies designed to evaluate the effectiveness of a technique to stimulate creativity is to determine when the technique has been given sufficient opportunity to demonstrate its usefulness—put more colloquially when has the technique been given "a fair shake." In a number of studies experimenters seem to have assumed that by instructing subjects to behave in a certain way they have, in fact, provided an appropriate set of conditions to study whatever technique it is that they wish to study. For example, it seems that when some investigators wish to study brainstorming, they believe that they are actually doing so when they tell subjects who have never brainstormed before that they should follow brainstorming rules. In some instances they tell subjects "do not evaluate," or they ask them "to defer judgment." By so instructing their subjects, it appears that some researchers actually believe that their subjects do, in fact, defer judgment or do not evaluate their thoughts. They may well be doing so, but no evidence that is independent of the associations produced is provided to show that subjects have indeed deferred judgment, etc. Anyone who has ever spent time with the procedure of free association knows that his first attempts at it are quite different from his later more experienced behavior. Anyone who has ever been in psychoanalytic therapy can certainly attest to the validity of this statement.

To expect that individuals instructed by the researcher to assume certain experimental sets in one session, at one meeting, can actually do so at an appropriate level of effectiveness strikes us as expecting much too much. It would appear that experimenters have a great deal of faith in the efficacy and magic of words and in their ability to turn their subjects on and off. Obviously, the ways in which the subjects are instructed are consistent with a time-honored tradition in psychological experimentation, but this tradition does also stress that the subject has to be capable of accepting the instruction and of giving the desired response. If these conditions do not exist, then the subject has to be trained properly before the experiment is begun. By way of historical example we would like to call attention to how the introspectionists worked hard to train their subjects to introspect. No one was expected to introspect merely with the instruction to introspect. True, a person instructed to introspect might behave differently from a person not so instructed or one who was instructed differently but he would also behave differently from a person trained to introspect.

Putting this in the context of the techniques and methods considered in this work, we should like to say that just because an individual is asked to brainstorm (or given some instructions along these lines) it should not be expected without further supporting evidence that he has actually done so or that he has performed as well as someone who is experienced in this process.

Lest someone assume that we make these suggestions because they would put creativity stimulating techniques in better light, we hasten to add that we believe that the same standards should be used for other techniques too. Specifically, if the question is whether deferment of judgment results in more creative ideas then it is important to select subjects who are well trained in this procedure. Since such a group will likely be compared with one using a procedure that does not involve deferment of judgment but uses judgment itself, then what was said for the first group holds equally well for the second. The second group must also be very well trained but in the use of critical judgment. To assume that all college students (the favorite subjects in most experiments) are quite adept at critical problem solving is obviously open to question. Just as one would want the creativity stimulating technique to be tested under the best possible conditions to set it off so it is important that any technique with which it is compared also be tested under conditions which set it off in the best possible manner.

To summarize: our first point is that it would be most desirable if future research efforts were so designed that they would test the relative values of different techniques for stimulating creativity by studying subjects who were well trained in the techniques. In addition, researchers should devote themselves to providing evidence as to the procedures their subjects actually used in working on their problems. If, for example, the experimenter has asked his subjects to brainstorm a problem, he should provide evidence that brainstorming was actually used that is independent of the nature of the result produced. And, if the experimenter has asked his subjects to be critical and evaluative as they seek creative solutions then there should be evidence that critical problem-solving behavior actually occurred. Without such evidence we are limited to outcomes such as number of ideas and quality of ideas, etc. We have no way of knowing how the subjects went about producing them, and we have no way of knowing whether they were indeed produced according to the instructions they were asked to follow.

The second matter that requires attention in future research is the nature of problems used to study the effectiveness of the various techniques for stimulating creativity. As we have seen most of the problems used generally fall into three categories. There are some problems, such as how many uses can the subject think of for a broom, which come from various tests developed to gather data on cognitive factors related to creativity. A second category of problems are so-called "real" problems such as ideas for increasing the number of tourists who come to the United States. And, then there are "unreal" problems which involve generating ideas as to what would eventuate if one had more than one thumb on each hand.

These different problems were used either because some previous investigator had used them or because they were expected to tap some psychological factor or capacity—such as ideational fluency—that was expected to be related to creativity. These are hardly the reasons that should be used in future research. Problems that are part of tests of cognitive functions presumably related to creativity should be used only when it has already been demonstrated that they do indeed correlate with creative behavior. If they do not, they should not be used. It would also seem to us that it is not necessarily a good reason to use problems simply because other investigators have used them. Meaningful and significant problems should be used. And they should be problems that the subjects are motivated to solve and in which they are involved. In the past little, if any, attention has been paid to whether or not subjects were involved in working on the experimental problems. The experimental design should include some measure, if only a questionnaire, answered by the subjects to indicate their level of involvement. And, if a desired level of involvement is not obtained then the subject might well be dropped from the whole or pertinent parts of the study. Finally, it would also be desirable for the needs of future research to have a system for determining the various characteristics of problems and to use such systems to determine whether a technique for stimulating creativity has been studied with a sufficiently wide array of problems. It may be that a creativity stimulating technique is equally effective with all kinds of problems but it is most likely that some techniques are better with some problems than are others. And if such be the case the obtained information is most valuable.

One of the important pieces of data that helps one decide about the value of a technique for stimulating creativity is its use in practical situations where a well-defined tangible product is produced. It is unlikely that even in the future will there be an appreciable increase in the number of studies where such data are possible. It is more likely that even in the future, experimenters will be limited to the study and use of problems where ideas for suggested solutions, rather than worked out solutions, will be available. These ideas will have to be evaluated by raters or judges of some sort who will have to determine whether or not an idea or suggestion is creative and if so just how creative it is. Such being the case it is important that data be gathered on the judges too, for it is very conceivable that judges' characteristics will affect the nature of the obtained evaluations and results. It is conceivable, for example, that some judges, who are themselves not very creative and who are tradition-bound, are likely to under-value some creative suggestions while more creative judges may be more sensitive to other kinds of material. Whatever the case, since judges do play important roles in the experiment, it would be necessary to obtain data on the nature of their characteristics. Since more than one experimenter is likely to use raters in the same or similar experiments, data about the judges would also be of help to these experimenters. For the same kind of comparisons they might not only want to replicate certain aspects of their colleagues' experiments, but they might also want to select their judges on the basis of the same characteristics as those used by their colleagues so that their design would also be comparable on this significant aspect. And, of course, it would also be of interest to study how subjects would behave and what kinds of end products they would produce when they were and were not aware of the criteria used by the raters.

Let us also hope that future research will bring the person back into the various processes for stimulating creativity. Just as different techniques for stimulating creativity may be applicable for different kinds of problems, so different kinds of persons may need different kinds of techniques to perform creatively. Both cognitive and personality data on the subjects in the experiments are most desirable and most critical. In the final analysis, we need to know what kinds of people should use what kinds of techniques with what kinds of problems under what kinds of conditions. This is an important challenge for future research to fulfill.

It would also be of much value if organizations that use various techniques for stimulating creativity would keep systematic records of their efforts and their results. Hopefully, they would make these available to others for future study and evaluation, as well as allow the reports to be used as possible bases for deciding whether or not, and under what conditions, an organization might consider participating in a specific creativity stimulating program.

When we speak of "organizations" in this context we have two kinds of organizations in mind. One organization is that one which has originated the procedure. This organization has an obligation to its clients, to the profession and the society at large to build evaluation procedures into their creativity stimulating programs so that judgments can be made of the value of these programs. The second type of organization is the one using each of the different programs. It is to their obvious advantage from an organizational and economic point of view to keep tabs on what benefits they derive from their various endeavors.

And, finally, there would be much to be gained if there were further experimentation and study not only of the various ways to overcome resistances to change but also of the various ways of having creative changes accepted without too much turmoil and upheaval. Possibly such work would require that attention be paid not only to the matter of accepting change but also to the factors involved in the readiness for change.

In Conclusion . . . and the Society

It is impossible to provide ideas, suggestions, procedures, and techniques for stimulating creativity that would be applicable to all situations. Although we have not covered all existing procedures, etc., hopefully readers will be able to make selections and combinations from that which has been presented so as to nourish and actualize their creative potentialities. The further development of creativity, however, is not dependent solely on the individual's efforts. As we

have so often stated throughout this work, creativity is a function of interpersonal as well we intrapersonal factors. Creativity occurs in a social context
and that context may vary in size from the smallest of groups to the larger
context of the society as a whole. That society is a most critical ingredient in the
creative process. It is far beyond the scope of this work to discuss in detail the
effects of various societal matters only touched upon in the text, and to demonstrate how they affect the creative process. All we can do at this point is to
provide some guidelines and to repeat what I said on a previous occasion about a
society that fosters creativity. I would have to say the same, with obvious
appropriate adjustments, for any subgroup or organization within the society
that is involved in creativity in the arts, humanities, sciences, and technologies.
On that occasion I (Stein, 1963) raised the following question, "What is the
nature of the environment that encourages, fosters, and facilitates creativity?"
and the answer I gave to that question at that time is still applicable to any
discussion of conditions that foster the creativity of individuals or facilitate the
acceptance of creative persons and the novelty they produce by others. I said
then,

> My focus is not on those societies which make creativity a privilege of a
> chosen few, or who concentrate on certain areas for creativity. My focus is
> on the free society that will allow for the release of the creative potentialities
> in all of us and which will accept creativity in all areas of human inquiry.
> A free society fosters creativity to the extent that it provides the in-
> dividual with the opportunity to experience its many facets and from which
> he may select what he desires. A society that limits a person's freedom to
> work, study, or experience, restricts his opportunity for exposure to the gaps
> that exist, keeps him from learning the necessary media through which he
> might communicate his feelings and ideas to others, and consequently de-
> creases the probability of creative contributions.
> A society fosters creativity to the extent that it encourages openness to
> internal and external experiences. Orientations that result in rigid inner per-
> sonal boundaries and lead to passivity and the expectation that ready-made
> solutions are available for new problems hamper creativity. Societies that are
> full of "don'ts," "shouldn'ts," and "mustn'ts" restrict freedom of inquiry
> and autonomy so important for creativity.
> On the biological level irritability is a sign that we are dealing with a living
> cell or organism. The counterpart of this irritability on the social level is
> criticism. When the cell is no longer irritable, when it is no longer responsive
> to the stimuli that impinge upon it from the external environment, it is dead.
> The society that puts a lid on criticism is a dead society. Creativity implicitly
> and explicitly involves criticism of that which exists. But it is not criticism
> for its own sake, it is not criticism that stems from hostile alienation but

criticism that will eventually result in greater growth and freedom. A society of free men, a society of creative men, has within it feedback and self-correcting mechanisms that keep it well balanced and integrated. Consequently, there is nothing to fear in criticism but there is a great deal to fear in the lack of criticism for it is a precursor of decay.

Society encourages creativity to the extent that it values change and novelty. It discourages creativity to the extent that social pressures to conformity are so intense that deviations are punished directly or indirectly through social isolation and ostracism. Change and novelty do involve risks because they are untested and untried. Mistakes have been and will be made. But these are only human as one seeks to grow. The fear of risks and the concern about mistakes are diminished in a society based on mutual trust and confidence and not in a society where suspicions and fears are dominant.

Creativity is fostered in a society where creative individuals have high status and are rewarded in a fashion congruent with their pursuits and not in a manner that will cause them to leave their specific lines of endeavor. A society in which scholars, scientists, poets, and artists are also invited to [Presidential] inauguration ceremonies will encourage creativity to a greater extent than one in which these individuals are exposed to inquisitions and ridicule. In societies that recognize creative men, individuals are encouraged to continue their inquiries and they become models to younger generations as they embark on their own developments.

A society encourages creativity to the extent that its social interactions, opportunities, and privileges are not determined by one's social status, school tie, family, race, color, or creed, but on the personal qualifications and attributes of the members of the society.

A society that fosters creativity provides its citizens with four basic freedoms—the freedom for study and preparation, the freedom for exploration and inquiry, the freedom of expression, and the freedom to be themselves [Stein, 1963, pp. 129-130].

References

Numbers in brackets refer to the chapters in which the references are cited.

Asch, S. E. *Social psychology*. Englewood Cliffs, New Jersey: Prentice-Hall, 1952.   [12]

Bavelas, A. A mathematical model for group structures. *Applied Anthropology*, 1948, 7, 16-30.   [12]

Bavelas, A. Communication patterns in task-oriented groups. *Journal of the Acoustical Society of America*, 1950, **22**, 725-730.   [12]

Bionics, Journal of Creative Behavior, 1968, 2, 52-57.   [14]

Bittel, L. R. Brainstorming: Better way to solve plant problems. *Factory Management and Maintenance*, May 1956, 98-107.   [13, 17]

Bouchard, T. J., Jr. Personality, problem-solving procedure, and performance in small groups. *Journal of Applied Psychology Monograph*, February 1969, 53 No. 1, Part 2.   [13]

Bouchard, T. J., Jr. Whatever happened to brainstorming? *The Journal of Creative Behavior*, 1971, 5, 182-189.   [13, 15]

Bouchard, T. J., Jr. Training, motivation, and personality as determinants of the effectiveness of brainstorming groups and individuals. *Journal of Applied Psychology*, 1972. 56, 324-331 (a).

Bouchard, T. J., Jr. A comparison of two group brainstorming procedures. *Journal of Applied Psychology*, 1972, 56, 418-421 (b).   [13, 15, 18]

Bouchard, T. J., Jr., & Hare, M. Size, performance, and potential in brainstorming groups. *Journal of Applied Psychology*, 1970, 54, 51-55.   [13]

286

Brilhart, J. K., & Jochem, L. M. Effects of different patterns on outcomes of problem solving discussion. *Journal of Applied Psychology*, 1964, **48**, 175-179.   [13]

Brim, O. G., Jr., Glass, D. C., Neulinger, J., & Firestone, I. J. *American beliefs and attitudes about intelligence*. New York: Russell Sage Foundation, 1969.   [12]

Bristol, L. H., Jr. The application of group thinking techniques to the problems of pharmaceutical education. *American Journal of Pharmaceutical Education*, 1958, **22**, 146.   [13]

Bruner, J. S. The conditions of creativity. In H. E. Gruber, G. Terrell, & M. Wertheimer (eds.), *Contemporary approaches to creative thinking*. New York: Atherton, 1962.   [15]

Bujake, J. E., Jr. Programmed innovation in new product development. *Research Management*, 1969, **12**, 279-287.   [17]

Campbell, J. Individual versus group problem-solving in an industrial sample. *Journal of Applied Psychology*, 1968, **52**, 205-210.   [13]

Caron, A. J., Unger, S. M., & Parloff, M. B. A test of Maltzman's theory of originality training. *Journal of Verbal Learning and Verbal Behavior*, 1963, **1**, 436-442.   [13]

Christensen, P. R., Guilford, J. P., & Wilson, R. C. Relations of creative responses to working time and instructions. *Journal of Experimental Psychology*, 1957, **53**, 82-88. [13]

Clark, C. H. *Brainstorming*. Garden City, New York: Doubleday, 1958.   [17]

Cohen, D., Whitmyre, J. W., & Funk, W. H. Effect of group cohesiveness and training upon creative thinking. *Journal of Applied Psychology*, 1960, **44**, 319-322.   [13]

Cramer, P. *Word association*. New York: Academic Press, 1968.   [13]

Creativity Program Center for Creative Leadership, Greensboro, North Carolina: Center for Creative Leadership, no date.   [18]

De Bono, E. *Lateral thinking: Creativity step by step*. New York: Harper & Row, 1973.   [13, 17]

Dillon, P. C., Graham, W. K., & Aidells, A. L. Brainstorming on a "hot" problem. Effects of training and practice on individual and group performance. *Journal of Applied Psychology*, 1972, **56**, 487-490.   [13]

Dunnette, M. D. Are meetings any good for solving problems? *Personnel Administration*, March-April 1964. **29**, 12-16.   [13, 18]

Dunnette, M. D., Campbell, J., & Jaastad, K. The effects of group participation on brainstorming effectiveness for two industrial samples. *Journal of Applied Psychology*, 1963, **47**, 10-37.   [13]

Edwards, M. O. Possibilities for professional development in creative problem solving at SRI. Final Report SRI Project IRD 188531-157. Menlo Park, California: Stanford Research Institute, 1966.   [13, 17]

Forehand, G. A. Suggestions for further research. In *Education for innovative behavior in executives*. Cooperative Research Project No. 975. Washington, D. C.: Office of Education, US Department of Health, Education, and Welfare, August 1962.   [16]

Forehand, G. A., & Libby, W. L., Jr. Effects of educational programs and perceived organizational climate upon changes in innovative administrative behavior. In *Education for innovative behavior in executives*. Cooperative Research Project No. 975. Washington, D. C.: Office of Education, US Department of Health, Education, and Welfare, August 1962.   [16]

Freedman, J. L. Increasing creativity by free-association training. *Journal of Experimental Psychology*, 1965, **69**, 89-91.   [13]

Freeman, L. (ed.) *Celebrities on the couch*. New York: Pocket Books, 1971.   [18]

Fuerst, K. & Zubek, J. P. Effects of sensory and perceptual deprivation on a battery of open-ended cognitive tasks. *Canadian Journal of Psychology*, 1968, **22**, 122-130. [18]

Gallup, H. F. Originality in free and controlled association responses. *Psychological Reports*, 1963, 13, 923-929.   [13]

Garcha, M. (ed.) "Synectics" analogies spark creative ideas. *Employee Relations Bulletin*, Report No. 1140. Waterford, Connecticut: National Foreman's Institute, 1969.   [15]

Goldfried, M. R. & D'Zurilla, T. J. *Assessment and facilitation of effective behavior in college freshmen.* State University of New York at Stony Brook: Final Report submitted to The National Institute of Mental Health, Research Grant No. MH15044, 1972.   [14]

Goldner, B. B. *The strategy of creative thinking.* Englewood Cliffs, New Jersey: Prentice-Hall, 1962.   [17]

Gordon, W. J. J. *Synectics.* New York: Harper, 1961.   [12, 13, 15, 18]

Gordon, W. J. J. *The metaphorical way.* Cambridge, Massachusetts: Porpoise Books, 1971.
                                                                                    [12, 14, 15, 18]

Gordon, W. J. J. Personal communication, 1972.   [15]

Gough, H. G. *Manual for the California Psychological Inventory.* Palo Alto, California: Consulting Psychologists Press, 1957.   [13, 14]

Gough, H. G. & Heilbrun, A. B., Jr. *The adjective check list manual.* Palo Alto, California: Consulting Psychologists Press, 1965.   [14]

Green, E. E., Green, A. M., & Walters, E. D. Voluntary control of internal states: Psychological and physiological. In T. Barber (ed.), *Biofeedback and self-control.* New York: Aldine-Atherton, 1971, 3-28.   [18]

Guetzkow, H., Forehand, G. A., & James, B. J. An evaluation of educational influence on executive judgment. *Administrative Science Quarterly*, 1962, 6, 484-500.   [16]

Guilford, J. P. *The nature of human intelligence.* New York: McGraw-Hill, 1967.
                                                                                    [13, 14, 17]

Harman, W. W., McKim, R. H., Mogar, R. E., Fadiman, J., & Stolaroff, M. J. Psychedelic agents in creative problem solving: A pilot study. In C. T. Tart (ed.), *Altered states of consciousness.* New York: Wiley, 1969.   [18]

Harris, R.H. & Simberg, A.L. *AC test of creative ability, test administration manual.* Chicago, Illinois: Education-Industry Service, 1959.   [13]

Hathaway, S. R., & McKinley, J. C. *Manual for Minnesota Multiphasic Inventory.* New York: Psychological Corp., 1951.   [14]

Hoffman, L. R. Homogeneity of member personality and its effect on group problem-solving. *Journal of Abnormal and Social Psychology*, 1959, 58, 27-32.   [12]

Hoffman, L. R., & Maier, N. R. F. Quality and acceptance of problem solutions by members of homogeneous and heterogeneous groups. *Journal of Abnormal and Social Psychology*, 1961, 62, 401-407.   [12]

Hoffman, L. R., & Maier, N. R. F. Valence in the adoption of solutions by problem-solving groups: II. Quality and acceptance as goals of leaders and members. In N. R. F. Maier (ed.), *Problem solving and creativity.* Belmont, California: Brooks, Cole, 1970.   [12]

Horowitz, M. W., & Newman, J. B. Spoken and written expressions: An experimental analysis. *Journal of Abnormal and Social Psychology*, 1964, 68, 640-647.   [13]

Hughes, S. Untitled summary of survey findings (mimeographed), and personal communication, June 2, 1970. (a)   [15]

Hughes, S. Manifest and latent functions of Synectics Problem Solving Laboratories. Paper presented at Boston University Human Relations Center Centennial Conference, May 7, 1970. (b)   [15]

Hyman, R. Some experiments in creativity. New York: General Electric Co., 1960.   [13]

Hyman, R. On prior information and creativity. *Psychological Reports*, 1961, 9, 151-161.
                                                                                    [13]

IBRIC, *Manual for alpha biographical inventory*. Greensboro, North Carolina: Prediction Press, 1969. [14]

James, B. J., & Libby, W. L., Jr. An experimental curriculum for studies in administrative innovation. In *Education for innovative behavior in executives*. Cooperative Research Project No. 975. Washington, D.C.: Office of Education, US Department of Health, Education, and Welfare, August 1962. [16]

James, B. J., Guetzkow, H., Forehand, G. A., & Libby, W. L., Jr. *Education for innovative behavior in executives*. Cooperative Research Project No. 975. Washington, D.C.: Office of Education, US Department of Health, Education, and Welfare, August 1962. [16, 18]

Krech, D., Crutchfield, R. S., & Ballachey, E. L. *Individual in society: A textbook of social psychology*. New York: McGraw-Hill, 1962. [12]

Leavitt, H. J. Some effects of certain communication patterns on group performance. *Journal of Abnormal and Social Psychology*, 1951, **46**, 38-50. [12]

Lewin, K. Group decision and social change. In E. E. Maccoby, T. M. Newcomb, & E. L. Hartley (eds.), *Readings in social psychology* (3rd edition) New York: Holt, 1958. [18]

McClelland, D. C., Atkinson, J. W., Clark, R. A., and Lowell, E. L., *The achievement motive*. New York: Appleton-Century-Crofts, 1953. [14]

Maier, N. R. F. Reasoning in humans: I On direction. *Journal of Comparative Psychology*, 1930, **10**, 115-143. [13]

McGuigan, F. J. The experimenter: A neglected stimulus object. *Psychological Bulletin*, 1963, **60**, 421-428. [13]

McLuhan, M. *Understanding media: The extensions of man*. New York: Signet, 1964. [18]

Maier, N. R. F. Assets and liabilities in group problem solving: The need for an integrative function. *Psychological Review*, 1967, **74**, 239-249. [12, 18]

Maier, N. R. F., & Solem, A. R. The contribution of a discussion leader to the quality of group thinking: The effective use of minority opinions. In N. R. F. Maier (ed.), *Problem solving and creativity*. Belmont, California: Brooks, Cole, 1970. [12]

Maltzman, I. On the training of originality. *Psychological Review*, 1960, **67**, 229-242. [13]

Maltzman, I., Bogartz, W., & Berger, L. A procedure for increasing word association originality and its transfer effects. *Journal of Experimental Psychology*, 1958, **56**, 392-398. (a) [13]

Maltzman, I., Brooks, L. O., Bogartz, W., & Summers, S. S. The facilitation of problem-solving by prior exposure to uncommon responses. *Journal of Experimental Psychology*, 1958, **56**, 399-406. (b) [13]

Maltzman, I., Simon, S., Raskin, D., & Licht, L. Experimental studies in the training of originality. *Psychological Monographs*, 1960, **74**, No. 6 (Whole No. 493). [13]

Maltzman, I., Belloni, M., & Fishbein, M. Experimental studies of associative variables in originality. *Psychological Monographs*, 1964, **78**, No. 3 (Whole No. 580). [13]

Mandler, G., & Cowen, J. E. Test anxiety questionnaires. *Journal of Consulting Psychology*, 1958, **22**, 228-229. [13]

Maslow, A. H., *Motivation and personality*. New York: Harper & Row, 1954. [14]

Meadow, A., & Parnes, S. J. Evaluation of training in creative problem-solving. *Journal of Applied Psychology*, 1959, **43**, 189-194. [13, 14]

Meadow, A., Parnes, S. J., & Reese, H. Influence of brainstorming instructions and problem sequence on a creative problem solving test. *Journal of Applied Psychology*, 1959, **43**, 413-416. [13, 14]

Mednick, S. A. The associative basis of the creative process. *Psychological Review*, 1962, **69**, 220-232. (a)   [16]
Mednick, S. *Remote associates test*. Ann Arbor, Michigan: Univ. of Michigan Press, 1962. (b)   [13, 16]
Merton, R. K. *Social theory and social structure*. New York: Free Press, 1957.   [12]
Myers, I. B. *Manual: The Myers-Briggs type indicator*. Princeton, New Jersey: Educational Testing Service, 1962.   [13, 14]
Nineteenth Annual Creative Problem-Solving Institute and Regional Extension, 1973. Buffalo, New York: Creative Education Foundation, 1973.   [14]
Noller, R. B., & Parnes, S. J. Applied creativity: The creative studies project. Part III—The curriculum. *Journal of Creative Behavior*, 1972, **6**, 275-294.   [14]
Ogilvy, D. *Confessions of an advertising man*. New York: Atheneum, 1963.   [18]
Osborn, A. F. *Applied imagination* (3rd edition). New York: Scribner, 1963.   [13, 17, 18]
Parloff, M. B., & Handlon, J. H. The influence of criticalness on creative problem solving in dyads. *Psychiatry*, 1964, **27**, 17-27.   [13]
Parnes, S. J. Effects of extended effort in creative problem solving. *Journal of Educational Psychology*, 1961, **52**, 117-122.   [13]
Parnes, S. J. The deferment-of-judgment principle: A clarification of the literature. *Psychological Reports*, 1963, **12**, 521-522.   [13]
Parnes, S. J. *Creative behavior guidebook*. New York: Scribner, 1967. (a)   [13, 14, 17]
Parnes, S. J. *Creative behavior workbook*. New York: Scribner, 1967. (b)   [13, 14, 17]
Parnes, S. J. Personal communication, February 8, 1972.   [13, 14]
Parnes, S. J., & Meadow, A. Effects of "brainstorming" instructions on creative problem solving by trained and untrained subjects. *Journal of Educational Psychology*, 1959, **50**, 171-176.   [13, 14, 16]
Parnes, S. J., & Meadow, A. Evaluation of persistence of effects produced by a creative
.   problem solving course. *Psychological Reports*, 1960, 7, 357-361.   [14]ˑ
Parnes, S. J., & Meadow, A. Development of individual creative talent. In C. W. Taylor & F. Barron (eds.), *Scientific creativity: Its recognition and development*. New York: Wiley, 1963.   [13]
Parnes, S. J., & Noller, R. B. Applied creativity: The creative studies project. Part I—The development. *Journal of Creative Behavior*, 1972, **6**, 11-22. (a)   [14]
Parnes, S. J., & Noller, R. B. Applied creativity: The creative studies project. Part II— Results of the two-year program. *Journal of Creative Behavior*, 1972, **6**, 164-186. (b)
                                                                                                                   [14]
Parnes, S. J. & Noller, R. B. Applied creativity: The creative studies project. Part IV— Personality findings and conclusions. *Journal of Creative Behavior*, 1973, 7, 15-36.
                                                                                                                   [14]
Pelz, D. C., & Andrews, F. M. *Scientists in organizations*. New York: Wiley, 1966.
                                                                                                              [12, 18]
Prince, G. M. Synectics: A method of creative thought. *Journal of Engineering Education*. 1968, **58**, 805-806.   [15]
Prince, G. M. *The practice of creativity*. New York: Harper, 1970. (a)   [12, 15, 18]
Prince, G. M. Personal communication, March 13, 1970. (b)   [15]
Prince, G. M. Personal communication from C. E. Anagnostopoulos, February 20, 1970. (c)
                                                                                                                   [15]
Rogers, E. M., & Shoemaker, F. F. *Communication of innovations*. (2nd edition) New York: Free Press, 1971.   [18]
Rokeach, M. *The open and closed mind*. New York: Basic Books, 1960.   [16]

Rosenbaum, M. I., Arenson, S. J., & Panman, R. A. Training and instructions in the facilitation of originality. *Journal of Verbal Learning and Verbal Behavior*, 1964, **3**, 50-56. [13]

Rotter, G. S., & Portugal, S. M. Group and individual effects in problem solving. *Journal of Applied Psychology*, 1969, **53**, 338-341. [13]

Shaw, M. F. Communication networks. In L. Berkowitz (ed.), *Advances in experimental social psychology*. New York: Academic Press, 1964. [12]

Shepard, H. A. Creativity in R/D teams. *Research and Engineering*, October 1956, 10-13. [12]

Schutz, W.C. Firo: A three dimensional theory of interpersonal behavior. New York: Holt, 1958. [13]

Stein, M. I. *Individual qualification form*. Available from author, 1959. (a) [12, 18]

Stein, M. I. *Personal data form for scientific, engineering, and technical personnel*. Available from author, 1959. (b) [12, 18]

Stein, M. I. *Research personnel review form*. Available from author, 1959. (c) [12, 18]

Stein, M. I. *Stein research environment survey*. Available from author, 1959. (d) [12, 18]

Stein, M. I. *Stein survey for administrators*. Available from author, 1959. (e) [12, 18]

Stein, M. I. Creativity and the scientist. In B. Barber & W. Hirsch (eds.), *The sociology of science*. New York: Free Press, 1962. [18]

Stein, M. I. Creativity in a free society. *Educational Horizons*, 1963, **41**, 115-130. [18]

Stein, M. I. Creativity and culture. In R. L. Mooney & T. A. Razik (eds.), *Explorations in creativity*. New York: Harper, 1967. [18]

Stein, M. I. Creativity. In E. F. Borgatta & W. W. Lambert (eds.), *Handbook of personality theory and research*. Chicago, Illinois: Rand McNally, 1968. [18]

Stern, G. G. *High school characteristics index*. Syracuse, New York: Syracuse Univ., Psychological Research Center, 1958. [18]

Stern, G. G., & Pace, C. R. *College characteristics index*. Syracuse, New York: Syracuse Univ. Psychological Research Center, 1958. [18]

Strong, E. K. *Vocational interests of men and women*. Palo Alto, California: Stanford Univ. Press, 1943. [14]

Synectics. Synectics: An intensive program in creative group problem solving. Cambridge, Massachusetts: Synectics, Inc. (no date). [15]

Synectics, Inc. *Making it strange*. Teachers manual. New York: Harper, 1968. [15]

Synectics. The anatomy of teambuilding a new course. Cambridge, Massachusetts: Synectics, Inc., 1971. [15]

Synectics Casebook. The department store experiment. Cambridge, Massachusetts: Synectics, Inc. no date. (a) [15]

Synectics Casebook. The Metropolitan Hospital experiment. Cambridge, Massachusetts: Synectics, Inc. no date. (b) [15]

Taylor, I. A. Creative production in gifted young adults, through simultaneous sensory stimulation. *Gifted Child Quarterly*, 1970, **14**, 46-55. [18]

Taylor, I. A. The effects of sensory stimulation on divergent and convergent thinking. Abstract Guide of XXth International Congress of Psychology, Tokyo, Japan, 1972, 364. [18]

Taylor, I. A., & Knapp, M. W. Creative artistic production of chronic schizophrenics through simultaneous sensory stimulation. *Proceedings, 79th Annual Convention*, American Psychological Association, Washington, D.C., 1971, 411-412. [18]

Taylor, D. W., Berry, P. C., & Block, C. H. Does group participation when using brainstorming facilitate or inhibit creative thinking? *Administrative Science Quarterly*, 1958, **3**, 23-47. [13]

Torrance, E. P., Rush, C. H., Kohn, H. B., & Doughty, J. M. Fighter-interceptor pilot combat effectiveness: A summary report, Lackland Air Force Base, Texas: Air Force Personnel and Training Research Center, November, 1957.   [12]

Tuckman, J., & Lorge, I. Individual ability as a determinant of group superiority. *Human Relations*, 1962, 15, 45-51.   [13]

Von Fange, E. K. *Professional creativity*. Englewood Cliffs, New Jersey: Prentice-Hall, 1959.   [17]

Wallach, M. A., & Kogan, N. *Modes of thinking in young children*. New York: Holt, 1965.   [12]

Weisskopf-Joelson, E., & Eliseo, T. S. An experimental study of the effectiveness of brainstorming. *Journal of Applied Psychology*, 1961, 45, 45-49.   [13]

Wispé, L. G., & Parloff, M. B. Impact of psychotherapy on the productivity of psychologists. *Journal of Abnormal Psychology*, 1965, 70, 188-193.   [18]

Witkin, H. A., Oltman, P. K., Raskin, E., & Karp, S. A. *A manual for the Embedded Figures Tests*. Palo Alto, California: Consulting Psychologists Press, 1971.   [16]

Subject Index

A

Abasement, 233
Abnormal psychology course, 212
AC Test of Creative Ability, *see* Tests
Acceptance finding, 143, 145, 150, 154, 155, 158
Achievement, need, 164
Achievers, 214
Adjective Check List, 169, *see also* Tests
Administration, 228
  test of, 273
Administrative cases, 226
Administrative effectiveness, 232, 233
Administrative potential, 206
Administrator, 273
  federal programs, 223
  role of, 14
  school, 260

Adopter categories, 266
Adoption process, 265
Advertisers, 84
Advertising, 103
  media, 266
  personnel, 86, 95, 99
Aesthetic, 186, 262
Aesthetic feel, 262
Aesthetically satisfying, 189
Affection, 143
Affiliation, 233
Age, 206, 268
Aggression, 191, 194, 233
Aggressive, 67, 164
Aidells, A.L., 91
Alcohol, 256
"Almost" individual, 206
Alpha Biographical Inventory, 169, *see also* Tests

Alpha waves, 258, *see* Brain waves
Amphetamines, 256
Anagnostopoulos, C.E., 216
Analogy, 4, 172, 184, 196, 199, 200, 209,
    219, 220, 263, 272, *see also* Synectics
  direct, 181, 182, 186–189
  distance on, 188, 199
  fantasy, 181, 182, 186, 190
  personal, 181, 186–189, 200, 219
    270, 272
  plus sequencing, 272
  symbolic, 182, 186, 189
Analysis, 197
Analyzing, 196
And-also method, 242
Andrews, F.M., 13, 14, 15, 19, 268, 277
Anticipation, 150
Anxiety, 263
Apparatus Test, *see* Tests
"Apple-polisher," 226
Arenson, S.I., 166
Art of the possible, 212
Artists, 215
Asch, S.E., 16
Assistance, 150
Associational fluency, 238
Associationism, theory of, 269
Associative range of responses, 220
Associative thinking, 201
Attititude of assistance, 206
Attribute analysis, 243
Audience, 264, 265, 266
Authoritarian, 231
Authoritarian environments, 274
Autonomy, 233
  of object, 185
Awareness, heightened, 161
Awareness training, 248

B

Barron Complexity Scale, 248
Barron–Welsh Figure Preference Test, 248,
    see also Tests
Batten, Barton, Durstine, and Osborn, 247
Bavelas, A., 5, 6
Bell, A.G., 181
Belongingness, 143
Benefit segmentation, 266
Berry, P.C., 73

Biofeedback, 257
Biology, 188
Bionics, 160
Bittel, L.R., 25, 240, 242, 243
Block, C.H., 73
Bonus, 209, 248
Book title, examination of, 186, 189,
    200, *see also* Synectics
Boss, 196
Boston University, 216
Bouchard, T.J., Jr., 58, 62, 63, 65–67, 69,
    70, 86–91, 93, 94, 100–102, 104–
    106, 108–112, 114, 138, 218, 219,
    269, 270, 272
Brain waves, 257, 258
Brainstorming, 3, 4, 7, 25–141, 48, 69,
    71, 83, 145, 148, 159, 163, 165,
    170, 219, 222, 224, 231, 238,
    239, 248, 268–271
  in action, 34
  compared with critical problem solving,
    63
  differences with synectics, 184, 185
  example of, 34, 35
  group, 30–37, 55, 58, 60, 61, 64–66, 270
  individual, 37
  instructions, 51
  plus personal analogy, 111, 112, 218
  plus sequencing, 109, 218
  principles of, 28, 29, 41, 44–52, 137, 148,
    268
  rules of, 28–30, 33, 41, 44–52, 137
  training in, 113–137
  uses of, 36, 37
Breadth of problem area, 14
Bridge, 212
Brilhart, J.K., 56, 63
Bristol, L.H., Jr., 31, 33, 35, 36, 53
Brunel, I.K., 180
Bruner, J., 183, 216
Buffalo, State University College at, 3, 26,
    142, 143, 160–163, 168, 171
Bujake, J.E., Jr., 211, 243–245
Bureaucratic environment, 28, 230–232
Bureaucratic personality, 12
Buzzards, 180

C

Caffeine, 256
Caisson, 180

Cajal, S.R., 181
California Psychological Inventory (CPI), *see* Tests
Campbell, J., 84, 98
Car wheels leaked, 203
Caron, A.J., 116, 123
Cartoon Apperception Test, *see* Tests
Categories, manipulation, 143, 146, 155–157
Catholic Community Church in Neuilly–sur–Seine, 53
Censorship, fear of, 26
Center for Creative Leadership, 246
Center for Programs in Government Administration at the University of Chicago, 4
Centralized networks, 6
Checklists, 146, 156, 158, 159, 170
China Lake Naval Station, 189
Christensen, P.R., 43, 45, 48, 51
Clark, C.H., 246
Clever, instructions to be, 48
Cleverness of ideas, 49, 52
Client-expert, 174, 192, 195–199, 202, 207, *see also* Synectics
Closed system, 229
Closure, 181
Coca-Cola program, 243–245
Cognitive, 144
  abilities, 170, 271
  approach, 224–228, 230, 233, 268, 278, 272–274
  factors, 254
  processes, 256–259
  tests, 169, 230–231
Cohen, D. 96
Cohesiveness, group, 13, 14, 96–98
College counseling service, 177
Combination and improvement, 28, 30, 137
Communication, *see also* Hypothesis
  pattern of, 5, 6, 268
  of results, 253, 259, 264–267
Company programs, 235, 249
Competition
  and age of groups, 14
  effect on groups, 15
  with team, 192
Competitive, 67
Complementary aspects, 206

Compressed conflict, 186, 187, 189, 200, *see also* Synectics
Compulsive talker, 193
Concept development, 211, 245
Concept expansion, 244, 245
Conceptual distance, 189, 213, 214
Conceptual strain, 189
Conditioning, 137
Confidence, 164, 239
Confirmation, 265
Conformity, 285
Congeniality of pairs, 72, 74
Conscious, 190
Consciousness altering, 256
Consequences, *see* Tests
Constructive strain, 188
Consultants, 245
Content Devices, *see* Tests
Control seminar, 233
Controlling, 67
Conventional conference, 25, 37, 55, 78, 83
Conventional thinking, 55, 84
Conventionality, 67
Convergent Thinking Test, *see* Tests
Coping Problems Test, *see* Tests
Courses in
  Creative Problem–Solving, 160–163
  Synectics, 174–179
Cowan, J.E., 124
Cramer, P., 136, 137
Creative Education Foundation, 3, 26, 31, 142, 161, 163, 246, 271
"Creative mind," 28
Creative Problem–Solving, 3, 26, 37, 49, 54, 139, 142–171, 222, 238, 242, 268, 271
  example of, 146–159
  Institutes, 26, 143, 161, 171
Creative Studies Project, 143, 160, 167, 168, 171
Creative–type questions, 152
Creativity
  defined, 253
  in arts and sciences, 179
Criteria, 41–44, 155, 157, 158
  acceptance by group, 67
  clarity, 73, 74
  effectiveness, 82, 83, 93
  evaluation, 24, 58

feasibility, 73, 82, 83, 93
generality, 82, 83, 93
interaction with problem, 92–95
limited, 28
primary, 29
probability, 74, 83, 85, 93, 94
quality, 79
secondary, 28
significance, 73, 83, 93
Criteria–ideas pattern, 56
Critic, 29, 79, 262
Critical problem–solving, 58–67, 73, 74,
    84, 98, 223
compared with brainstorming, 68
training, 166
Criticism, 56, 153, 259, 284
fear of, 15, 26
ruled out, 28, 29, 44, 137
Cultural inventions, 212
Culturally deprived students, 214
Curiosity, 239
Customized materials, 179

D

Darwin, C.R., 180
De Bono, E., 34, 246
Decentralized networks, 6
Decision, 265
Defensiveness, 193
Deferment of judgment, 190
Defining a problem, 196
Democratic, 228, 230
Democratic environments, 274
Depression, 263
Descriptive facts, 199
Description of emotions, first person, 187
of fact, first person, 187
Detachment, 190
Diagnostic Surveys, 18, 19, 260
preparing for, 20–23
Dialog, 262
Dillon, P.C., 91, 92, 104–106, 114
Discovery, 253, 263
"Distance" between the individual and
    the problem, 187
Divergent Thinking Test, *see* Tests
Diversity of groups, 15
Dogmatism (D–Scale), *see* Tests
Dominance, 66, 164, 169, 170

Dominant, 67
Dreaming, 201
Dreams, 256
Dunnette, M.D., 84–87, 89, 90, 93–95, 99,
    103, 104, 113, 138, 270
Dyads, 11
D'Zurilla, T.J., 169

E

Education, 59, 69, 70, 206
Edwards, M.D., 53, 238, 239, 247, 248
Effectiveness, interpersonal, 108, 113, 138
Ego-involving problems, *see* Problems
Einstein, A., 180, 266
Elaboration, 196, 214, 223
Electromagnetic wave theory, 180
Elephant, 212
Eliseo, T.S., 43, 44, 58, 61, 62, 71, 78
Embedded Figures Test, *see* Tests
Embeddedness, 263
Emotional, 179
Emotional constitution, 206
Emotional involvement, 188
Empathic identification, 187, 188
Energy level, 193, 206
Engineering courses, 76, 241
Engineers, 132
English courses, 169
Enterprising, 67
Enthusiastic, 67
Entrepreneurship, 206
Environmental questionnaire, 228
Environments, working, 274
Essential paradox, *see* Paradox, *see also*
    Synectics
Esteem, 143
Evaluation, 26, 40, 94, 143, 150, 157,
    158, 165, 169, 195, 259, 261, 268,
    280
brainstorming, 37–137
conventional, 78
creative, 158
creative problem–solving, 163–170
critical, 245
deferred, 26, 57–58
group, 35–36
procedures, 61
raters, 76–80
standards, 71–76, 94

studies, 163–170
synectics, 214–219
Evocative question, *see* Analogy, Synectics
Examination, 199, *see also* Synectics
Example, 186, 188–189, 199, *see also*
Analogy, Synectics
Excess stimuli, 263
Excursion, 172, 184, 199, *see also* Synectics
Executive Apperception,Test, *see* Tests
Experience cycle, 144, 146, 154, 155, 159
Experimenter
female, 89
presence of, 89
sex of, 89, 90
Experts, 265, *see also* Client–expert
Expressed–affection, 66
control, 66
inclusion, 66
Extended effort, 50, 51
Extroversion–introversion, *see* Tests

F

Fact-finding, 27, 143, 145, 146, 151,
155, 156
type of question, 152
Federal agencies, 273
Feedback, 59–61, 63, 65, 69, 70, 90–91
Feelings of others, concern with, 67
Fiddler crab, 187
Figural factors, 169
FIRO-B, *see* Tests
Fixed role play, 227
Flexibility, 69, 214, 239
Flow chart, 197, *see also* Synectics
Fluency, verbal, 67, 121, 164, 170, 214,
239
in thought, 67
Forced relationships, 146–149, 155, 157–
159, 170, 184, 193, 196, 200, 201
practical (PFF), 200
fantasy (FFF), 200
Ford Motor Co., 244
Forehand, G.A., 230, 232, 233
Forgetting, 203
Franconia College, 213
Freedman, J.L., 125–127
Freedoms, 212
four basic, 285
Freeman, L., 255

Freewheeling, 28, 29, 44, 137
Freud, S., 266
Fuerst, K., 258
Functional fixity (fixedness), 200, 263
Funk, W.H., 96

G

Gallup, H.F., 116, 119, 130, 131
Garbage can method, 242
Garcha, M., 196, 205, 209
Gas, 216
Gatekeepers, 265
General Electric Company, 45, 76,
127, 132, 240, 241
General science, 178
General Telephone and Electronics Corp.,
248
Get–fired technique, 201
Ghetto students, 214
Global rating scale, 229, *see also* Tests
Goals as understood (GAU), 198, 200,
see also Synectics
Goldfried, M.R., 169
Goldner, B.B., 246
Goodrich, B.F. Co., 248
Gordon, W.W., 3, 4, 7, 110, 160, 172,
173, 177, 184, 185, 187, 188, 196,
197, 199, 200–202, 205, 208, 209,
212–216, 219, 221, 260, 261, 269,
271, 272, *see also* Synectics
Gough, H., 66, 67, 109, 164, 169, 170
Grades, elementary and junior high
school, 12, 179
Graham, W.K., 91
Greater Lawrence Chamber of Commerce,
53
Green, E.E., 257, 258
Greene, G., 255
Grind, 226
Group
aging, 12–15
communication and cohesiveness,
13–14
scientific contribution and usefulness,
14
brainstorming, 37, 71
centered environments, 228, 230, 231
centralized, 6
characteristics of, 4–17

climate, 7, 268
cohesiveness, 269
communication patterns, 5–6
competition, 14, 15
composition, 31
decentralized, 6
diversity, 15
dynamics, 4, 191, 192
effects on brainstorming (nominal
    versus real groups), 80–104
homogeneous and heterogeneous, 7–11,
    268
increasing effectiveness of, 104, 108
leaderless, 15–17
moral, 269
perceived similarity, 14
procedures
    arranging for, 17–24
    diagnostic surveys, 18, 20–22
    evaluation criteria, 24
    in-house training, 22–23
    personnel to select, 23,
    program to select, 23, 24
    psychological testing, 18, 20–22
processes, 173
relations, 161
role of administrator, 14
secretiveness, 15
size, 88–89
source of information, 133
technique, 267–279
work, 238
Guetzkow, H., 232
Guidebook, 144, 149, 161
Guilford, J.P., 39, 43, 92, 120, 143,
    166, 167, 169, 229, 238, 247,
    258
Guilford–Zimmerman Temperament
    Survey, *see* Tests

                              H

Habits, 146, 148
Handlon, J.H., 41, 61, 71–74
Happening, 201
Hare, M., 89, 90
Harman, W.W., 256
Harris, R.H., 39, 47, 54, 99, 242

Harvard Freshman Seminar Program, 215
Hathaway, S.R., 169
Healing, 203
Hedonic response, 185, 186, 220, 272
Heilbrun, A.B., Jr., 169
Hesse, H., 255
Heterogeneous, *see* Group
Heuristics, 227
Hidden Figures Test, *see* Tests
Hierarchy, 143
Hindley, R., 213, 214
Hindu religious teachers, 27
Hitch–hikes, 33
Hoffman, L.R., 8, 9, 17
Homework, 242
Homogeneous, *see* Group
Horowitz, M.W., 88
Hotpoint program, 242
Hughes, S., 216, 218
Human context, exercises for, 224
Human relations, 228
Hydrophobia, 181
Hyman, R., 45, 46, 74–80, 126–128,
    133–136
Hypnosis, 255
Hypothesis, *see also* Communication
    formation, 46, 76, 253, 259–262
    testing, 253, 259, 262, 263

                              I

IBRIC, 169, *see also* Tests
Idea
    best, 48
    commonplace, 48, 256
    criteria pattern, 56
    effectiveness, 57
    evaluation, 30, 31, 56, 63, 72, 269
    feasibility, 57
    finding, 27, 31, 36, 143, 145, 146,
        152, 155, 156
    fluency, 229, 230, 258, 282
    generation, 26, 30, 40, 56, 58, 63, 72,
        73, 77, 149, 150, 223, 269
        separate from evaluation, 57, 61
    good, 55
    impractical, 60
    novelty, 73
    number, 47, 52, 54, 56, 60, 109, 111, 112

penalty for bad, 54, 55
practical, 60
quality, 52, 56, 71
selection, 211, 223
spoken, 70
spurrers, 146, 156–158
unique, 48
unusual, 48
usual, 48
Idea Laboratory, 246
Illumination, 238
Illusions, 155
Illustrated lecture, 242
Immediate suggestions, 200
Implementation checklist, 150
Inchworm, 212
Incubation, 100, 158, 223, 236
Indian rope trick, 189
Individual techniques for creativity,
    254–267
Industrial arts program, 214
Information, 270
Ingenious, 67
Inner city, 177
Innovations, 213, 248
Innovative forced choice scale, 229
Innovative rating scale, 229
Innovative Steve, 227
Innovativeness, 232, 233
    organizational, 162
Innovator's personality, 226
Insight, 238
Insightful problem-solving, 253, 263
Inspiration, 186, 262
Instructions, 40, 41, 140
    appropriate, 48, 49
    brainstorming, 55
    clever, 49, 54
    creative, 46, 54
    critical, 54
    evaluative, 47
    nonbrainstorming, 55
    original, 118
    practical, 46
    problem–solving, 57
    quality, 45
    written, 58
Intellectual, 179
Intellectual background, 206
Intellectual tension, 15

Interjudge reliability, 75
Intermediaries, 264, 265
Interpersonal dependency, 233
Interpersonal effectiveness, 66, 67, 107–
    110, 112, 270
Interpersonal effects, 53, 65
Interviews, 19
Intuition, 186, 223, 225, 227, 262
Invent-O-Rama, 179, 212, 215
Inventions, 208, 212, 248
Inventive elegance, level of, 188
Inventory, 212
Involvement, psychological states, 190
    and detachment, 185
    four degrees of, 187
Irrelevance filter, 186
Irritability, 284

J

Jaastad, K., 84
Jacking mechanism, 189
James, B.J., 223–227, 231, 273, 274,
    276, 278
Jochem, L.M., 56, 63
Johns–Mansville, 216
Journal of Applied Behavioral Science,
    247
Journal of Creative Behavior, 143, 160,
    247
Judges, 77, 78
Judging–perceiving scores, 66
Judging solutions, 73
Judgment
    critical, 38, 61, 72
    deferred, 26, 28, 29, 38, 40, 44–47, 54,
        57, 58, 61, 72, 74, 75, 84, 87, 137,
        139, 145, 148, 149, 151, 152, 155,
        157, 159, 166, 167, 170, 184, 185,
        261, 268, 269, 280, 281
    instructions to defer, 165
    studies of deferring, 44–47
Judicial versus creative thinking, 242
Judicial mind, 28
Judicial type of question, 151, 152
Junior high–school level, 212

K

Kangaroo, 212
Kekulé, J.B.P., 181, 257

Keller, H., 212
Kimberly-Clark, 216
Kindergarten, 179
Kinesthetic, 188, 206
Knapp, M.W., 258
Knapsack, 212
Knowledge, 212, 265
Kogan, N., 7

L

Laboratory, dissimlar tasks, 271
Lamarck, J.B.P., 180
Language devices, 225
Language skills, 212
Laplace, P.S., 180
Leader, 31, 32, 184, 185, 190, 192–200,
    220
  associate, 31, 32
  in brainstorming, 184
  in synectics, 174
Leaderless groups, *see* Group
Leadership
  creative, 161
  training in, 177
Learning theory, 137
Leavitt, H., 5, 6
Leek, 196, 205, 209
Lewin, K., 265, 267
Libby, W.L., Jr., 223–227, 230, 232, 233
Life-styles, 266
Listener, 193
Little, A.D. & Co., 173, 216
Litwin, G., 134
Location, 150
Lorge, I., 85, 98
Love, 143
LSD, 256
Lyell, C., 180

M

McClelland, D.C., 164
McGuigan, F.J., 90
McKinely, J.C., 169
McLuhan, M., 266
Magnify, *see* Categories
Maier, N.R.F., 8, 9, 15–17, 268
Make the familiar strange and strange
    familiar, 173, 179, 187, 197, 213,

261, 272
Making It Whole, 179
Making Objects Test, *see* Tests
Maltzman, I., 114–123, 127–137
Mandler, G., 124
Manipulation, *see* Categories
Marijuana, 256
Maslow, A.H., 143
Mathematics, 211
Maxwell, J.C., 180
Meadow, A., 47, 50, 51, 54–56, 68, 74, 84,
    87, 88, 91, 92, 98, 163, 164, 166
Mechanical axes, 216
Media, 266
Mednick, S., 120, 123, 225
Member, best, 86
  group, 184, 191, 193
Memory, tests of, 169
Mental dazzle, 263
Mental energy, 190
Merton, R., 12
Mescaline, 256
Mess, 147
Metaphorical approach, 214, *see also*
    Synectics
Metaphorical capacity, 206
Metaphorical potential, 206, 219, 220
Metaphorical value, 224
Metaphorical Way, 173, 189, 197, 211–213,
    see also Synectics
Metaphors, 4, 172, 173, 180, 181, 184, 196,
    207, 212, 213, 215, 220, 260, 263,
    272, *see also* Analogy, Metaphorical,
    Synectics
  forced, 201
Metropolitan Hospital Experiment, 210
Meyer, H.H., 134
Mind-expanding drugs, 256
Mini-book, 167
Minify, *see* Categories
Minnesota Multiphasic Inventory, *see* Tests
Missile loading hazards, 216
Monsanto Company, 216
Morale, 53, 63
Morphine, 256
Morphological matrix, 244, 246
Motivation, 65, 92, 106, 109, 239
Muller, G.H., 244
Myers-Briggs Type Indicator, *see* Tests
Mystique, 262

N

National Association of Social Workers, 53
National Training Laboratories, 247
Need, basic hierarchy, 143
Negative entropy, 180
Negative training experience, 135
Nerves, 181
New product service, 174
New products, 266
Newman, J.B., 88
Noller, R.B., 143, 160, 161, 167–169, *see also* Parnes
Nonbrainstorming instructions, 48, 51, 69, 71, 72, 86, 99
Nonconscious, 144, 223, 225, 227
Noncritical, 62
Nonfeedback, *see* Feedback
Nonrational, 179, 211, 222, 227, 263
Nonverbal skills, 239
Nouns, 149
Novelty, 253
Nurses, 96

O

Object synthesis, 229, 230
Objectives, 145, 176
Observation, 143
Ogilvy, D., 266
Open-mindedness, 239
Operational mechanisms, 173, 183, 184, 186–191, 196, 199, 219, 272
Opinions, 62, 104
  questionnaire, 59
Opportunity, 197
Optimal size of a brainstorming group, 88
Optimism, 207
Order
  of instructions, 99
  nominal and real groups, 86
  of work, 98–104
Organizational conditions for creativity program, 283
Organizational environment, 232
Organizational Performance Questionnaire, 229
Organizational programs, 274
Organizational stereotypes, 225, 226
Organizing for creativity, 277

Original, 67
Originality, 69, 121, 136, 137, 214, 239
  criterion, 79
Osborn, A.F., 3, 23–33, 36, 37, 53, 56, 63, 65, 88, 98, 142, 143, 151, 170, 240, 246, 268, 271
Outgoing, 67

P

Pace, C.R., 277
Pairs of individuals, 96
Panman, R.A., 116
Paradox, essential, 186, 189, 203, *see also* Synectics
Parloff, M., 41, 61, 71–74, 116
Parnes, S.J., 3, 26–29, 37, 47–51, 54–56, 74, 79, 80, 83, 84, 87, 88, 91, 97, 142–144, 149, 150, 153, 154, 156–161, 163, 164, 166–171, 247, *see also* Noller
Participants, 192, 195, 205, 279
  brainstorming 30–37
  experiments, 31, 52
  synectics, 191–196, 205–209
Pasteur, L., 181
Patent applications, 248
Patents, 208
Patrons, 265
Patterned approach, 240
Pelz, D. C., 13–15, 19, 268, 277
Penetration, 229
Perceived similarity, 14, *see also* Group
Perceptual problems, 224
Personal analogy, *see* Analogy, Synectics
Personality
  characteristics, 52, 66–68, 106, 109, 144, 169, 170, 222, 254–256, 270, 271
  measures, 66, 164
Personality–insight approach, 4, 224, 226–228, 230, 233, 268, 278
Personality tests, 231, 232
Persuasion, 265
Physiological, 143
Picasso, P., 266
Playboy, 226
Pleasure, 186, 212
Plot Titles, *see* Tests
Poetic response, 189
Polar expeditions, 207
Popularity, 264

Portugal, S.M., 85, 101–103
Positive training experience, 135
Practice, 104–106, 109
Practice of Creativity, 174
Prai-Barshana, 27
Precautions, 150
Prejudice, 203
Preparatory (educational) stage, 259, 260
Primary process, 59
Prince, G.M., 3, 4, 173, 174, 180, 184,
    189–192, 194, 196, 202, 216, 219,
    221, 272, *see also* Synectics
Problem(s)
  as given, 27, 52, 143, 147, 158, 196–198,
    200, 223
  as understood, 198, 200
  finding, 143, 152
  labs, 174, 218
    evaluation of, 217
  order of, 68
  preparation, 27
  related solution, 52
  research studies, existing in, 39, 40
  sensitivity to, 46, 47, 76, 146, 229, 240,
    244
  solution pattern, 56
  solving, 243
  specific kinds, 74, 91, 92, 97
    automatic warehousing, 127, 133–135
    brick uses, 229–231
    broom, 48, 54, 55, 68–70, 84, 92, 99,
      231, 281
    consequences, 46, 47
    discharge, 97
    ego-involving, 96–98
    hypothesis–formation, 47
    laboratory, 52
    library, 57
    one–solution, 123
    other uses, 46, 76, 164
    people, 85, 100
    real, 52–54, 68–74, 91–93, 104, 271,
      281
    supervisory, 54
    teacher (education), 57, 60, 72, 73, 83,
      85, 86, 90–94, 102, 103
    thumbs, 59, 60, 69, 70, 73, 81, 83, 85,
      89, 90, 92, 94, 97, 100, 101, 107–110,
      281
    tire, 108, 109

toothpaste, 107, 109, 110
tourist, 52, 72, 81, 83, 85–87, 91–93,
  97, 102, 103
treatment, 97
unreal, 68–70, 72–74, 91, 93, 100, 101,
  281
unusual uses, 164
wire coat hanger, 48–51, 54, 55, 68–70,
  84, 99, 164, 166, 167, 231
Process studies, 70–104
  raters of responses, 71
  spoken ideas, 70, 71–76
  standards of evaluation, 71–76
  written ideas, 70, 71–76
Production of ideas
  effort, 48
  time, 48
Profits, 248
Programmed exercises, 212
Programs, in house, 275
Progressive Concept Refinement, 227
Protective thinking, 150
"Protoplasmic kiss," 181
Psilocybin, 256
Psychiatric patients, 97
Psychographics, 266
Psychological climate, 190
Psychological distance, 207, 263
Psychological states of synectics, 183, 185,
  191, 196, 219, 272
Psychological testing, 18
  preparing for, 20–22
Psychotherapy, 255
Public, 264–266
Purge, 196, 198, 200

Q

Quality
  average, 56, 58, 60, 61, 69, 71, 90, 91,
    94, 100, 101, 269
  best idea, 80
  definition of, 42, 52
  ideas, 46–48, 50–52, 54, 56–58, 60–62,
    71, 72, 76, 78–80, 84–86, 90, 92,
    94, 95, 99, 104, 108, 164–167, 184,
    269, 271
  instructions, 165
  low, 61

measures, 49, 51, 82, 83, 109, 110, 112, 164
rather than quantity, 58
subjective rating, 77
Quantity
breeds quality, 28, 29, 137
good ideas, 60–62, 66, 67, 87, 95, 96, 100
ideas (responses), 28, 29, 52, 54, 57, 58, 60, 61, 74, 76, 78–80, 82–86, 90–95, 101, 104, 105, 164, 166, 167, 184, 269, 271
unique, 97

R

Racial tension, 210
Raters' evaluation, 42, 71, 77, 78, 79
criteria, 76–80
reliability, 94
Rational, 179, 211, 263
RCA–Whirlpool, 216
Recital of Assignment, 243
Reese, H., 54, 164
Reinforcement, 117
Relaxation–reflection, 161, 256
Remington Arms Company, 196, 209
Remote Associates Test (RAT), 120, 123, 126, 225, 229, 230
Representation, 205
Research
introduction to, 37–44
subjects, 38–39
Research and development organizations, 19
Research considerations, 278–283
Research personnel, 95, 99
Research scientists, 84, 86, 103
Responses
appropriate, 54
clever, 48
infrequent, 42
not critical, 54
practical, 54
remote, 48, 49, 52
silly, 101
spoken, 101
uncommon, 48
unique, 49
value, 51
written, 71–76, 88
Results, *see* Communication

Retail employees, 177
Reverie–hypnagogic behavior, 257, 258
Reversible, figure, 155, 156
Risks, enjoyment of, 206
"Risky–shift," 7
Rock Pool Experiment, 173, 215
Rogers, E.M., 265, 266
Rokeach, M., 229, 231
Role playing, 187, 255
Rosenbaum, M.I., 116, 118, 122
Rotter, G.S., 85, 101–103
Rule–centered group, 228, 230–232

S

"Safe attack," 181
Safety, 143
Satiation, 137
School using synectics, 211
Schrödinger, E., 180
Schutz, W.C., 66
Science, 211
Science program, 212
Secretary, 31, 32
Secretiveness, effects of, 15
Self–acceptance, 66
Self–actualization, 143, 144
Self–assurance, 67
Self–control, 164
Self–deceptive, 199
Self–doubt, 263
Self–instructional programs, 177
Self–preparation for creativity, 276
Self–reliance, 164
Selecting personnel for programs, 23, 24, *see also* Group procedures, arranging for
Selling
idea, 155, 158
solution, 224
Semantic redefinition, 229, *see also* Tests
Sensing problems, 147
Sensitivity, 191
Sensitivity training, 248
Sensory awareness, 161
Sensory and perceptual deprivation, 258
Sensory stimulation, 246, 258
Sequencing, 105, 106, 108, 110, 112, 138, 269, *see also* Analogy
with personal analogy, 270

Serendipity, 253, 263
17-Solutions method, 242
Shipworm, 180, 188
Sleeping bag, 216
Sociability, 66, 67, 95, 96
Social change, 267
Social-emotional factors, 66
Social influence, 267
Social institutions, 229, 230
Social participation, 67
Social presence, 66
Social studies, 212
Socialization, 67
Socrates, 213
Solution
  development, 223
  finding, 27, 143, 145, 146, 153, 157,
    224
  quality, 165
Shaw, M.F., 6
Shepard, H.A., 12, 13
Shoemaker, F.F., 265, 266
Shop-invention, 179
Simberg, A.L., 39, 47, 54, 99, 242
Singer Sewing Machine Co., 216
Society, 283
  characteristics that foster creativity, 284
Solem, A.R., 15, 16
Southern Bell Telephone Col, 248
Space suits, 181
Spatial arrangement, 263
Spectrum policy, 192, 193, 195, 217,
    see also Synectics
Speculation, 185, 190, *see also* Synectics
Spoken responses, 102
Spontaneous, 67, 162
  flexibility, 229, 230
Stages of the creative process, 253,
    259-267
Standards, 41, 72, 74
Stanford Research Institute, 238-240
Status, 66
Stein, M.I., 253, 277, 284, 285
Stern, G.G., 277
Sticks, 224
Stony Brook, 169
Strong Vocational Interest Blank, *see* Tests
Studt, A.C., 242
Subject
  involvement, 282

kinds of, 283
  selection, 67
  sex of, 103
Substantive inquiry, 212
Succorance, 233
Suggestions, 193, 196
Superfacts, 199
Supervisory personnel, 54
Supporters, 265
Sylvania Electric Products, Inc., 248
Symbolic factors, 169, *see also* Tests
Synectics, 172-221, 248,
  for education, 211-215
  example of, 181-183, 202-204
Systems analysis, 179, 244

                           T

T-group, 212
Taping, *see* Videotaping
Taylor, D.W., 73, 82-88, 90, 92, 93, 98,
    102, 108, 114, 258
Taylor, I.A., 258
Teachers' Manual, 187
Teaching Is Learning to Listen, 178
Teambuilding, 175
Teamwork, 238, 243
Tear-down method, 242
Teaspoon, redesign of, 34
Telephone, long distance calls, 53
Test anxiety, 124
Tests, *see also*, Adjective Check List,
      Barron Complexity Scale, Barron-
      Welsh Figure Preference Test,
      Semantic redefinition, Symbolic factors
  AC Test of Creative Ability, 39, 44, 46,
      47, 54, 99, 164, 166, 167, 238,
      242-243, 247, 248
  Apparatus Test, 166, 167, 229, 230
  California Psychological Inventory
      (CPI), 66, 67, 95, 107, 109, 113,
      164, 169, 170, 270
  Cartoon Apperception Test, 225
  Consequences, 49, 76, 238
  Content Devices, 225
  Convergent Thinking, 169, 258
  Coping Problems Test, 169
  Divergent Thinking, 169, 258
  Dogmatism (D-Scale), 229, 231, 232,
      273

Embedded Figures Test, 225
Executive Apperception Test, 225
Extroversion–introversion, 65
Figure Concepts, 49
FIRO–B, 66
Guilford–Zimmerman Temperament
  Survey, 8
Hidden Figures Test, 155
Making Objects Test, 238
Minnesota Multiphasic Inventory, 169
Myers–Briggs Type Indicator, 66, 169
Number Association, 49
Plot Titles, 45, 49–51, 164, 166, 167
  reliability of, 20
Strong Vocational Interest Blank, 169
Thematic Apperception Test (TAT), 164
Torrance Test of Creative Thinking, 214
Unusual Uses Test, 48, 120, 122, 129–
  133, 166, 167
Vocabulary scale, 166
Wechsler Adult Intelligence Scale, 166
Thematic Apperception Test (TAT), *see*
  Tests
Thermodynamics, 180
Theta waves, *see* Brain waves
Tiffany prize, 215
Time, 51, 52
Timing, 150
Titles
  appropriate, 40
  clever, 40
Toredo, 180
Torrance, E.P., 12
Torrance Test of Creative Thinking,
  see Tests
Total grasp, 207
*Toward Supersanity: Channeled
  Freedom*, 160
Trained subjects, 50, 61, 109, 164, 165,
  167
Training, 96, 97
  in–house, 22, 23
  in originality, 123, 137
  by repetition, 123
  transfer of, 117, 119, 120, 136, 167
  271
Training and Development Journal, 247
Trauma, books of, 207
Trial and error, 253, 263
Trigger sessions, 244

Trojan horse, 200
Tuckman, I., 85, 98
TV, *see* Videotaping
Typologies, 266

U

Uncommonness, 43, 52, 77
Unconscious, 180, 190
Unconventional answers, 79
Underachievers, 214
Understanding, 196
Unger, S.M., 116
Unified learning, 179
Uniqueness, 43, 47, 51, 55, 69, 79, 82,
  93, 99, 143, 239
University of Chicago, 223, 273
Untrained, 50, 84, 96, 165, 167
Unusual Uses Test, *see* Tests
U.S. Army Management School, 248

V

Vacuum cleaner, 212
Valence index, 16, 17
Value, 49, 55, 79, 99, 143
Verbal idea fluency, 239
Verbal problems, 224
Verbs, 147, 149
Videotaping, 70, 73, 74, 82, 84, 87, 89,
  100, 104–106, 186, 192, 196, 208,
  210, 211, 220
Viewpoint, 184, 194, 196, 202, *see also*
  Synectics
Visual arts courses, 211
Vocabulary scale, *see* Tests
Von Fange, E.K., 246

W

Wallach, M.A., 7
Wanted–affection, FIRO–B, 66
Warm up exercise, 86, 99, 103, 242
Wechsler Adult Intelligence Scale, *see* Tests
Weisskopf–Joelson, E., 43, 44, 58, 61, 62,
  71, 78
What Color Is Sleep, 173
Whitmyre, 96
Williams, T., 255
Willingness to report idea, 71–76
Wilson, 43, 45, 48, 51

Wispé, L.G., 255
Witkin, H.A., 225
Word Association, 136
Word finding, 225
Workbooks, 144, 157, 161, 179
Working environment, 223

Workshop, 175
Wright brothers, 180
Writing, 70, 86–88, 101, 102

Z

Zubek, J.P., 258

A   5
B   6
C   7
D   8
E   9
F   0
G   1
H   2
I   3
J   4